MY 35 YEARS IN UNIFORM

A MEMOIR

By
RAYMOND F. WRIGHT JR.

Copyright © 2013 Raymond F. Wright Jr.

All rights reserved.

ISBN: 1489537953

ISBN 13: 9781489537959

Library of Congress Control Number: 2013909784

CreateSpace Independent Publishing Platform

North Charleston, South Carolina

CONTENTS

1. Family Background 1
2. Teenage Jobs 5
3. Teenage Trouble 9
4. Joining the Marine Corps and Boot Camp 19
5. Values Ingrained for Life 31
6. Advanced Training 43
7. Zooming to the "Nam" 51
8. Kilo Company, Third Battalion, Seventh Marines 55
9. Getting Wounded 85
10. Charleston, West Virginia 99
11. Marine Barracks, Philadelphia 107
12. Embassy Duty 113
13. Parris Island Again 121
14. Second Recruit Training Battalion 127
15. Civilian Life 159
16. Becoming a Police Officer 163

17. The Police Academy 191

18. SCAT Team 195

19. METRO 219

20. First Job as a Sergeant 267

21. Criminal Investigations 283

22. Patrol Squad Commander 335

23. Judicial Operations 355

24. DEA Task Force 379

25. METRO Again 397

26. Assistant Chief of Police 429

27. Family Tragedy 445

28. Back to Work 455

29. Retirement 473

30. My Promise to My Children 479

FORWARD

I BEGAN WRITING THIS BOOK AT THE SOMEWHAT advanced age of sixty-three. Since retiring from law enforcement in April of 2011, I began to reflect on my thirty-five years in uniform and decided to write this book. The time went by so fast that I do not think I ever really reflected on how my six years in the Marine Corps defined my twenty-nine plus years as a law enforcement officer. More than twenty years ago, I began a book on my experiences in Vietnam and recently found my abandoned work while cleaning out my garage. I decided to redirect my book idea to cover my later teenage years, followed by my entry into the Marine Corps, which ended up providing the groundwork and core values for my career in law enforcement and my entire life.

I was born in The Bronx, New York, and moved to New Jersey before I was a year old and spent the next sixteen years growing up in a small town right across the Hudson River from New York City. My childhood dream, for as long as I can remember, was to become a marine. I joined during my senior year of high school in the delayed-entry program and went to Parris Island, South Carolina, to begin six years of life-changing training in the United States Marine Corps. After my discharge, and while going through the emotional readjustment to civilian life—and experiencing the serious thoughts of reenlisting—I began my own trucking company and trucked the east coast for six years.

Family issues brought my family of five to Charleston, South Carolina, in 1979, where I was finally able to fulfill my second goal in life of becoming a police officer. I was fortunate enough to complete twenty-nine plus years in law enforcement, and retired in 2011.

This is my story of a smartass kid from New Jersey, who did some crazy and stupid things as a teenager and who would have been put in jail had I ever been caught. I will share how I barely made it through high school and played around more than I should have until I made the life-altering decision to join the United States Marine Corps.

I intend to share the values ingrained in me by the Marine Corps that became the basis for guidance in my entire personal life and professional career.

I intend to share some of the bad acts of my teenage years and the sometimes humorous, sometimes sad, sometimes life-threatening events, and narrow escapes along the way during my thirty-five years in uniform as a marine and as a police officer.

I deliberately used only the first names of most persons, except when deceased, since many of the stories I refer to may prove embarrassing to them or to their families. There is some profanity used in this writing, which is not meant to offend anyone, just meant to get the point across and to inject reality.

My mother saved the dozens of letters I sent home while in Vietnam, which to my good fortune I was able to reference in this writing. I have used incidents listed in my letters to jog my memory and have confirmed my memory of most of those events through Battalion Command Chronology provided by Headquarters Marine Corps Archives. I quickly found out that unless an incident was a major event at the platoon or company level, it was never reported at the battalion level. Consequently, I discovered that a major firefight or battle to us at a squad or platoon level just was not serious enough to be reported to a higher command by battalion for entry criteria purposes in its daily diary.

Being involved in a firefight was common, and many times, we were involved several times per day. I have shared only some of the incidents that were particularly memorable to me. We went on daily patrols, participated in ambushes, and established listening posts as well as participated in company and battalion-sized operations.

FAMILY BACKGROUND

1

I WAS BORN IN THE BRONX, NEW YORK, in September of 1948 to Raymond F. Wright Sr. and Mary Lou Wright. My dad served in WWII in the Pacific in the US Army Air Corps and was discharged in early 1946. He then went to work for Bendix Aviation, just across the Hudson River in Teterboro, New Jersey. He was a machinist who made aircraft parts by hand on a metal lathe and commuted daily by either bus and or train.

In 1949, before I was year old, the three of us moved to the quiet bedroom community of Hasbrouck Heights, New Jersey. This home was now within walking distance to work for my dad. Even though it was a two-mile walk, he did it every day, no matter the weather. Rain or snow, he did it five and sometimes six days a week. He had to walk because he did not have a driver's license, and we did not have a family car until the mid-1950s. Sometime around 1955, after he took driving lessons from a local driving school, he finally got his license in his late thirties and purchased his very first vehicle. This purchase now allowed him the luxury of driving to and from work. Having a vehicle also allowed him the flexibility of having transportation to and from his second job, which was a local repairman to the mostly widowed older women of the church who needed small repair jobs around their homes.

Prior to getting a car, we walked to church and local stores and brought groceries home in my little, red wagon or in a collapsible grocery cart that everyone used in those days. If we had to travel anywhere, it was by bus, which could take you just about anywhere you wanted.

I have vivid memories of listening to war stories from my dad and all three of my uncles, who all served in the war in the Pacific. I grew up watching the weekly documentary *Victory at Sea*, narrated by Walter Cronkite. Watching it was a weekly ritual with my dad, going back as far as I can remember. We also watched the TV show *Combat* every week, which really intrigued me, and every war movie or war documentary ever made.

In addition to working fulltime at Bendix and doing the small repair jobs, he also worked every Sunday in his mother's and stepfather's luncheonette in town. We used to look forward to Sundays because my dad had someone deliver a bag of hamburgers and milkshakes for the entire family, especially enjoyed since my mother was a very poor cook. Reflecting back now that he is gone, I understand why he always fell asleep in his chair after dinner each night. My dad was the hardest-working person I ever knew, and I respected him for his work ethic, then as I do now that he is gone.

My mom, Mary Lou, was born in Alabama and moved to The Bronx, New York, with her mom and dad and two brothers. Her dad worked for the Con Edison power company in New York City, and her mom worked in the city as well for a Chilean Export company, Corporation de la Fomento.

When World War II broke out, my mom's two older brothers Leroy and Thomas Langdon both left school early to join the Marine Corps. Both brothers saw a lot of action in the Pacific, and both were wounded. Leroy was awarded the Silver Star for his actions and was discharged as a sergeant. Both brothers were fortunate enough to meet up with each other on Guadalcanal and both survived in one piece.

Her dad, my grandfather, served in the US Army as a sergeant during World War I and saw much action. He also spent many years suffering from the lingering effects of mustard gas. He almost never spoke about the war, and as a result no one asked him about it either. It was not until after I returned from Vietnam that he ever spoke with anyone in any detail about the war.

In hindsight, it is easy for me to understand why I wanted to be a marine since I was a small boy. With a father, grandfather, and three uncles who all served, they shared some of their stories from time to time; my ambition was clearly connected to my upbringing.

My mom met my dad as a pen pal while he was serving in the Pacific. When he was discharged, they dated and were married in 1947 in a joint wedding with her brother Thomas Langdon and his wife, Frances, who was also from The Bronx, New York.

The house I grew up in always seemed so big to me while growing up, but it really was not. My mom and dad paid $13,500 for the house, with a $1,000 down payment that they borrowed from a family member. A sign of the times, after my dad's death, my mom sold the house in 1989 for well over $200,000. The house had three bedrooms. I shared my room with my two brothers, Dick and Jim, the two girls Sallie and Emmy Lou were in the smallest bedroom, and my parents had the master bedroom. Seven people shared the upstairs bathroom, and it would be many years before I ever had my own room.

Hasbrouck Heights, a small town of about 14,000 people is located in Bergen County, about eight miles across the Hudson River from New York City. It is about two and a half miles long and less than a mile wide. The school district split the town in two with two grammar schools at either end of town, so everybody walked to school and came home for lunch. Grades seven through eight were in the junior high school located in the middle of town. The walk was a little longer to the junior high, but a little longer lunch period accommodated those who went home for lunch. Junior high now combined kids from both grammar schools, so everyone in the entire town went to the same school and got to know one another in this new setting, where we all stayed together as a class until graduation from high school. Fortunately for me, the high school was just around the corner from my house.

The police department was a force of about twenty-four. Everyone knew the name of every cop in town, and vice versa. The town had a volunteer fire department with state-of-the-art equipment. There was a whistle system in three or four separate towers around town that would alert volunteers to respond. The police and fire departments were in the same building in the center of town, right across the street from the junior high school. Virtually all of the business in town was on one the main street called The Boulevard. Until the surrounding area was built up and large chain grocery stores popped up, most people shopped on The Boulevard in the mom-and-pop stores in town. State Highway 17 ran north and south at the eastern edge of the town's boundary, which had the usual gas stations, furniture stores, car dealerships, and office space.

Unbelievably, the size of the town was such that if you did something wrong, it would get back home before the end of the day through a family member or neighbor. It is amazing to me that some of the things I will tell you about never made it back to my parents through the Hasbrouck Heights pipeline.

TEENAGE JOBS

2

MY DAD'S PARENTS, HIS BROTHER, MY MOM'S PARENTS, her brother, and their families all lived in close proximity to where we lived, so I saw them often. My dad never made much money, which is why he worked two extra jobs. As a result, I do not recall ever going on a family vacation. My only memory of ever going out as a family to dinner was one time per year when my dad received his vacation pay. He would take the entire family to a local restaurant for supper on the Friday night he began his vacation. He used his vacation time to rest somewhat, in that he did sleep later, but he ended up using that time to take on bigger odd repair jobs to earn extra money to make ends meet. By 1960, I had two younger brothers and two younger sisters. I never realized how poor we were, but in hindsight, I realize how close to the edge my family was financially. I know that both sets of grandparents helped my parents financially from time to time.

I saw my dad work hard all of his life, which established a work ethic in me that lasted for my entire adult life. I always did something to earn money for myself since my parents did not have anything extra to give us. I helped in my grandfather's luncheonette, where he fed me well and gave me a few dollars here and there, so I had some spending money in my pocket. I never asked my parents for anything because I knew they did not have it. I never received an allowance because my parents did not have any extra to give.

During the summer, my grandfather would take me to New York City on his day off. We would take the bus into the city and usually go to Radio City Music Hall, and after the movie or show, we would go to a nice place for dinner. I looked forward to these weekly summer outings with him.

I had a paper route, a six-day commitment, which lasted a couple of years. I also cut grass around town, but had no gas mower because all my dad had was an old push mower. One summer my grandmother offered to buy me a power mower from Sears, with the understanding that I pay her back the $85 a little at a time. This business became very lucrative, which put the most money in my pocket that I had earned to date. I managed to pay my grandmother back in six weeks.

Of course, anyone who ever wanted extra cash went door-to-door when it snowed to shovel snow around town. I recall one year, about three days before Christmas, it snowed about two feet. I earned more than $200 shoveling snow, and I was able to buy everyone in my family, including grandparents, a gift—perfect timing for sure! One of my regular snow-shoveling jobs was a funeral home. I was paid well, but an additional bonus was that the owner would give me tickets to Yankees games when he could not go because he had season tickets. Yankee Stadium was a thirty to forty-five-minute bus ride in those days.

Being the hard worker that I was, I also worked at a gas station at the head of my street. I hung out there, emptied trash, and painted parking space lines by hand around the station. I also caught an occasional car-waxing job, which the owners allowed me to do on their property. The owner of the gas station was also a season ticket holder to the New York Yankees and often took me with him to games. Since I was a huge Yankees fan, this was a thrill for me to sit in box seats.

I also worked at a German delicatessen around the corner, where I stocked shelves. Minimum wage in the '60s was only seventy-five cents an hour, but the money went a long way then. Earning this extra money allowed me to dress like the other kids because I was able to buy my own clothes and shoes. I do recall a time when I was around fourteen or so that my mom told me that being able to buy my own clothes was a big help to her and my dad, and she told me that I would be expected to continue to buy for myself because they didn't have the money. As I recall, this news did not bother me. It just made me work harder and allowed me to buy what I wanted without any parental control about what I wore.

The best and most lucrative job I had as a teen was working for a locally owned chain of dairy stores that opened in my town. The minimum wage was seventy-five cents an hour, but my best friend, Gil, and I were hired as clerks and started at $1 per hour, big money in 1964. The job required that I wear a white, short-sleeve dress shirt and tie with slacks. I recall having to wait about a week after I was hired to begin work because I had to raise the money to buy at least two dress shirts and pants. My grandparents who owned the luncheonette were mad at me for a little while because my new employer sold ice cream by the half gallon, which cut into their homemade ice cream business. The store was open from 10:00 a.m. to 10:00 p.m., and my job generally had me there from five or six to closing time and all day Saturday and alternating Sundays. After a few months, the manager thought so much of the job that Gil and I were doing that he gave us both a raise to $2 per hour and later to $2.50 per hour. None of our friends was making as much as we were, and we were in the money!

I bought my first car for $50, a four-door, 1956 Pontiac, which I drove up and down the driveway until September of '65 when I turned seventeen and got my license. The engine blew up about a month after I got it on the road. Before getting it towed to the junkyard, I had friends come by the house and charged a quarter a shot with a sledgehammer to do as much damage as they could. I made five or six bucks and then had a friend tow it to the junkyard for me.

My next car was a 1950 Ford four-door sedan, with a flathead V-8 and stick on the column. I paid the great sum of $40 for this car, which I had for about a year before I bought the next one. I bought it from the mother of a girl in my class, and it was a very dependable ride.

This new monetary freedom I had with my new job allowed me to buy a hot '57 Chevy convertible, black with red interior and a white top. The engine had some work done on it, and it had a Hurst three-speed shifter. I paid $750 for this car, and it was my pride and joy. This is the car I had my entire senior year in high school. One Saturday morning I allowed Gil to drive it while I sat in the shotgun seat. As he caught second gear, he hit an oncoming car. The left front fender caught the left front of the other car. Fortunately, a '57 Chevy is built like a tank, and I was able to get it fixed by just replacing the fender.

TEENAGE TROUBLE

3

From the day I turned seventeen and had a driver's license, I had my own car, and prior to that when I was fifteen to seventeen, I always hung out with guys who had cars. They picked me up for school and took me home, and we cruised our town and adjoining towns, sometimes getting into trouble. The area we lived in was a group of adjoining towns with distinct boundaries. For example, the City of Newark was about ten miles from Hasbrouck Heights, but there were eight municipalities between Newark and us. A full cruise would be from our town through all eight towns with a turnaround when we got to the city limits of Newark. Then we would cruise back through the same towns we just came through.

Growing up I had two distinct groups of friends. Since I had come up through the Cub Scouts, Boy Scouts, and Youth Fellowship at church, I had friends I had established through the church. We were a group of guys who never got into trouble and followed the straight and narrow. The other group that I was involved with was called "The Boys." We were the ones who did the crazy things that would have landed us in jail or juvenile court, had we ever been caught. "The Boys" were all my age or a year older.

We used to stand on the corner of the main drag in town and sing the latest soul music. The business district was lined with gas stations, delis, drugstores, soda shops, banks, hardware stores, etc. The Boulevard was connected to the other main streets of the eight municipalities between "The Heights," as we called it, and Newark.

One friend worked at a gas station nearby that sold some groceries, including local, farm-fresh eggs. I recall the eggs were only about thirty cents per dozen, so a favorite sport would be to load the car up with dozens of eggs and ride around and throw eggs at people walking on the sidewalk. One night we were out egging in my '50 Ford and had about three dozen eggs left after hitting a few people in an adjoining town. Well, one of our victims must have called the police and given a description of my car, which was easy to spot since it was a brown '50 Ford loaded with five guys. A cop in Wood Ridge stopped us, and while I was preparing to stop, all of the remaining eggs were quickly put under the backseat, something very hard to do with three guys in the backseat. The cop could not find anything, and, of course, we denied having thrown any eggs, so he had no alternative but to let us go. We also purchased loads of eggs to throw at cars after Friday night football games. It was tradition for kids from the school we played to ride down The Boulevard blowing their horns if they were fortunate enough to beat us. The natural thing to do was to throw eggs at them.

Before any of us had a license to drive, we would often go joyriding in friends' family cars. My buddy Gil, who lived next door, and I along with others would often roll his mother's car out of the driveway and roll down the street and start it, then drive around for hours, being sure to stay on the back streets of town so police would not see us. Since we lived on a hill, we would put the car in neutral and coast down the hill and into the driveway so we would not wake his mom or anyone in my house because his driveway was fifteen feet from my kitchen window.

One of my friends had a '56 Ford that he wanted to race at a quarter-mile drag strip, but the driver's door lock did not work, so he could not lock the door, which was a rule requirement by the NHRA, the sanctioning body of racing. This was on a Saturday night, and the races were on Sunday, so we drove around and looked for another '56 Ford. After driving around a while, we found one parked in someone's driveway, so we stole the driver's door while it was in the owner's driveway. The stolen door would not fit in the car we had, so two of us carried it about six blocks and installed it on my friend's car. We removed the molding, which did not match and quickly spray-painted the door, and off we went to races the next day. He actually won his class and took home a trophy.

The same few guys who were in on the stolen door caper were friends with a guy named Steve who was like the mad scientist because he liked making things. He started making a homemade bomb in his garage where he had a '37 Chevy he was building for the street. Well, one Saturday night he announced he had this small makeshift bomb designed to make more noise than damage. He had the brilliant idea to place it in the cellar of Town Hall. Our Town Hall was a large building, which housed the Fire Department, the Police Department, and the Municipal Court. The Fire Department was volunteer, and the town offices, of course, were empty, leaving the only occupant of the building after hours the desk sergeant at the Police Department, who also answered the phone to dispatch officers to calls—definitely before the days of 911. We checked out the building and went around all four sides to make sure the sergeant was the only one there, and "Mr. Bomb Maker" entered an unlocked door and went down into the basement and placed his device. He came running out, and we ran across the street to hide near the junior high school to wait for the bang. Sure enough, it went off and made the loudest sound we ever heard. Within a minute or two, the two cops on duty on the street came speeding up. Then volunteer firefighters began showing up, having been activated. We decided we had seen enough and got the hell away from the area, lucky again.

The following weekend "Mr. Bomb Maker" had made another device, and this time we had the idea to tape it to the inside of a huge old bell on display in Memorial Park at the traffic circle on The Boulevard. The bell had been used at the turn of the century to alert volunteer firefighters when there was a fire, and it was as big as the Liberty Bell in Philadelphia. This was a little harder to place than the bomb in the first caper because the street was heavily traveled and was close to houses. We used a car this time and let "Mr. Bomb Maker" out where he taped his device to the inside of the bell. We were several blocks away when it went off, and it was unbelievably loud. That was the last of our bomb escapades—lucky again. Just think if this had been done post-9/11, we would have been charged federally because of all the strict new laws enacted after 9/11.

In those days, bars and liquor stores were not closely monitored by law enforcement, so it was common to walk into a local bar and purchase a quart container of draft beer. We all frequented a pool hall in a nearby town since we were all into pool at the time, and we all pretty much had our own cue sticks. One night a few of us were leaving the pool hall, and a gang from that town did not like the fact that we were in their town. A nasty fight broke out, and several cue sticks were used defending ourselves. Since they knew what town we were from, they pretty much declared a temporary war to guys in Hasbrouck Heights. There were at least two other gang fights we got into. The last one was at a party in our town, and as we pulled up outside of the house, a group approached us with knives. We fought out in the street, and it still amazes me that none of us was cut—lucky again.

None of my friends or anyone I knew for that matter ever did drugs. It just was not the thing to do yet in the mid-'60s. We all drank alcohol, and did so every weekend at least through my junior and senior year in high school. It was not uncommon to go out on a date on Friday night, then meet the guys and go somewhere to drink. Saturday nights were usually reserved for drinking. One night in my senior year, my buddy Gil dropped my drunk butt off in front of my house, and when I went inside my mother was waiting up for me. She could easily smell the alcohol on me and immediately asked for my driver's license. She ripped it in half and threw it back at me. This was significant because my license was laminated in plastic, and she had easily ripped through it!

Another bar served underage and was pretty much the best and closest place to go and hang out in a nearby town. The best part was that we were able to drink hard liquor there, which we did regularly. One night one of my friends got into a fight at one of the pool tables, which ended up in a knockout, drag-down fistfight. My buddy was getting his ass beaten pretty well, and it was just him and me there by ourselves, so I dived into the middle of the fight and dragged my buddy out of there, and we ended up in the famous Bendix Diner in Hasbrouck Heights. The Bendix Diner has been featured as one of the best diners in New Jersey and has not changed its appearance in more than fifty years. It has also been a backdrop in many movies over the years. It was the only place open in town, other than a bar, and was frequented by the local cops who came in for coffee. Obviously, we had been drinking, and my buddy and I were all bloodied. We sat at the counter, ordered a burger and coffee, and in came a Hasbrouck Heights cop. He became overly inquisitive about my friend's appearance to a point where our demeanor could have gotten us locked up for disorderly conduct or public intoxication. The cop got his coffee to go and finally left us alone—lucky again.

I had always gone to the Christmas Eve Candlelight church service with my dad, which was at 11:00 p.m. and ended near midnight with lit candles. Well, on Christmas Eve 1965, I went to several Christmas parties and got drunk and never met my dad at our church as planned. I actually ended up at the local Catholic church with a girl I knew named

Fran. The church was full to capacity, and we had to stand for the entire hour-long mass. After walking Fran home, I showed up at home around one o'clock in the morning. My mother was not very happy, and my dad was somewhat amused, but deep down probably a little disappointed in not knowing where I may be the following Christmas.

We had a class trip while I was either a sophomore or junior in high school and went to New York City to see a popular movie that was out at the time. A group of about four or five of us sneaked away, walked over to Seventh Avenue, and went into the famous McSorley's Ale House where we drank fifteen-cent draft beers. We managed to hook up again with the group as they were exiting the movie to go to the buses—another close call. McSorley's was a well-known location, and we frequented the bar when in the City.

Growing up in the area placed us close to the pulse of new musical groups and entertainers, mostly because many of the groups began in suburban New Jersey due to the close proximity to New York City. There were many nightclubs in our area, and our love for the great sounds of the '60s allowed us to see Chubby Checker, Frankie Valle of the Four Seasons, The Four Tops, The Temptations, The Dupree's, The Drifters, Ruby and the Romantics, The Thymes, Marvin Gaye, and many others. We were able to see them for as little as a $3 or $4 cover charge. Frankie Valle used to drive through town in his brand-new Thunderbird and wave to the guys standing on the corner.

Once we all piled in a car and decided to go to the famous Apollo Theater in New York City, which was well known—and still is—for its great black entertainment. We thought nothing of making the trip, which was a short twenty-minute ride across the George Washington Bridge and into Harlem. We ended up being the only white guys in the entire theater. We got a lot of dirty looks and looks of disapproval, but we did not care because we were seeing the latest Motown music of the times. As the show disbanded there were some words directed at us, so we got to our car and got the hell out of Dodge!

The reason we thought nothing about making this trip was the fact we really were not attuned to the racial climate going on at the time. What did we know? We were from a small New Jersey town that did not have one black person living or working there. We were in our own teenage world loving the music and were oblivious to the fact that what we did may not have been the safest thing to do. At the time, we lived our sheltered lives in a town where everyone knew everybody else. Italians predominantly populated Hasbrouck Heights and a mishmash of other various ethnicities. We did not know or care that just ten miles away in Newark there were shootings, stabbings, and murders on a nightly basis.

***

The mid-'60s was the greatest time for muscle cars, and a favorite pastime was street racing. I did not own anything worthy of racing until I got the '57 Chevy, but that did not keep us from attending the street races, wherever they happened to be. A favorite hangout at the time was a hamburger stand on Route 17. We would go to there to hang and wait for someone, usually from another town, to come with his car to find someone with a similar size motor to race. In the age of 409 Chevys, 406 Fords, 428 Hemi Dodges and Plymouths there was never a Friday or Saturday night where there wasn't a race to go to or see. There was a lot of serious money involved in betting on the winner. We had many close calls with the police showing up during races, which many times resulted in them chasing the two cars that had been racing.

In the summer of 1966, there was a big push by the police in our town to enforce loitering laws on the main drag, which was the business district. I had already enlisted in the Marine Corps in the delayed-entry program and was due to go to Parris Island on September 2. I had already been sworn in and had been issued my service number. Well, one night about four of us were hassled, and the cop decided he was going to take down our names and addresses and other contact information. The cop, of course, knew who we were because, as I have stated before, everybody knew everybody in our town. The cop pulled over to the side of the street, and we leaned into the car while he stayed seated. Two of us were at the driver's window, and the other two leaning into the passenger window. In those days, the lights on the roof of the police car were screwed directly into a rack on the roof. Well, while the cop was busy trying to pull information out of us, I was unscrewing one of the lollipop-looking lights out of the roof bracket. A guy on the other side saw what I was doing, so he did the same. When it became my turn to give my information to the cop, I did so but gave my already memorized service number as personal information. This pissed the cop off so badly that he told us to go the hell home, threw the car in drive, and quickly drove away. Well, as you can imagine, as he pulled away both of the lights that we had removed from the bracket banged the roof and hung by wires over the side of the car. We hauled ass, and nothing was ever said to us again—lucky again.

I say that nothing happened, but the cop who had us stopped got back at me in particular a week or so later. I had parked my '57 Chevy on The Boulevard and gone into a nearby candy store for a soda, and someone said a cop was outside looking closely at my car. I quickly learned that cops have a way of getting back, a lesson I learned twenty years later as a cop myself. He proceeded to write me four tickets—one for being too far away from the curb and the others for various equipment violations. We had embarrassed him, so he was taking care of business—lesson learned.

Another caper that went over well at school happened a few guys and I went out into the back parking lot at school and picked up a little foreign car owned by a teacher nobody liked. It was parked in an end spot next to a fence, so after we turned it, we parked one of our cars closely next to it so he could not leave at the end of the school day. We came back a few hours later to get the car, and he was pissed. The word of our caper quickly got around the school, and he never found out who did it. We regularly made life miserable for that teacher by letting air out of at least two tires, since he, naturally, had only one spare. I heard that he took a job the following year at a different school.

Another caper to pull was to roll someone's car, usually owned by a person we didn't especially like, and take it down the street and fill it with piles of dead leaves left in the street for pickup by the town's sanitation trucks.

Too much time fooling around and drinking, caused my grades in school to suffer, and I ended up failing history, which meant that I would need to attend summer school to obtain my diploma. Based on my smart-ass personality at the time, I walked into the classroom of the teacher who failed me during a class and yelled, "You are an asshole." This class was a short roadblock and cut into my last summer of freedom. My only regret was that I never graduated with my class. I went to the graduation parties, of course.

About two weeks before I left for boot camp, I was out in front of my house waxing my '57 Chevy. A few weeks prior to that, a guy who was in another group in town had been busting my horns for some reason known only to him. He would drive by, flip me the bird, and yell profanities. He was known as a tough guy among his group of friends, but I was not about to let him humiliate me, especially in front of my own friends. While I was in front of my house, I saw a car coming down my street loaded with four guys and noticed that the guy who had been busting my balls was a passenger in the front seat. I stood out in the middle of the street and waved the car over to the curb, and words were exchanged. As this asshole got out of the car, I coldcocked him once right in the face, and he went down. As he went down, I saw that I had broken his nose and moved it to the side of his face. He was covered with blood and shocked at what I had done as he realized all of that blood was coming from his face. Everybody got back in the car and quickly hauled ass.

I never heard a word about the altercation from anyone, and I went on into the Marine Corps two weeks later, went to Vietnam, and spent my extended time in the hospital after being wounded. I ran into him in a bar in New York State more than a year and a half later. He came up to me, apologized, and shook my hand. After I returned from Vietnam, I ran into another guy who was in the car, who told me that nobody wanted to call the police on me. He said they knew I was going into the Marine Corps and probably to Vietnam. They figured I was half-crazy anyway for joining the Marine Corps, and nobody wanted to mess with me, so why bother?

That was about the last of the things I did as a teenager that would have gotten me arrested. All of these incidents were in the summers before and after my senior year of high school. I was not really a bad guy, but I was a follower not a leader—that would change later. I had a good family life, went to church, and worked hard at numerous jobs to earn money to have my freedom and buy what I wanted. In hindsight, I think because I worked hard and earned my own money and was the oldest of five children, my parents let me stay out later than they would ever let any of the other kids. I was on a long leash, but had my parents had ever known about any one of these events, I would have been grounded for life!

As stated earlier, whenever a family member asked me what I wanted to do when I grew up, my response was always, "To join the Marines." I also had silent ambitions about wanting to be a cop one day.

JOINING THE MARINE CORPS AND BOOT CAMP

4

For those old enough to remember, the war in Vietnam was just starting to escalate in 1965 and 1966. The evening news devoted most of its coverage to the war. It was obvious that this was the first war where people saw battles in real time. TV was not available during WWII, and at that time, the news was censored and sometimes did not get to the States for many weeks. It was common for parents to see their wounded son minutes after their injury and long before family notification. Some parents actually found out that their loved one was killed in action on the news. I had an intense interest in seeing the news each night because of my interest in joining the military and understanding the latest news about the war.

I already knew one friend killed in Vietnam who was a year ahead of me in school who joined the Army and went right to Vietnam. He lived with his dad in an apartment on The Boulevard, and his mother had died a few years earlier. I felt extremely sorry for his dad, who was now very alone, and I remember going to his funeral and thinking that I could be next.

In February or March of '66, there was a career day in the gymnasium at school. The boys were separated from the girls, and our half of the class, about seventy-five guys waited in the bleachers to be addressed by four recruiters from each of the armed services, from left to right Air Force, Navy, Army, and Marine Corps. The airman, sailor, and soldier were standing at ease and, you guessed it, the marine was standing at parade rest. The marine was a gunnery sergeant, with a chest full of ribbons from WWII, Korea, and Vietnam.

The principal introduced the four recruiters one at one time before the beginning of the program. As the airman, sailor, and soldier were introduced, they all took a step forward and waved individually. You guessed it, when the marine was introduced, he came to attention and did not say a word. Each recruiter gave a presentation of three to five minutes, and as each finished his talk, the marine stood erect and held his right arm straight out with his thumb down. Nobody in the room laughed. You could hear a pin drop in the room. The marine did the thumbs down three times and then gave his speech. Nobody asked him a single question. When all four had spoken, the principal announced that each recruiter would be at four small tables against the wall to answer any inquiries. I was the only guy in the class to go to talk to the marine. Everybody else was scared shitless! I made an appointment to meet him at the recruiting station and filled out all of the necessary paperwork to enlist for three years. Because I was only seventeen, my parents had to sign to give permission for me to enlist. I made at least two trips to New York City for testing and physicals, and on my second trip in May of 1966, I was sworn into the Marine Corps in the delayed-entry program. I was provided with my service number and given the date of September 2 to report to the Newark Recruiting Station at 7:00 a.m.

The draft was in effect at the time, and there was little interest on the part of high-school graduates to join the military because of the great possibility of going to war. Most graduates did everything they could to get into college so they would get their college deferment. Those without the grades to enter college pursued the military reserves or National Guard. Other than the class Valedictorian, Fred, who had been appointed to West Point, I was the only person in my class to join the military.

I definitely partied the entire summer of '66, not to mention working for the cash to do the partying. The week before I left, I traded my prized '57 Chevy to a friend for a 1960 Plymouth, which I left my dad to use as the family car. On the night of September 1, my buddy Gil and I started out by hitting the famous hot dog joint Rutts Hut, where we each had a couple of their great deep-fried dogs

Our next stop was a thirty-minute drive to the Brauhaus, a regular watering hole just across the state line into New York State. We met a few friends who were expecting us, and I never purchased one drink with my own money the entire night. I started out drinking draft beer, but then my friends started buying shots of whiskey to drop in my mug to make boilermakers! I remember getting into the backseat of Gil's car and had my head out the window the entire trip home, throwing up. Gil deposited me on the front step of my house at about one in the morning. and I was due in Newark at 7:00 a.m., so there was little time for sleep. My dad woke me at five thirty before he left for work. We hugged and said our good-byes. I then walked next door to get my ride. Gil and I stopped at a diner on the way and had some greasy bacon and eggs. When he dropped me off at the induction center, I immediately deposited the bacon and eggs at the curb before entering.

Within minutes, we were sworn in by a Marine captain and later bused to Newark Airport for the trip to Charleston, South Carolina. I recall a fellow recruit who had some college as being in charge and responsible for carrying our records. This was the first time on a plane for me, but only the first of many that I would experience as a Marine. This entire group of about forty ended up being in the same platoon all through boot camp. I befriended a few of the guys and actually had my first ever contact with blacks. Several of the guys in the group were blacks from the Newark area, and we ended up close throughout our training. We landed in Charleston, South Carolina, and it was hot as hell. We were herded outside to a small, grassy area to wait in the heat. Long after dark, a bus arrived for our hour-long ride to Parris Island.

The entire ride was loud with everyone talking loudly, but when the main gate to Parris Island came into view, everyone became silent. We were silent until we stopped and a drill instructor from the receiving barracks entered the bus and yelled at us in profanity-laced terms that we had thirty seconds to get off of his bus and out onto the yellow footprints painted on the pavement outside!

Once addressed as a group outside, we were herded into the barracks and told to stand in front of tables with individual bins and to empty our pockets and any bags anyone had so the drill instructors could inspect for contraband. I was surprised to see that people had brought knives, brass knuckles, and condoms! What did they think they were going to do for nine weeks? The bins had a small board on top where the drill instructors walked back and forth looking down at us and of course yelling profanities the entire time.

I do not know why I remember this, but one bald guy had brought a small briefcase-looking bag that contained numerous bottles of liquids and creams. When the drill instructor asked him what the contents of the case were, he responded that it was to make his hair grow. There was a large, open garbage can next to the back door to the squad bay, which was propped open to where we had entered from the footprints, and I recall the drill instructor let loose with about ten lines of expletives as he heaved the briefcase from his position above us and right into the open can. He finished by saying he would not need that shit here!

We left there, got our thirty-second haircuts, went out to supply, and were issued our utility uniforms, underwear, boots, sneakers, and toiletries. We returned to the room with the bins now containing the civilian clothes we had worn to boot camp. We were shown how to package the items, and we filled out labels for them to be mailed home. We were then herded into a mess hall for breakfast, where I again lost that meal as I exited. I had now been awake for over twenty-four hours with less than five hours of sleep in two days and had not yet held down any food in that entire time, and it appeared we were destined to be awake until we all went to bed that night.

I had always been told by my dad and uncles to be quiet, never to volunteer for anything, and to follow orders explicitly. Even though I had consumed half of the beer in New York and New Jersey, I was in fantastic physical shape. My high school gym teacher, a former marine, told me to run as much as possible, and I was able to run four miles without a problem. Being a former marine, he taught all of his classes to march as a platoon. I knew all of the facing movements and marching commands, a distinct advantage in boot camp. I was six feet two inches tall and weighed only 145 lb. I had been drinking plenty of beer, but had also been taking an over-the-counter pill from the drugstore called Wate On and had been taking the pills and drinking milkshakes all summer to gain weight. I managed to gain 5 lb. and weighed in at a whopping 150 lb. when I left for boot camp!

I was assigned to Platoon 1055 in the First Battalion, one of the three male Recruit Training Battalions on Parris Island. The forty or so of us who made the trip from Newark were assigned with more than forty others, mostly from the south, to complete our platoon. I quickly found that the military does everything alphabetically, and my last name, Wright, made me the eightieth recruit of eighty in the platoon. All through boot camp, whenever we did something alphabetically, I was called to the front of the platoon and ordered to call out each laundry number until I got to eighty.

My drill instructors were badass dudes. My senior drill instructor was a staff sergeant, and his two assistant drill instructors were a staff sergeant and a sergeant. I actually found that I enjoyed boot camp, something that not many people can admit to. Call me weird, but I relished the training and ate up the Marine Corps history and tradition taught to us throughout our training. I also loved the food and ate everything in front of me every meal—and finally began to gain some weight.

About the first thing taught to us by our drill instructors was the fact we would no longer use the terms *I*, *me*, or *my* while in recruit training. We were instructed to speak in the third person. For example, if you needed to go to the bathroom, you would say the following: "Sir, the private needs to make a head call." If you needed to go to sickbay because of a blister, you would say the following: "Sir, the private needs to go to sickbay because the private has a blister on his right heel." This manner of speaking was not hard to learn, but some had issues with it and did not get it right until well into training.

One of the things that the Marine Corps instilled in us was to memorize our chain of command, starting with our three drill instructors, series gunnery sergeant, series commander, company commander, battalion commander, regimental commander, commanding general, commandant, secretary of navy, secretary of defense, vice president, and president. Each name had to be learned and recited each night prior to hitting the rack (going to bed). I do not think any other branch of service emphasized or taught its chain of command from bottom to top. The Marines have done this for years and years and continue to do so today.

Marching was a breeze to me, which kept attention by the drill instructors away from me and onto those with two left feet who could not walk and chew gum at the same time. I kept my nose clean and followed orders to the letter and can recall being singled out only one time in nine weeks of training. Marine Corps training in the '60s had not changed much over the years, even after the famous 1956 Ribbon Creek incident in which a drill instructor deliberately marched his platoon of recruits into a marsh, resulting in several recruits being drowned. A high-profile and highly publicized court-martial ruined the instructor's career and resulted in more supervision of drill instructors. Marine Corps boot camp was still the harshest of all four services, and I can tell attest to the fact that it became necessary at times for some recruits to have their attitudes physically adjusted by certain drill instructors.

In 1966, we were issued bayonets to go to our assigned M-14 rifles. It was common for one of the assistant drill instructors to hold a bayonet with the scabbard removed and the tip pointing at the stomach of recruits that he singled out as they did pushups over the blade. To do this we had our toes on the edge of the table and our hands on the floor in the middle of the squad bay. Years later, the Marine Corps discontinued the issuance of bayonets to recruits after several stabbing incidents.

The one time I was called out as an individual happened in front of the battalion mess hall while waiting to enter. We lined up in what was known as "asshole to elbow," meaning our nose almost touched the back of the neck of the recruit in front of us. The First Battalion was located on the edge of a marsh, and when the tide was out, the South Carolina sand fleas were unbelievable to endure. They were the smallest bug I have ever seen and were small enough to go through the small squares of a window screen. While standing at attention, asshole to elbow, a sand flea went up my nose, and I had to quickly reach up and kill it. Well, the assistant drill instructor saw me do it and ordered me to find the sand flea and bring it to him. That was just an impossible task, so I just killed another one and brought it to him. As I held it up on the tip of my finger, he closely inspected it and proceeded to tell me that the one I killed was a male and this one was a female. One thing was certain most drill instructors could easily be comedians, and most had a great sense of humor.

Our platoon entered the mess hall and had our chow, and after we were dismissed from formation at our barracks, the drill instructor said, "Wright begin." The order *begin* meant to drop where you were and begin to do the dreaded Bends and Thrusts, which was the punishment of choice by most drill instructors. I did them for quite some time—a tough thing to do on an extremely full stomach—and left a large pool of my sweat on the deck. I never, ever swatted a sand flea again while in formation—lesson learned.

A prime example of drill instructors' sense of humor was on display very early in training during the first week. The drill instructors needed to determine the religious denomination of each recruit to ensure that everyone made it to his respective service on Sunday. While counting heads and forming a list of Catholics and Protestants he quickly determined that only seventy-nine recruits were on his list. Once he determined who the one recruit was who had not claimed a religion, he questioned him in front of the platoon about his undeclared religion. The drill instructor said, "Well, we have plenty of Catholics and Protestants, but I don't have any Jews, so you are now a Jew! On Saturday when I call for my Jewish recruits, you will answer up, and you will go to Jewish services!" Therefore, for the next nine Saturdays this recruit went with the few other Jewish recruits of the series of over three hundred to their respective services. Only in Marine Corps boot camp could this ever happen. I still laugh when I think about it today.

Physical exercise was always in unison, and if any one of the eighty recruits in our platoon failed to comply, his noncompliance would result in all eighty recruits being punished, which was just one example of discipline being taught to us. The sand flea incident was also a lesson in discipline. Discipline is the groundwork in the training of Marine recruits. Along the way, the little lessons in discipline were slowly sinking in with everyone, and as training progressed, the discipline became second nature.

During the third or fourth week of training, our cycle of recruits was required to serve seven days on mess duty in one of the numerous mess halls on the island. When our week came along, we served our time in our own First Battalion mess hall. I was assigned the serving line, which was a good assignment. When chow was being served, my job was to place whatever I was serving on the tray of the recruit who extended his tray to me, indicating he wanted what I had to offer. Being on mess duty required us to get up at 3:30 a.m. instead of 5:00 a.m., so we had that much less sleep for those seven days.

During the week, one of the recruits was caught taking ice cream without permission. He happened to be a guy who was overweight and was on a weight-control program. Well, another lesson in discipline was about to be given. The entire platoon of eighty recruits was herded out onto the grass in the rear of the mess hall, and the drill instructors ordered us to do push-ups in unison, twenty-five at a time. We were allowed to rest only in the up position, with our arms extended and locked. The recruit who took the ice cream did not have to do the push-ups and stood in front of his seventy-nine fellow recruits while we were punished for what he did. We continued and continued, resting only in the up position until we completed one thousand in increments of twenty-five. I never in my life thought I was capable of doing one thousand push-ups, but we did this as a platoon. Yes, it was punishment for the transgression of one, but in hindsight, this was one more lesson of discipline. I recall that the recruit guilty of stealing was a very lonely guy until the day we graduated in November.

Platoon 1055 was shaping up to be a great platoon and had already won the First Phase Drill Competition. The Second Phase of training was the rifle range. The first week at the range, which required the entire platoon to move to new barracks, was all classroom, which were two-sided, lean-to-type buildings with a chalkboard and benches. The entire first week was spent "snapping in" when we were not in the classroom. Snapping in was aiming at a stationary target while sitting, lying, standing, or kneeling in a circle on the grass. The target was an old fifty-five-gallon drum on a wooden stand about two feet high. On the barrel were small black bull's-eyes painted all around the barrel. We dry fired at those barrels for many hours the entire first week. This exercise was to simulate firing at a target using the different shooting positions at each yard line.

The second week was the actual firing of the weapons from Monday to Friday. Friday was qualification day and Platoon 1055 qualified every recruit for a 100 percent. Accomplishing 100 percent was a big deal and had not been done by any platoon in recent memory, which resulted in another trophy for the platoon. Now that we had completed six weeks of training, we were now moving to Third Phase, and we were really beginning to click as a group. We all respected our drill instructors immensely, and their hard work instilled in us extreme loyalty and dedication to them.

The Third Phase of training was the most interesting to me and involved things such as the Confidence Course, force marching with all of our gear, camping overnight at Elliot's Beach, more advanced classes, fittings for dress uniforms, close-combat training, Series Commander Inspection, Company Commander Inspection, Final Drill Evaluation, Battalion Commander Inspection, and Graduation. Platoon 1055 completed its training as an Honor Platoon and won every award offered during our nine weeks of recruit training.

Recruit graduations were held one time per week on the Parade Deck just across from First Battalion. We had seen eight graduations, and now it was our turn. We graduated on November 2, 1966, and wore our Class "A" green uniforms since the entire Marine Corps on the east coast at that time had switched to the woolen green uniforms on November 1. The evening before graduation, I had the opportunity to meet my mom and dad who had made the trip, their first time ever out of state or away from the kids since 1947, when they were on their honeymoon.

While going through a box full of letters preparing to write this book, I ran across three letters my dad sent me. They are the only three letters he ever wrote to me or to anyone else, for that matter. In his first letter, dated September 11, 1966, he wrote, *"I think this is the first personal letter I have written at all, since I was in the service myself, twenty-one years ago."*

I cherish these letters now that he is gone and am reminded of my dad's hard work by an excerpt in a letter dated October 5, 1966, where he wrote,

"The most important thing that I will say is that we will be there sometime. Planning to leave Sunday night so that we can have Monday evening with you as well as Tuesday, graduation day. Can stay over Wednesday if necessary from work, you know I have 5 sick days a year, can use 3 at a time. This is one trip I am not going to miss for anything." He then closed his letter by saying *"Looking forward so much to trip down to see you. It'll be the first vacation since married, (19 years) next week from Friday."*

My parents had never taken a vacation, and he considered their long eight hundred-mile trip to see me for one evening and the day of graduation a vacation. I know the cost of the trip set them back financially, but I was glad they came and, as I reflect back on it, appreciate their effort even more now.

I spent graduation day with my parents, and we walked everywhere. They flew down and took a bus to Parris Island, which is why we walked. In those days, the day after graduation was a long bus ride on Greyhound buses to Camp Lejeune, North Carolina, for infantry training, then to other specialty schools for those who were not designated infantry or grunts. I was designated infantry, so my specialty school was more infantry training. The next morning there were about eight buses lined up in front of our barracks to carry the more than three hundred newly minted marines to their destination almost three hundred miles north.

Overall, I was proud that I was now a marine and happy that this, the hardest portion of training, was over. I had succeeded where others before me had failed, and I must say that each and every recruit was treated as an equal in that we were *all* treated like shit! We were not black or white, we were all *green*.

VALUES INGRAINED FOR LIFE

5

Leadership
The art of getting someone else to do something you want done because he wants to do it.
DWIGHT D. EISENHOWER

LOYALTY IS DEFINED AS THE QUALITY OF BEING loyal to someone or something or a strong feeling of support or allegiance.

I certainly did not recognize it at the time, but the previous nine weeks of intense training had changed me immensely. I had developed an unwavering loyalty not only to the three drill instructors who trained me, but to the Marine Corps itself. I found out in subsequent years what a loyal fraternity that the Marine Corps is. I would spend the next five years, ten months, and twenty-eight days as a member of our elite institution.

If one former marine meets another, instant conversation begins. They find out when and where each other served, and with what unit. Loyalty taught in the Marine Corps intensified my already ingrained patriotism for my country, which had been years in the making through my dad and the other former service members in my family.

The Marine Corps went to extremes to instill loyalty in its recruits by drilling into them their chain of command, all the way to the president of the United States. Every recruit knew exactly whom he was to be loyal to and exactly whom answered to in your life —as a marine. No other military service does that.

Loyalty to my future bosses, either in the Marine Corps or my twenty-nine plus years in law enforcement, was a trait that has lasted my entire life. As a result, I would also extend loyalty to my friends over the years. Any one of my friends, bar none, can tell you that if I am your friend, we are friends for life. I have at times extended my friendship to people to a fault trying to help someone if he or she got into trouble on the job, but my friendship is everlasting and not conditional in any way shape or form. I owe this trait to my Marine Corps training.

Trustworthy is defined as able to be relied on as honest and truthful.

Based on all of the things I did as a teenager that could have gotten me thrown in jail, I guess I could not have considered myself honest or truthful. Being trusted is not just about telling the truth. Our training proved that we had trust in those who trained us, in particular, our drill instructors. We had to believe that they were teaching us what we needed to know to be Marines and to keep our sorry asses alive one day, which was true of all of our superiors. We would never lie to a superior because we all quickly figured out there would be consequences. Going back again to the recruit who sneaked the ice cream while on mess duty—he did not lie; he just did something he had been told was not allowed, so he was dishonest. His dishonesty cost the entire platoon an hour's worth of our sweat, and I can promise you that no recruit in our platoon would ever risk doing what he did after that incident, so the disciplinary action taken, in fact, worked.

Being trustworthy was something I learned in the Boy Scouts because it was part of what we memorized as scouts, but the concept did not mean much to me until now. After boot camp, I can say that this trait was firmly embedded in my being. I have carried this value through my entire life and have taught my children the same. If you are known as an honest person and someone who can be trusted, you will gain the respect of your peers and subordinates as well as your family. I have always taught my children that if you always tell the truth, you will never have to think about a lie you may have told in the past. A liar needs to have an exceptional memory.

Discipline is defined as the practice of training people to obey rules or a code of behavior, or to use punishment to correct disobedience.

My uncles who were marines told me prior to going into the Marine Corps that everything that you do in training is for a reason, even the things that may seem stupid or ridiculous at the time. During boot camp, we were taught to do things a certain way. There is the wrong way and the Marine Corps way.

The practice of doing exercise as punishment for what others did wrong was given to develop discipline as a group and as an individual. It developed cohesiveness, camaraderie, and esprit de corps. Knowing that you will be punished for not following directions, orders, policy, or procedure is a distinct deterrent.

I was smart enough to figure out as a young recruit more than forty-five years ago that the discipline given was for a reason. I did not necessarily like it at the time, but knowing there was a distinct goal made training easier for me, which is probably why I enjoyed the training. The most significant example described and remembered by me was the previously mentioned one thousand push-ups done for the transgression of one person sneaking ice cream.

I spent my entire thirty-five years in uniform being the disciplined person I learned to be in just nine weeks of boot camp. Speak to anyone who ever worked either with me or for me, and he or she would tell you that I was a by-the-book person, and I believe for that, I had their respect. Those who received disciplinary action from me also knew that they received a fair shake, were treated respectfully, and deserved their punishment for whatever their transgression may have been.

Responsibility is defined as the state of having a duty to deal with something, or the state or fact of being accountable or to blame for something.

The Marine Corps taught me to be accountable to myself and for others once I was in a position that required that I be responsible for others. Either as a fire team leader, gun team leader, squad leader, non-commissioned officer in charge, or sergeant of marines.

In my law enforcement career, I was a sergeant, a lieutenant, and most recently an assistant chief of police. The Corps taught me to take charge and control of situations as they arose and to handle them with professionalism and pride, no matter how unpopular the task may be. I credit the Marine Corps with instilling that trait in me from the very beginning, and no doubt, the ability to get others to follow unpopular orders without question..

There were numerous instances when I gave an unpopular order or instruction that required immediate action or resolution. The discipline and responsibility ingrained in me at the age of eighteen has lasted through an entire career and has carried over to my personal life. As a result, the unpopular order must be given and acted upon without hesitation.

Respect is defined as a feeling of deep admiration for someone or something elicited by his or her abilities, qualities, or achievements.

The trait of respect began as a child because of having so many family members who served in either WWI or WWII. Because of their accomplishments and my knowing what they had been through, I had deep admiration and respect for them. Being a baby-boomer and being so close to those who served also made me one of the most patriotic people you will ever meet, then and now. Now that I am older, just hearing Taps played at a funeral will bring tears to my eyes because of the deep respect that I have for my country and for the flag that represents her. The first time I ever saw my dad cry was during President John Kennedy's funeral service when Taps was played at his grave site.

I mentioned earlier that my fellow recruits deeply respected our drill instructors and would follow them into hell. If one of them ordered us to do anything, there was never any hesitation whatsoever. We trusted and respected them to the level that no order was ever questioned, which was intentionally ingrained so when you found yourself in a life-or-death situation, you obeyed orders from superiors without a second thought. As a result, there was no other human being I feared, which was put to the ultimate test many times in my life.

I learned early on that respect is earned, and as far as the Marine Corps was concerned, anyone above the rank of Private First Class had my respect. Later during my subsequent time in the Marine Corps, I ran across higher ranking NCOs, (Non Commissioned Officers) and Commissioned Officers who were horses' asses, but I showed them the respect that their rank deserved. When saluting an officer, their rank rates the salute, not the person wearing the rank. I can tell you that the people I am referring to were rare, especially in areas of training because those NCOs and officers appeared to be a cut above others with whom I came into contact later.

While in law enforcement, a female lieutenant was promoted to captain the same day that I was promoted to lieutenant. She had a terrible reputation and had been responsible for at least two incidents: one that resulted in death and one that resulted in an officer being wounded. In my agency, we did not salute superiors, but you would, of course, greet them according to rank when passing each other in the hallway or outside.

Because of her reputation and the fact that she had been promoted, in my opinion, above her level of competence, I never referred to her by her rank. I called her *ma'am* but never *captain*.

Punctuality is defined as the quality or habit of adhering to an appointed time.

Being punctual is an automatic; recruit training is nine weeks of intense, nonstop training. Each minute in the day is accounted for, and drill instructors must strictly adhere to their schedules without being a minute late. Being late would result in the entire series of more than three hundred recruits starting late for a class or activity. Not to mention that being late caused the drill instructors issues with their superiors, i.e. series gunnery sergeant, series commander or company commander.

There was not one single thing that we did as recruits that was not controlled by time, from waking up, to shaving and showering, to eating, getting into formation, free time, and, yes, sleeping. One technique drill instructors used to get things done was to count backward, generally starting by just saying "ten," the entire platoon would automatically respond by counting down to zero. Whatever the command given prior to saying ten meant that we had ten seconds to complete the task. I practiced counting down from ten with my two oldest boys, and I have seen them from time to time practice the countdown with their boys. If it works, use it! We went to bed (rack) by the numbers, with the command "Prepare to Mount" and got in our racks at the command of "Mount," and upon getting into the rack lay at the position of attention while the drill instructor gave us his last words of wisdom for the day until given the final order of "Sleep."

When eating our meals, we quickly learned to eat fast since we had to be done and outside in platoon formation by the time the drill instructor finished his meal and came outside. The drill instructor did not get his meal until his last recruit was served his meal and seated. To this day, I still eat fast.

Punctuality goes hand in hand with discipline. Having a certain amount of time to accomplish a task or being at a certain location or checkpoint is especially important in battle. The military succeeds by being punctual and disciplined to have personnel where they are supposed to be at an appointed time. People can be killed or wounded if a person or a unit fails to be on time. Being late for an appointment, to me, indicates that a person must not have thought the meeting was important enough to be on time. I consider it a serious form of disrespect.

To this day, I hate to be late to go anywhere. If we are going on vacation, for example, my wife asks me the night before departure what time we are leaving the next day because she knows if I say we are leaving at 0600, that's when we leave. I am always at least fifteen minutes early for any appointment or function. It drives my wife crazy, but she has accepted the fact that I am never going to change.

Organization is defined as the act of organizing something or the structure or arrangement of related or connected items.

Being organized or neat is a trait that anyone who knows me can attest to, almost to a fault. Boot camp could not and would not function without organization. Everything issued to us had a function and proper place to be stored. We were even taught how to pack our sea bag and believed that unless we packed them the way we were taught, our issue of uniforms and equipment would not fit. We, of course, believed that because our trusted and respected drill instructors told us so.

Receiving our thirty-second haircuts within hours of our arrival on Parris Island was probably the very first act of organization taken upon us, which was designed to remove our former civilian identity so we all looked the same and reduced every individual back to zero, with no visible personality. This was the Marine Corps way of starting to rebuild the individual and indoctrinate him or her into well-disciplined young fighting machine who would act decisively upon command, without hesitation. This was and still is the way of the Marine Corps.

Learning to be neat and organized has become second nature to me. Growing up I did not have much in the way of worldly possessions, except for the clothes or whatever car I owned at the time.

Marines were taught from the very first day in boot camp how to do things their way to ensure uniformity, discipline, responsibility, and organization. No other service spends the time that the Marine Corps does on how to prepare a uniform to be worn, not to mention the numerous uniform fittings throughout the training cycle to ensure that their uniforms looked their best on their marines at graduation from boot camp and their release into the real world. Recruits who were somewhat overweight lost weight during training, and the thin recruits tended to gain weight and muscle mass. As I stated earlier, I entered the Marine Corps weighing 150 lb. and left weighing 180 lb.

The Marine Corps teaches each recruit that to wear the uniform of a Marine is a privilege because many parts of the uniform represent part of our unique history.

Before the first day of boot camp ended we were taught the proper way to shave. Yes, the Marine Corps had its way of shaving too. We were shown to shave the face in sections, how far down the neck we were to shave and where to pay particular attention. A black grease pencil was used by the drill instructor on a recruits' faces and necks to illustrate how and where to shave the proper way, the Marine Corps way. We were all required to shave daily, even those who had never shaved before. Since we shaved at night before showering, shaves were inspected nightly, as each recruit stood in front of his rack (bed). Recruits stood, freshly showered and shaved, and as the drill instructor passed each recruit, the recruit held his hands out, palms down so cleanliness and fingernail trimming and cleaning could be inspected.

I have three grown sons I taught to shave by teaching them to shave their faces in sections. If it works, use it—and I did.

Just this past week I was talking to my oldest son, Doug, and we were discussing the hygiene issues that my daughter in-law is having with their oldest son who is almost thirteen. Doug said that he could not understand why he was having issues because he buys only gold Dial deodorant soap. That is the brand of soap issued to recruits, and he has been using it ever since he was in the Marine Corps himself.. I told him that gold DIAL was also the only soap that I used and have done so since 1966. He is thirty-seven years old and I never knew that he had continued the family tradition, but I certainly was not surprised. If the Marine Corps uses it, it must be good, so I have never switched. These very small idiosyncrasies do not seem out of the ordinary to either of us. Call us crazy. We decided that the hygiene issue was not a result of the brand of soap he was using, but was just something that all boys go through at that age. The issue quickly resolves itself once " once boys discover girls"

Hour upon hour was spent teaching recruits how to remove Irish pennants (lose threads) and measuring with a match the distance between ribbons and the top of the left breast pocket. Shoes and boots were laced left over right and how to shine them was an art form. To this day, I never leave the house with dirty or scuffed shoes. The belt had to be cut to specifications with military alignment, of course. Proper military alignment is when the seam of the shirt is aligned with the seam of the trousers and the right side of the belt buckle is aligned with those seams. All buttons on the uniform are always buttoned, without exception. To this day, I am conscious of having proper military alignment, even in my civilian clothes, and my children teach their sons the same.

The proper method of tying a tie was also taught. The tie had to be tied so its tip stopped at the waistband with the smaller portion of the tie shorter than the wide portion shown. The gold tie bar with the Marine Corps emblem had to be placed between the third and fourth button down from your collar. I will sometimes retie a tie several times to get it adjusted to the specifications taught to me in 1966. If I wear a tie, I will never loosen that tie until I get home and remove it. The top button of my shirt is never unbuttoned until I remove the tie, because I consider myself to be out of uniform if it is undone.

These facts might seem ridiculous to an outsider but any active-duty marine or former marine reading this will nod and smile. When was the last time you saw a sloppy marine in public? Go to an airport or bus station and compare marines with other members of the armed services—there is no comparison. Drill instructors taught us that if we ever saw marines out in public with something amiss on their uniform, that we were to approach them and advise them accordingly. Later in my career, when I was a sergeant, I was in the airport in Washington, DC, and saw a newly minted marine second lieutenant wearing his Class "A" green uniform and quickly noticed that he was wearing his shooting badge and National Defense Ribbon over his right breast pocket instead of over the left pocket. I approached him, advised him of his error, and suggested that he quickly go into a nearby men's room to make the change. He was embarrassed, but who cared?

I do not remember being especially neat or organized prior to entering the Marine Corps, so I can attribute this trait only to my Marine Corps training. My entire family says that I have OCD (Obsessive Compulsive Disorder) to the point where I am "freaky," to quote my daughter. I do not feel that this is a fault and now laugh at my son Doug, who was a marine, and his daughter who both appear to be afflicted with this terrible trait. I do not believe that being neat and having everything in place is a bad thing because it is the way I have lived my life for more than forty-five years.

I am certain the seven values that I have listed in some detail have served as the foundation to my professional career and personal life. I am sure that there are other traits, but these seven have had the most influence on me personally. None of the values individually makes a good leader, but collectively they make a difference and begin to prepare a person for the awesome responsibility of taking charge of people and accomplishing an objective, whether it is in the military or in my case years later—my long career in law enforcement.

I have listed my values in no specific order, but I would have to say that *trustworthy* is probably at the top of the list in importance to me personally. Being trusted by others causes people to follow, so I would say that this is the most important value in being a good leader. If you are trusted, the other values come easily.

My friends and family also know that they can count on me to give them an honest answer or opinion when asked. I have raised four children to be trustworthy and honest and now see that they have instilled those important values in their children, my seven grandchildren. A man only has his good name, and if he is not trusted, what good is his name?

ADVANCED TRAINING

6

OUR BUSES ARRIVED IN NORTH CAROLINA, AND WE were off-loaded at Camp Geiger and ordered into formation. Camp Geiger was and still is a portion of Camp Lejeune designated for the training of newly graduated recruits, now called marines. We would all receive basic infantry training then move on to whatever school needed for our assigned MOS (Military Occupational Specialty). We were quickly broken down into platoons and given barracks assignments and told when to be in formation outside for chow.

We were marched everywhere by so-called Troop Handlers, usually sergeants and sometimes corporals and, for the most part, all recent veterans of Vietnam. Most of them were there in that capacity until their respective enlistments expired. Our housing appeared to be post-WWII, one-story, cinder-block buildings, which each housed one platoon. We had to go to a different building to use the bathroom or shower, which was a bitch in the cold North Carolina November and December.

Our training was interesting and all taught exclusively by Vietnam vets. We had some classroom training but almost all was outside in the field. We had been used to marching in boot camp with everyone in step all of the time. We were now in much larger formations and because of the size of the formations, it was nearly impossible for the guys in the rear to be in step with the others. In the field, we were most often marching at route step, which meant that we all did not have to be in step but needed to stay in formation and keep our proper interval.

All marines attended the first several weeks and when we split up the 03s, which are the first two digits of a four-digit designation of an infantryman's MOS. My designation was 0311, which was the designation of a basic rifleman. The 03s went on to AIT (Advanced Infantry Training), where we were transferred to another location after bidding good-byes to the friends we had made since September 2 at Parris Island.

AIT involved the firing of almost every weapon in the Marine Corps arsenal. After having M-14 rifles in boot camp, our WWII vintage M-1 rifles assigned here took some getting used to. They were great weapons but heavier and harder to clean. We fired Browning Automatic Rifles, LAWs, (Light Anti-Tanks Weapons), .45 pistols, bazookas, M-60 machine guns, and .50-caliber machine guns, and we threw hand grenades. We also had many live fire exercises crawling under barbed wire with live machine guns firing three feet over our heads. There were long compass courses and radio training as well as many overnights in the field and war games.

We ate C-rations and had a hot meal from time to time in mobile field kitchens, which is where I grew to love SOS (shit on a shingle) which was the best thing to eat for breakfast when it was cold out. SOS is cooked chopped beef in heavy, white gravy served over a piece of toast, hence the name, shit on a shingle.

Everyone looked forward to the end of this training because, for one thing, the cold and snow of northern North Carolina made training miserable. We knew we were more than likely heading for the jungles of Vietnam, so we all wanted to get the hell out and get going.

The Marine Corps gives everyone a twenty-day leave upon completion of training, and for those who were headed to the war via California, five days of travel time was added to our twenty-day leave to get to the west coast. There was no graduation ceremony, and we did not care. We just wanted our Greyhound bus tickets home and our orders to our next assignment. On December 23, we loaded onto Greyhound buses to our respective hometowns, in my case New York City to the Port Authority Bus Terminal. Our bus was almost full, and I recall making one stop in Virginia where we picked up five or six soldiers who were also headed to New York. I felt sorry for those poor bastards because we made life miserable for them the rest of the way to New York by singing the "Marine Corps Hymn" most of the way. My friend Gil who had dumped my hung-over, puking butt at the curb in Newark several months prior, met me at the bus terminal.

We took the short drive back home to New Jersey, and I spent maybe an hour with the family, then we were off to meet my friends in a bar, where else, back in New York City! I had a good time seeing my buddies and drinking a few with them, but I quickly noticed that we were vastly different now. Most were home on Christmas break from college, and some were working, waiting for the dreaded draft to catch them. I certainly did not feel like I was in any way better than they were, but there was now a distinct and noticeable difference. They were doing everything they could to avoid military service, and I was now a trained killer, who, in twenty-five days was on my way to more training before going off to war.

While I was at home on leave, a girl named Betty, who was going to school to be a beautician needed someone to practice giving a manicure to. I do not know what she did wrong, but my right pinkie became infected and swelled to double its size. I knew I needed to go to the doctor and told my mother. I was again reminded that money was still tight for my family. She told me that because she owed our longtime family doctor money that I would have to pay whatever the bill was on my own. I ended up needing to have my finger lanced to drain the infection and was given antibiotics. I offered to pay the bill on the way out, but Dr. R. would not take my money. He knew the deal and had been our family doctor for many years. He delivered my two brothers and two sisters, and in those days still made house calls in his Corvette.

Except for Gil, who picked me up and who had been my best friend most of my life, I never socialized with the guys again after this leave. Gil ended up being the best man in my first wedding, and I was in his wedding party. He remains my oldest and dearest friend, and although he now lives three thousand miles away in Washington, we continue to correspond regularly.

After twenty-four days of spending time with siblings and family, several family gatherings, Christmas parties, New Year's Eve parties, and guys just hanging out, it was time to take my second plane ride. I had orders to report to Camp Pendleton, California, to Staging Battalion, which was additional training in preparation for Vietnam. My orders stated after training I was to be ordered to WESTPAC GRNDFORCES, which is the military abbreviation for West Pacific Ground Forces. I flew into San Diego on January 16, 1967, spent a night there, and shared a hotel room with a marine I knew. Then I took a bus to Oceanside and changed buses for the last connection to Pendleton.

Upon my arrival at Pendleton, we had to turn our orders over at a building with two windows, one marked 1st Marine Division and the other 3rd Marine Division. I could not believe that I would actually have a choice of where I would serve. Because of the fact that one of my uncles served in the 1st I naturally chose the 1st. We were assigned a barracks and were now housed with enlisted marines of all ranks. Most all of us just out of training were all PFCs (Private First Class), and we were now housed with marines from private to staff sergeant. Now we were with marines who were trained on the west coast and some marines who had obviously been in the Corps for a while.

Meeting guys from all over the place was interesting, to say the least. I recall one old guy who was at least in his forties and was a sergeant. He told us that he had been busted to sergeant three times and had been in the Marine Corps for twenty-two years. He had a cook MOS and had been a cook since 1945, and, of course, his nickname was "Cookie." I ran into him several times in Vietnam where he had again been promoted to staff sergeant. Whenever I went to see him, he would put me at a table in the kitchen and have someone cook me a big meal. He would sit with me and wanted to know about the guys we trained with and who had been wounded and who had been killed. He was great guy—old enough to be my father—but that did not matter.

We trained for a month, climbing up and down the hills of Camp Pendleton and later Camp Las Pulgas, a more desolate area that too was part of Pendleton. We trained Monday to Friday and were able to get liberty on Friday night until dusk on Sundays. We were now able to wear civilian clothes on liberty, and we went to places like Disneyland, the San Diego Zoo, and Tijuana, Mexico.

Part of our training was escape and evasion classes, which was interesting. We were cut loose after dark in the boonies of the mountains of Pendleton and were required to find our way back to a designated location without being detected. If we were caught, we were taken into custody and treated as thought we were a prisoner of war. From the drop-off point, the distance back to camp was fifteen miles. We had a canteen of water but no food.

We had survival classes in outdoor training areas and went through mock Vietnam villages with amazingly accurate setups to simulate the real thing. One class I vividly recall was when an instructor stood in front of us, while we were seated in bleachers, and he took a white rabbit out of a cage, held it upside down by its hind legs, and suddenly gave a quick chop to the back of the rabbit's neck, killing it instantly. He then skinned and gutted the rabbit, demonstrating how to eat portions of the rabbit and to use the skin turned inside out as a boot if necessary. I would like to add that I never saw one single rabbit while in Vietnam.

Because of the imminence of going to war and because we had an image to uphold, guys would go out and get bowl-hugging drunk as often as possible. A favorite too was to go out and get drunk and come back with wild tattoos. I later saw many of those tattoos get torn up by gunshot and shrapnel wounds. I also saw many guys get their girlfriends' names tattooed on their arms or chests then get the Dear John letter later in Vietnam where they sorely regretted ever getting a tattoo. I was surprised at the large number of guys who went home on leave and married their high-school sweethearts. Those newly married guys were the ones getting the dreaded Dear John letters, not the ones who had been married a while.

One weekend my favorite uncle, Uncle Tom, arranged for a business trip from his home in Kansas to Los Angeles, and we hooked up for the weekend. He was able to get on base and picked me up and we drove around the base. When he got out to Camp Las Pulgas, he said it looked very familiar from when he passed through in the '40s on his way to the Pacific. The barracks on the main portion of the base were the same wooden, prewar buildings as well as the sheet metal Quonset Huts on Las Pulgas. We went to Los Angeles and drove to see his old house in Canoga Park, as he used to work in the LA area. We went out to eat, and he passed on wise and helpful advice to me, knowing that I was just a week or two from heading to Vietnam. Now that I was a marine, he spoke more candidly to me about war than when I was just an awestruck kid asking dumb questions. The only difference was that this time he would pass on valuable information that would very likely keep my young ass alive for a little while.

My uncle saw a lot of action on Guadalcanal and Okinawa and was badly wounded by a large caliber bullet to the leg in the battle for Sugar Loaf Hill on Okinawa in 1945. He was a Browning Automatic Rifleman (BAR Man), which was our modern version of an automatic rifleman in the '40s. He told me that he saw the "Jap" soldier who shot him, and his buddy was able to kill him after he shot my uncle. We recently found a letter he wrote to my mother, while hospitalized, where he wrote that Okinawa was the most scared he had been to date. We spent two nights in a hotel in the LA area and just enjoyed each other's company. I spent many summers as a kid at his house on Long Island when he worked for an aircraft company, and I respected him as much as I did my own dad. He dropped me off at my barracks Sunday evening as I prepared to enter my last week of training before leaving the country.

Several days before our departure there was a shakedown of our barracks by several officers and staff NCOs. We were advised that we would have the opportunity to turn in any illegal weapons with no questions asked, and if any weapons were found later, that marine would be arrested and charged. I was amazed at what weapons came out of the woodwork—guns, pipes, chains, switchblade knives, and brass knuckles. There were no metal detectors in those days. I managed to keep a small, spring-loaded, lead-filled blackjack given to me by my godfather who was a cop in New Jersey. The blackjack was not considered to be illegal.

ZOOMING TO "THE NAM"

7

WE LEFT CAMP PENDLETON AT THE END OF our training on February 14, 1967, and were bused to the Marine Corps Air Station at nearby El Toro. We had our individual orders to specific division commands to be later assigned to smaller units upon our arrival in-country. We waited for quite some time at the airport and finally boarded a commercial airliner, a Continental Airlines Boeing 707. We flew forever and made a quick stop in Hawaii for refueling and were allowed to stretch and walk around the terminal and were back in the air in less than two hours. Our next stop was Okinawa, where we were then trucked to Camp Hansen. We were now on our own, so to speak—no formations, no marching to chow, and no yelling. We were, however, assigned to work parties and spent the next several days doing manual labor around the base.

We had the opportunity to give blood, which I did, and spent several nights hanging out in the E-Club (Enlisted Men's Club). We also stored our dress uniforms and any civilian clothes we had there, which were stored for safekeeping until our Vietnam tour was over, either by death or end of tour.

Marines from the group were selected based on our MOS (job classification) and the need at the time in Vietnam for particular units. Once we received word we were on the manifest to leave, we again boarded another commercial jet that would fly us to Danang Air Base in Danang, Vietnam, a three-hour flight. We approached the airport in the dark and were instructed to close all window shades for obvious reasons. When we taxied up to a stop at the wooden terminal and the door opened, the heat and humidity hit us like a wall. As we exited one by one, we inhaled the soon-to-be familiar smells of the country and experienced the intensity of the heat and fetid air that hit us right in the face. As we filed off of the plane, there were marines who had completed their thirteen-month tours waiting to board for their well-earned trip back to the world because, for obvious reasons, the aircraft stayed on the ground only long enough to empty the cargo holds and refuel. Some yelled, "You'll be sorry," but most kept quiet, just wanting to get out. You could instantly tell who had seen combat and who had been in the rear areas almost never seeing or hearing a shot fired. The combat veterans all had the deep, sunken eyes from lack of sleep, which made them look older than their years. Most were thin, underweight, and gaunt, not in the mood to play or joke around. The extreme heat and humidity was oppressive, something that we would soon be getting used to.

I spent one night at the Danang Airport, received my unit assignment the next day, and awaited transportation by C-130 to Chu Lai to the Seventh Marines Regimental Headquarters. Once there I received more specific orders, telling me that I would be going to the Third Battalion Seventh Marines (3/7), which was located south of Chu Lai. I was told that I would be in Chu Lai in a day or two and assigned a "hooch" to stay in, which was a wooden platform with a wooden frame with a canvas tent over the frame. In Chu Lai, I walked into the mess hall for chow and saw "Cookie," the cook I befriended from Camp Pendleton. He was in charge of the galley crew and had been in-country only a few days, so we talked, and he told me to stop in any time I was in the area, and I told him I was going south in the morning to 3/7. He told me there was a lot of fighting going on down there.

The next day after morning chow, I caught a CH-46 helicopter to Duc Pho in Quang Nam Province, which is where the Third Battalion was at the time. I still had not yet been issued any gear and was still in a stateside utility uniform with leather boots. I was told that as soon as the chopper landed to exit as quickly as possible in case there was an attack when they landed. The handful of us who made the ride hauled butt down the back ramp, and the supplies that made the trip with us were quickly off-loaded. During my exit, I noticed that there were several black rubber body bags that were hastily loaded for the trip back. This was a sobering observation and a reminder that we were now very close to the action.

A gunnery sergeant, who I later found out was in charge of the landing zone incoming and outgoing, met me. I was directed to the battalion headquarters office and assigned to Kilo Company, Second Platoon, and was told that my platoon was out on a long-range patrol and was not due back for a few days. I was told that it would be ten days to two weeks before I would report, though, because all new replacements are assigned to the landing zone to load and unload helicopters to become acclimated to the weather. My company office then processed my paperwork and sent me to supply, where I was issued my M-16 rifle and all of my web gear, flak jacket, and helmet. I also got one set of jungle boots and one set of the new tropical lighter weight utilities. From that point on I did not go anywhere without my weapon until the day I left country.

I spent the next thirteen days, along with some other new replacements, working my ass off. Since our battalion was crammed in a relatively small area to accommodate an entire battalion, there was no airport or landing strip. The area occupied by the battalion could accommodate only helicopters, which meant unloading and loading supplies by hand. We were still trying to get acclimated to the weather, so our asses were dragging at the end of each day. We not only moved supplies but also had to unload dead and wounded marines as they arrived for medical care at the Battalion Aid Station. The wounded were quickly placed on stretchers and into a waiting ambulance for a one-minute ride to the Battalion Aid Station, which was just a large tent with an outer wall of sandbags about three feet high. Many Viet Cong prisoners were brought in almost daily, and we were instructed that photographs were prohibited.

I recall one time we were alerted that a chopper was incoming with a severely wounded pilot. The chopper, an old CH-34, ones in which the pilots sat high up with most of their body exposed, came in about as fast as I had ever seen. The pilot sitting in the right seat was slumped in his seat, and as soon as the chopper landed, the pilot climbed down, ran around to his copilot's side of the craft and climbed up to unstrap his buddy and help him down to us. It was obvious that the copilot was wounded badly with a frontal head wound from a large-caliber weapon. He had been shot through the windshield, which had been blown out on his side of the cockpit. The pilot said he thought they were hit by a .50-caliber machine gun. Carrying someone already in a body bag or helping a wounded marine was much different than pulling a freshly wounded marine pilot out of his helicopter straight from a heated battle. Unfortunately, the pilot died before he ever got to the Aid Station. About thirty minutes later another load of wounded marines was brought in after their chopper was shot down less than a mile away.

I soon found out that the helicopter pilot and the wounded and dead marines that we had off-loaded in the past three days while assigned to the landing zone were from my newly assigned Company K or were fighting in support of our company. After almost two weeks, I was removed from working the LZ, and I reported to my platoon.

KILO COMPANY, THIRD BATTALION, SEVENTH MARINES

8

I WENT TO MY PLATOON AREA, WHICH WAS situated behind some 105 mm artillery batteries. My new squad leader was a corporal, and the first things he asked were "Where are you from?" and "Do you smoke?" I responded with "Jersey" and "No, I don't smoke." He came back with a quick "You will." I never smoked, but I did trade what cigarettes I got in my C rations for a can of fruit or a better meal.

My platoon had been out for three or four days, and were all busy cleaning weapons and gear. Because of that, we did not have to stand perimeter watch that night. I was paired up with another guy, and we shared a two-man tent by snapping our shelter halves together. My squad leader came to get me to take me to meet our lieutenant. We spoke for a few minutes, and he told me to get my gear squared away because we were going on another patrol in a day or so. He also told me that I was replacing a man who had been killed the day before by a booby trap. My tent mate and I became friends, and he filled me in on what I needed to do to prepare for the next patrol. Since we were right behind batteries of 105s, sleeping was very noisy because they fired off and on through the night as they received fire missions from other units out in the bush.

Our battalion was actively involved in Operation Desoto and had been ongoing for almost two months. Two days after joining my platoon, I went on my first patrol, which resulted in two, wounded from a booby trap. A chopper flew out both wounded—unfortunately, one lost an arm. We returned late in the afternoon and in time for chow. The next day was my second patrol, a little longer than the day before, which was uneventful; no contact meant no casualties, which was fine with me.

My third day and third patrol was a different story. This was an entire platoon-sized patrol with a Viet Cong prisoner walking point. The prisoner was wearing black pajamas and had his hands tied behind his back with a thirty- to forty-foot-long rope tied around his neck. The rope ensured that he did not run, and the length was so if he stepped on a booby trap only he would be the only one wounded. Through an interpreter, he had been instructed to guide our platoon safely to a certain location around the enemy. My squad was the first of three, and I was back about halfway in the column across an open area on a rice paddy dike when all of a sudden we were ambushed by automatic weapons at a range of less than seventy-five yards. We went down immediately, taking cover where we could find it and returned fire. When we looked up, the prisoner was standing up all alone on the rice paddy dike. I remember the company commander running up to see what was up and gave us the order to take out the prisoner. He went down quickly after several of us cut loose with rifle fire.

This battle ended up being a heated firefight, where we were pinned down in an open rice paddy for three hours. The last squad in the column worked its way around and flanked the enemy, which ended that battle and resulted in three confirmed enemy kills, with evidence of more. To confuse our count and us for reporting purposes, the VC (Viet Cong) were known for quickly removing their dead, but the best part of this action was that no marines were wounded. When this firefight ended, we continued to our original destination, walked into a village and were again ambushed. This fight lasted almost two hours, resulting in three more confirmed enemy kills. After this second firefight of the day we headed back again with no casualties.

The best way to describe a firefight is to say it is organized bedlam and chaos, and the adrenalin rush is unmatched by anything I have ever experienced, to say the least. When involved in a firefight, there was no time to be scared because you were fighting to do the right thing and to follow shouted orders to the best of your ability. The firing of numerous weapons and explosions made it impossible to hear what was being said, so we depended heavily on our fire-team leaders, squad leaders, and platoon leader to direct us to do the right thing. You had to yell to be heard over the firing of the weapons.

Lack of sleep was another issue that I quickly identified as a constant. We just never got enough sleep, because when in the field, we had to take turns doing two-hour watches, and when in the rear area, we had to stand duty in perimeter foxholes. God help the poor soul who was ever caught sleeping on duty.

Until a person has been battle tested under fire, he or she will not completely understand that your life depends on the buddies on either side of you. We were all well trained and knew what to do. Our squad buddies and the training kept us alive, and we learned quickly to trust our fellow marine without question.

One thing I immediately noticed when I got to the field was that most all of the grunts were wearing an Ace of Spades playing card in the elastic around their helmet liners. I inquired and found out that the Vietnamese were very superstitious, especially about the Ace of Spades image. As soon as the government found out about this, they began issuing whole decks of cards to commanders, which consisted only of Ace of Spade cards. They were handed out to squad leaders and then to individual marines. When we had a confirmed kill of an enemy soldier, we would place the card on the body in a prominent place, sometimes right over the wound. It apparently had a positive superstitious effect on the enemy and went on as long as I was in-country.

Well, my first eight days in Kilo Company resulted in seven patrols and no rest, but time passed quickly. After being out seven days, we welcomed getting back to hot chow in the battalion mess tent.

Back in the rear in the battalion area, our mess hall was an open area with handmade picnic-type tables with benches and one large tent with tables for cover and a second tent, which was the mess tent or kitchen. Before eating, there were large garbage cans filled with water with a kerosene heater to heat the water to boiling. Before going through the chow line, we had to dip our clean mess kits into at least two of these cans of boiling water. This was necessary to avoid sickness, especially dysentery. When our meal was finished, we dumped any leftover food out of our mess kits into a garbage can then went through a series of three garbage cans of hot boiling water. The first had soapy water with a long handled brush and the other two were for rinsing.

Sometime during my first month in the unit, we were standing in line waiting to rinse our mess kits before eating. Some rear area marine ahead of me had his .45 caliber Colt pistol out of his holster when all of a sudden the weapon went off and shot a marine in front of him in line in the back, which exited his stomach then hit a marine ahead of him in line. I know the first marine hit died immediately, but I'm not sure what happened to the second, who appeared to be seriously wounded. The .45s issued were old and worn, as were their safeties. That was the first accidental discharge resulting in death that I would witness in Vietnam. A sad situation, with one dead, a second severely wounded. The marine responsible surely ended up in the brig.

On March 16, Kilo Company was a blocking force on the high ground overlooking a valley being cleared by marines of Foxtrot 2/7.

There was a large village in the valley. All of a sudden, all hell broke loose on the marines in the valley, with heavy automatic weapons fire from an unknown number of VC. There were snipers down there with them and snipers on an opposite hill from us with large-caliber machine guns, identified as a .30 and a .50 caliber. The .50 caliber had a distinct sound and they were firing only one to two rounds at a time, which made them very hard to locate for a while. There were major firefights ongoing in several places within our view. Once the choppers came in to medevac our wounded, we started taking the heavy caliber fire from the opposite hill, which resulted in at least two choppers being shot down. Once the firing started, we returned fire in attempt to suppress their fire on our fellow marines that we could plainly see were being chopped up badly.

On this day, I got my first confirmed kill. A sniper in the village shot at me, and I happened to see where the shot came from as it whizzed over my head. I waited a few minutes, and sure enough, he showed himself again. I fired five or six rounds from my M-14 and saw him go down. The .50 caliber on the mountain was finally removed by Marine Corps fixed wing and helicopter air strikes. Marine Corps aircraft came in right over our heads in their path to the target and were so close we could almost read the pilot's name painted on the side of the cockpit. I had been in-country for only a month but had quickly learned that Marine Corps pilots, jet and chopper, had balls the size of grapefruit. Before this gun was eliminated, it had shot down choppers loaded with casualties and shot through eighteen-inch-wide rice paddy dikes, killing personnel seeking cover behind them.

The fight lasted all morning and afternoon, and we eventually went down in the valley to sweep the village clear. It was dark by the time we finished. The guns on the mountain were eliminated, and all of our casualties and shot-down choppers were removed. This battle was very costly in terms of lives and equipment lost.

3/7 Command Chronology reported 8 marines Killed In Action (KIA) and five Wounded In Action (WIA). There were 7 confirmed VC KIA and 9more confirmed KIA by air strikes to the guns on the opposite hill. More than 200 two hundred rounds of support artillery were expended in this battle.

When we got down into the village that evening, a marine saw that I had "Which way to Jersey?" written on my helmet liner and asked me where I was from. When I told him Hasbrouck Heights, he said, "My girlfriend lives there." After talking a few minutes, we figured out that his girlfriend lived across the street from me, and I grew up with her brother. Dick turned out to be a good guy and looked up my parents when he went home several months later.

Although we were following our orders as a blocking force on the high ground and firing at targets of opportunity, we had to lie and watch Foxtrot 2/7 accomplish its assignment of moving through that village and clearing it of any enemy that they encountered. It was a large fight that lasted from midmorning to darkness, with active and fierce firefights ongoing, choppers and fixed-wing aircraft attacking the opposite hill to take out the two machine guns, not to mention the hundreds of rounds of supporting artillery fire, and at least two medevac choppers going down while trying to get the dead and wounded out.

The following year I ran into a guy in Embassy School, and when we compared notes, I found out he had been in Foxtrot 2/7. I told him we were on the mountain watching the whole thing unfold and helped them clear the village at the end of the day. He thanked me immensely, and we became instant friends.

A couple of weeks later several of us came down with what was described as yeast poisoning from eating a bad batch of C ration canned bread. We were in sickbay for several days and sick as dogs the entire time. Easter Sunday was approaching, and the Thursday before Easter, we were released from sick bay and sent to our company area to wait for our company to return from the bush. My buddy Tony and I stayed in a tent that night, so that we would have room to move around, we both put all of our gear into a tent next to ours, only six to eight feet away.

At about one thirty on the morning of March 25 (Good Friday) we were awakened by a large volume of incoming mortar and rocket fire. We bailed out of our tent, went to get our weapons, and discovered that a direct hit by a mortar round had hit the tent containing all of our gear. There was nothing left but some debris and a small crater where the tent had been. It appeared as though the VC had all of the vital areas of the battalion area zeroed in. The first rounds hit the ammo dump, fuel dump, artillery batteries, and battalion headquarters. The attack lasted for one to two hours, but marines on the perimeter kept the enemy out of the wire. The marines of 3/11 fired their cannons pointed straight at the perimeter with anti-personnel flechette rounds, which are shells loaded with thousands of little darts intended to kill personnel. Flechette is a French word that means little arrow, and a 105 mm howitzer had 5,000 flechettes per round. India Company 3/11 took at least two direct hits to gun batteries, but they kept their remaining guns going throughout the battle. Tony and I were helpless without our weapons, so we just helped where we could and carried some wounded and KIA to the aid station.

As soon as the battle was over, I went to the area where we had our gear and weapons stored, and I managed to salvage a small portion of the receiver of my trusty M-14. The piece I salvaged was the base of the receiver that had the rifle's serial number engraved on it, so I took that piece to the armorer. Because the number was on the piece, he immediately gave me a new weapon, magazines, and ammo. For that time we were under attack, I never felt so helpless. A marine without a weapon in the middle of a fight is not an experience I care to re-live.

When daylight came on Good Friday morning, the battalion area was mess. I was able to salvage a few Polaroid photos from home, which I still have today, with shrapnel cuts and powder burns on the edges. I lost everything else, but who cares? I was alive and could easily get new equipment, a camera, a writing portfolio, and shaving gear. There were holes in the tent that we were sleeping in from the mortar shrapnel that destroyed our equipment, and we were amazed that we were not wounded from such a close hit—another close call.

3/7 Command Chronology reported that we were attacked by 60 mm and 82 mm mortars and 57mm and 75 mm recoilless rifles. incoming rounds were estimated to be between 200-250 rounds. Two gun pits of India Company 3/11 received direct hits. The tactical fuel dispensing system, mogas, (*unleaded fuel*),and aviation gasoline dumps were destroyed by fire.

Intelligence later indicated that twelve recoilless rifles were used in the attack. I know that three marines of 3/11 were killed, and at least twelve wounded, but records provided did not list the specific numbers of marines either WIA or KIA that night. I saw the KIAs, so I know that to be a fact.

In a letter I wrote home to the family dated March 28, 1967, I was reminded of my concern for my parents' financial situation. They were my beneficiaries, and I had most all of my money sent home to them. I was earning only about $105 per month in base pay, with an extra $100 per month in combat pay. I said in my letter please use my money if you need it. I know they needed to tap into my account from time to time, but I was eighteen years old and ten thousand miles away, and without a care in the world, so money was not an issue to me at the time.

The first week of April we went out on a company-sized operation in some of the mountains in our area of responsibility. We were out for seven and a half days, and the temperature got up over 120 degrees. In the first two days, there were twelve cases of heat exhaustion, which all required medevac out of the field. I recall a marine I knew from New York who was overcome by the heat. I saw him coming down the last mountain running in a stupor. He was as pale as a ghost, his lips were blue, and he somehow made it to the bottom without going over a ledge to his death. He was medevac'd by helicopter as a heat casualty. When we returned several days later, he seemed fine and later returned to the platoon as if nothing ever happened.

It was on this operation that I lost my first friend. We got into a fierce firefight in a large village with snipers shooting from several directions. My buddy Lawrence was my squad's automatic rifleman. When we had the M-14s, only one or two marines per squad had the automatic selector switch on their weapon. Well, in the middle of the fight, Lawrence took a burst of bullets to his chest and died quickly. We ended up capturing the sniper alive and threw him into a well followed by a grenade. The loss of Lawrence was a bummer to the entire platoon because he was so well liked by everyone and was considered a short-timer, with only a few months remaining on his thirteen-month tour.

When we returned from this operation, we were issued the controversial new M-16s. We all received several hours of classroom training, were issued ammo, and were able to fire our weapons to familiarize ourselves with their operation. After lugging the heavy M-14 around with ten to twelve loaded magazines, the difference in weight was astonishing. The weapons were much lighter and the ammo was lighter, and the magazines were an aluminum alloy so humping a patrol was now much easier for the grunts. How they performed in battle was yet to be tested. We had already heard horror stories of rounds becoming jammed and marines being found dead with cleaning rods in their hands, killed while trying to clear their jammed weapon. None of us could wait to get back out on patrol and see what damage the new 5.56 round would do to the enemy—we had been told that the M-16 round would tumble once it entered the body.

Our battalion had been in Duc Pho conducting long- and short-range patrols in Operation Desoto since January 26, and it was now time to move out. We went out on one more patrol with our M-16s, but for a change, we made no contact with the enemy. We were preparing to leave Duc Pho and were to be relieved by the Army's 1st Air Cavalry (Airmobile), which started bringing in massive amounts of equipment. I mentioned earlier that our entire battalion of over 1,200 marines was inside of a very small perimeter and had an area large enough to accommodate only two helicopters at a time. Outside of the edge of our barbed-wire perimeter were Vietnamese villages, which we, of course, passed through each day on our way out on patrol. Well, the 1st Air Cav. was huge and brought in a great deal of equipment, including bulldozers that quickly graded an airstrip to accommodate fixed-wing aircraft, such as C-123s and C-130 aircraft. The last marine left Duc Pho on April 7 after suffering 76 KIAs, and 573 WIAs. During Operation Desoto, marines were responsible for killing a reported 383 enemy soldiers.

As everyone knows, the Marine Corps has used hand-me-down equipment from other services for years. Our packs were WWII vintage, our C rations were canned in the late 1940s, and our hot chow was primitive at best. Well, we started seeing what the Army was bringing in for its troops, and we Marines just could not resist doing a little shopping at the expense of the good, old US Army. We were able to convert ownership of new A-Frame backpacks, jungle boots, and Sundrie Pack C rations, which was a large case of canned food with enough to feed a platoon of thirty. We were also able to get our hands on the new dehydrated long rats (rations), which were foil bags of great meals, which only required that you add water and stir. We were sure glad to see the Army take over, for more than obvious reasons.

We left the area and were flown by CH-46 choppers to Chu Lai, about forty miles north, while the Army expanded our battalion area so much they ended up having the enemy inside of their wired perimeter. We quickly heard that their first night of occupancy in Duc Pho resulted in a large fight with heavy Army losses because of its rapid expansion to accommodate all of their personnel and equipment.

As soon as we got to Chu Lai, I went immediately to the mess hall where my friend "Cookie," the mess sergeant worked. He sat me and few of my buddies down, had someone cook us steaks, and kept the milk coming. He wanted me to fill him in on who had been wounded and or killed. He was a great guy and always took care of me when he saw me.

Officially, 3/7 was transferred from Duc Pho in Quang Ngai Province to the Dia Loc District, relieving the Second Battalion Fourth Marines just south of Danang. We spent several days in Chu Lai eating good mess-hall food and swimming in the ocean.

We ended up on a hill near Dia Loc and ran daily patrols and nightly ambushes off of the hill. This was nothing new to us. If you were not on a patrol or an ambush you were on the hill pulling perimeter watch two hours at a time. I quickly came to find that sleep was the most precious commodity to a marine, and you never had enough. Every spare moment was used taking a nap to try to catch up on sleep, but catching up was never a reality.

About a week after arriving in Dia Loc, I was one of two guys assigned to a listening post (LP). We went out after dark and set up about three hundred yards outside of the perimeter. Our purpose was to be the eyes and ears for the marines on the hill and to alert command if we heard or observed the enemy attempting to infiltrate the area. In the middle of the night, we heard a major firefight ongoing off in the distance and over our right rear that appeared to be at the location of a CAP Unit (Combined Action Platoon). This was a program that only the Marine Corps was crazy enough to institute. CAP was a program in which a small unit of marines, usually the size of a squad (twelve men) and commanded by a sergeant, lived in villages with the local population. They were extremely vulnerable but were successful in providing for the needs of the villagers. There was one hell of a fight going on, and we could hear the distinct difference in the sound of the M-16s vs. the AK-47s of the VC. There were numerous explosions at first. Then we heard our artillery and mortars coming in. We were also providing 81 mm mortar illumination support from our hill. We then heard the tank on our hill start up and move away from our hill to the main road. Trying to figure out what was going on just by the sounds of battle we were hearing was driving us crazy.

All of a sudden, we received excited orders over the radio for us to return quickly to the hill because we were going to the CAP Unit as a reactionary force. The tank and one squad already had about a fifteen-minute head start because they left as soon as the CAP unit reported being under attack. We force marched the entire way down the road, approximately two miles, and set up a perimeter. The CAP Unit had been overrun by an estimated two platoons of Viet Cong. Five marines were killed, and four were wounded, which was 75 percent of their manpower. They had managed to kill at least ten to fifteen VC during the intense fight for their lives. There was much evidence that a fierce fight had taken place. The enemy attacked from all directions as most of the squad slept in a large tent. They attacked, firing AK-47s and throwing satchel charges into the two bunkers in the perimeter, collapsing them.

Our platoon stayed in the area, set up a perimeter around the village, and sent out patrols at first light to follow the drag marks and blood trails left by the fleeing enemy. They were able to capture Chi-Com hand grenades, rifles, magazines, and a magazine from a Thompson Sub-Machine Gun, as I recall. Our squad stayed on the perimeter while the other two went out on patrols.

Lieutenant General Lew Walt, the ranking marine in-country at the time was known to visit the field regularly after fights to see firsthand what we were up against. He was a veteran of WWII and Korea and was famous in Marine Corps history. Sure enough, around midmorning we were told that General Walt was coming in and to be prepared. When he and his choppers landed, we were in the process of filling sandbags to rebuild a CAP bunker that had collapsed from an explosion the night before. He exited his chopper and came right to us from the chopper, asked a few questions, and moved on to inspect the rest of the damage.

3/7 Command Chronology reported an estimated 100 Main Force VC attacked CAP B-4 at AT943664 with grenades, satchel charges, S/A (small arms), and A/W (automatic weapons). Penetration occurred in the SW part of the perimeter. The CAP unit returned over 1,000 rounds of 5.56 and called in artillery and 81 missions for illumination and to interdict likely VC withdrawal routes. A reaction force of tanks and one squad arrived within 10 minutes of the initial assault and restored the perimeter security. The casualties included 5 USMC KIA, 4 USMC WIA, 5 PFs (*police forces*)WIA, 2 bunkers destroyed, 7 M-16 rifles were lost, as was one M-79 and 7 LAAWS. Eight VC bodies were observed to have been dragged away.

A day or two after that incident, our platoon was on perimeter watch just outside of the village of Dia Loc, and, as usual, we took turns at two-hour watches. Not long after dark, we took incoming fire from a tree line, and we all returned fire after a short firefight. I recall that I slept on top of my plastic poncho liner in a soft area. I stood my two-hour watch and went back to my poncho to finish the remainder of the night's sleep. When we woke up the next morning, I picked up my poncho to fold it up and saw that I had slept on top of a bed of baby pit viper snakes, one of the most poisonous snakes in the country. They looked like a bowl of spaghetti all curled up. I just wondered how far away mama pit viper was all night. We had been taught that Vietnam had 127 species of snakes, and 126 were poisonous. We had seen foot-long lizards, poisonous centipedes, and snakes eight inches in circumference and fifteen feet long. This was definitely another close call for me.

Several days later while on patrol one of our guys stepped on a booby-trapped grenade. He had arrived in-country as a lance corporal and had been in the Corps for a while, so he had taken the unusual route to Vietnam, having been in for almost two years already. He had been an Lance corporal for a while and said one day that he would give his left nut to make corporal. As luck would have it, or not, he ended up losing his left testicle after stepping on that booby trap, but did not make corporal!

By now, I had been the squad's grenadier and now carried an M-79 grenade launcher. Our next major operation lasted seven days. CH-46 choppers inserted us into the mountains on an operation called Bald Eagle. We were inserted with a 1st Reconnaissance Battalion Unit (1st Recon) walking point.(*first man in the column*). We came upon what was identified as a VC training area. There were numerous houses and caves with much livestock. The caves contained uniforms, anti-American leaflets, and medical supplies. We also located a large cache of rice and bundles of black clothing. We stupidly broke open the bundles and put the black pajama-type tops on but were quickly told to remove them because we could be mistaken from the air as the enemy. We put them on mainly because they were dry, and we were wearing nasty, sweat-soaked shirts. Engineers were called in to blow the caves and to destroy the buildings. We also destroyed the rice and livestock in place.

3/7 Command Chronology reported On 071700H a Co. K Bald Eagle came upon 5 VC in green uniforms with weapons. The VC were taken under fire but fled into the dense brush and jungle. A search of the area at 814637 found an apparent VC training area. The complex consisted of twenty houses with 15 ft. caves nearby; pigs and chickens numbered about 100; clothing, included camouflaged utilities, anti-American propaganda, and a handwritten journal was uncovered. Co. K continued their Bald Eagle search/ destroy at 815631, and uncovered a large rice cache in what appeared to be a VC staging area. Three huts were found along with bundles of black clothing and 250 rolls of black cloth bearing Chinese markings.

While on this operation, we were so far up in the mountains covered by heavy jungle vegetation that we were unable to be resupplied. Helicopters tried to get to us, but heavy fog and bad weather continued to prevent us from receiving much-needed food and, more importantly, water. It was on this operation that we went three and a half days without food and more than two days without water. While in the jungle, we came upon banana trees that were loaded with miniature bananas. They were much smaller than any I have ever seen and were still green on the vines. We did not care; we were hungry and made the fateful mistake of gorging ourselves on these tiny, green bananas. In no time at all, we were all suffering from acute diarrhea and were all off into the jungle to relieve ourselves. That very same afternoon we were finally resupplied with water and C rations.

Later in the day with 1st Recon walking point, we came under heavy automatic rifle fire at the head of the column. The area we were in was dense jungle, with canopies over one hundred feet high. The only light we had was the little sunlight that shone through the cracks of openings in the jungle canopy. In the subsequent firefight that followed an ambush, two recon marines were killed and three wounded. The point recon marine took one right between the eyes, but Kilo suffered only one wounded. We managed to assault their positions without finding any enemy dead or wounded. We carried our wounded and dead to the top of the mountain. When we got to the top the trees were sparse, but it was obvious that to get choppers in for a medevac, some trees had to be blown to allow room for a chopper.

Trees were blown, and an Air Force chopper arrived to medevac the troops, which was extremely unusual. Marine choppers almost exclusively provided our chopper support, and we had never even seen an Air Force chopper in-country. The chopper hovered about fifty to seventy-five feet over our position over the blown tree stumps as they lowered a litter basket to remove the dead and wounded one by one. After retrieving all of the dead and wounded marines, the chopper all of a sudden dropped from the sky and into our laps, with the blades twisting wildly into the blown tree stumps. Those in the chopper took one hell of a wild ride. Even though their altitude was relatively low, the blades kept spinning and hitting the tree stumps and every time they hit a stump, the chopper was thrown about violently. We quickly pulled out the wounded marines and the now-wounded Air Force pilots and their shaken up crew. I recall that the pilots had broken bone-type wounds and cuts but none were life threatening. We now had two KIA marines and three WIA marines and an additional two WIA Air Force personnel on the ground. Of course, this happened at the end of the day, and darkness was near. Because of impending darkness, the decision was made to stabilize the wounded and set up a perimeter around the chopper and set in for the night. I recall that the Air Force pilots were not too crazy about spending the night in the bush with marines, but they had no choice. They gave away their side arms and rifles they had on board, their survival gear, and we also took the ammo and machine-gun barrels that they had on board their chopper.

We knew the enemy knew where we were, and they obviously saw the chopper go down, so we had to be prepared to protect the most valuable asset, the chopper, which would have been a great prize had the enemy gotten their hands on it. We spent what turned out to be an uneventful night with no further probes by the enemy, and when daylight came half of the Air Force and Marine Corps Air Wing were flying overhead. We were able to get all of the dead and wounded out and destroyed the Air

Force chopper by blowing it in place. The pilot of the downed chopper was a major and the last one out. He had a broken leg and cuts, and I vividly recall as he was being pulled out by a harness at the end of a cable that he looked down at all of us and waved. Then he gave us a big thumbs up and saluted us. I guess if you are going down in enemy territory, it's not a bad thing to land in the lap of a company of marines.

3/7 Command Chronology reported Company K Bald Eagle with a reconnaissance unit from 1st Recon Bn. Acting as point came under heavy automatic weapons fire from an estimated 6 VC at 814631. A platoon from Co. K assaulted the VC positions but the VC fled and no further contact could be made. The reconnaissance unit suffered 2 KIA and 3 WIA, Co. K 1 WIA.

A medevac helicopter on 08133H sent to remove the reconnaissance unit casualties at 812631 lost power and crashed reinjuring the medevac's and two crewmen. The helicopter was destroyed.

By now, I had been in-country for three months, and because of attrition, I was now the third senior person in my squad. Near the end of May, I gave up the grenade launcher to become the platoon radioman, a good job with a great lieutenant. , who just transferred into our platoon. He was from Teaneck, New Jersey, about three towns away from my hometown. He knew several people I knew, and we often talked about mutual places we used to frequent. He was a good leader and was highly respected by all. He was new in-country but had the good sense to rely on seasoned NCOs in the platoon until he felt comfortable enough to do things on his own.

We went on another operation, this time lasting about five days. We had a few skirmishes, killed three VC, and took one prisoner. My squad leader and I got the prisoner after he began to run away from us, and we fired our weapons at him. All of a sudden, he stopped dead in his tracks and put his hands in the air.

It was on this patrol that we lost two more great guys. We were moving off a hilltop after being there overnight, and as we left in column, the point man, a buddy from Texas, tripped a booby trap, and the second guy, "Champ," walked right over the explosive device as it detonated. I was third in column behind "Champ" and by the grace of God was not hit. Stan, whom we all called "Champ," sustained a sucking chest wound and died in my arms as Doc worked hard to save him. "Champ," who was black, knew every song ever recorded and was one of the guys I used to sing Motown songs with to pass the time. He was a great guy and funny as hell. He had just returned from R&R and had only three months left in-country. We called in a chopper, and I helped carry "Champ" to the first leg of his long trip home to Saint Louis. We heard a week or so later that Galvin, who had tripped the booby trap, took some shrapnel to his face and had some partial paralysis. He had been sent back to a hospital in Texas to recuperate, which is where he was from.

When we returned from this patrol, we moved to another hill about two miles closer to Danang than where we had been since early April. Part of being on this hill was to share security responsibilities a month at a time with the other platoons of the company. When not at the bridge, the other two squads took turns going on patrols and ambushes. There was never a day during my entire tour in Vietnam that we ever did nothing.

About this time, I had to go back to the battalion area to see a dentist so he could fill a cavity for me. I had been out in the field and was dirty—and let's say ripe—no shower in at least a week. I went to the mess hall and ran into another cook, named Dean, whom I knew from ITR in Camp Lejeune. He had always told me that he would take care of me if I ever came to see him. At the time, I was dead tired and just wanted to sleep. He showed me his hooch (tent), which was a raised wooden platform all screened in with a canvas roof. All of the cooks slept on regulation Marine Corps folding cots with air mattresses (rubber ladies) as we called them. He told me to sleep in his cot and left. I had been in the field so long, the thought of an entire night's sleep was unimaginable, so I threw my gear down on the wooden floor and crashed on the floor using my helmet for a pillow. Hours later Dean came in and could not believe I was on the floor when I could have been in his cot. He tried to get me to move, but I told him I was fine. I could overhear the other cooks mumbling about us crazy grunts sleeping on the hard, wooden floor. If you had a buddy who was a cook, he always looked out for his friends because he knew that he was in the rear with the gear and appreciated what we did.

I had now been given the responsibility of fire team leader, my first such role of leadership as a marine. Each full-strength squad had twelve marines with a corporal as a squad leader. The squad was further broken down into two or three fire teams of four, with a senior marine in charge of each fire team. I was elated at the responsibility bestowed upon me and intended to do everything I could to excel. Although being the platoon commander's radioman was a very fine job, I was happy to move on to the next level of responsibility.

We continued our nightly ambushes and patrols and always tried to catch up on sleep. Doing so was a constant in that we never got enough. We put up with the leeches, snakes, infected bug bites, scratches, rashes, foot rot, and extreme cases of sunburn. Every spare moment, though, was used to take a catnap or to rest our eyes. Fatigue, exacerbated by the extreme heat, never left us, but it was a condition that we all understood was part of the deal. There just never seemed to be enough time in a day to fit in an adequate amount of rest. Of course, as marines, we all complained, but higher-ranking marines expected that. We kept true to the old adage: "A bitchin' marine is a happy marine"!

In mid-June, during our time on the bridge, I was up in my assigned hole for the midnight to 2:00 a.m. watch. I had just relieved my buddy AJ when I heard some slight movement out to my front, about fifty to sixty yards out. I waited and watched, and all of a sudden, I saw four VC no more than fifty yards away. I tapped AJ and silently pointed to what I saw. As he grabbed his rifle, I popped an illumination flare, and we both opened up on full automatic with our M-16s. When the illumination popped, I could plainly see a hand grenade in the hand of one of the VC. There was no time to alert the lieutenant in his sandbag protected tent not two hundred feet from us. Our firing, of course, drew return fire, which in turn resulted in an entire platoon of marines firing where they saw our tracers going. We called in illumination for the rest of the night to assist us in making sure no other advances were made against us or the bridge we were assigned to protect.

At first light, we went out and observed much blood and many drag marks, which indicate wounded VC being removed from the area. They were good at doing this, mainly because they wanted to reuse the equipment that the wounded and dead were wearing. They quickly buried their bodies in shallow graves too to hinder the US in reporting how many of the enemy we had killed. Marines would never leave a fellow marine dead or wounded—but for much different reasons.

3/7 Command Chronology reported that the new MCB Bridge located at 943588 received 30 rounds of S/A and A/W fire from an estimated four4 VC at 920585. The VC were driven off by M-60 and M-16 fire along with 4 3.5 rockets. The bridge was not damaged.

On July 14, the huge airbase in Danang, less than 20 twenty miles to our northeast, was rocketed and mortared, which resulted in heavy losses of aircraft and other equipment. The rockets were launched from sights between our position and the airbase. We were assigned to the bridge at the time and at the bridge was a tower with an M-60 machine gun mounted on a tripod on the sandbagged roof. During the attack, we were asked to provide directions by aiming stakes in the tower to assist in getting exact locations for Spooky.

The morning following the attack, we went out in search of the launch sites and located many, along with freshly dug graves of enemy soldiers, with bloody bandages and loose equipment. We had the unfortunate task of digging up the graves in order to get an accurate count of dead VC. These casualties were the result of Spooky, an old Air Force DC-7 equipped with Gatling guns that fired .30 caliber rounds fast enough to cover every inch of an area the size of a football field in seconds. After counting the bodies and documenting their units through paperwork, we reburied them. I recall that one had a pack of Vietnamese Ruby Queen cigarettes in his pocket, so when we reburied him we left his right arm sticking up out of the ground and put a Ruby Queen between two fingers. Just a little more sick, black Marine humor!

On July 19, while on a squad nighttime ambush, we were lying in a hedgerow watching an open area to our front, which was used as a path for resupply routes by the enemy. At about one o'clock in the morning, we heard loud movement coming from our left front. As we waited, we saw twelve to fifteen uniformed enemy soldiers passing by and moving quite quickly. These were North Vietnamese troops (NVA) in uniform, and if there were fifteen, there were definitely a lot more where they came from. We opened up on them and fired every weapon the ten of us had. We managed to kill four and wound many others and were surprised to find out that one KIA was a female dressed in black pajamas. The command chronology entry that most closely resembles this action follows. I know it happened on July 19, based on a letter I sent home the next day.

3/7 Command Chronology reported a Company K squad ambush encountered 14 VC. Approximately 20 rounds of M-16 and 40 rounds of M-60 were fired at the VC. An area search found 1 VC (conf.), 1 VC

KIA (prob.), 1 cartridge belt with first-aid pouch, I notebook, and 2 pieces of .45-cal. pistol grip.

VC are Viet Cong not NVA and I am unable to locate any 3/7 Command Chronology that represents what we all experienced that night. We had fought NVA before but from a distance, and this was the first time that we had encountered NVA troops at close range. This was within days of the massive rocket attack on Danang Air Base, and their presence coincided with that very closely.

Sometime from mid- to late July while on patrol off our assigned hill, a very good friend of mine in another squad named Stan stepped on a booby-trapped grenade and lost one of his legs from the knee down. He and I had been through the ITR in North Carolina and Staging at Camp Pendleton together. Luck was responsible for us being assigned to the very same platoon in Vietnam. We had stopped to take a short break, and when Stan asked a buddy for a cigarette, he took a step to get it and stepped on the explosive device. He was very lucky to be alive and was quickly evacuated. He ended up in the Philadelphia Naval Hospital Amputee Ward. Once he stabilized, he wrote to me regularly, and I kept him abreast of what was going on in-country. I wrote to his parents right after he was wounded to assure them that Stan was fine and was on his way home, meaning the United States. He was from Massachusetts, so Philadelphia was a little inconvenient for the family, but better than ten thousand miles. Little did I know that I would be joining him in Philadelphia in the very near future.

3/7 Command Chronology reported the second man in a squad column from Company K detonated a pressure-type of AP mine. Two marines were wounded and required an emergency medevac.

Near the end of July, we were on a squad-sized ambush, with my fire team acting as point for the night. It was a crazy practice of Marine Corps commanders—after having men set up for hours at a good ambush position—to give an order to move to a predestinated position at a specific time during the night. This practice was at the time the cause of many casualties, which usually occurred when the move was made.

We were moving to our second position at approximately 11:00 p.m. and were moving across a dry rice paddy in column. My guy Bill from Chicago was walking point, and I was second, followed by the other two guys in my team and the rest of the squad in column behind us. As we were walking quietly across this open area, I immediately saw four heads peering over a hedgerow about four feet high to my front. My point man Bill did not see them, and I yelled, "Ambush front!" and began firing my M-16 on automatic at them. I shot first, and they quickly returned with automatic fire from their AK-47s. As they returned fire, they shot Bill at close range while he was on his belly returning fire. The VC were on slightly higher ground than we were, and they got Bill in the back and shoulders. He was no more than thirty feet from the enemy, and I was about forty-five feet away. The rest of the squad behind me were repositioning to gain fire superiority and firing at full automatic to keep them down while I attempted to get closer to Bill. I suddenly realized that I had some grenades with me, and I grabbed one, pulled the pin and heaved it into the hedgerow, which silenced the return fire permanently and gave us the opportunity to retrieve Bill.

One of the guys from another fire team and our corpsman came up, and we carried Bill back to the safety of a group of trees where he was given immediate medical aid. For the life of me, I cannot remember Bill's last name. I just recall that he was Bill from Chicago. He had not been in the squad that long, and it was hard to get too close to guys because they sometimes did not last long, and we purposely did not get too close, knowing that they may not be around tomorrow. He was badly wounded, taking several rounds into his shoulders, which traveled through his body and exited his back. He received great medical care from Doc Benson and survived to talk about it.

Although I had been a fire team leader for about a month and had been involved in many other fierce firefights, this incident was surely my closest call yet. I felt that I passed the leadership test, even though one of my guys was taken out of the picture, but he survived. We got a priority medevac chopper in and got Bill out. Then we packed up and started following blood trails at first light. There was a lot of blood where the VC had waited for us and there were trails of blood and loose equipment left or dropped as they escaped. Blood evidence indicated that all four were more than likely badly wounded. This was a close one, and I felt lucky as hell to be alive. When we returned from this patrol, the lieutenant told me that I had been promoted to Lance corporal, not much of a raise, but I was glad to make it.

It is curious that this incident was highlighted the following month in the *Navy Times* newspaper, not because of the action that took place, but because during the firefight a bullet went through Doc Benson's helmet. It seemed that a bullet through a helmet was more newsworthy than the firefight where a marine was severely wounded.

3/7 Command Chronology reported a squad ambush from Co K at 903673 was hit by 50 rounds of automatic S/A fire from a position at 910675. Returned fire included 10 M-79, 200 M-16, and 200 MG rounds. The VC broke contact, and a search revealed evidence of VC casualties. One Marine received minor wounds.

After getting back in from this patrol, I was asked by the machine gun squad leader if I wanted to be a machine gun team leader. I had always asked to shoot the gun whenever I had a chance and now jumped at the opportunity. This meant that I would be in charge of a machine gun team consisting of a gunner (me), and two assistant gunners (A-Gunners), who carried extra ammo. One was assigned to feed additional ammo by clipping it onto the fifty or so rounds that were always kept locked and loaded in the gun while out on patrol. I relished the opportunity and loved to shoot the gun. It is unfortunate that this opening became available because the best gunner in our platoon, a guy named Dave, had recently accidentally drowned while swimming near the bridge.

I spent a lot of time with the machine gun squad leader, who was a school-trained machine gunner. Cleaning an M-60 machine gun took two to three hours minimum, and we cleaned them twice a day. While on the bridge security detail, we fam-fired (familiarization fire) every day. We got the three guns from the entire platoon and fired from one riverbank to the other. The tanks assigned to the bridge did the same, which was done to ensure that the guns were in working order. While on the bridge, my machine-gun team was assigned to the tower that I mentioned earlier. Being in the tower was great. We caught a good breeze if there was one and had great visibility and a cover for shade. We spent the better part of the month of August on the bridge with daily probing by VC and random incidents of VC probing us each night. After spending August on the bridge, we moved to the hill around September 1.

Losing Dave to a senseless accidental drowning was indicative of other freak accidents or injuries that took guys out of the fight. Some of these may just as well have been a gunshot wound or a shrapnel wound because the marine affected had to be medevac'd out just as though he was a casualty of a firefight.

Another such accident occurred while on a patrol. One of the guys in my platoon was bitten in the testicles by a poisonous centipede through a hole in his pants. In Vietnam, you see, we never wore underwear because we were always wet and in the process of trying to dry off. My uncle had told me this on our weekend together, so it was not something new. Within minutes of being bitten, his testicles had swollen to a point where they looked like they would explode. He was immediately medevac'd out and was well enough to rejoin the platoon within a week.

Another freak, but serious, injury that I recall happened one evening while we were setting up a perimeter out in the field to set up for the night. One of our M-79 grenadiers was unslinging the M-79 and placing it down to take his gear off when it suddenly went off with his right hand over the barrel. The round went through the palm of his hand and exploded nearby inside of our perimeter. The round looks like a huge bullet but was 40 mm and was a miniature high explosive designed to maim and injure enemy personnel. The flesh of his hand was torn and bones were broken. He was in danger of going into shock, but the quick-thinking corpsman took good care of him and got him safely medevac'd out of the field. This was yet another freak, but avoidable injury that took a good marine out of the fight forever. He more than likely lost the use of his hand forever.

*On September 5, I wrote a letter home describing an incident that happened the night before. I mention this because I was unable to find any mention in 3/7 Command Chronology or 1/7 Command Chronology of this incident. The report of 1/7 Command Chronology is almost totally unreadable, and 3/7 Command Chronology is slightly better, but not by much.

My company, part of 3/7 was assigned to a hill under the command of 1/7, which is why this incident could be documented in one of two different chronologies. We ran patrols and ambushes off of their hill and crossed paths of squads from 1/7 all of the time. As I mentioned earlier, the Marine Corps wanted ambushes that were set up to move to a predestinated area at a specific time so you would end up covering two locations per night. Regulations required that we provide SITREPS (situation reports) every thirty minutes over the radio to ensure that units were where they were plotted to be at a specific time on a map. These

SITREPS were reported to the command post back in the rear. This practice was dangerous and caused needless casualties, usually by the enemy, but on occasion, there were friendly fire incidents, the result of this ridiculous practice.

On the night of September 4, we went out on a squad ambush and were already set up at our predestinated second ambush site. We reported when we were moving and advised by radio transmission when we arrived at our destination. About three in the morning, we observed a column of what appeared to ten to fourteen enemy troops moving from right to left about 150 yards to our front. Our squad leader called in on the radio to make sure they were not friendly troops, and when it was confirmed that no friendlies should be there, we opened up with everything we had. I fired approximately 150 to 200 rounds of M-60 when, all of a sudden, we realized by the orange tracers firing back in our direction and the sound of the return fire, that we were having a firefight with a friendly marine unit from another command. The enemy used green-colored tracers, and the sound of their AK-47s sounded much different from our weapons. Every fifth round in a magazine of ammo was a tracer, which aided the shooter when firing in the dark to see where his rounds were headed. Two marines were wounded by what I later found out were from my M-60. The marines fortunately survived and were immediately flown out by chopper.

There was an investigation, which may explain why this incident is not documented in either 3/7 or 1/7 Command Chronology. I know that it happened and felt bad enough that I had shot marines and not the enemy. Our squad and the squad from 1/7 were questioned at length. Within two days, we were advised that we were not at fault and were cleared of any wrongdoing.

Patrol leaders, especially those who were short-timers (not much time left in-country), sometimes short-cut the system by lying out in a safe area to avoid contact, not realizing that two friendly units could cross paths, causing unnecessary incidents such as this. We had been trained to kill and had been involved in daily firefights. I had been responsible for my share of killing and wounding of the enemy, so the fact that I had seriously wounded two marines was bothered me for quite a while. The 1/7 squad leader is the one that has to live with his decision to cut corners and in fact caused the serious injuries to his two marines.

We managed to put all this behind us, but I can tell you that living on their hill caused some animosity between the two units. All of the 1/7 marines knew that we shot their guys, so there were many smartass comments thrown our way. We knew we were in the right and had been cleared, so we sucked it up and ignored their bullshit.

I was scheduled to go on R&R (Rest & Recuperation) to Hong Kong, which had been canceled and rescheduled several times before the final date of September 8 was etched in stone. The Marine Corps allowed each person one five-day R&R per thirteen-month tour in-country. The flight to and from the destination chosen was free. Whatever you did for five days was at your expense. I had two more days in the bush before I left for my R&R to Hong Kong.

On September 6, we went out on patrol and on our way to our designated ambush sight, we observed six VC to our left hiding in the bushes. We yelled to alert the squad of our sighting and began firing at them as they returned fire and attempted to run away. I immediately set up the gun on the bipods and my A-Gunner on my left began linking more ammo to the belt I carried in the gun. I fired about 100 to 150 rounds and saw at least two VC go down from my fire. We advanced forward and found two dead VC and blood trails to indicate some of the other four were probably wounded. We called in mortar fire in their direction of travel and did not pursue. Another close call and one more day before R&R!

3/7 Command Chronology reported Company K squad security at 948599 received 100 auto/weapons fire from estimated 5-6 VC at 947600, 25 meters from point man resulting in point man WIA medevac'd. Returned fire and received 80 rounds sniper's fire from 946604. Called in 81 mm fire mission, receiving 16 HE and 4 WP rounds. Fired 15 M-16 rounds, 125 M-60 rds. 40 M-79 rds. 2 VC KIA.

*Every 3/7 Command Chronology entry used in this writing is in exact words and terms used in their report.

GETTING WOUNDED

9

ON SEPTEMBER 7, MY NINETEENTH BIRTHDAY, WE DID what we usually did after being out the previous night. We caught some chow at the mess hall, cleaned our weapons, and slept for as long as nobody bothered us or as long as the oppressive heat allowed. I shared what was left of my birthday package from home—crackers, cheese, and pepperoni—with guys in the squad. Our orders for the night of September 7 included another patrol and ambush to an area that was very familiar. This was to be my last patrol. Then I would go to Seventh Marine Regimental Headquarters on the eighth for orders, back pay, and transportation the following day to Danang Air Base for a flight to Hong Kong.

September 7 was no different than any other day in Nam: patrol, ambush, security watch, sleep, eat, sleep, and eat. Not getting enough sleep and being exhausted was something that never changed from the day I arrived in-country. There was just never enough time in the day to get the amount of sleep necessary and to be near exhaustion. This fact of war hasn't changed in centuries. I have spoken to WWII, Korean War, Vietnam, Iraq, and Afghanistan vets, and all agree that there was never enough time for sleep, and exhaustion was a relentless foe.

The squad saddled up, and we moved out at about eight o'clock in the evening, planning to arrive at our ambush site just about the time it turned dark. After walking in column across the never ending, but familiar, rice paddy dikes and dry ground, we approached what can best be described as an island of trees with a clearing in the middle. It was about the size of a small baseball field and was a place we had often used because we could set up a perimeter and observe the open area surrounding this island of land for several hundred yards in all directions.

As we entered the tree line and began to set up our positions, we were hit with small arms fire and a large explosion, later identified later as a satchel charge. As we all went down to return fire, I immediately felt a burning in my stomach. I immediately set up the gun and began to fire, spraying a wide area because we did not know exactly what direction the enemy took to get away. I fired 100 to 150 rounds and slowed down my firing because I could hear that everybody else seemed to have stopped shooting. We assessed the situation and were confident that the enemy had left the area. Now we had to deal with the wounded.

There were twelve of us, and, unbelievably, nine were wounded. The most seriously wounded was a guy named Benny from Georgia, who ended up losing a leg from the explosion. Benny was the radioman, and the blast that took his leg also disabled the radio because the explosive device landed near his location. We now had no way to request assistance medically or otherwise. Our corpsman was wounded and unable to get around well enough to provide aid, so he instructed one of the unwounded guys what to do. They wrapped up Benny's legs, which were both broken and stabilized him and patched up the others as well as they could.

We were all lying wounded, talking back and forth to each other, and trying to decide what we would do to get help to us. The squad leader decided that "Woody" would work his way back to the hill and get help.

Until now he had been assisting in providing first aid to the guys. At this point, about an hour had passed and Woody was just leaving on his blind trek back for help. It took us about an hour to get to where we were and knew it would take him at least that long. He also had the dilemma of keeping the perimeter marines from shooting at him as he approached friendly lines.

Two hours passed and no help. Benny was not doing well, and some of the others were feeling worse due to loss of blood. We all talked to each other as though it were daylight and did not care if anyone heard us. I then reminded everyone that it was my birthday, and the guys all began to sing "Happy Birthday" to me—crazy! The enemy obviously knew we were there but did not know how badly incapacitated we were. My wound was getting gradually worse as far as the pain was concerned. Having a stomach wound and internal bleeding can best be described as the same feeling a male gets when kicked in the testicles, only the pain is constant and never lets up; and now my stomach was swelling from the internal bleeding as well. My good luck and string of close calls had finally run out—Happy Freak in' Nineteenth Birthday!

After approximately three hours, we started hearing tracked vehicles, and as they got closer to our position, we could tell that they were Amtracs. Our lieutenant and a reactionary force of two squads and a corpsman were riding on top of the Amtracs. Woody had made it back and guided the lieutenant back to us. He was later awarded the Bronze Star for his actions. Woody was a very funny black guy, who could have easily been a comedian. I heard through the grapevine that Woody died several years ago of a heart attack. I will forever be indebted to him and was able to see him and thank him the following year at a small reunion in Jacksonville, North Carolina.

Lieutenant Nelson immediately called in medevac choppers and went to every one of his wounded marines and asked us each by name how we were. Before we knew it, there were two CH-34 Marine helicopters landing to fly us to the Naval Support Activity Hospital in Danang.

*Neither 3/7 nor 1/7 Command Chronology has any record documenting this incident that I could determine. As stated earlier, 1/7 Command Chronology was illegible, and 3/7 was only slightly better. My guess is that the incident was documented by 1/7, since we were attached to them at the time, and this happened in its area of responsibility. Along with me, eleven other marines can definitely attest to the details of this incident.

The next thing I remembered was all of us under a roofed open triage area, and we were giving thumbs up to each other. We were all extremely concerned for Benny, who did not look to be doing very well. A corpsman then came over to my gurney and started cutting off my bootlaces, removing my boots and socks. Then he cut off my green T-shirt and pants. There I was naked as a jaybird, but who cared? We were now all safe. After an IV was put in my arm, I was gone until I woke up the following day in an air-conditioned surgical ward. Benny was across the aisle from me, and I was able to signal to him by waving with my right arm. I had tubes in my nose, IVs, a catheter, and a huge bandage covering my stomach and lower back from surgery. Benny was able to talk, and we conversed somewhat in low, whispered tones. He knew he had lost a leg and was extremely down and depressed, which was understandable. One leg was saved but was severely broken and casted. He had also taken some shrapnel to the torso. The following day, Benny was told that he was flying home to the United States, which made him crack a little smile, but he remained very down and depressed as we talked back and forth.

On September 9, my second day in the hospital, a Brigadier General, who we were told was General Herbold, the Commanding General of the Force Logistics Command, came around to each patient and awarded us our Purple Heart by pinning it to our pillow. He stopped and talked to me for about two minutes and wanted to know what unit I was in and where I was from and so forth.

After five or six days, Benny got the word that he was heading home that day. I saw Benny smile from ear to ear for the first time since being wounded. I was extremely happy for him; he was out of the fight for good. As they loaded Benny onto a gurney, we waved to each other as he was wheeled away. I never saw him again. Benny and I had met in California, and he and I were assigned to Kilo Company within days of each other and had been on the same squad and had fought together for eight months.

On September 15, I was told I was leaving later that day and was being transferred to the USS *Repose*, a hospital ship. The *Repose* was one of two hospital ships that took turns stationed off the coast to accept wounded by helicopter, especially when there were some heated ongoing battles. The two ships, the *Repose* and the *Sanctuary* traveled up and down the coast of Vietnam to be closer to where the action was for more rapid medical evacuation. The *Repose* was presently in the Danang harbor, and I was transported to a dock and expected to walk down a flight of steps to a lower dock and into the boat to get to the ship. At the ship, I was expected to walk up a long gangway down at the water level up to the deck. When it came time for me to make the climb, I needed help from a sailor to make it up to the deck of the ship because I had no strength.

I was assigned to a surgical ward and was in the ward with some of my buddies and others I knew from training. The ward was a mix of battlefield wounded to routine hernia patients. I recall a gunnery sergeant who was in for hemorrhoid surgery, and he went everywhere with a blowup donut to sit on. It did not matter that he was an E-7 or not because marines from E-1 to E-9 razzed the shit out of him for being in the ward for hemorrhoid surgery!

I was feeling better and appeared to be improving slowly on a daily basis. I was able to walk to the mess hall on the ship and thoroughly enjoyed the great chow and cold milk. I had gone from 185 lb. out of boot camp to 165 just by virtue of the lack of steady food, humping in the bush, and constant heat, but I was now down to about 135 lb., and at six feet three, I was downright skinny. I was expected to stay on the ship until I was fully healed for full duty and looked forward to going back to my old unit once fully healed.

There was a chief petty officer stationed on the ship who was married to a girl I knew from my hometown, so I looked him up, and we caught up on family news. Before leaving home her family told me that if I ever made it to the hospital ship *Repose* to be sure to look up Skip. I told them I appreciated the information but sincerely hoped I would not have an opportunity to be on the *Repose* because that would mean that I had been seriously wounded.

The ship was heading to the Philippines for two weeks, so when the ship pulled anchor in Danang, it headed for Subic Bay, Philippines. When we arrived, Skip took me out to the old city of Olongapo for some beers. I was able to walk fairly well and had to scrounge a khaki uniform to wear on shore, which I did. I had no money, but Skip took care of me.

I was on the mend and getting my strength back a little at a time. The *Repose* stayed in Subic Bay for about two weeks before returning to the coast of Vietnam for its turn to retrieve wounded. A month went by, and after retrieving more wounded, the ship now headed for Hong Kong, my original R&R destination. My records and pay had not caught up with me yet, but I recall receiving a very small advance in pay.

When we got to Hong Kong, we anchored way out in the harbor and had to take a small launch to get ashore. I immediately went to a pay phone, called my parents, and assured them that I was all right. We had not spoken to each other since the Sunday in California before I left for Vietnam in February. They had expected to hear from me when I went on R&R in September, but that never happened. We then went immediately to a bar, hooked up with some Australian marines, and started drinking beer and throwing darts, a favorite pastime of the Aussies. I ended up in a tattoo parlor and had *USMC* tattooed on my right forearm for $5, the exact same one my senior drill instructor and idol had at Parris Island.

Within a week of being in Hong Kong, I developed an infection in my wound, which started with sharp abdominal pains and high fevers of over 105 degrees. For some reason I did not respond well to the antibiotics they were giving me. By now, the ship was back off the coast of Vietnam, and the doctors made a decision to send me back to the States to recuperate.

I would have gladly gone back to my unit and missed being with the buddies I knew best. I had now been in the country for ten months of a thirteen-month tour and was notified that my remaining time had something to do with their decision, not to mention the fact that the infection just was not going away, and my stomach wound was still open.

After sixty-six days on the *Repose*, my day had come, and I was going home. I was transported to the Danang Air Base, where I saw a huge, shiny C-141 Air Force Hospital aircraft waiting for us to be loaded. We were all in awe of this aircraft because it was new to the military, and none of us had ever seen one before. The aircraft had two-tiered bunks strapped on either outer wall, with a double row down the middle. There appeared to be about five rows of airliner-type seats facing backward then steps up to the cockpit from there. When it came time to take-off, we started down the runway, and the pilot immediately aborted. The lid to the water supply to the aircraft's restrooms was not properly locked in place, and when the aircraft started down the runway at takeoff speed, water started gushing out into the passenger seating area. The crew thought they fixed it, but the pilot's second attempt was again aborted, with water going all over the place. We were lying on stretchers, strapped in and helpless and pretty freaked out, thinking we were going to die while trying to leave this godforsaken country. The third try was the charm, and we landed at Clark Air Base in the Philippines several hours later and spent two or three days in the Air Force hospital there.

On the next leg of the trip between the Philippines and Alaska, I began to feel wetness under the bandage on my stomach. A nurse checked the bandage and found that my wound had reopened, probably from the pressure of being in the air, and infected fluid had drained all over me. The nurses cleaned me up as best they could and kept an eye on me for the remainder of the trip.

We landed in Alaska for re-fueling, then went on to Travis Air Force base in northern California to an Air Force hospital there. We stayed there a few days and flew to Texas to pick up more patients. Then we went on to Great Lakes, Michigan, where we spent a night or two at the Navy Hospital there. So far, we had zigzagged across the country and were finally going to the east coast. We landed at McGuire Air Force Base in southern New Jersey and were taken by hospital bus by the Army to the Naval Hospital, Philadelphia, Pennsylvania.

This was my final destination, and I was sent immediately to the tenth floor Isolation Ward because of my lingering infection. All of the patients in this ward had infected wounds, and extreme control was used with gowns and masks required by anyone entering.

My parents were able to come and visit and took the bus from New York City to Philadelphia, an eighty-five-mile trip. My dad was so glad to see me that he hugged and squeezed, me not realizing he had hurt me. I was so glad to see them, but could not ignore the pain, which greatly upset my dad. This bus trip was very different than the trip to visit me a little more than a year ago for my graduation from Parris Island.

I eventually beat the infection and moved to a surgical ward occupied by about fifty patients, pretty much all ambulatory. It is hard to explain how big Philadelphia Naval Hospital was, but it took up an entire city block squared. Fairmount Park was directly across the street, and on opposite corners was the Phillies baseball field and John F. Kennedy Stadium, where the Army–Navy football games were played. Just down the street was the bustling Philadelphia Navy Yard, loaded with warships and thousands of sailors and civilian workers.

The head nurse in the ward on night shift was a tough lieutenant commander who ran the ward as tightly as any drill instructor. She was great with the guys and did not take any crap from anyone. More than twelve years later, after relocating to Charleston, South Carolina, she became the leader of my daughter's Girl Scout Troop. Her daughter grew up with mine, and she was the nurse at our family doctor's office. She was married to a Marine helicopter pilot, which is how they ended up in Charleston when he retired. Now, more than forty-five years later, I still see Nora at church occasionally.

As soon as I had the freedom to walk, I had to get to see my buddy Stan, who had lost his leg to the booby trap months before. There was an entire one-story wing for the amputee patients, which was almost a city block long. There were, of course, hundreds and hundreds of amputee marines and sailors being treated, rehabilitated, and fitted with prosthetics. All of the wards were on the left side of the long, never ending hallway, and the prosthetic shops were lined up opposite each ward where craftsmen worked tirelessly with each amputee, making his prosthetic. There were also many occupational therapy rooms between each prosthetic shop. Since the amputees used wheelchairs to get around the entire block-long hallway, there was a series of ramps, which the guys used to have wheelchair races. Some of these patients were in this ward for as long as two to three years—longer for the more seriously wounded.

I saw Stan in his ward, and we spent countless hours over many trips there catching up and spending time together. He had not yet been fitted with a prosthetic, so his means of getting around was his wheelchair. As patients, if we were ambulatory, we were allowed to leave the hospital, but had to return by midnight and were allowed to wear civilian clothes. Stan wanted me to go to downtown Philly to drink at a bar he knew, which was several miles away. Our first trip out, I pushed him in his wheelchair to the corner to catch the subway, which meant that we had to go down a long flight of steps. I could not lift so Stan pushed the collapsible wheelchair down the steps and we went down with him hopping on one leg and me slowly making it down the steps. We went through the turnstiles and onto the train and made our way downtown. We had to reverse the deal to get back up the steps, only this time we had to ask a Good Samaritan to carry the chair up the steps for us. It was never a problem on any of the trips we made because the locals knew where we were from and never turned down a request for help with the wheelchair. We sometimes took a cab back to the hospital.

While taking a nap one day at the hospital, I was surprised by my old platoon commander, Lieutenant Nelson from Vietnam, standing at the foot of my rack. He was standing there with his right arm in a hard cast from his wrist to his shoulder. He had fallen off an Amtrac and broken his arm so badly that he was flown back to the States to convalesce. He was the same lieutenant who had come to our rescue the night we were wounded. He visited several times, and we caught up on what had happened to the guys since my last night in the field. All wounded officers stayed in the same area on the eleventh or twelfth floor.

Sometime during December the hospital had a visit from the previously mentioned Lieutenant General Lew Walt, who had been the overall Marine Commander in Vietnam from 1966 to 1967, and who had visited the overrun CAP Unit and briefly spoken to me when he got off his helicopter. He came to our ward as we stood in front of our hospital beds. I was in my civilian clothes, and he asked me what unit I had been in and how my wounds were healing. I have a prized eight by ten photo of him shaking my hand, which he inscribed, **L/Cpl. Raymond Wright, Warm Regards and deep appreciation, Lew Walt, Lt. General**. That photo hangs proudly in my den with my other military and police memorabilia. He went on to become the Assistant Commandant of the Marine Corps and was awarded a fourth star.

In late December I was given orders on how to keep my wounds clean and was given a thirty-day convalescence leave to go home until mid-January. The great part about this leave was that it was not charged against my accrued leave, so it was free paid leave. My pay records had still not caught up to me, so I had no cash to speak of, but my grandparents took care of that for me with wads of cash stuffed into my pockets when no one was looking. Both grandmothers and grandfathers were good for this, but I wanted my back pay because I wanted to buy myself a car.

The leave at home was great because it had been almost a year since I had left and Christmas was a truly thankful one this year for our family. By now, the people I had gone to school with were off doing their college thing, and the politics of the war, the pictures of the war in every issue of *LIFE* magazine, and the nightly killing on the TV news were now turning the opinion of the people. Several of my friends had lost their school exemptions because they failed, or the ones who were working were now being caught by the draft. After being the only person in my high school class to date who had been to Vietnam, these guys were now reluctantly going into the Army for two years after being drafted and were badmouthing the war.

I returned from leave to the hospital and was allowed to leave the hospital every evening if I wanted, which resulted in more trips downtown with Stan and his wheelchair. We were allowed to leave on Friday evening for the weekend. I usually took a train to the downtown Greyhound bus station and took the bus to the New York Port Authority Bus Terminal.

Either a family member or my buddy Gil would meet me there to avoid another bus ride to Hasbrouck Heights.

***

On one of my weekends home from the hospital, I had just been let off at the house by a friend after a night on the town. As I was walking through the front door, I heard distant police sirens that seemed to be getting louder and much closer. I went inside and was talking to my mom when I heard the sirens abruptly stop and brakes screech down the street. I opened the door and heard several gunshots and the cop yell at the driver he was chasing saying, "Stop or I'll blow your brains out!" My mother said that it sounded like firecrackers, and I said, "No those are gunshots." I ran down the street to see if I could help the cop. He had been chasing a stolen car from Passaic, a city from another county about ten miles away. This incident quickly reminded me of the ambition I had of become a police officer, but at the time, I was still only nineteen.

While hanging out in the cold with some of the neighbors who had come out to see what was going on, I was surprised to see my buddy Dick, who I had met the previous March when Foxtrot 2/7 had been hit hard. The chase had ended right in front of his girlfriend's house and we ended up standing in the cold for thirty minutes catching up on things. What a small world we live in.

***

My back pay finally caught up to me, so my huge monthly salary of about $103 per month and my $100 per month combat pay put money in my pocket again, the most I ever had at one time. I bought a sweet '55 Chevy with a built 327 engine with a 4-speed transmission. I loved that car and wish I still had it today. I left the car at home while going back and forth to Philly on the bus, but I had wheels for the weekend and now had some cash to spend without having to hit up my grandparents.

One weekend while home from the hospital, a group of guys went out to Highway 17 and parked on the side of an entrance ramp to the highway to watch a buddy race his Corvette against another Corvette. We had races there all of the time, and the straightaway in that stretch of highway was perfect. The end of the quarter-mile stretch was right where we were parked on the side of the highway. There were about ten to twelve of us parked, and I was the last in line in my '55 Chevy. When the racing Corvettes came flying by at about 115 m.p.h. we all proceeded off of the next exit ramp to go back into town onto The Boulevard.

Just as we were exiting, a Bergen County cop saw what had just happened and came flying across the overpass and did a power slide in front of the lead car by pulling his emergency brake, thus blocking our exit from the ramp. He started at the first car and walked to each car and collected driver's licenses and registrations. By the time he got to me, I remembered that many of those county cops were former marines, so when he got to me I handed him my license, registration, and between the two slid my military ID. We all sat for quite some time, and after about forty-five minutes, he started handing out tickets. When he got to me, he handed me my paperwork with no ticket, said "Semper Fi," and walked back to his car. My gamble had been correct—he was obviously a former marine.

***

After being out of commission since September 7 and under the control of the Navy, I was itching to get out of the hospital and back to the Marine Corps again. I still had eighteen months left on my three-year enlistment. After appearing before a board of Navy doctors to determine whether I was fit to return to full duty, I was released from the hospital on February 27, 1967, and was transferred to Marine Barracks, Philadelphia Navy Yard, two blocks down the street. I had spent five months and twenty days recuperating and was now able to be an active marine again.

CHARLESTON, WEST VIRGINIA

10

I RECEIVED ORDERS TO REPORT TO MARINE BARRACKS, Philadelphia Navy Yard, less than a mile down the street from the hospital. I reported to the company office in my winter Class "A" green uniform. After meeting with the sergeant major, I was told that I was squared away in my appearance, and I was going to receive additional orders to escort a fallen marine to his home in West Virginia. I was given a bunk in the barracks and instructed to store my gear and to pack only what I needed for several days. I was given orders and an hour- long class on what my responsibilities would be and what was expected of me on my assignment.

My orders were to accompany Lance Corporal Steven Emrick from Dover Air Force Base in Dover, Delaware, to Charleston, West Virginia, on March 1. The expectations were to stay with him until arrival at the funeral home, and I was expected to stay with him for the wake and funeral. Marines from the local Charleston Inspector and Instruction Staff (I & I Staff) were to provide pallbearers for full military honors at graveside with a rifle salute.

My responsibility was to make sure that ribbons and shooting badges were properly attached to the dress blue jacket worn by the deceased and to make sure that no issues during the flight from Dover had affected his appearance. I was told that the deceased died as a result of being shot multiple times in the chest and that he had been awarded the Bronze Star for his actions while assigned to a reconnaissance unit. No other information was provided. It would be more than forty years before I would find out about the battle he was involved in and in which he was killed.

I had no idea when given the assignment that it would have such a profound effect on me personally and the way I felt about my own mortality.

I was provided a small amount of advance money for meals and was given an address of a motel, which was prepaid and within walking distance of the funeral home. We arrived in Charleston, and the casket was placed on a conveyer truck for a short ride to the hearse. I too rode the truck standing at attention with one hand on the casket as we rode across the tarmac. This was not something we were instructed to do, but it seemed like the right thing to do at the time. I rode in the hearse to the funeral home and upon arrival, we checked to ensure that the deceased's appearance was in order.

I checked in to the nearby fleabag motel, showered, shined shoes, and ironed my uniform to prepare for the wake. I walked over to the funeral home and was immediately met by Lance Corporal Emrick's mother and father, who introduced themselves to me. The family had known for some time that their son had been killed on February 16, 1968, and had anxiously awaited his return for almost two weeks after his death.

Mr. and Mrs. Emrick introduced me to their three daughters, all teenagers still in high school. The family could not have been friendlier and more hospitable to me, knowing that I had just been discharged from the hospital myself. They were genuinely interested in my well-being and wanted to know all about my own family, trying to make me feel at ease, even though they were going through a trying family crisis of their own.

I was essentially the first marine they were able to speak with at length, so they had many questions about Vietnam, which I was pleased to answer. The first evening of the wake went smoothly with many family and friends visiting. At the end of the evening, I walked to the motel and slept fitfully.

The following day a second wake was scheduled with the funeral the following day, which was to be in Parkersburg, West Virginia, almost seventy miles away. At some point during the day Mr. Emrick came to the motel and knocked on my door and insisted that I move out of the motel and stay with his family at his house. I tried to explain that the Marine Corps expected me to stay at the motel and had paid for the room. He was insistent and would not take no for an answer, which exhibited the kind of family that the Emricks were. They were a very close-knit family of faith, who thought of me as a friend of their son, which I was, since he was a fellow marine.

I have previously referred to Lance Corporal Emrick as "the deceased," but the family had now shared their son's life with me and made me feel as though Steve and I had been school buddies. I packed my gear and went with Mr. Emrick to his home. The entire family greeted me and made me feel at home, which was a wonderful feeling during a difficult assignment. A college friend of Steve's named Bill was also a houseguest. He was in the Navy and had been burned on the now famous fire on the USS *Forrestal* in 1967. He and I became instant friends, and he shared stories of Steve with his sisters.

Mr. Emrick saw action in Europe in WWII, and had only been told that his son had been involved in a major battle as a member of a Recon unit, and he questioned me at length about Recon and what they did and where they went. I gladly answered all the questions I could for him, and he intently listened to every word of response. This information was all he had at the time since no other details of the battle had been released or made public.

The second wake that afternoon was again well attended, and we all went back to the house. When we awoke the following morning, Bill and I were noticeably low key and more quiet than usual out of respect to the family for the upcoming solemn church service followed by the long ride to Parkersburg to the cemetery. Mrs. Emrick quickly saw that we were acting differently and tried to get us to be more talkative, which I thought was very telling about the kind of family that Steve came from. Through their own grief, they noticed that we were not ourselves and were trying to cheer us up while they were preparing to bury their only son and brother.

The family insisted that I ride with them in the limousine with the family. I told them that I should be riding with Steve in the hearse, but they wanted me with them. I think now after years of reflection I understand why much more clearly.

The church was packed, and the service was a moving one. We then made the long seventy-mile ride to the cemetery. The I & I Marines carried Steve's flag-draped casket up a steep hill to the gravesite and a short, emotional military service was held, which culminated with the traditional rifle salute and taps.

When I left the gravesite, I rode back to Charleston with the marines from the I & I Staff, and they made arrangements for my return to the airport for my flight back to Philadelphia and my new assignment at Marine Barracks.

On the flight back to Philly, I thought of what a great honor it had been to represent the Marine Corps to this family and hoped that their grief would soon pass. Having spent time with this special family was an experience that made me think that this very well could have been my family attending my funeral, and it reminded me of how close I came more than once to being a statistic myself. While in Vietnam, we used to express our Marine black humor by joking about how our family would be notified that we were killed by singing telegram and had our own tune with lyrics that made it a song. While in-country, this humor was a defense mechanism to offset the everyday close calls with death we had. In reflection, this black humor does not seem very funny now.

I have been to the Vietnam War Memorial in Washington, DC, many times. I do not need a written list with names on it because I can remember each name of those I knew whose name is engraved on that wall, including Steven Emrick.

For many years, I kept in touch with the Emrick family, and we remembered each other with Christmas cards and letters for at least the next five years. After I got married and had my own family, the correspondence dwindled to just a card at Christmas. Then, as often happens, we lost touch with each other for more than thirty-five years.

In November of 2009, I was reading my monthly issue of *Leatherneck Magazine*, which I have subscribed to since 1966. I was reading a very well-written article titled "Last Full Measure of Devotion, Extraction of Team 'Box Score,'" 16 February 1968.

As I read, the article and details of the battle forty-one years after the fact, the name Steven E. Emrick was listed as a member of the patrol, and the details of his death and how he was posthumously awarded the Bronze Star.. The battle was one that was spoken about around the Marine Corps at the time, but names were never mentioned.

There were only three survivors of this squad-sized Recon Patrol, which resulted in the following awards:

Medal of Honor
Second Lieutenant Terrence C. Graves

Navy Cross
Private First Class James E. Honeycutt

Captain Bobby F. Galbreath
Captain David F. Underwood

Silver Star
Corporal Danny M. Slocum
Hospital Corpsman Third Class Stephen B. Thompson
Corporal Robert B. Thompson
Private First Class Adrian S. Lopez
First Lieutenant Paul A. Jenson
Staff Sergeant Jimmy E. Tolliver
Corporal Harry W. Schneider
Captain Carl E. Bergman

Bronze Star
Lance Corporal Steven E. Emrick
Private First Class Michael P. Nation

After reading this article, I felt like I needed to reconnect with the Emrick Family because I wanted them to be able to read the article. I was able to locate Mrs. Emrick, and we caught up on forty years of family news. She informed me that Mr. Emrick had died some years ago, and the youngest of three daughters too had died just a few years ago, the result of an automobile accident.

She stated that the family was aware that a story was being written and that it would appear in *Leatherneck* but had not seen it yet, so I mailed my copy of *Leatherneck* to her. We spoke for more than an hour and now regularly correspond via e-mail and Facebook. She is now in her mid-eighties and raising a young granddaughter by herself.

My oldest son, Doug, is a former marine who served eight years in the reserves and is now a lieutenant at a local police department. I shared this reconnection with him, and after telling him the whole story, he said, "You never told me this before" to which I replied, "There are a lot of things I never told you, son."

MARINE BARRACKS, PHILADELPHIA

11

The Philadelphia Navy Yard in early 1968 was like a mini-city with thousands of civilian shipyard workers and thousands of sailors assigned to ships in port and permanent base personnel. The Navy Yard opened in 1801, and all of the buildings were old, well-constructed brick buildings, including our barracks. The base ultimately closed in 1996, the result of cost-cutting measures.

Our barracks was a three-story building with the Mess Hall and Enlisted Club on the ground floor and two floors of barracks. The top floor was for Brig Guards who manned the large Navy Brig (military jail) on base. The brig was quite large and was the destination for many AWOL (Absent Without Leave) sailors and marines who had not returned from leave, most generally because they did not want to go to war, which had become even more unpopular in 1968. The middle floor housed the marines who manned base security, which was where I was assigned. We provided twenty-four-hour base security in eight-hour shifts, eight on and sixteen off, with every other weekend off.

Working the busy front gate, the main entrance onto the base, was the best and busiest post to work. There were two lanes onto the base and two lanes off. With thousands of sailors and shipyard workers on the base, the incoming gate was the busiest, and each car had to wait to be waved in by the marine in each lane. Many times the wives who had just let their sailor off at his ship handed a marine on the outgoing gate a piece of paper with a name and phone number. Many marines made that phone call and met the wives after getting off duty.

There was a guard building that stood a story above the gate, and all pedestrian personnel had to pass through this building to be inspected by a marine on duty in the guard shack. The corporal of the guard and the sergeant of the guard occupied the desk. If a sailor passed through the guard shack and was found to be out of uniform, the marine on duty turned him away until he returned in the proper uniform. Civilian workers even had to open their lunch boxes to ensure that no contraband left the facility.

In early 1968 the battleship USS *New Jersey* was being refitted in the deep-water dock located at the farthest point on the base from the main gate, which was at least a mile and a half away. On Friday afternoons many of the *New Jersey's* 2,500-plus enlisted sailors would walk to the gate in uniform to pass through the guard shack to be inspected by the marine on duty for proper attire. We would make them lift up their blouses to see if they had a belt on. If they didn't, they were out of uniform and had to go all the way back to the ship and get one. When this happened, they would have already walked six miles before ever getting off base and to the bus stop just outside of the gate for their trip downtown. Just a little Navy/Marine Corps rivalry kept alive and well!

I spent less than two months at the Marine Barracks and received orders in April to report to the Third Battalion Second Marines, Second Marine Division in Camp Lejeune, North Carolina. After taking about a week's leave at home, I reported to Camp Lejeune and was assigned to a rifle company in 3/2, that was undergoing training for a Mediterranean cruise near the end of the summer. Our Regimental Commander was the famous Colonel Bill Barber, who had been awarded the Medal of Honor in Korea. We trained daily in the field and even conducted amphibious landings on Onslow Beach from old WWII LSTs (Landing Ship Tanks) off the coast of North Carolina.

I kept my nose clean and was a fire team leader again. I was recommended to attend an NCO (Noncommissioned Officer) Academy and completed that weeklong course with high grades. Being selected was an honor because it meant that someone thought I had the leadership capabilities to be an NCO.

There was not much to do at Camp Lejeune at night except go to the Enlisted Club and drink the watered-down beer. To go off base, we took a bus to the closest town, Jacksonville, (J-Ville). Camp Lejeune is so large that from the main gate to the bus depot closest to our barracks was a thirty-minute ride. The bus from J-Ville back to base at the end of the night was, understandably, loaded with intoxicated marines. You always wanted a seat in the very front of the bus because once the drunks started puking on the floor of the bus, it flowed down toward the front every time the bus stopped at a traffic light or stop sign. Those sitting way up front knew to keep their feet up to keep from getting their shoes full of puke, if it reached that far by the end of the trip..

Another funny and somewhat scary story happened while conducting our amphibious landings at Onslow Beach. We made our landing in Amtracs, which we were all familiar with from Nam, but in Nam, we never did water operations. The front of the LST would open from the bow, and the tracs would drive down the ramp and into the water. Well each trac was loaded with a squad of marines with weapons and full packs sitting on benches facing each other in the closed, cramped and stifling hot compartment. When the trac went into the water, the driver did not clamp down his hatch and when the trac went into the water, the entire trac submerged completely before it bobbed back up.

When it went under, the open hatch allowed about a foot of water to enter our compartment. Now, there were a bunch of pissed off marines sitting in a foot of water, and some started puking in the water because they were seasick. Now we were all sitting helpless in a foot of water with puke floating around our legs. The smell was unbearable, and we could not wait to hit the beach to breathe and wash ourselves off. The driver of the trac caught a lot of grief from us on the ride in, and he was none too happy!

The summer of 1968 was a very trying one for the country and was one of major discontent, especially with the antiwar protestors.

On April 4, 1968, Martin Luther King was assassinated in Memphis, Tennessee, which set off immediate riots and protests around the country. We were training to go on a Mediterranean cruise, and all of a sudden we were conducting riot-control training every night to be trained if needed somewhere in the country to conduct crowd control.

Sometime during my time at Camp Lejeune, Lieutenant Nelson, who was now stationed at Camp Lejeune too, had managed to locate and contact about a dozen guys on base who had been in our platoon in Nam and had invited us all to a house he was renting just off base in Jacksonville. He had a keg of beer, and we spent the afternoon reminiscing and catching up. Woody, who had gone back to our hill to get help for us the night we were all wounded, was there, and we all thanked him immensely.

Even though the Marine Corps was known for being well disciplined, responsible, and organized, Martin Luther King Jr.'s death brought about racial tensions on base. There were nightly incidents of black marines jumping whites while walking to their barracks after being at the club or at the base theater. The problem escalated to the point where white marines had to walk with a buddy back to their barracks to avoid being jumped. I wondered what the world was coming to and started thinking of ways to be stationed elsewhere.

Just a little over two months later, Robert F. Kennedy was assassinated in Los Angeles after giving a speech in the same building. This event sort of put the country over the edge, in my opinion, and made current situations on base and off even more serious.

By late July, I was now almost twenty years old and had a little over a year until my enlistment ended, and I was not looking forward to going on a Med Cruise, and all the bullshit training that went with it. I had spoken to a career advisor, and we discussed embassy duty. Embassy duty was a two-year commitment, and I only had thirteen and a half months left of my enlistment, so I would need to extend my enlistment to be eligible. I decided I would extend my enlistment by two years, which would mean I would have three years and one month of service until my obligation was complete. I would be twenty-three instead of twenty-one and would then be able to pursue my next career goal of becoming a police officer. I signed the extension paperwork and awaited orders to Embassy School.

EMBASSY DUTY

12

WITHIN WEEKS OF EXTENDING MY ENLISTMENT, I RECEIVED orders to Embassy School, Henderson Hall, Arlington, Virginia, to report on August 28. Embassy School was known as one of the hardest schools in the Marine Corps, which included Drill Instructor School and Recruiter School.

All Embassy marines had to have a top-secret clearance to be able to work in a foreign embassy. My parents told me that federal investigators had already come to the house and had interviewed many of my former neighbors, conducting my background investigation. I am glad my neighbors did not tell them any of the bad things I ever did!

Embassy School was run by a bunch of top-notch former Embassy Duty Marines. We had daily personnel inspections and had classroom training from eight to five. We were taught everything from table etiquette to security violations to how to handle a person who wanted political asylum. We went to Quantico, Virginia, for weapons training and fired shotguns and .38-caliber revolvers, which were the weapons of choice for Embassy Marines. There were at least two trips to the State Department in downtown DC, after hours, where we actually went through each office looking for security violations. One of the offices I swept through was that of the Secretary of State. Another trip to Marine Barracks Eighth & I in downtown DC for a Friday night sunset parade was also on the agenda.

There were several trips to downtown DC to Bonds Clothing Store to be fitted for civilian suits and sport jackets that we were issued, as well as shoes, dress shirts, and ties.

Near the end of training, we had to appear before a board of officers and senior staff NCOs who decided whether we would be assigned to a post or not. I remember walking out of that board sweating bullets.

The school was not only interesting but was located in a great place for liberty. With Washington, DC, within walking distance, if you cut through Arlington Cemetery, there was plenty to do on the weekends. Henderson Hall was a small facility bordered on one side by Arlington National Cemetery. Just down the street was the Navy Annex Building, which housed Headquarters Marine Corps, the office of the Commandant of the Marine Corps, and the Office of the Sergeant Major of the Marine Corps, as well as most of the administrative office support required to run the Marine Corps and the Navy. You could stand at the Navy Annex Building and look out over the Pentagon and all of Washington, DC. Once assigned to school, I did not go home to New Jersey again. I soaked up the liberty in DC and occasionally visited a great aunt and uncle who lived in northeast DC.

Since the Pentagon, the largest office building in the world, and the Navy Annex Building were nearby, there was no lack of female availability. There were always parties to go to.

On graduation day, I was promoted to the rank of corporal, which made me an NCO. Anyone who was ever an enlisted marine can tell you that attaining the rank of corporal was special. It was and remains a respected enlisted rank in the Marine Corps chain of command. In battle, dating at least back to WWII, it was common for a corporal to be in command of an entire platoon of fighting marines when superiors were taken out of the fight. We had our wetting down (promotion) party at the Enlisted Club and all had a good time.

I had been assigned to spend the next two years in Santiago, Chile, which was a very desirable post indeed. Some of my buddies were not as fortunate, but the less-than-desirable posts were only one-year assignments with a choice within the company area for the second year. At the time, my grandmother still worked for a Chilean Export Company, and she had great plans for visiting me while on business trips to Chile.

Since we had to wait for background checks to be completed, passports, visas, and airline tickets, most of us had to wait up to a month before we left for our individual assignments. During my month-long wait, I worked in the Awards and Medals Office at Headquarters Marine Corps at the Navy Annex, so I walked to work from Monday to Friday while I awaited my departure to Chile.

Sometime in early December 1968, I flew out of town on a Brantiff Airways flight from Baltimore, Maryland, to Santiago, Chile. I arrived in-country and was met by the NCOIC (Non-Commissioned Officer in Charge) and his wife. He was a first sergeant and had seen action in WWII and Korea. They drove me to the Marine House, which is where all of the Embassy Marines resided. It was a large house located in the suburbs of Santiago, about eight to ten miles from the embassy. My assigned room in the house was great because this was the first time in my life that I had a room of my own, and I was twenty years old. The other seven marines there all made me feel right at home, and we all got along famously.

We were required to take at least one hundred hours of the language to the country we were assigned, so three times a week I took Spanish classes in the embassy. To be able to do anything in-country you really needed to know some Spanish, or you were sunk. I quickly learned our address so I could tell the taxi driver where to go in order to get home if we were downtown. The marines were assigned a Chevy Suburban with a three-speed floor shift that was used to get the guys back and forth to stand duty in the embassy. The embassy was located in a high-rise office building in the heart of the city, and we occupied three entire floors of the building. The guys quickly learned of my proficiency with the three-speed shifter and experience driving in the congested city and elected me to drive whenever I was part of the group. There was no speed limit, so driving was an experience.

The culture of the city was like no other I had ever experienced, and the fun of speaking a different language made it more interesting. The police force of the country was a national guard called the Guardia Nacional and was highly respected by the citizens and known for not taking any crap when there was trouble. It had its own police academy, and we were allowed to use the gym to play basketball and often played against some of the Guardia. We were issued a Chilean driver's licenses and special diplomatic identification. Whenever we had to show that ID, we usually received a click of the heels and a salute from the officer in return.

I had been in Santiago for three months when suddenly I was notified that since I was the newest marine assigned in the company, which encompassed the entire area of Central and South America, I was to be transferred to Panama City, Panama, where that embassy was shorthanded. The headquarters for Company D was also located in Panama. I bid farewell to my friends in Santiago and reluctantly made the flight north to Panama City, Panama.

I was welcomed in Panama by several of the guys from the embassy as well as the NCOIC, a staff sergeant. The post was just five marines and the NCOIC. Three of the enlisted marines from the company office also lived in the house with us.

Again, the guys were friendly, and I fit right in and got to work. The weather in Panama was similar to Vietnam, hot as hell and a lot of rain. It was no doubt a tropical climate. I shared a room with a great guy from Philadelphia, who was a clerk in the company office. Panama was a unique post because of the nearby Panama Canal Company, which controlled the Panama Canal. Unfortunately, the Panama Canal was given back to Panama during President Carter's administration. The company had its own stores, PX, gas stations, theaters, churches, hospital, and housing, to which we had full access.

There were also two large Army bases, a large Air Force base, and a Navy base, along with a Marine Barracks. Each of these bases had its own facilities, which we also had access to because we had a military ID card. This was the best of both worlds: we were in a foreign country but had access to military shopping on their bases. We actually purchased all of our food for the house from the Navy commissary.

On top of our salary, we were provided with housing and food subsistence by the State Department. We never saw any of this money because we signed that check right over to pay the rent on the house and the food purchased for us at the house.

Several months into my stay in Panama, I ended up in the hospital in the Canal Zone to remove internal metal sutures used to patch me up in September 1966 when I was wounded. The sutures pinched and were painful, so a Navy doctor at the Rodman Naval Station arranged for the surgery.

Things went well in Panama, and I was promoted to the rank of sergeant, with the ceremony held in the office of the American Ambassador to Panama, Ambassador Adair. Being promoted twice in seven months had made up for my lost records while hospitalized and the fact that I had been a lance corporal longer than normal. When I had been in the Marine Corps for two years and ten months, and twenty-eight days, I canceled my two-year extension, which had allowed me to be eligible for Embassy Duty and re-enlisted for three years and received a monetary bonus of a little over $3,000. I was now a sergeant of marines, had three grand in the bank, and was happy as hell. Right after making sergeant, the NCOIC told me he was replacing the ANCOIC (assistant) with me. He said he had been waiting for my promotion just so he could make that move. The ANCOIC was essentially in charge of the house where we lived, and I was now responsible for paying the house help, which consisted of a cook and a house boy who were Panamanian nationals, and to prepare menus for all meals and to purchase all of the food. I enjoyed the added responsibility, and the change worked out with no issues from the person I had relieved. The switch also resulted in me having my own room again.

Being stationed in the same location as company headquarters allowed me the opportunity to travel to many different countries in the region on special assignment. When the company office needed a marine to go on a special assignment, it first checked with our availability, which was convenient for them for preparation of orders and travel arrangements. As a result, I visited almost every country in South America, except Paraguay and Uruguay.

In 1969, former governor of New York Nelson D. Rockefeller made a trip to Panama on behalf of the Nixon administration. He traveled on one of the president's fleet of jets, and I was fortunate enough to be able to assist the Secret Service agents with security during his visit.

I went to the embassy in San Jose, Costa Rica, twice to assist when the embassy had troubles in the city. One trip coincided with the May 4, 1970, shooting at Kent State University by National Guard troops. The Kent State incident caused many American exchange students in Costa Rica to protest outside of the embassy, which generated a lot of unrest.

Although I would rather have stayed in Chile, the transfer to Panama turned out to be a good one for me as far as my career was concerned. During my twenty-four months on Embassy Duty, I completed more than a dozen Marine Corps Institute (MCI) Courses, which was a continuing education of sorts for marines. All of the courses were oriented to being a better marine and included subjects such as Marine NCO, Tactics of a Marine Rifle Squad, Individual Protective Measures, Tactics of a Marine Rifle Platoon, etc. These courses were mailed directly to each marine. We had to read the enclosed soft cover book and take a test. The completed test was returned by mail to the MCI. Every course I ever completed is listed on the Form DD214, which is the individual record for all members of the military. I am certain that these courses are now all available online, and tests are probably sent electronically from the MCI in Virginia.

I was also fortunate to have excelled in my assignment and always received high proficiency and conduct ratings in my annual performance evaluations. During my tour, I received two Letters of Commendation from the ambassador, which also became a permanent part of my Service Record.

When I re-enlisted in 1969, I was required, as all marines are, to list three choices of duty station for my next assignment in December of 1970 when my two years on Embassy Duty were complete. My third choice was Drill Instructor School, Parris Island, South Carolina. In mid-November I received my orders to take twenty days annual leave at home then report to—yes, my third choice—Drill Instructor School, Parris Island, South Carolina, in late December.

My second day home I went to the nearest Chevrolet dealer and purchased a slightly used 1967 Chevy Chevelle Super Sport, with a big 396 motor and four-speed transmission. The neighbors definitely knew that I was back in town.

I spent my leave at home and caught up with the family, saw what friends there were left to see, and attended my sister's wedding. At my sister's wedding I announced my engagement to the girl I had been corresponding with for the previous year. She was a nurse and had attended nursing school with my mother, which is how we met.

Several days after Christmas, I loaded the Chevelle with all of my gear and made the eight hundred-mile trip to my next duty station, Parris Island, South Carolina.

PARRIS ISLAND AGAIN

13

I REPORTED IN AT THE HEADQUARTERS & SUPPORT arracks with my orders for Drill Instructor School and met an old buddy Bob who went through boot camp in my series in 1966. He was from New York and worked at Officer Candidate School, (OCS) in Quantico, Virginia. He was the OCS version of a drill instructor there and needed to attend the school to remain in that assignment. He ended up staying in the Marine Corps and retired as a sergeant major.

The following morning we both dressed in the uniform of the day and checked each other's appearance. Then we both went to the base barbershop, and got a "high and tight" and drove to the school to meet with the chief instructor, a hardened gunny and former drill instructor himself.

The gunny accepted our orders and told us when and where to report on the day that school started and looked at both of us and said, "And get a damn haircut!" We could not believe what he had said, but we were not about to tell the gunny we just came from the barbershop. We both responded with "Aye Aye" and left. As we walked away, we looked at each other and said in unison, "Holy Shit!"

That afternoon I went to the base credit union to open a checking account, and while standing in line to be waited upon, I noticed a gunnery sergeant in front of me who looked familiar. When the gunny turned and spoke to the teller, I immediately recognized him and his voice as my senior drill instructor from my own recruit training platoon in 1966. I got out of line so I could approach him when he was done with his banking, and we ended up talking for twenty minutes. He started out as a drill instructor in early 1966 and was still there, although in a different capacity more than four years later. He was now part of a unit that was manned by experienced drill instructors who checked on and inspected other drill instructors while they were working. I later found out that they were referred to as "spies"! The gunny clearly remembered Platoon 1055 and the fact that we won every award possible during our training. I often ran into the gunny and would talk about the Marine Corps and, of course, the drill field. He was later promoted to master sergeant but stayed in the Inspector Section as the SNCOIC (Staff Non-Commissioned Officer in Charge). Master Sergeant Altizer had been my idol and mentor since boot camp, and now I was able to speak with him regularly for advice and direction. One of my assistant drill instructors went on to attain the rank sergeant of major himself and, I believe, retired as the base sergeant major at Camp Lejeune, North Carolina. I heard through the grapevine that the other assistant drill instructor in my platoon was killed in Vietnam.

Bob ended up sharing a cubicle with me in DI School, which was seven weeks long. There were four of us to a cubicle, which consisted of two double bunks separated by wall lockers. Bob and I shared the cubicle with Bill an air wing sergeant who had been a helicopter gunner in Vietnam, the fourth was an older staff sergeant, whose name was also Bill, who was an instructor at Navy Flight Training School in Pensacola, Florida. His job was similar to that of the character that actor Lou Gosset played in the movie *An Officer and a Gentleman*.

Bill, Bob, and I were inseparable and spent our off time together, although there was very little off time. We got up at 5:00 a.m. and had to shower, shave, dress, and get to the chow hall by 6:00 a.m., which we shared with the Women Marine Training Battalion, Admin School, and Recruiter School. We had to be seated in the classroom by 7:30 a.m. Our classes were all taught by drill instructors, with a captain as the commanding officer. Every instructor was a unique individual with the outgoing personalities you would expect. Those selected to become an instructor at Drill Instructor School were the cream of the crop of the six hundred or so drill instructors on Parris Island. An example of this is that one of the gunnery sergeant instructors when I went through later became the sergeant major of the Marine Corps, Sergeant Major David Somers. The other Recruit Training Depot in the Marine Corps was located in San Diego, California, which had its own Drill Instructor School.

The training was rigid and as hard as going through boot camp more than four years earlier. We, of course, were expected to do everything that a recruit was expected to do, so there was a major emphasis on physical training (PT). There was organized PT daily, which ended in a run of three to five miles. We were required to memorize the entire Marine Corps Drill and Ceremonies Manual and to present or teach individual marching and facing movements to each other, as well as the manual of arms with an M-14. We were broken down into groups and took turns presenting individual movements to the group with the watchful eye of an instructor assigned to each group, who made appropriate suggestions when necessary.

We were also taught the sword manual of arms because duties as a drill instructor required that we carry a sword at all recruit graduations. We also spent a week at the rifle range and the same amount of time a recruit did drown-proof training at the pool.

We had daily personnel inspections and always had the big one with our rifles on Saturday morning. After the Saturday inspection, we were free, so to speak, until 5:00 a.m. Monday morning. If you failed the

Saturday inspection or a test, you were dropped from training, which shows how high training expectations were.

I recall a staff sergeant in the class who came from the Marine Air Wing in nearby Beaufort, South Carolina. On one Saturday morning inspection, he was asked why he did not shine the back of his brass belt buckle. His response was "I don't know; I didn't shine the inside of my shoes either." He was gone and dropped from the class before we ever got back to the barracks. We lost at least one-third of the marines who started by graduation day.

As you can imagine there was a lot of studying involved, so we did not leave the barracks very often. There was a restaurant in Beaufort, though, that served steak dinners for $5 a plate, and Bill, Bob, and I went there each Saturday evening.

In those days, it was very common for a recruit to escape from Parris Island and make his way into Beaufort or Port Royal before being apprehended by local police. One Saturday evening Bill, Bob, and I were in my Chevelle on our way to that $5 steak dinner when, all of a sudden, a police car was stopping us. Then we were surrounded by several police cars and ordered out of the car at gunpoint as if we were bank robbers! We, of course, did as ordered and began to explain that we were three marine sergeants attending Drill Instructor School at Parris Island. Since most of the cops in the area were former marines, they quickly understood the mistake. There had apparently been three recruits who escaped Parris Island, and the cops thought we were they because of our high and tight haircuts.

Years later, after becoming a cop myself in a military town, I found out that the military paid cops a $50 bounty per head for returning AWOL military personnel to their command. These cops were looking to split $150—that I am sure.

After seven long weeks, we finally graduated and were awarded our coveted Campaign Cover and given orders for our next assignment. Bob, of course, went back to OCS at Quantico, and Bill was assigned to the Third Recruit Training Battalion, which in those days was still referred to as Disney World because up until mid-1971, the Third Battalion was the only one of three that had air-conditioned barracks. I received orders to the Second Recruit Training Battalion but took a week of annual leave at home before starting.

For those who were staying on Parris Island, the week of graduation they were issued what was considered Organizational Clothing. Since we were always expected to wear a fresh uniform, we were issued extra uniforms and were able to get those uniforms laundered and dry cleaned free. We received an extra five sets of utilities and at least five or six khaki shirts, long and short sleeve. They were stamped in the collar in red ink ORGANIZATIONAL CLOTHING. I later found out how much help it was financially to receive these extra uniforms and free dry cleaning.

I flew home and spent a week relaxing and preparing myself for the grind of eighteen-hour days seven days a week. I knew that I was well trained and felt the same way I did after my boot camp training while on my way to Vietnam more than four years earlier. I was ready.

I had now been a marine for more than four years and had my core leadership values instilled in my being, which controlled my life the way I wanted them to. I had been putting them to use as a leader of marines myself, and it was now going to be my turn to be a drill instructor and to instill those same values in new recruits myself.

*I have deliberately not used the term "DI" to refer to drill instructors in this writing. The Army freely throws around the term "DI" when soldiers refer to their drill sergeants. The Marine Corps does not use the term DI, so I did not. If two former or present marines were having a conversation about drill instructors, they would never use the term "DI."

SECOND RECRUIT TRAINING BATTALION

14

I RETURNED FROM ANNUAL LEAVE, CHECKED INTO THE Bachelor Enlisted Quarters (BEQ), and reported to F Company, Second Recruit Training Battalion. At the time, the Second Battalion was the only recruit battalion still housed in the old WWII wooden barracks, as the First Battalion had just moved across the parade deck to its new brick, air-conditioned barracks. I was going to train recruits in the identical style barracks that I was trained in back in 1966.

I was quickly assigned to a platoon that was already several days into training. I was replacing someone who had abruptly left for some unknown family emergency. The senior drill instructor and the assistant were both staff sergeants, and they welcomed me with open arms and guided me in the right direction. Both were good guys and had been around a while.

Each platoon started with approximately sixty-eight recruits and varied by as much as 10 percent by the time graduation came. Each platoon had three drill instructors. The senior wore a black garrison belt to signify his position, and the other two wore green web belts that had a large brass buckle with a Marine Corps emblem, with two brass keepers.

On the belt, we wore only one thing, a three-by-six-inch first aid pouch centered between our two rear pockets.

Four platoons of sixty-eight recruits made up a series, so each series had twelve drill instructors, and one series commander, a lieutenant, and each series also had a series gunnery sergeant. The entire series conducted the same daily training that was generally split with two platoons at a time going to class together. There were some scheduled portions of training that mandated the entire series of four platoons attend together. Three series made up a company commanded by a captain.

Drill instructors alternated duty by staying with the recruits every third night. Training functions dictated whether one, two, or three drill instructors needed to be present, so even though a drill instructor may have spent the previous twenty-four hours with the recruits, certain functions required that he stay over an additional six to eight hours, or more. A twenty-four-hour shift can easily turn into a thirty to thirty-two-hour stretch. As a single guy living in Bachelor Enlisted Quarters (BEQ), I spent more hours with the platoon than necessary in order to learn more quickly. The BEQ was at the end of the street that housed Second Recruit Training Battalion with Receiving Barracks on the opposite corner. The married guys appreciated my dedication, which sometimes allowed one of them to go home to his family.

In 1971, we were still involved in Vietnam, so our mission was the same as it was since 1965. We were preparing these recruits to be deployed eventually to Vietnam, so we had to get it right. Unfortunately, standards had been lowered for entry into the military services in the late '60s and especially in the early '70s, which resulted in some who never graduated from high school or with low IQs making it to boot camp. I had one recruit in my second or third platoon who had used LSD, and he admitted that he regularly tripped out as result of using it. How he ever made it past a recruiter is beyond me. I had another recruit one time from

Philadelphia with an IQ in the sixties. He was unable to pass any written tests at Parris Island, so I do not know how he ever passed the required testing for pre-enlistment with the Recruiter. He was so slow that it took seconds for verbal commands to register in his head before understanding what was said. He tried hard, but he never made it through and was eventually dropped from training and discharged.

By February 1971, recruit training was virtually the same as it was when I went through myself in September of 1966. Nothing had changed, which pretty much resulted in drill instructors doing to recruits what drill instructors did to them, dating back to the late '50s.

In April of 1956, there was an incident I mentioned earlier that resulted in the drowning of six recruits. The drill instructor, Staff Sergeant McKeon had marched his platoon into the marsh in Ribbon Creek and had gotten into deep water, which resulted in the drowning of the recruits. He was, of course, court-martialed in a highly public proceeding. This incident changed recruit training from what it had been since the '40s, to what I experienced in the sixties until the present, 1971..

That incident and his subsequent court-martial drew daily never-before-experienced press coverage for the times and involved the Secretary of the Navy and Congress. General Lewis "Chesty" Puller, the most decorated marine in the history of the Corps, testified that the incident was a "deplorable accident" that did not warrant a court-martial, even though he had some harsh words regarding McKeon. He also testified about the training methods of the Marine Corps and stated that discipline was the most important factor in military training.

Each and every recruit in the platoon of seventy-one was interviewed, and each and every recruit spoke in favorable terms of his drill instructor and claimed that he was not the sadist that was portrayed to be by the prosecution. This simple fact is a result of their basic trust in following the orders of their drill instructor, and the discipline to follow Staff Sergeant

McKeon into the water. In my opinion, even though their training was not yet complete, the TRUST, LOYALTY, and DISCIPLINE had not been completely instilled in their training to date unfortunately may have contributed to the incident, and the fact that they had never been on any nighttime training exercises.

As a result of this incident, changes in recruit training were immediately enacted. Two drill instructors per platoon was increased to three; an officer, the Series Commander was instituted; drill instructors were more carefully screened; and new Drill Instructor Schools were established in each command. Additionally, a Special Training Company (STC) was instituted to provide recruits with remedial training in physical training and motivation, and drill instructors now wore the distinctive Campaign Cover in recognition of the new norm of professionalism and specialization. Prior to that incident drill instructors wore the same hats (covers) that any other marine wore.

I can personally attest to the fact that lessons in TRUST, LOYALTY, DISCIPLINE, and RESPECT helped me survive my time in Vietnam. Without these traits, survival would not have been an option. These traits or values were planted in my brain by my own drill instructors in 1966, and the additional values of RESPONSIBILITY, PUNCTUALITY, and ORGANIZATION were gradually instilled in our being, which became a way of life for most recruits who successfully completed recruit training. The Marine Corps will push a person to his or her extreme limit, and the Corps believes that the mind can control how much a person can put his or her body through.

I enjoyed every minute of being a drill instructor and was with the recruits as often as possible. I was eager to learn and to master the trade of my new Military Occupational Specialty (MOS) of 8511., drill instructor.

The training of this, my first, platoon was moving quickly, and I slid into my expected role as the most hated assistant drill instructor.

The senior, the most senior in rank of the three, was expected to be hard on the recruits but at the same time to be a father figure of sorts. For the training to work effectively one of the assistants was expected to be a slightly more strict disciplinarian, and the third was expected to be a hard-ass, the one drill instructor disliked the most by recruits. This policy was unwritten and would never, ever fly as a written directive, but it had worked for years and continued for decades. The subject was never spoken about or referred to, but each crew of drill instructors was selected for their strengths and weaknesses, and the terms *heavy* or *easy* were never discussed.

Being the hard-ass was a role that I enjoyed, and as I stated earlier, new drill instructors tended to train the way they were trained. My goal as the hard-ass was to make the recruits hate me, which I must admit was not hard to do. If it became necessary to put my hands on a recruit to get his attention, I did. We were loud and profane and did what we had to do to mold disciplined troops. We did to them what had been done to us, such as making a recruit who didn't want to share a birthday cake with his fellow recruits be made to eat the entire cake while sitting in front of the entire platoon, with only a canteen of water to wash it down. For those whose did not like to shave, they now shaved without shaving cream and with a bucket over their heads. For those who did not like to shower, there were blanket parties that took them to the shower and scrubbed them with scrub brushes, at the suggestion of the drill instructor. When one recruit left his footlocker unlocked, all footlockers were turned upside down and recruits' beds (racks) pulled apart. These things were done to us, so we just returned the favor.

Senior drill instructors generally selected their team prior to forming a series for training, and they knew who the easy and hard-asses were and selected accordingly. Series senior drill instructors met with the company commander, series commander, company first sergeant, and series gunnery sergeant to select their teams for the next series of recruits to begin their training cycle. There was a board hanging in the company office that had each platoon with its specific chain-of-command nametags hanging. Every drill instructor in the company had two sets of nametags that were placed on the team with which he was presently working and on the team he was selected for in preparation of newly forming platoons.

Near the end of recruit training, generally in the last week, the senior drill instructors asked their recruits to put in writing whatever they wanted to say anonymously about what they thought of their drill instructors. These writings were referred to as "Love Letters" and were a tool used to determine whether there was a problem with a certain drill instructor or not. This was done unofficially, of course, and the letters were passed around between the team of three drill instructors. Some were amusing, and some let you know you were doing the right thing, and some showed the respect that each individual had for you. There were very few derogatory comments made about anyone. They may have hated us during training but in the end respected us for what we did for them and knew it was all for a reason. We had planted the seeds of LOYALTY, TRUST, DISCIPLINE, RESPONSIBILITY, RESPECT, PUNCTUALITY, and ORGANIZATION.

***

In 1971 with Vietnam still ongoing, there was very little time off between platoons. We graduated my first platoon in mid-March, and there were maybe four days off before I picked up my second platoon. There were times that a platoon would graduate in the morning, and I'd have a new one by the same afternoon. Time off was rare, but that was the nature of the beast.

When a platoon of recruits is ready to leave the Receiving Barracks to go to the assigned platoon with its drill instructors, an event takes place called "Pickup." The three drill instructors assigned to the platoon, two drill instructors from each of the other three platoons in the series, the series gunnery sergeant, and all company personnel in a drill instructor billet meet the group of unsuspecting recruits to take them officially to their barracks. There are usually ten to twelve drill instructors who participate in a platoon pickup.

The recruits are already suffering from sleep deprivation, are confused, and know nothing of what they are about to experience. They are ordered to take their full sea bag of issued clothing, issued supplies, their steel buckets of cleaning supplies, and gear and fall into formation outside for the forced march to their respective barracks. Along the way, they are yelled at for any insignificant infraction, especially when someone drops a piece of issued gear or falls behind the formation. The recruits are then herded into their barracks where they are put in front of their racks (beds) while the team of drill instructors verbally work them over psychologically. They continued their tirade, usually for not properly standing at attention, or by moving while at attention, or for any other insignificant transgression they may have violated.

The Pickup process has a function, just like everything else that is done for the nine weeks of boot camp. After thirty to sixty minutes of frenzied drill instructors using their best verbal material, the large group of drill instructors abruptly leaves the platoon with its three assigned drill instructors who will live with them for the next nine weeks.

The purpose of the pickup as I saw it was to scare the crap out of the recruits so that they became disoriented, then skillfully left to the custody of their senior instructor who, by design, is the father figure and the easiest on his recruits.

The senior drill instructor then sternly, but professionally, introduces himself and his two assistant drill instructors, who immediately move into teaching the proper way to make their racks and procedures for how their lives will be run for the next nine weeks.

I picked up the next platoon and was assigned to a senior who had been around a while, and, as described earlier, I was the hard-ass with a weaker assistant. I employed what I had learned from my mentors in the first assignment, did well, and completed the entire training cycle with no issues. This platoon graduated, so I had a long weekend off. I went home and got married on May 2, 1971. I went home on Friday, got the marriage license, planned a small wedding, got married on Sunday, and I was back on Parris Island on Monday afternoon.

I took $500 in cash, which was part of our wedding money, on Monday afternoon and went into Beaufort to Earl's Mobile Home Sales. I purchased a new two-bedroom trailer and arranged for it to be moved onto Parris Island and into the Argonne Trailer Park. This was my wife's and my first home with a monthly payment of $65. The rent in the park was $40 dollars and included water and electricity, so for $105 a month, with the $500 down payment, we were in a home.

Within days, I started with another platoon, and this time I was assigned with a senior who had no more time on the field than I did. He was very squared away and came from the Air Wing, but was a little harder on the recruits than most seniors were. He was a stickler for giving physical exercise as punishment. We collectively, though, gave no more physical training than normal and did nothing out of the ordinary to that point.

We had a good team, but complications arose not long after training began. We began as usual and had the normal issues that arise while training. All of a sudden, out of nowhere, we started having recruits complaining that they were urinating blood. Since this is something that we would allow a recruit to go to sick call for, we allowed them to go individually, not knowing what the problem was. I seem to recall that eight recruits ended up in the Beaufort Navy Hospital, which drew the attention of Navy doctors, who immediately notified our command. Because we as drill Instructors were suspected of doing something to them to cause this, the three of us were relieved of our duties while the matter was investigated.

Whenever there was a complaint lodged against a drill instructor, for whatever reason, he was relieved until the allegation was fully investigated and resolved. The recruits were so new that we had not had a chance to develop LOYALTY, TRUST, and DISCIPLINE, which resulted in the affected recruits exaggerating the severity and level of physical training we had inflicted upon them. Before it was all over, the problem of bloody urine had affected about 10 percent of the platoon. The medical term for the problem was Rhabdomyolysis, which is when protein from torn muscles floods the bloodstream, caused sometimes by overexertion. We just referred to this new malady by using the term Rhabdo.

This matter made the world news and was investigated fully, resulting in all three of us eventually being exonerated of any wrongdoing, which took about five to seven days, as I recall. It was a nice break at home with my wife, but nerve-racking with the thought that this could potentially ruin my career. We had done nothing wrong as drill instructors, and we were somewhat vindicated when several recruits from the other three platoons in the series came down with Rhabdo too.

Doctors said that the problem could be eliminated if the recruits were allowed to drink water more often, thus allowing them to go the bathroom more often to urinate. A lot of water put into the body results in a lot of urine out of the body at some point. The result of the incident was that a second canteen was issued to each recruit, who was now required to carry two canteens of water and was now required to drink a canteen of water every thirty minutes to flush out his system. All of this water was a nightmare for drill instructors, who now had to stop what they were doing to make sure every recruit drank the appropriate amount of water. Think about the logistical problem this caused because each hour recruits ended up with two empty canteens, so the entire platoon now had to find a place to refill them.

This affected all training across the entire island. Classroom instructors had to stop in the middle of their lessons to deal with the water issue, and not all classroom facilities even had bathrooms, thus no running water was available.

Drill instructors have historically used the privilege of a bathroom break as motivation, and the simple fact is that if recruits are not ingesting a lot of water, the need to use the bathroom was more infrequent. That little piece of psychological leverage was now gone.

We returned to work and reassumed supervision of our platoon, which had been covered by other drill instructors in our absence. The recruits had definitely been affected because the investigation interfered with their training, and we had to bring them back in focus and up to speed.

Not much later in training with this same platoon, we accepted a recruit who we were told had been transferred after being set back in training due to an injury. This practice was common and. drill instructors called them "retreads" because they came from other platoons that had dropped them for one reason or another. This recruit—I can still remember his name and his face, although it probably wasn't his real name—was nothing but trouble from the minute he arrived. He was an obvious troublemaker and a malcontent. We believed that he was planted by the Criminal Investigative Division (CID) to infiltrate or spy on us to see if we were abiding by the new changes and to ensure that we were not punishing or paying back the recruits for what had happened.

Now a second major Issue arose in which I was accused of excessive force by the retread recruit and relieved of duty again while the allegation was fully investigated. Now, for the second time with the same platoon, I had been relieved. I knew that I had done nothing to worry about and was cleared quickly and sent back. Very suspiciously, the recruit we had suspected of being a plant was gone just as quickly as he had appeared, with no explanation. The incident was very fishy because recruits never left a platoon unless the drill instructors made it happen.

I was glad when this platoon graduated because it had been a hectic journey for seven plus weeks. By this time, my wife and I found out that we were pregnant with our first child due to arrive in April of 1972. This was hard on my wife because we were newlyweds and now pregnant in a state eight hundred miles from home. Several relatives came to visit from time to time, who kept my wife company while I worked my long days in the field.

I worked another platoon with two great guys. The senior was a staff sergeant, and the other assistant was a sergeant. The three of us worked well together and put out a good product. The senior was a little overweight and had some problems when running with the platoon in formation. He more than once fell out of formation and had to be treated by a Navy corpsman who was always present for formation runs in the event medical aid for a recruit became necessary. I would often run around the platoon as they ran in formation, which meant that I ran more than twice as far as they did. I was in such great physical condition I could have run forever. When I did this, it drew attention away from the struggling senior. I am certain that his issues with running were responsible for him being passed over for promotion. We graduated this platoon and took a few days off before we picked up again.

Because I was off between platoons, I was ordered to go to a platoon that was already six weeks into training. I filled in for a drill instructor who had to go on emergency leave for a death in the family. I spent about ten days with the platoon and waited for my next assignment. As a side note, more than twenty years later, I worked with an investigator from a police department in North Carolina to capture a fugitive for murder who was hiding in our area. When we met, I immediately recognized him as the senior drill instructor I worked with for those ten days in 1971. It is truly a small world we live in.

A particular senior drill instructor was known for having the best marching cadence on Parris Island. He was a short, black staff sergeant about five feet five inches tall who sang his cadence as he marched his recruits, which turned heads all over the island when he passed by. He was a senior in my company and had specifically asked me to be in his next platoon that was to begin shortly. This staff sergeant had been on the drill field since he was a corporal, some four years prior. He had been promoted meritoriously to sergeant and to staff sergeant and had a great reputation as one of the best drill instructors on Parris Island.

There are unique opportunities for advancement on the drill field because each battalion is allowed to promote one meritoriously per quarter. A company commander or series commander nominates a deserving drill instructor to appear before a Meritorious Promotion Board at the battalion level. One was selected each quarter of the four nominated from each company, so the opportunity was there for unscheduled promotions. The staff sergeant told me that I had developed a reputation as a good drill instructor, and he was stuck with the other assistant he had to settle for to get me. This made me feel good, knowing that I had at least been noticed for my leadership skills, and this post was a reward. He told me what he expected from me, which was the first time this had happened since I had been a drill instructor. He was known for his exceptional skills in teaching a platoon how to march, and almost every one of his platoons had won its respective drill competitions. There was not a drill instructor on the island who did not want to work for him, and I was happy as hell to have the opportunity.

We picked up the platoon and began our training, and I watched as the master taught the recruits every facing and marching movement as well as the rifle manual. He wanted to be the one to teach all of that, not relegating it to assistants. I can see now how he won all of those competitions—he taught it all himself. This was definitely a lesson to me for the future if I ever intended to be a senior myself. This platoon was unique in that all sixty-eight came from the state of Ohio, and many of the recruits came from the same area, even the same huge, regional high school. This coincidence caused somewhat of a problem, however, in training because so many of them knew each other. This platoon was very much like my own recruit platoon in 1966 that won every competition available. Platoon 284 was by far the best platoon I had trained or seen to date as a drill instructor, and it certainly rivaled my own boot camp Platoon 1055.

When it was my night to stay in the barracks with the recruits I would give motivational speeches after lights out, praising the senior. These recruits would walk on water for him and were reduced to tears at times by my speeches of the respect that I had for him and the fact that I would go to battle with him and follow him anywhere. The command to march through a wall could be given, and I would bet they would try before they would ever fail their senior drill instructor.

One of the last major hurdles prior to graduation was the Command Inspection, which took place two or three days before graduation. This was a full-dress rifle inspection in Class "A" uniform conducted by the regimental commander, a colonel, and his staff. It was generally held out on the parade deck, unless it was raining. Because it was raining that day, it was to take place in the barracks under fluorescent lighting. As the four platoons waited for the inspection party to arrive, the lights in our squad bay suddenly went out. Our platoon was scheduled to be inspected first, and the inspectors were approaching the front door of the barracks. They were directed into our dreary, unlit squad bay and conducted only a cursory walk-by inspection, never looking at one rifle and asking questions only of random recruits. The inspectors then went on to conduct their inspection of the other three platoons. When the colonel and his staff left the building, the lights in our squad bay suddenly came back on. The senior whispered to me that he had pulled the switch in the power box for our portion of the building. He had successfully pulled one of the oldest drill instructor tricks in the book—no lights, no inspection!

My duties as the hard-ass required that I make certain adjustments by hand to almost all of the recruits in this platoon. Drill instructors were forbidden to touch a recruit, other than to adjust their position of attention. No issues arose, and we moved on to graduation practice for graduation the following morning.

The next morning while we were forming in the back corner of the parade deck with about twenty minutes before our pass in review, our company first sergeant came up to the three of us and told us an allegation had been made. The parent of a recruit in our platoon alleged that the senior and I had assaulted a recruit when he was caught smoking without permission. The first sergeant was very adamant that this matter needed to be taken care of or we would be relieved, pending an investigation of the allegation. The senior told me to take the recruit out of formation and have a little talk with him, saying, "You know what to do." He trusted me enough to know I would take care of the matter.

It was foggy that morning. Because we were so close to the watery marsh, we could not see the grandstands that were full of parents to watch their sons graduate from recruit training. I took the recruit back behind a nearby building that housed supply and told the recruit in no uncertain terms that the Marine Corps was a small place, and he would be a marked man if he cost us, particularly the senior, our careers. I told him that if the allegation was not rescinded immediately, we were going to be relieved of duty at the conclusion of graduation. The recruit assured me that he would make sure the complaint went away and that the complaint was generated over a conversation between another recruit and his parents. His own parents were unable to come to graduation, so he was with his friend and his parents when they overheard him talking about the day he had been caught smoking and what happened to him as a result.

In hindsight, the story is funny and is part of the culture of recruit training from the late '50s. The recruit had been caught smoking by me in the bathroom (head), and when the senior came in, we both went to work on him. The recruit was about six feet five inches, and the senior was all of five feet five inches, so he pulled out a footlocker so he would be face to face with him. As he yelled at him face to face, I was at the recruit's ear yelling at the same time. Well, while yelling, which was a show by us to deter the other recruits from sneaking a smoke, the senior saw that the recruit had a torn pocket flap over his right breast shirt pocket. The senior started growling like a dog and grabbed the torn pocket flap in his teeth and tore the pocket flap off as he continued to growl with the pocket flap clenched between his teeth. This story sounds bizarre, but that is, honest to God, what happened. I can assure you that no other recruit ever tried to smoke without permission again because this display got everyone's attention.

After the graduation ceremony, the first sergeant came up to us and said the parent who had filed the complaint had changed his mind, stating that there was a misunderstanding. The first sergeant asked me what I had said to the recruit, and my response was "You don't wanna know, First Sergeant!" He walked away shaking his head. We may have pushed the envelope with this particular incident, but I must say that this was one hell of a great platoon of marine recruits—lesson learned. , we had gone too far.

We had a little time off between platoons, and the senior I had just worked with had arranged for me to work with him again. This situation was extremely unusual, but I sure did not complain and was elated at the prospect of working for him again. We picked up the recruits and went through the motions doing what we were expected to do, and halfway through training, the senior was promoted to gunnery sergeant. Imagine coming to Parris Island as a corporal and a little over four years later being a gunnery sergeant! The promotion was great for him because, in conjunction with the promotion, he was transferred to the Inspector Section that drill instructors called the "spy section." He was transferred there and now worked for my old senior drill instructor who was now a master sergeant. It is weird and ironic how my two mentors in life ended up working with each other. Sadly, as abruptly as he was promoted, he was transferred. I will forever treasure the opportunity to have worked with and for Gunnery Sergeant N. W. James, training two platoons of recruits.

In the middle of this platoon's training, we had a "Field Day," which is when the entire barracks is scrubbed from deck to ceiling. The decks were scrubbed by hand with scrub brushes and then mopped. The mattresses were rolled up, and even the springs of the beds (racks) were dusted. The bathroom (head) was scrubbed and showers and sinks scrubbed. Well, in the middle of these sixty-eight recruits feverishly cleaning to make their deadline, I saw a recruit lying under a rack not doing anything. Out of the corner of my eye, I continued to watch him because he was not known as one of our better recruits. As I watched him, I saw that he was trying to deliberately cut his wrist on one of the sharp, metal springs under one of the racks. He gouged a nice laceration into his wrist, which started to bleed profusely, and he came to me to tell me that he had accidentally cut his wrist while cleaning and needed to go to sickbay. I got a towel to wrap around his bleeding wrist, and I guess he thought I was going to flip out over his bloody injury, but my response was to berate him for getting blood all over my clean deck and that I saw him deliberately cut his wrist. I made him clean up his blood before I let someone escort him to sickbay. Fortunately, we never saw him again. He was medically discharged from the Marine Corps because I wrote this incident up as a suicide attempt.

There was one other smoking incident that I recall was quite funny and imaginative on my part. The drill instructors' hut or office/sleeping quarters was just twenty feet from the main squad bay where sixty-eight recruits were supposed to be sleeping. I heard some low whispering coming from the head, specifically the room that held eight toilets. As you walk in from the squad bay, the head was set up so that the first room houses approximately a dozen sinks and mirrors. The next room is the room with trough-type urinals, and the next is the room with the toilets. The farthest point of the head was the shower room. It was one large room, approximately twelve feet by twelve feet, with multiple showerheads for communal showering.

During training, recruits wore what were referred to as "chrome domes," which were fiberglass helmet liners, painted silver, designed to reflect the hot sun. Recruits wore the "chrome dome" everywhere.

Recruits were required to stand fire watch, rotating two hours at a time, while their fellow recruits were sleeping. It was the responsibility of the fire watch to alert me if anything out of the ordinary occurred and to loudly knock on my door to wake me up. When I heard the commotion in the head, I knew something was up. I was wearing what the fire watch was wearing—boots, utility trousers, and a white T-shirt, so I waited for the fire watch to make his tour down my hallway, and I took the "chrome dome" off of his head and his flashlight and went into the head as though I were the fire watch. When I walked into the dark room that contained the toilets, I found four recruits in the dark, sitting on the commodes smoking, so I sat down on one of the empty commodes and asked them in a whisper if I could have a smoke. They, of course, handed me one. Then I let loose and herded them all into the shower room and PTed (physical training) the shit out of them for a while. I also went and got the fire watch who failed to report the smokers, so he joined the party too. I never had a problem with unauthorized smoking again.

The graduation of this platoon was bittersweet without the gunny there with us. During the training cycle for this platoon, the series commander had approached me and told me there was talk of me becoming a senior drill instructor. There were a handful of sergeant (E-5) seniors on Parris Island, but not many. There may have been five in my entire battalion. We talked about it, and I did not commit one way or the other. Not long after this and during the previous platoon's training cycle I was nominated to appear before the Meritorious Promotion Board. I went before the board and did well, but a sergeant from another company got the promotion to staff sergeant. One thing was for sure, my work was being noticed, first by the fact that the most respected senior drill instructor in the battalion had selected me twice to be his assistant, that the series commander had discussed my becoming a senior as a mere E-5, and that I had been nominated for meritorious promotion.

In this period, the company first sergeant struck up a conversation with me one day and wanted to know whether I had ever considered becoming a warrant officer. He told me I was squared away and the kind of marine that they were trying to recruit to become a warrant officer. I had to break his bubble and tell him that I was considering getting out of the Marine Corps the following June. I told him that I appreciated his interest in my career, though.

I was nominated again to the Meritorious Promotion Board but declined to participate because, by then, I had decided that I would get out of the Marine Corps when my enlistment expired on June 30, 1972. I told the series commander that I planned to get out in six or seven months and did not want to take a promotion away from someone staying on the drill field. My decision to get out was because, even though I had been out of the country for four of the five years I had been a marine, I knew my next duty station was either to Okinawa or back to Vietnam. This decision was easy to make because I was newly married, had been working eighteen hours a day, and had a baby due in April.

On Christmas Eve in 1971, I was the duty drill instructor when all of a sudden we heard female voices singing Christmas Carols outside in the street. I was in the middle of speaking to my recruits as they stood at ease in front of their racks. I walked to the front door of the barracks and saw that the singing was coming from a formation of women recruits who were outside in the street facing our barracks that housed our series of male recruits.

When I saw what the distraction was, I immediately said, "Bah humbug" in a way that my recruits knew to repeat loudly the same thing in unison. To uphold my reputation as the badass of the three drill instructors, I then had the entire platoon fall in outside on the grass adjacent to the female carolers and proceeded to PT (physical training) the shit out of them. I made them PT until the carolers were forced to move on down the street to another company. Two days later, my series commander, a lieutenant, came to me to inquire about my PT session while the carolers were singing. I, tongue in cheek, explained that I was conducting corrective action for someone who had screwed up, and it was customary to make all pay when someone screwed up. He walked away from me and said half smiling, "OK, Sergeant Wright, bah humbug." He knew what I had done and let it slide. Naturally, this incident was mentioned a few times when the senior collected love letters from this platoon.

This platoon was the last with which I actively worked. During this training cycle, I applied to be considered as an instructor in the Academic Section. The Academic Section was a unit composed of drill instructors who traveled around the entire island and taught military subjects in classrooms in all three of the recruit training battalions. The unit was made up entirely of staff NCOs, staff sergeants, and gunnery sergeants. I was interviewed and required to give a short presentation to the panel of a military subject that they handed me on a piece of paper. I was selected for the job, the only sergeant in the unit and the only one ever selected. I felt good about the move, even though I had worked only a little over twelve months as a drill instructor. I now had the opportunity to be home every night and to work Saturdays only once in a while.

The move to the Academic Unit was a good fit, and right after my move there, I found out that I was on the list for promotion to staff sergeant, but where I was on the list meant that I probably would not make it unless I was still around in September or October. I was due to complete my enlistment on June 30. The promotion was not enough of an incentive for me to stay in, however.

The new assignment was still an important part of a recruit's training. We were responsible for teaching them everything from the .45-caliber pistol nomenclature, to Marine Corps History, to First Aid, to Mapping. There was a lot of preparation involved by studying lesson plans and rehearsing in my living room at home. I generally taught two platoons at a time, so I had a captive audience of more than 120 recruits at a time.

There was one class in particular that was taught in the Base Theater where we taught three entire series of 1,200 to 1,300 recruits at one time. One of the classes they had to take was health related, and they all had to be lectured on Sexually Transmitted Diseases (STDs), which was taught the first Saturday of their training. I ended my very boring subject matter on a note that got their attention and made their drill instructors laugh in the back of the theater.

When my lecture was complete, I told them that I was going to take a poll of the recruits in the room, so they all had to put their heads down in their laps, close their eyes, and raise their hands to answer my questions.

Question #1: How many of you have ever had a sexually transmitted disease? At least 25 to 30 of the 1,200 raised their hands, so I said put them down.

Question#2: How many of you have ever had gonorrhea? At least fifteen to twenty raised their hands, so I said put them down.

Question #3: How many of you have ever had syphilis? Maybe one or two raised their hands, so I said put them down.

Question#4: How many of you have had sexual relations with another recruit since you have been here at Parris Island? Of course, no one raised his hand, so I told them to put them down and class was dismissed. All 1,200 recruits immediately looked up and looked around to see who had raised their hands and did not know it was a joke. In the back of the room were at least twelve drill instructors laughing their asses off!

We taught the .45-caliber pistol. We showed recruits how to take one apart and met them at the range where they fired one magazine of ammunition for familiarization purposes. This demonstration coincided with the time that their platoon went to the rifle range. Well, I recall one time a recruit committed a major violation of safety by turning around with a loaded .45 and aimed it toward others standing behind him. I immediately pulled him from the line, and he was dropped from training and forced to be transferred to another platoon behind his in training. His drill instructors were not too upset because he was probably not a model recruit. This happened in 1972.

Some fourteen years later when I was a police officer in the area of the Charleston Naval Base, a guy who yelled, "Hey, Sarge!" approached me, and

I responded that I was not a sergeant. He said, "Oh yes, you are. You kicked my ass off the pistol range at Parris Island back in 1972." He remembered me, shook my hand, and said he deserved what he got—no hard feelings.

***

For years, the completion of recruit training meant that recruits traveled by bus to Camp Lejeune for Infantry Training. The Marine Corps decided for whatever reason that they would extend boot camp to include much of the training they previously received in Lejeune. To accomplish this additional training required our unit set up Mapping and Compass Courses, which would be set up on the property called Page Field, which was a deserted WWII airstrip, with surrounding woods full of snakes, namely rattlesnakes, water moccasins, and copperheads. We had to blaze the trail, so to speak, and run the courses ourselves to ensure that all of our compass data was correct. We ran into numerous snakes and other varmints in doing so.

The addition of this infantry training, whose responsibility fell mostly on the Academic Unit, was just another good reason to end my enlistment. I am glad that I was on the ground floor of making it happen but glad to be leaving at that point in time.

I thoroughly enjoyed teaching and enjoyed the fact that I was still considered a drill instructor receiving my monthly $100 proficiency pay, which all drill instructors received over and above their salary. The extra money came in handy, since the light of my life, my daughter Christy Elizabeth was born on April 1, 1972. She was born in the Beaufort Naval Hospital and was the first grandchild born to her generation. She was a sweet baby—blonde hair, blue eyes, and beautiful.

Being assigned to the Academic Unit meant that I was under the command of the Headquarters Support Battalion (H&S), which required that

I stand duty approximately once per month at the Receiving Barracks, which is where all civilians start their time as a marine. I had several opportunities while on duty to get up on the bus, get the recruits off the bus, and out onto the yellow footprints just outside of the Receiving Barracks. My career as a marine had come full circle. I was standing duty in the Receiving Barracks at the Marine Corps Recruit Depot, Parris Island, South Carolina, as a sergeant of marines, in the exact spot where I had started the whole deal almost six years before.

On June 29, the guys in the unit gave me a little going away party at Elliot's Beach in the picnic area. They gave me a very nice plaque with a miniature sword and wished me well in my new endeavor in civilian life.

I had no regrets about getting out. I had been fortunate enough to serve my country in battle, even though the war was an unpopular one, and lucky to get out alive. I had the opportunity to travel to many countries that I never would have had the opportunity to see otherwise. I successfully completed two of the hardest schools in the Marine Corps and started my family with a beautiful baby girl.

I served for a little over six months in the Academic Unit and was discharged from the Marine Corps on June 30, 1972, five years, ten months, and twenty-eight days after beginning on September 2, 1966. My wife, three-month-old daughter, and I got into our new Datsun station wagon with a U-Haul trailer hitched to the back bumper and headed north to New Jersey.

We were fortunate in that I sold our trailer and left the Marine Corps with absolutely no debt. We had a brand-new car that we had paid cash for and had money in the bank, but I now needed to find a job, hopefully in law enforcement.

My grandfather, LeRoy Price Sr., circa WWI.

My uncle, LeRoy Price Jr. in dress blues, note his Silver Star and Purple Heart.

My Uncle Thomas Langdon Price, wounded on Sugar Loaf Hill on Okinawa.

My dad, Raymond F. Wright Sr., in uniform of US Army Air Corps.

My official Parris Island Drill Instructor photo, Raymond F. Wright Jr.

My oldest son, Douglas R. Wright.

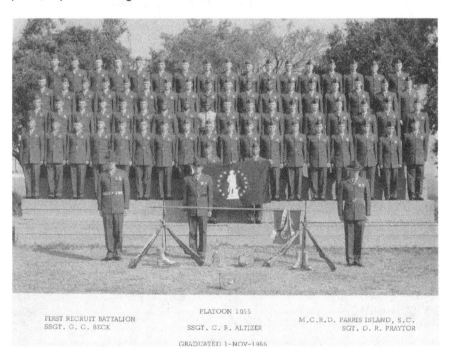

My boot camp graduation photo, Platoon 1055, graduated November 1, 1966. I am in the middle of the top row.

Cleaning my M-16 after an overnight patrol.

Me in the observation tower at the bridge.   *From the tower, looking down at a passing Army self-propelled 175 mm cannon.*

Injured Corpsman Carries On

DA NANG, Vietnam (ISO) — In need of a corpsman himself, Hospitalman Harry T. Benson suppressed his own pain to relieve that of a wounded Marine on a night ambush south of Hill 10.

Benson, a member of "K" Co., 3rd Bn., Seventh Marine Regt., 1st Marine Div. and six Marines of the same unit, moved from their hill at dusk, set up their ambush at 8 p.m., then moved again to set in elsewhere at midnight.

One hundred meters from where the Leathernecks thought they'd be stopping, they discovered the Viet Cong were already there.

A heavy volume of fire from enemy automatic weapons was directed at the Marines, and the point man was hit in the initial burst. Benson, who was near the rear of the column, rushed forward as the Leathernecks laid down return fire.

Twenty-five meters from the casualty Benson was hit and hurled to the ground as an enemy bullet smashed through his helmet, creased his forehead and stuck in the side of the steel pot.

Benson was undoubtedly saved by the bullet's upward deflection as it ricocheted off the helmet's rim. Maneuvering forward a second time, Benson reached the wounded Leatherneck and began treating him under fire.

Benson moved the casualty to the protection of a rice paddy as the Leathernecks gained fire superiority.

While the VC started their retreat, Benson, with the aid of another Marine, carried the wounded man to the rear and called for a medevac helicopter.

A search of the area revealed three dead VC. A later report confirmed that three more of the group were killed as they ran into another Marine patrol, 200 met...

Navy Times article about our ambush where our corpsman had a bullet go through his helmet.

My home for sixty-six days, the USS Repose.

Lieutenant General Lew Walt and me at Philadelphia Naval Hospital, December 1967.

Walking in the front door for the first time in almost a year, December 1967.

My proud grandfather and me after church, December 1967.

After church at my grandparents' apartment, December 1967

My promotion ceremony to sergeant in 1969. L to R, Ambassador Adair, Corporal Wesley, Gunnery Sergeant Tolliver, Corporal Robbins.

Walking through the ranks during bayonet training in 1971.

With recruits at rifle range during "snapping-in week."

My mentor, Gunnery Sergeant N. W. James.

GySgt. N. W. James
Senior Drill Instructor

At rifle range, looking at scoring board with Gunny James and me, with unknown third drill instructor joking about James's height.

Graduation of platoon 284, Pass in review, eyes right!

Me waxing my '67 Chevelle in parking lot of Drill Instructor School at Parris island.

CIVILIAN LIFE

15

WHEN WE ARRIVED HOME TO NEW JERSEY, WE stayed with my parents in Hasbrouck Heights until we found a place to live. The first thing I did was to go to the Veterans Hospital in Newark and apply for disability for my Vietnam wounds. I had been having stomach problems for some time, and as I got older, the problems had gotten increasingly worse.

Within a week of being with my parents, I remembered that since I was in boot camp in September of 1966, I had been having money deducted from my paycheck to purchase a monthly US Savings Bond and had been doing this for the past seventy months. After settling in, I asked my mother about them because she had received them each month. She informed me that she had cashed most of them in and used the cash to pay bills. I was not upset because I had told her in my letters while I was in Vietnam to use any of my money that was needed while I was away. This conversation again reminded me of how close to the edge financially my parents still lived.

I then pursued a job in law enforcement and took a civil service exam to become a police officer in the town I grew up in, but there was no prospect of a job opening in the very near future. I had been promised the next opening that became available, but no time frame on when, as no one was planning to retire anytime soon. I inquired with the New Jersey State Police, and, at the time, there was a hiring freeze, so working there was not an option. These were my only two choices at the time.

I had to feed my family and did not want to be a burden on my parents and accepted the fact that to be a cop would require waiting for the right time financially. I immediately found a job with the same dairy chain that I had worked for in high school, only now I was a manager trainee. Due to my prior experience with the chain, my training was short, and I was assigned my own store to manage in East Paterson, New Jersey, in an ethnically Italian section of town.

Even though I found a job immediately and things were going well, I really missed the Marine Corps. By now, I had been out for about five months and sorely missed the everyday challenge and rush of training— and being a marine—my only job as an adult. I went as far as inquiring with a recruiter about what the Marine Corps could do for me if I decided to go back in. At the time, because I had been out for over ninety days, I would have to go back through boot camp and start from scratch, which sealed the deal—going back would not be an option.

After a year as a store manager, an opportunity arose within the company for an owner/operator trucker subcontracting back to the company. The deal required that I purchase the truck and lease the refrigerated trailer at a cost of $29,500. The company would finance the equipment entirely and deduct payments from my billing. I was now in the trucking business, a complete turnaround from what I had been doing. The business went well and was very profitable. I drove to the ice cream plant near the Pennsylvania border six days a week, which originated in New Jersey, and was home every night.

The company then built a new plant in northeastern Pennsylvania, which required that we move there, so I could originate from that plant and deliver daily to New Jersey. By now, we were expecting a second child, a boy, Douglas Roy who arrived on June 13, 1974. He showed up just before the move to Pennsylvania. The business remained very profitable, but the cost of fuel was slowly escalating. When I started in 1973, diesel fuel was nineteen cents per gallon, and by 1977, it was fifty cents per gallon, which was eating deeply into the profit margin. At fifty cents per gallon for diesel, my yearly fuel cost was $40,000, so I sold the equipment and the route to another guy and took a short break for a few months.

I then purchased another new truck and leased out to a large, New Jersey-based dairy company and hauled raw milk in a tanker trailer from Pennsylvania and New York State into New York City and Long Island six days a week. This job was even more profitable than the last, and I did this for a few years but was unable to overcome the ever-escalating cost of diesel fuel.

I ended up selling in 1977 and went to work as a union trucker making fabulous money driving someone else's equipment, with no headaches, such as payments, maintenance, and taxes. I traveled Pennsylvania, New York State, and New Jersey pulling forty-five foot long double trailers. Then our third child, another boy, Peter James, was born on February 21, 1978. I was gone from early Monday morning and returned late Friday night or Saturday morning. The pay was great, but the hours took a toll on my marriage, so we ended up splitting in late 1978. We got a quick divorce, and my ex-wife moved to Charleston, South Carolina, with the kids to live with her mother. I missed my kids terribly and drove the eight hundred miles to visit them every several weeks.

We ended up getting back together in mid-1979, and I left my job in New Jersey and made the move to Charleston myself, where we remarried. Moving to the south removed the Hasbrouck Heights Police Department as a job possibility, as well as the New Jersey State Police, when its hiring freeze ended.

Jobs in the south did not pay as well, but I did get a trucking job right away hauling gasoline and ended up in the sales field within four months of coming to Charleston. The sales job was extremely profitable and allowed us to buy a nice house, but I still had the bug to get into law enforcement. It is obvious that the past seven years had not been too conducive to changing professions because law enforcement did not pay as well as trucking or sales.

I have glossed over the years in my life from 1972 to 1982 because they really do not pertain much to my story of thirty-five years in uniform. I did venture into the trucking business, which spanned seven of the past ten years. To do so took organization and discipline that I learned in the Marine Corps. My purpose in writing about this time period was to fill in a ten-year span for readers.

The birth of my three children was and remains the shining accomplishment of that period, and my life continues to be rewarded by them and their children.

BECOMING A POLICE OFFICER
16

IN 1982, AT THE AGE OF THIRTY-FOUR, I made up my mind that it was time for me to do what it took to become a cop. I signed up to attend a six-week course to become a reserve police officer with the Charleston County Police Department. I enjoyed the training and worked as a reserve cop during evenings and weekends to get in my forty required hours per quarter. At some point while I was a reserve, there were openings in the department for fulltime officers, and I was the first reserve police officer ever hired full time.

I had worked hard to pay off my bills and sold my house in preparation for the much lower salary I would assume once I started. I had earned between $35,000 and $50,000 annually for the past several years, and I was now going to be a police officer for the princely sum of $14,500 a year. One of the police officers on my hiring board asked me if I was nuts when he was made aware of this information during the interview.

At the time, the Charleston County Police Department was one of only two county police departments in the state. The other forty-four counties were sheriff's departments. The department was highly respected, and at the time it consisted of 186 sworn officers and approximately 40 civilian personnel.

At the time, the department conducted its own six-week, "mini" police academy. Other departments in the area also attended the academy, which mirrored all aspects of training at the state police academy. In those days, someone could work on the street with just this training for up to a year before actually going to the state police academy. The police departments managed to extend that year often, so it was common to be working on the road for up to eighteen months before ever attending the state academy. The law now requires officers to attend the state police academy within two weeks of being hired.

I was hired and started the mini-academy. I was selected to be the class leader based on my military experience. The class consisted of about twenty-four students, approximately five of whom were US Navy personnel who were base security personnel at the nearby Charleston Navy Base. Since law enforcement agencies are all paramilitary, the class was run accordingly, including uniform inspections, formations, chain of command, etc.

The first time one of the two fulltime instructors punished me with pushups for something someone else in the class did, I immediately figured out the deal, and I was not going to be their guinea pig. It happened twice the first day of training, so I asked the instructors if I could have a few minutes with the class with the door closed. They agreed, and I proceeded to tell the entire class directly that I was not going to do one more pushup because of their screw-ups. I told the class that if someone screwed up, and I was punished, they too would suffer the consequences. I told them that teamwork and discipline started right here and now, and I would not stand for any more bullshit.

The next time someone screwed up and I was ordered to do pushups, the entire class in unison dropped down and began to do pushups with me—my goal exactly. The training sergeant came to me later wanting to know what I did or said behind closed doors to cause the class to respond the way it did. I smiled and said, "You don't wanna know, Sarge!"—shades of the incident on graduation day at Parris Island twelve years before.

Different knowledgeable and highly experienced people within the department taught the various classes, which were extremely interesting. Investigators and crime-scene techs showed actual photos and slides of crime scenes to enhance the training. We even went to the Charleston County Hospital to attend an autopsy and walk through the cooler that housed unclaimed corpses. On the day that our class went to the autopsy, coroners were conducting one on a male subject who had been dead for almost a month and was found in his house with no air conditioning. Several members of the class got sick, and the training had the effect on the class that was intended., to see who had a weak stomach for the job. Based on the quality of the training, most Charleston County police officers who later attended the police academy did extremely well academically, and many were awarded the highest academic award for being first in their classes.

The class went well. We lost one or two because of grades, and I managed to come in first in the class academically, which gave me the choice of where I wanted to be assigned. I chose the West District, which was the busiest of the entire county and the district that I lived in. I would first need to ride with a Field Training Officer in several different areas. Then I would end up in the district that I requested.

Charleston County is a coastal county that runs ninety miles from Beaufort County to Georgetown County and encompasses nine hundred square miles. The police department had the county broken down into four districts: North, South, East, and West.

My first assignment was to go North, which started at the Charleston City line and encompassed the area around the busy Navy Base, which included low-income, minority housing near the base to middle-income homes further north in the county. Near the Navy Base, there were dozens of prostitutes who worked the area, and illegal drugs were abundant. At first, I was partnered with an older cop named Bill, who had been around a while and had been an investigator for many years. He taught me the area and shared his experience as we responded to our assigned calls for service.

On one particular day in my first week of training, we responded to a call of a reported suicide in a subdivision of middle-income homes. We entered the home and found a white, male subject, approximately twenty-two years old, sitting deceased in his car in the garage. He had apparently committed suicide by rolling his car windows down and sealing off the garage and starting the car. He died of carbon monoxide poisoning. An ambulance was standing by, and paramedics transported the subject to the nearest hospital while attempting to revive him. We walked around the house, and I quickly discovered a suicide note sitting on the dining room table, propped up so it would be noticeable. As I had been instructed, I did not touch it, but read it and advised my training officer Bill of what I had discovered. He picked it up, read it, then folded it, and placed it in his shirt pocket. I could not believe what I had just witnessed, but I was the new guy and kept my mouth shut.

We called the crime scene personnel to respond and left an officer to secure the scene while we went to the hospital to meet with the wife of the deceased to get some information. When we went back to the house, the Crime Scene sergeant, a former marine named Ernie, a hard-ass, and one of the officers who taught us many of our classes in the mini-academy, was processing the scene.

The Crime Scene sergeant came right up to me and said that he heard there was a suicide note. I acknowledged that there was, and he wanted to know where it was. I told him that my training officer, Bill, had it in his pocket. The sergeant proceeded to get into my ass for what happened and reminded me that he had just taught that class. I was between a rock and hard place, but I quickly told the sergeant that I knew what to do based on what he had taught us and that he needed to speak to Bill, my training officer. A lesson learned—just because you have been around a while does not mean you necessarily always know the right thing to do.

I have since worked directly for and with that sergeant, who later rose to the rank of chief deputy.

I worked in that district for two or three weeks, then went to the South District and was assigned to be trained by another former marine. Ray and I hit it off immediately, and he cheerfully shared his law enforcement experience with me. I had ridden with him several times as a reserve officer, and we had already gotten to know each other. Once, while riding with him as a reserve officer, we stopped a car one night after clocking it on radar at 112 miles per hour. While the driver was sitting in the backseat of the cruiser, he attempted to bribe us to let him go. When he said he had $40 in his pocket for us, we both laughed.

The South District is a rural area with a lot of farms and homes on large pieces of property. Because the district was so big, calls for service were at times many miles apart. There were times that you had to travel thirty miles to respond to a call, and if it was serious call, you had to run at high speeds.

One Friday not long before getting off at 3:00 p.m. on a 7:00 a.m. to 3:00 p.m. shift, we responded to a black, male subject suspicious person call near an old bar. We responded along with another officer working the area, and we spotted the suspicious subject wearing a trench coat. The subject had his hands in his pockets and was slowly approaching, so we ordered the subject to put his hands in the air, but he failed to comply. I was closest to the subject and saw the outline of a long weapon on his right side under his coat. I yelled "Gun!" to my partners and jumped behind the trunk of a car for cover. They covered me, and I threw the subject to the ground and disarmed him of a sawed-off shotgun, which is why he could not show his hands. Both cops thanked me for doing what I did, and the word quickly got around that I knew what I was doing.

Several weeks later, we were working an 11:00 p.m. to 7:00 a.m. shift on a Friday night and were working the entire weekend. This was my last weekend in training, and I was due to appear before a review board of a major, a captain, and a lieutenant on Monday afternoon to decide whether I should be released from training. The temperature was in the teens, and it was as cold as it had been in Charleston in quite some time.

We were riding around our district. I was driving, and we were just talking when we observed a Honda Civic occupied by three black male subjects, who kept looking out of the back window at us. We called in the tag number to check the status, and, all of a sudden, they started to accelerate, attempting to get away from us. My partner stayed on the radio while I drove and pursued the Honda. We went through several residential neighborhoods, and they could not shake us. Then they went back onto the main highway and then onto a paved road that turned into a dirt road, when the vehicle started to slow down as though it was going to stop. In the five to six minutes of pursuit, there had still been no status of the vehicle over the radio until we were getting ready to get out as the vehicle slowed almost to a complete stop. As the Honda slowed, we received a response of our license inquiry: "The vehicle is stolen and was used in a kidnapping and armed robbery ten days prior." Great, now you tell us. Then the vehicle stopped, and the driver turned to us and fired a shot at our vehicle. Then the driver got back in and went several hundred feet further down the road and slowed. As the vehicle slowed, the three occupants started to bail out of the car, and we both exited and fired our Model 10 .38 revolvers at them. My first shot shattered the left taillight, and my second, after adjusting, shattered the rear window. As we were firing, the three occupants ran into the woods to our left. They had left the car in gear and it continued to roll, so we had to stay with the car to ensure there were no more occupants or and that there was no one wounded inside.

I had emptied my weapon of the six spent cartridges, dumped them, and reloaded as I had been trained. My partner did the same, and we cleared the car and quickly reported that shots had been fired and the subjects had bailed into the woods. This type of a response is exactly the way the Marine Corps had taught both of us—when fired upon, return fire and advance toward the enemy. We had been fired upon and had returned fire and advanced as we fired.

The lieutenant on duty for that shift arrived on the scene within minutes, and based on where we were and where the suspects had gone, he elected to cancel anyone else from responding to our location. He was a by-the-book guy who quickly exhibited some fine leadership skills that I never forgot and used myself years later.

The lieutenant, whose name was Larry, told us to pick up our spent casings, and he personally inspected every casing. He said he wanted to make sure that we both had fired legal, department-issued ammunition and offered to replace any unauthorized rounds with the proper ammo that he had in his trunk. He said, "I want you two to be right in case investigators come to start checking things out." He did not have to do that, and he quickly showed me that he was a leader who looked out for his people. Well, it was so cold nobody wanted to respond from their warm beds. We had shot the hell out of a Honda and had wounded no one that we knew of, so investigators elected not to respond. While we waited for a tow truck to respond, it actually started snowing—something that rarely happens in Charleston.

We finished out our weekend, which was spent writing the lengthy report required for the incident. Again, my training officer thanked me for my quick thinking and good driving. The word got around that I had my shit together.

On Monday afternoon, I had my board as previously mentioned, and I was released to full duty and was now able to work alone. I was issued my police vehicle and was officially the *police*! In our area of the country, it is common that individual police officers are issued vehicles and allowed to take them home. The police agencies feel that officers are highly visible going to and from work, and if something happens and officers are called out for some reason, the vehicle is already in their driveway. Having police vehicles parked in driveways in neighborhoods is also a crime deterrent. This policy started with my agency in our area of the state. It was considered a boost in pay over the departments that did not yet allow this benefit because they provided the gas and allowed officers to use the vehicle while off duty. The requirement to drive a police vehicle off duty is that you had to have your badge and ID (identification), handcuffs, and weapon in your possession. In my career, there were countless times that I took police action while off duty.

The take-home vehicle was definitely a benefit because, at the time, it allowed me to get rid of the second car we had, thus saving a car payment. Today, more than thirty years later, I see some of the young kids who are starting out in law enforcement, and they cannot wait to be issued the take-home police vehicle because many of them do not even own a vehicle.

I was assigned my shift, and in the West District where I had requested, and went to work. Each squad for each district consisted of approximately eight officers, two sergeants, and one lieutenant. My lieutenant was the very same lieutenant who came to the scene when we had the chase and shot up the Honda Civic. I ended up working for Larry later in another assignment as a lieutenant, again as a captain, and as a chief some years later. I worked in the busiest district in the entire county, which is why I chose to be assigned there. It did not hurt either that I also lived in that district, so I was able to police in the area where I lived.

The district involved everything from poverty-stricken neighborhoods, middle-class, upper-middle class, and luxury, high-end neighborhoods, as well as migrant farms, trailer parks, government housing, and many schools and businesses. There were many domestic disputes, burglaries, car break-ins, and robberies, with an occasional stabbing, shooting, or homicide. I quickly discovered that I had a keen interest in drug enforcement, and I made more than the average number of drug arrests. Some people did not like messing with drugs and quickly figured out that if they happened upon some drugs during a traffic stop or street contact with a subject, they could call me, and I would gladly make the drug case for them. Some people liked enforcing traffic violations, some liked to handle accidents, and some liked to enforce drug laws.

The Charleston area is unique in that just about every kind of illegal drug was available in our area—from marijuana, to cocaine, to heroin, to LSD, to hashish, to pills. Because of the many barrier islands, there was a great deal of marijuana and cocaine smuggling going on from the waterways to uninhabited islands, marinas, boat landings, and docks in the area where I worked.

***

Any cop will tell you, if he or she has a heart, that anything involving children has an effect and bothers you inside. Cops, like military personnel, tend to hold their emotions within. I had been driving by this one particular house in a neighborhood not far from where I lived and had observed, before ever becoming a cop, that the house was a mess, and there were always children around the house who appeared to be dirty and not clothed very well.

Well, not very long after I became a cop and working that district, we had a call at that house to check on the welfare of the children. When we walked in, the smell coming from within was unbelievable. Feces and urine were throughout the house, the kitchen sink was full of dirty dishes, and cockroaches were running everywhere. The garbage was piled high in the corner of the kitchen, and the bathroom was disgusting. The bedrooms had only mattresses, no dressers, and very little clothing visible. I went back into the kitchen, opened the cupboards, and found no food, except for a jar of jelly. I opened the refrigerator and saw just a few items, but nothing that I would even consider consuming.

There were no adults present, and the kids said that they were at work. What my partner and I witnessed was enough to decide that the kids had to be taken into emergency protective custody so they would have an opportunity to get fed and cleaned up and to stay in a clean foster home until their parents could rectify the mess that we had witnessed. We called the Department of Social Services (DSS) to respond. They did so quickly and removed the children from the squalor they had been forced to live in. As the children were leaving, one of their parents arrived home, and the children began to cry because they loved their parents and did not understand that they were going to a better place than they could ever imagine.

I went home that night, hugged my own three kids, and thanked my lucky stars that they would never know or experience what those poor five children did. It took many months for that house to be cleaned to a point where it was acceptable to DSS to allow the children to return. Once they returned, I kept a special eye out and watched closely to ensure that the parents did not allow the situation to get back to where it had been. I always made sure to slow down and wave to the kids, and they always waved back.

The three to eleven shift is 3 p.m. to 11 p.m. and is always the busiest shift to work in any district. It was common to respond to a dozen calls for service in an eight-hour shift. One Saturday night we were working the three to eleven when a call went out that a naked male subject was going door to door, kicking in doors in a neighborhood, running into the kitchen of each house and drinking water directly from the kitchen faucet. He would then run back out of the front door and on to the next house. Rick, a guy on the shift with me, and I were patrolling the neighborhood actively looking for the suspect. I asked over the radio if we had any further description of the suspect, and I recall the dispatcher saying, no, other than he is completely naked. Rick had come up on the suspect in a major, five-point intersection that connects to the neighborhood and tried to radio his position, but he was busy fighting the suspect when I found him a minute or two later.

I bailed out of the car and was able to call in on the radio that we were out at five points with the suspect. Rick had the guy against the left front fender of his cruiser and was attempting to gain control of him. I jumped in and grabbed his right arm, and Rick had his left arm, but he refused to allow us to take control of him. He was apparently high on LSD and had super-human strength. We had his back against the fender, so he was facing us, and we were unable to turn him around. We fought with him for several minutes and were so busy that we were unable to get on the portable radio to ask for assistance.

Unknown to us at the time, while we were fighting, another officer in an adjoining district had gotten into a fight and had asked for assistance. As a result, every available unit traveled miles to assist the other officer. Whenever an officer puts out a call for assistance, every available cop responds, whether he or she is on or off duty. In the confusion of two major incidents at one time, nobody came to assist us. We had now been fighting this guy hard for over five minutes in the middle of a busy intersection, so we started drawing a crowd.

While we were fighting him, a woman from a nearby home actually came up and tried to throw a blanket over the suspect to keep people from seeing him naked. I yelled at the woman and said, "Get the hell out of here, lady! You are in the way!" Just then a male citizen came up and asked what he could do to assist, and my only thought was to say, "Kick him in the nuts." He seemed dumbfounded that I said that and he repeated, "You want me to kick him in the nuts?" I yelled, "Yes, do it now!" The citizen did as asked and had to be told to do it several times before the suspect lost his will to continue the fight, finally going down to his knees to be subdued and controlled.

We were finally able to handcuff him and use the radio to tell the dispatcher that we were OK, just as three or four cruisers rolled up to assist us. When the other incident had been resolved, they suddenly realized that we were still out at the intersection and had been unable to raise either of us on the radio. Even though we each had a radio on our belts, we were too busy to give up the use of one hand long enough to call for help.

The suspect definitely required medical attention, so Rick brought him to the emergency room, where he spent most of the night. Rick injured his knee during the incident, so he had to be checked out too. I then had to go to each house the suspect had entered and sort out what charges we were going to bring against the guy. He ended up with numerous counts of Housebreaking and Malicious Damage to Property as well as Assaulting Police Officers.

The next morning at the suspect's bond hearing, he was escorted into the courtroom with arms in hard casts, several broken ribs, and some facial lacerations. The hospital also confirmed that he was high on LSD, just as we had suspected.

We went home in one piece that night, and he stayed in jail for quite some time.

I was thoroughly enjoying my work and looked forward to going to work each day. I had picked the best place to work, and it was definitely a busy district.

In April of 1984, a bank alarm sounded in a bank in my district. A patrol sergeant was the first to arrive, but had failed to follow procedure and entered the bank in the middle of the robbery. He was disarmed and taken hostage and placed in a room with other bank employees. The second officer to arrive followed procedure but encountered three of the bank robbers leaving as he arrived. A male and female accomplice got away, but the officer was shot twice in the neck and shoulder at extremely close range by the third suspect. The officer, whose first name is Larry, was a weightlifter and in super physical condition. He was able to subdue the suspect after being shot twice. As he struggled with the suspect, he managed to shoot him. He did not know that his one round was fatal to the suspect, but exhausted from the hand-to-hand fight for his life, he managed to roll the wounded suspect over and handcuff him, then rolled back himself, totally exhausted.

A concerned citizen who had witnessed the fight, came to Larry's aid and used his portable radio to call for assistance. Cops from everywhere swarmed the area, set up roadblocks, and searched everywhere. I was not due to work until 11:00 p.m. that night, but I quickly dressed in my uniform and went to work to help. I remembered staying out more than eighteen hours, but when a fellow police officer is shot, fellow officers really do not care about the time. The other two accomplices were subsequently located, arrested, and charged with Armed Robbery and Murder because the killing of their accomplice was a result of their actions.

Only Larry's exceptional physical condition allowed him to live through this injury and to be able to talk about what happened that day. I rode with him as a reserve officer. We later became partners, and he was one of my closest friends. The South Carolina Police Academy began to use this incident in its Officer Survival and Practical Problems Training for bank robbery response.

One night while working the 11:00 p.m. to 7:00 a.m. shift, I observed a pickup truck coming from the beach on a main thoroughfare. I got behind it and followed it far enough to determine that the driver was probably Driving Under the Influence (DUI). I stopped the truck and determined that the driver was an active member of the local chapter of the Hell's Angels. The area he was coming from had a bar there that was frequented by the Angels, and this was my first encounter with one. He was wearing his colors, meaning he was wearing his leather vest with "Hell's Angels" across the back and various patches that signified illegal acts he had committed. I had been taught that when members are wearing their colors, they are usually armed.

I got him out of the truck and looked up since he was about six feet six inches tall and weighed in at about 325 lb. I was six feet three inches and about 225 lb. at the time, and I knew if he broke bad, I would certainly have to shoot this guy to put him down, but he ended up being a pussycat. After I searched him thoroughly and put him in the backseat, which he filled, I began asking him questions. I got the information from his license and started asking about tattoos and nicknames. He said his nickname was "Animal," and I responded, "I can understand how you got that nickname." While on the twenty-minute ride to the jail, he asked me if I was sure that I had gotten all of the weapons off of him when I searched him. He made me think very hard—did I search this guy properly? When I got him to the jail, we conducted a strip search of "Animal" to ensure that I had searched him thoroughly. I was relieved to find out that I had.

A little lesson learned from a Hell's Angel—I always checked a little more thoroughly than usual after that night, even though I didn't find anything.

Charleston, South Carolina, does in fact have active members of the Hell's Angels living here. They also have a fortified clubhouse just out of

Charleston County that Angels use as a safe house for those who have troubles with the law or need a place to hide out. It is built like a bunker with barbed wire and concertina wire at the top, with steel doors at each end.

In August of 1984, I was working the 3:00 p.m. to 11:00 p.m. shift on a payday Friday. My cruiser was gassed up prior to roll call, and when released to the road, I went immediately to the bank to deposit my paycheck, definitely before the days of direct deposit. I made the deposit at my bank just across the bridge onto John's Island and quickly returned to James Island, my primary district for that day. Minutes later a major call came across the radio, stating that there had been an armed robbery and shooting at a liquor store on John's Island. I was the closest unit, so I advised the dispatcher that I was responding. I knew that the liquor store owner cashed paychecks on Friday afternoons and had large amounts of cash on hand. He would cash a check in return for the purchase of a small bottle of liquor.

As I responded by the quickest route available, I was traveling at approximately one hundred miles per hour down a long straightaway that ran parallel to a golf course, but I slowed down to thirty-five to forty as I approached the traffic light before leaving James Island. The light was in my favor, and I was, of course, running lights and sirens, but as I slowed to enter the intersection, a vehicle coming from my left was preparing to proceed through the intersection, hesitated, and decided to scoot across before me. He did not make it because he broadsided me, striking my cruiser square between the two left doors, referred to as a T-bone impact. As he struck me, the impact pushed my vehicle into the cement curb, and my two right tires hit the curb, causing me to flip to the right and go airborne. I went airborne on my right side, and the roof struck a nearby Magnolia tree, crushing the roof. If I had been wearing a seatbelt, not required in those days, I would have been killed. Upon impact, I held onto the steering wheel with my left hand and leaned over in the seat to the passenger side. The vehicle came to a stop on its right side against the tree. My only thought was that I had just gassed the car up, and it was going to explode. I was unable to get out until a buddy of mine climbed on top of the car and pulled the jammed door open for me to get out. As he was tugging on the door, I was yelling, "Get me the fuck out of here!"—a close call, indeed.

My back was cut from scraping against the cage that separated the front and rear seats, and I was banged up from the impact and subsequent banging around until the car came to a rest. Now my wreck was causing traffic to back up in both directions, which blocked the intersection for two-way traffic between John's Island and James Island. Other units went on to the liquor store and found the owner badly wounded, suffering from a gunshot wound in the neck. The victim stated he had over $35,000 in cash stolen after being shot. They got a good description of the suspects and their vehicle and immediately broadcast that information.

While various members of the command staff showed up, and we waited for personnel to come and handle the accident and take photographs of the accident scene, crime lab techs also had to get through to respond to the scene of the robbery. As traffic moved slowly in each direction by alternating lanes, we now had a good description of the suspects and their getaway vehicle. You guessed it—the getaway vehicle was stopped in the backed-up traffic caused by my wreck! When the vehicle was seen in the line of bumper-to-bumper traffic, we all ran about one hundred feet to the vehicle, ordered the three suspects out of the vehicle at gunpoint, and had them out spread-eagled on their bellies on the hot, August blacktop. We arrested all three suspects, recovered two guns, and more than $37,000 in cash in paper bags.

This whole scene sounded like a comedy of errors, but if I had not been involved in the wreck, I would most likely have passed the suspects on my way to the liquor store before we ever had a description of the vehicle. They just happened to choose a bad getaway route.

I met the owner of the liquor store some weeks later, and he was very appreciative. The lesson I learned was that I now understood why supervisors were always telling officers to slow down over the radio when responding to call.

In those days, we drove fast Chevys with 350 engines, but the light bars on our roofs were just a bar attached like a luggage rack with a large, blue domed light mounted to it. When the cruisers were traveling at one hundred miles per hour or more, the light bars caused a whistling sound that could be heard when officers were transmitting over the radio. The whistling sound alerted the supervisor of the vehicle's speed, and the supervisor would then tell the officer driving to slow down. Another lesson learned for future reference was that getting into a wreck while responding to a hot call takes an officer and the resources used to help the officer away from the original call.

Just two weeks later on a Saturday afternoon, while I was working the same three to eleven shift, we received a holdup alarm at a different liquor store on James Island on the same road where my wreck had occurred. When the alarm went out, I was just blocks away and was at the location in less than a minute. When I arrived, I saw a vehicle leaving, but I had no description of the robbery vehicle, so my responsibility was to get to the store to check on the clerk and to determine whether a robbery had, in fact, occurred. Unfortunately, the traffic squad was out working traffic checkpoints that day, and the radio was busy with radio traffic asking the dispatcher for license information. I stood outside for several minutes covering the store as prescribed by policy, still unable to get on the radio to talk.

I looked around, and there was a pay phone fifteen feet away, so I called 911 and told the dispatcher my situation and berated her for not clearing the radio while a holdup alarm was ongoing, which was department policy. Protocol required that upon an officer's arrival, the dispatcher are to then call the clerk on the telephone and instruct him or her to exit the store and come to the officer. The clerk finally came out and gave me a description of the vehicle and suspect, and it had been the vehicle I saw leaving as I arrived in the parking lot. I bitched to the supervisor, who took action that ended up with disciplinary action taken against the dispatcher. The first responding officer violated this same robbery policy when Larry was shot at the bank robbery I previously described.

The information was broadcast, and we began looking for the car. In less than two hours we had located it in the back of a house not a mile from the scene of the robbery. We had a clothing description and now had a name to go with the vehicle. The suspect was not at home, but my partner, Chuck, and I tracked him all over the place for the next two hours. Every place we went, he was just minutes ahead of us. We finally tracked him back to the house and flushed him out after setting up a perimeter around the house. We were fortunate to be able to make a quick arrest, and we turned the suspect over to the Criminal Investigative Division (CID) to prepare arrest warrants and to interview the suspect. I received an Officer of the Month Award for making that arrest. It felt good to be able to handle a case from beginning to end, which was unusual for a uniformed patrol officer.

***

One Friday afternoon I was dispatched to a lower-middle-class neighborhood in response to a family dispute between grandmother and grandson. A second unit was not yet available, but two officers were required to respond to domestic calls for service. Upon my arrival, I met with the grandmother who explained that her grandson had pulled the phone wires out to all but one phone in the house and was now in her bedroom on the only remaining phone. Her husband was an amputee, and I could see that he would have been unable to intervene physically.

She pointed me to the room. I told them to stay in the living room, and I entered the room and observed her grandson, approximately eighteen years old, sitting on his grandmother's bed, talking to what sounded like a girl. He saw me and kept on talking as though I were invisible. He then proceeded to spit onto the carpet. He had to be removed from this house, but in 1984, there were not yet any domestic violence laws that he could have been charged with. When cops encountered an incident of domestic violence, we had to find a way to get the person or persons outside and find a way to arrest them for disorderly conduct by getting them to curse loudly or yell to be able to constitute disorderly conduct, which had to happen in public.

I asked the guy to get off the phone, and when he did not, I reached down and unplugged it from the wall, which got his attention. I asked him to walk outside, and he reluctantly complied. When outside I asked him if he had torn the phones from the walls inside, and he said, "Yeah, so what?" I told him that if he had done that in my house or had spit in my bedroom, I would beat his ass. I got the response I was looking for because he started cursing loudly enough so neighbors could hear, so I told him he was under arrest. When he resisted, I had to throw him down on the front lawn to handcuff him. Just as I put the cuffs on, my backup arrived.

Sometimes officers just have to do what is necessary to get the job done. Fortunately, a domestic violence law was enacted two years later, which allowed an officer to arrest someone if any evidence of violence was present. I took his driver's license from him because it was suspended, and I put it in a rubber band in the visor in my cruiser because, by law, he was not allowed to possess a suspended license.

About two months later, there was a murder one night on the front lawn in a neighborhood several miles away. The responding officers secured the crime scene and called detectives to investigate. After the detectives arrived, they developed a suspect name for the murder and gave a last name over the radio. I remembered the name, pulled his license out of my confiscated driver's licenses, and read his name and date of birth over the radio. He was the one who had shot and killed his best friend with a rifle and left the scene. I met with the detectives, gave them the license with his photo, and he was arrested within the hour when he was found hiding in bushes not far from the crime scene. I knew when I arrested him that he was a bad person, but I did not know he would soon be an accused murderer.

Another problem in our district was that there were many unlit rural roads, especially on John's Island and Wadmalaw Island. As a result, there were many serious accidents to handle, with a high percentage of fatalities involved.

In one twenty-eight-day midnight shift that summer, we had four separate major wrecks resulting in fatalities. One wreck that occurred in extremely cold weather earlier in the year was extremely unusual. My partner that night, JD, and I received a call over the radio at about four o'clock one morning that a subject near Seabrook Island was reporting that he had hit a deer and said medical attention was necessary. It was common to respond to car versus deer calls, so this did not sound like anything out of the ordinary. We decided that we would both take the ride, which was about twenty miles away. We arrived at the parking lot of a condominium complex where we were supposed to meet the complainant. I walked to the car on the passenger side, and JD walked to the driver's side, and we both shined our flashlights inside. We then observed a deceased male subject sitting in the front passenger seat with a perfect four-by-four-inch square hole right through his head, apparently caused by a wooden four-by-four mailbox post that went through the windshield, through his head, ending up in the rear cargo compartment. We both looked over the roof at each other and said in unison, "Call the traffic squad."

We spoke to the driver of the car, and he appeared to have been drinking because we could detect a strong odor of alcohol. We immediately placed him in the rear of my cruiser and awaited traffic-squad personnel who were trained to handle accidents involving fatalities.

It took quite some time, but we located the scene of the accident about a half mile back up the road on a curve in the road. The driver and his buddy were out drinking in downtown Charleston and were extremely intoxicated but decided to drive the twenty-five miles to Seabrook Island anyway. As the driver approached the curve, he failed to negotiate the curve and struck a bank of rural mailboxes on the side of the road, snapping a post that went through the passenger side windshield, killing the passenger instantly. There were no skid marks anywhere, so the impact speed was about fifty miles per hour.

At that time, a new law, Felony DUI, had just been enacted, making the crime a felony with major prison time. This case went to trial, and the driver was sentenced to major time in prison for recklessly killing his friend.

On the same shift, I was dispatched to a wreck on a road very near my home. It happened on a sharp curve lined with huge oak trees. When I pulled up, all I saw was debris and what was left of a car wrapped around a huge oak tree. There was a soccer field adjacent to the tree, and it was littered with debris, including the engine. I did not even have to get out of the car to tell that this would be a fatality.

I called the dispatcher on the radio and told her to send the traffic squad and the coroner.

***

In those days, especially working in the county, it was common for us to carry our shotguns in the front compartment with us, in a handy place for quick use. This practice is frowned upon now, and in many larger departments, long rifles are now issued to officers rather than shotguns. This transition was the result of the famous Los Angeles Bank of America bank robbery in which two heavily armed crooks shot many police officers because the officers were outgunned in the early '90s.

In the mid-'80s we had our Chevy Malibu's, and most guys kept their shotguns wedged between the driver's seat and the middle post between the two side doors. It was easy to grab as we got out of the car and when we did not have the time to unlock it from a shotgun rack or get it from the trunk.

I can think of several instances in which having a shotgun handy helped to resolve situations quickly. The first one that comes to mind occurred during the 11:00 p.m.to 7:00 a.m. shift. We received a call that a large crowd was causing an escalating disturbance in a neighborhood in District 7. We were at roll call when the call came out, and I still had to gas up before I left, but the other guy in the district with me said he was heading that way. I told him to wait until I could go in there with him because it was an extremely rough neighborhood. I quickly got gas, and when I tried to call my partner, he told headquarters he was out with an unruly crowd. Then a minute or so later he came across the radio and said, "Step it up!"

I located my partner and immediately saw that he had his back against his cruiser and was surrounded by at least fifteen male subjects ready to cause trouble. I pulled up, grabbed my shotgun, racked a round into the chamber, and aimed it directly at the crowd, the sound of a shotgun racking a round will always get someone's attention. This did, and all subjects scattered. My partner and I had a quick word about him going in alone and the situation was over.

On another midnight shift months later, I was working Districts 9 and 10, which includes James Island, John's Island, and Wadmalaw Island. I was working with a young rookie with less than four months on the job. He was sort of a "loose cannon" and had already wrecked two cruisers, and been in some trouble involving some citizen complaints. He was on John's Island, and I was on James Island at the time. The rookie (I cannot remember his name) rode up on a black male subject breaking into a business. He called it in on the radio and stated the suspect had a knife, which should not have been a problem since the rookie had a gun. Duke was the sergeant on duty that night, and because of the nature of the call, I was already heading that way to back him up.

While on my way, the rookie came across the radio, again sounding like his situation was escalating. Duke told me to step it up, which meant Mach 3 in police terms. I was now on John's Island and doing eighty to ninety miles per hour on unlit and winding River Road to get to him. When I slid up on scene I observed the suspect holding a knife in his right fist over his head as though he were ready to attack, and the rookie was standing like Wyatt Earp not five feet away with his legs spread and his hand over his holstered handgun like he was getting ready to draw at the OK Corral. I immediately saw the situation, grabbed the shotgun, racked a round in the chamber, and aimed it at the suspect's head. I told the rookie to back away for safety purposes because he was already way too close to the suspect. It was as quiet as being in church now, and the suspect was still holding the knife in a threatening manner when I clicked the safety off the shotgun and said, "Drop the knife, asshole, or I will blow your brains out!" He dropped the knife, and the rookie jumped in and tackled him. Sometimes there is no time for niceties in dealing with suspects. What I said to him to resolve the situation was in the language that he understood without question.

As one might expect, this rookie did not last another six months before he was fired. He was just not cut out for this type of work.

The third incident in which having a shotgun handy happened a year or so later while I was working on another assignment. I had gotten off work at 3:00 a.m. and was passing through District 7 on my way home when a report of an armed robbery at a local strip club went out over the radio. There were three suspects involved, and they had stupidly left the scene in a taxicab. Just as the report was being broadcast over the radio, I spotted the taxi and radioed in that I had spotted it and was attempting to stop it. The taxi stopped in the parking lot of an apartment complex and before any of the occupants could exit the taxi, I was out with my trusty shotgun. When the first units arrived, I had all four occupants, including the driver, spread-eagled on the ground with the shotgun aimed directly at them.

My old squad was the one working that night, and as my buddies pulled up, one of them stated, "I like your style, Ray." This situation is another reason local police agencies allow officers to take their vehicles home with them. These three incidents too are living proof that shotguns are a helpful tool in law enforcement.

***

My lieutenant, Larry, who was the first to arrive at the scene of the chase and shooting my last weekend in training, continued to exhibit leadership traits I had not seen among other lieutenants. You knew if you screwed up you were in for a butt-chewing, but only of you deserved it.

He kidded around just enough but knew how to draw the line between friend and boss. He would ensure that guys locked their cars while on service calls by checking while you were in on the call. If an officer left the cruiser unlocked, he would sometimes get in and drive it around the corner, or he would go into the cruiser and take the officer's shotgun, then would call an inspection and ask to see everybody's shotgun. We were supposed to check businesses in our district at least once per shift. He would sometimes sit for hours to see if we were conducting building checks. If he knew an officer was not that busy and he had not seen him or her check assigned businesses, he would let the officer know. It was his funny way to make sure all were doing their jobs and following policies and procedures. He was one of the most respected officers in the department, and his people would do anything for him.

As time went by, I started to watch the good supervisors, observe the few bad ones, and make mental notes of who I would emulate if ever given a leadership role. The good old boy system of promotion still existed, which resulted in quite a few substandard supervisors still within the department.

As for the two sergeants assigned to my squad, they were like night and day, complete opposites. One was named Duke, a good old boy sergeant, but he was the better of the two by far. He was genuinely concerned with his subordinates and checked on us from time to time. He made sure that we had what we needed and was understanding when people put in for time off. Duke was well liked and had been around for over twenty years at the time and later transferred to the Vice Unit, from which he retired several years later.

Personally, I did not take a day off for the first two years on the job because I loved it so much. We worked five-day weeks with set days off given out by seniority. I was off on Tuesday and Wednesday and the second year graduated to Wednesday and Thursday.

The other sergeant, Dale, was a completely different story; he was egotistical and cocky and was not a very well-liked person in the department. He was, however, respected and not hard to work for. He was the one who went to bat for me when I arrived at the liquor store robbery and was unable to get on the radio to announce my arrival.

Not long before I left the squad to attend the police academy, Dale and I had a situation that came up, which put me in a bit of a predicament. Since I did not start out on the job until I was thirty-four years old, I was older than most new cops and a little more mature. Well, Dale kept complaining loudly about the fact that his relief sergeant named Bill for the next shift was always late to relieve him, and he had heard Bill always left his house in North Charleston late and raced to the station, speeding through several districts. He knew that I was radar certified and had radar in my cruiser.

One day Dale came to me and told me to go up on St. Andrew's Boulevard and to clock the other sergeant on my radar and report his speed back to him. It was a known fact in those days that cops exceeded the speed limit all the time, and this particular sergeant had a lead foot. Dale was putting me in a situation that I did not want to be in, and I told him that he needed to find someone else to do his dirty work. He did not like my answer, but I was not intimidated and was not going to do it, simple as that. I did tell him that he could take the radar out of my car and clock his speed himself. What I did do was go to that sergeant, Bill, who I really did not know very well, and told him he might want to slow down when relieving Dale, and I explained what I was asked to do. From that day on he and I were instant friends, and we ended up working together years later as lieutenants.

As stated earlier, I took a major pay cut to follow my life ambition, so my family always lived from paycheck to paycheck. To supplement my income, I volunteered to work off duty as often as possible depending on what shift I was working at the time. I often worked security at high school football games, which was $35 for four hours work, which collates to $8.50 per hour, which was more than my hourly pay rate as a cop at the time. I worked concerts, county fairs, wrestling matches, restaurant security, store openings, drugstore security, horse races, and grocery store security. In those days, every little bit of extra money to be made was a huge help to a cop's meager income. I almost never had a day off because I worked extra off-duty work whenever I was able to do so.

Leaving my squad for nine weeks to attend the police academy was a welcome break, and I planned to return to the same squad after I graduated, which was normal policy. Squads just worked a person short until their cop came back from their required training. For nine weeks, I was unable to work much off duty, but I did work drugstore security on the Saturday evenings that I was home for the weekend.

THE POLICE ACADEMY

17

I HAD NOW BEEN A COP ON THE road for twenty-one months, counting the six-week Reserve Officer Training class under my belt and the identical six-week mini-academy put on by my department after I had been hired full time. I had been involved in a shooting incident and a half dozen high-speed chases. I had responded to numerous armed robberies and dozens of domestic disputes, stabbings, fights, and been involved in a major wreck, and I had been awarded a Patrolman of the Month Award. Now I was going to attend the South Carolina Criminal Justice Academy.

We drove our assigned cruisers to Columbia, the capital of South Carolina, which was about 110 miles away. We had to be in formation each Monday morning, so getting up at 4:00 a.m. was a must. We came home each weekend after the last class on Friday afternoon. For nine weeks I had every weekend off, which would certainly change after I got back to work.

I looked forward to attending and did well academically. There were several tests per week and a major legal test each Friday in the first three weeks. If an officer failed any one of those, he or she was immediately sent home to his or her police department and in most cases fired.

The physical portion of the training was a piece of cake, with daily three- to five-mile runs. We had defensive tactics, which involved hands-on self-defense as well as PR-24 training, which was the designation for our issued nightstick with a handle. There was much emphasis on firearms training, which lasted a week, and the driving range, which also lasted a week. There were at least two weeks of practical problem training, which was true-to-life scenarios using real police officers as role players to play the bad guys. Most scenarios were no-win situations but extremely helpful and true to life.

When I went through the academy, there was a new instructor who had come from a nearby police department in the Charleston area. He was responsible for teaching bank robbery response in the classroom and then teaching the practical problem for the class. In one scenario that I was involved in, the story line seemed familiar. Then I realized we were playing out the same bank robbery I described in the previous chapter in which the officer was shot twice but fought the shooter and killed him and had the presence of mind to handcuff the dead suspect before he collapsed, exhausted. I kept quiet, and when it came time for the shooting to occur, I shot the suspect and handcuffed him.

After the scenario was complete, the instructor critiqued our group and said that I was the first recruit who had ever gotten the scenario correct by handcuffing the suspect after he was wounded. He asked me how I knew what to do, and I explained that I had responded to the robbery and was familiar with what happened there. Lesson learned.

Coming from a busy police department and having spent twenty-one months on the road handling as many calls as some in the class from small departments handled in five years was a unique contrast to others in the class. Many of the people in my class were working for departments smaller than the squad I worked on. I met many great people and made friends in the brotherhood and sisterhood of cops that still exist today.

When it came time to graduate, I was near the top of my class and just missed being an honor graduate for the nine-week class, with a 94 percent average. We graduated on a Friday morning, and that was my last weekend off for a while.

While at the police academy, I was interviewed for a new unit being formed in my department. The new team was called SCATT, which stood for Special Crime Area Tactical Team. After being interviewed, I was notified that I had been selected for the position and was to report there after graduation, not to the squad I had spent my first twenty-one months with, but to the North SCAT Team.

I had made everlasting friendships on the squad I came from before going to the police academy, but I was delighted to have been selected for the newly formed unit.

SCAT TEAM

18

THE SCAT TEAM (SCATT) WAS TWO TEAMS OF five officers, consisting of one sergeant, one K-9 with handler, and three officers. The SCAT Team was formed to respond only to in-progress calls and to all open doors and alarm calls. We were allowed to work any area in the North/East districts and the other team had the South/West districts. I was selected to be a member of the North/East team and reported there the day after I graduated from the academy. We worked 7:00 p.m. to 3:00 a.m. Tuesday to Saturday, with Sundays and Mondays off.

The north area of our district included the Charleston Navy Base where over 20,000 sailors and their ships were based at any given time, as well as a large Air Force Base that housed many thousands of airmen.

Just outside the several gates of the Navy Base were swarms of prostitutes to accommodate the male Navy personnel. The prostitute's ethnicity was split by about 50 percent white and 50 percent black. We received periodic mandates to arrest them whenever we saw that they were outwardly soliciting for prostitution. It was common to arrest four or five per night, per officer. Because we were making so many arrests for prostitution, we became friendly enough with the prostitutes to use them as informants from time to time. We knew that they were the eyes and ears of the street and were very helpful to us when necessary.

Our sergeant was an old school guy named Tommy, with over twenty years on the job. He had much experience in Vice and Narcotics and subscribed to the my-way-or-the-highway doctrine. He was laid back and had a very dry sense of humor but knew his job. We were all fine with that, as this was now the third sergeant I had worked for.

The command staff of the police department never had a unit like ours at its disposal, so the command staff used us to go into bad areas in force to eradicate drug dealers. I was the only one in my group who enjoyed making drug cases, so I gladly took all the cases that came up or developed. Our commander, who was a captain, told our sergeant not to worry about any complaints we received because they were expected. He told us to get the job done and to do whatever it took to accomplish the task. He would handle the complaints. These were pretty open orders in the mid-'80s, and we accomplished our assignments accordingly. We had no lieutenant in our chain of command and reported directly to the North/ East Patrol Commander, a captain.

Having the use of a police dog was unique too, and we trained nightly with the dog and his handle. Our dog was a German shepherd named "Sam," and his handler, Don, a veteran of the Air Force, had been a dog handler who guarded the fleet of presidential aircraft at Andrews Air Force Base. He also worked for a short time at the North Charleston Police Department. We practiced nightly wearing the padded sleeve, allowing "Sam" to chase us down and to practice biting the arm wrap.

Chuck was a veteran too and had previously worked for the North Charleston Police Department. He had much investigative experience. He was very adept in quickly preparing the wording for arrest warrants, and he was the person responsible for teaching me that very important aspect of law enforcement. Chuck was the brains of the team, Don was the K-9 handler, and Larry and I were the muscle, so to speak.

Larry was the same Larry who had been shot in the bank robbery and had returned fire, killing his assailant before collapsing. He had been a patrol officer his entire career and was happy in our newfound job description. He did express interest in dog tracking, especially with bloodhounds, but presently, our department had only two patrol dogs that were both on the SCAT Teams. Larry was an avid gun and knife collector and a bodybuilder.

Tommy was usually with us when we were on specific assignments from the captain, but generally, he let the four of us out on our own if there were no specific orders.

***

Just weeks into my new assignment in January of 1985, my dad went into the hospital for routine surgery to his neck. He had several unexplained fainting spells while driving, which caused several minor accidents. The surgery was to remove plaque blockages from the veins in his neck to his brain from his heart, which would alleviate the fainting. I drove up to see him, and he seemed to be recovering normally. I was due to drive back home on Monday, so I decided to go to the hospital on January 26 and sit and watch the Super Bowl with him. While I was sitting there with him, I noticed that he seemed to be acting differently, and when I checked him more closely, it appeared that he had had a stroke while watching the game with me. His face drooped slightly, and he appeared to be partially paralyzed on one side. I immediately called a nurse. Then I called the house to advise my mother, who was a nurse in the same hospital.

I had to return home the following day and was only home a day or so when I got the call that my dad had passed away. I loaded the car again, and my wife and three kids and I made the trip back to attend his funeral. Several hundred people whose lives he touched attended his wake, and it was great to see all of his friends come to pay their respects. I still miss him every day and would give a million dollars to have a conversation with him today to thank him for the life's lessons he taught me. We returned home, and I was in a fog for a while getting over my dad's untimely and unexpected death at the age of sixty-seven.

***

Our team quickly became known for getting the job done, and we were making nightly arrests for everything from prostitution to robbery. When major crimes happened, we went to work talking to our prostitute informants. If they gave us helpful information for an investigation, we generally had pending court cases against them that we could give them help with. They cooperated because having a charge dismissed saved them money.

The narcotics unit used our assets whenever it went into a bad area, and we were usually used as outside security while those officers conducted search warrants in the projects, which always generated problems outside with crowds that gathered to see what was going on.

Not long after the teams were formed, we all received notification that we were attending an FBI Hostage Negotiation School, which lasted five days here in Charleston. None of us wanted to attend and were upset that the class would essentially remove us from the streets for a week. We all attended and sat through the sometimes boring training connected to the course. We finished on Friday and collectively said that it was a waste of time because we would never have the opportunity to use the training. In those days, there was no organized Hostage Negotiation Team in the department yet, so we were it.

Not two weeks after completing this course, we were dispatched to James Island in the West District to back up the other SCAT Team at a mobile home where a father had barricaded himself with a small child in the master bedroom. Both teams surrounded the residence, and I believe Chuck conducted the verbal negotiations with the suspect. After about two hours, Larry and I were able to quietly gain entry into the house and force our way into the bedroom. Larry put the father down and handcuffed him as I snatched the child from the crib and ran outside. Well, so much for never having an opportunity to use the training.

One of the first nights of our existence as a SCAT Team, we accompanied narcotics, known as METRO short for Metro Major Case Unit. We went to its briefing and got our assignments. The team was going to enter a two-story apartment with the stairwell to the second-floor portion of the apartment directly behind the front door. They hit the unit and made their entry, and a male subject upstairs ran right to the bathroom at the top of the stairs to flush his cocaine. The first narc into the door ran up the steps and encountered the bad guy attempting to flush. While I was at the front door for security, the bad guy who was flushing was struggling with James, the METRO sergeant, and just as quickly, the bad guy came tumbling down the steps, with a little help from James, who yelled down to me, "Cuff that piece of shit," which we did.

METRO was known as a hardcore unit that had the ability to investigate illegal narcotics anywhere in Charleston County and did not have to abide by boundaries of other police jurisdictions within Charleston County. This search warrant was in the boundaries of North Charleston, which had its own police department. After this incident, we all agreed that we might just have some fun working in this new unit.

We met each night after roll call at a local Waffle House for a cup of their dishwater coffee before hitting the street. Our sergeant, Tommy, was addicted to their lousy coffee, so we had to meet him there nightly.

The dispatchers knew where we were and sometimes called the Waffle House to get us if there was something they could not say over the police radio—before the days when everybody had cell phones.

One night, while finishing our coffee, we got a phone call from a dispatcher who said that the department had a request from the daughter of a woman who had been discharged from the hospital, saying that family members were unable to get the woman out of the car and into the house. They asked for police assistance, and we were requested to help. While finishing our coffee, we decided that Larry and I would be the ones to do the lifting. One of the guys was just recovering from a hernia operation, the K-9 handler was small in stature, and the sergeant said he would, of course, supervise. Larry was a bodybuilder but had a very squeamish stomach about certain things. Knowing this, I said I hoped that the patient did not smell, and he wanted to know why. I told him that some diseases have an odor, and she would probably stink, which set Larry off worrying about what we might encounter and asking a million questions. Just another example of some of our sick police black humor.

We pulled up at the house and met family members, who introduced us to their mother sitting in the passenger seat of a car parked at the curb in front of their house. She was obese—probably 350 lb.—and unable to stand on her own. We decided that we would place a wooden kitchen chair next to her, and we would slide her onto the chair and then carry her on the chair into the house. We slid her onto the chair and slowly carried her up to the front porch and set her down to catch our breath before entering the front door and into her bedroom. As we took a breather, I looked up at Larry and held my nose as though there were an odor. There was none, of course. He started to laugh uncontrollably, and we started into the house with Mama, laughing the entire way. Family members were looking at us and wondering why we were laughing, but they did not say anything. We got her into her room and set the chair down next to her bed with the plan to slide her from the chair onto the bed. We got her into the bed and rolled her over, and as we did, her dress went up over her head, and we saw that she was not wearing underwear. As she rolled over, she let out the longest and loudest fart we ever heard.

Her family thanked us profusely, and we exited as quickly as possible, laughing the entire way. I had no idea what the woman had been in the hospital for, but letting Larry think that she had an odor made this boring call for service turn into a laughable incident.

***

The captain wanted an area cleaned up in East District. For county vehicles to get gas for their vehicles in the remote areas of the county, there were several fenced-in areas that had gas pumps that county employees had access to. Our captain lived in the area, gassed his vehicle up every day, and saw drug dealers selling right in the street that led to the gas pumps. He gave Tommy emphatic orders that he wanted the area cleaned up right away. We checked it out and determined they were dealing early in the day seven days a week, so we decided to pay them a visit one Saturday morning. Don, with "SAM," and Chuck were to provide security as Larry and I approached the one dealer out there at that time. He was a big guy, and as we approached, he decided that he was going to stand his ground and take his chances fighting two cops. This was an extremely bad mistake on his part because as soon as we reached for him, the fight was on. While we were fighting the drug dealer, a group of his friends came running out of the house from across the street. Don got "Sam" out of the car on a long leash to hold back the friends, and Chuck pulled his PR-24 nightstick out because it looked like he might have to use it.

Larry and I fought this guy for several minutes and finally managed to get him subdued and handcuffed. His shirt was torn off, his pants were ripped, and he had cuts, scrapes, and bumps all over his body. Larry and I were OK, just dirty and disheveled. The bad guy was fighting over a large paper bag containing cocaine and marijuana. I did the arrest warrants and processed the drugs, and the dealer was taken to the hospital for later release to the jail. Later that afternoon at his Bond Hearing, he looked like he had been through a war. The judge raised his eyebrows to me until I explained the extent to which he had resisted our arrest. There was no war, just a short battle that we had won.

***

If you have not figured this out yet, there are as many funny stories to tell about my career as there are serious ones. I have always told people that you *must* have a sense of humor to be a cop. If you do not, you will never be able to make a career out of it because of all the bad and sad incidents that we regularly handle, we counteract by using our own sick, black humor, the same thing we did in Vietnam when referring to our possible death or serious injury.

I am certain that many professions have their own form of black humor that they use to cope with what they do for a living. I know nurses do, EMS technicians, teachers, and others, I am sure. It is not that the professionals do not respect the people they serve; it is just a mechanism to make the job more acceptable when times are bad.

***

The next assignment our captain gave us was to clean up a corner in an area called Maryville in the East District. It had a reputation for people congregating on the corner and selling illegal narcotics. We drove by the corner as a group the first time and saw four young, male subjects standing on the corner. As they saw us stop and exit our vehicles, they slowly walked away from where they were standing. I looked down and picked up numerous small nickel and dime bags of marijuana, worth $5 and $10, respectively. We had just seen all four subjects standing where the marijuana was found so we detained all of them. Of course, all four denied ownership of the narcotics, so we took all four into custody and charged each of them with Simple Possession of Marijuana, punishable by a fine of about $350 or thirty days in jail. Collectively, the drugs were enough to charge any one person with Distribution, but the drugs were found in several different spots, which indicated that that all four were in possession, and when they saw us, they dropped the small amount each had.

We immediately took the four to the nearest magistrate, who was a newly appointed retired female English teacher from the high school that all four subjects had once attended. We were hesitant to go to a magistrate that none of us knew anything about, but we were required at the time to go to the magistrate nearest where the crime was committed.

We walked into the magistrate's office, escorted our four handcuffed subjects into the courtroom, and sat them in the front row to await an appearance before the magistrate. In walked the magistrate, wearing a black robe, and we introduced ourselves to her and told her why we were in her court. The magistrate's first name was Jeanette, and she proceeded to speak with the four teenagers in custody. She appeared to recognize each one of them and asked how they were doing and how their parents and siblings were by name. We all looked at each other and just knew these guys were only getting a slap on the wrist for our trouble.

They all stood up before the magistrate, their case was heard, and she found them all guilty as charged. When she read her sentence all of our jaws dropped as she sentenced them all to thirty days in jail and said, "Take them to the pokey." We were elated at her sentence because we knew that once the word got around that they were sentenced to straight time in jail, our job would be easier from that day on.

***

One cold Friday night in February 1985, we got a call to travel to the southern part of the county along with the South West SCAT Team to respond to what appeared to be a triple homicide. To make a long story short, the husband of a woman returned home to find that his wife's former husband had arrived at the house while he was gone, and when he returned, he witnessed the ex-husband outside near his truck who appeared to be punching his father in-law, when he was, in fact, stabbing him multiple times. The ex-husband had already stabbed and killed his young stepson and his wife in the same manner, throwing and putting all three in the bed of his pickup truck. The husband was unaware that his stepson and wife had already been killed, but he tried to get into the house to get his handgun.

The ex-husband drove away when the husband went into his house and discovered that nobody was inside and that there were signs of a major struggle. He immediately called the Charleston County Police Department and both SCAT Teams responded. As I said, it was bitterly and unseasonably cold, probably in the teens. A perimeter had been set up, and we began a search of the nearby area and soon discovered the pickup truck that the husband saw the suspect drive away in after he saw his father in-law killed before his own eyes. The bed of the pickup was full of frozen and coagulated blood with some physical evidence present to indicate that the son and wife had also been killed.

Keep in mind that the temperature was frigid, and we were in a rural area of the county. Additional personnel began to arrive to process the scene and to assist in setting up a perimeter. We knew the identity of the suspect and knew that he had lived in the area and knew his way around. We stayed out throughout the night and into the following day with no sightings or additional information developing.

Just about 1:00 p.m. the following afternoon a female police officer came across the radio stating that she thought she may have spotted the suspect walking along the side of the road. I was the closest officer to her and was to her location in less than a minute. I pulled up next to the suspect, jumped out, threw him on the ground, and handcuffed him. By the time I had him cuffed, there were probably fifty cops surrounding us. The suspect was immediately put in the back of an investigator's vehicle and whisked to headquarters for questioning. He appeared to be exhausted and was wet and muddy. Our job was over for the time being, and we all went home to get some well-deserved sleep. We had been out working since the previous evening at 7:00 p.m., so we had worked eighteen hours. We returned to work that evening at seven with very little sleep and went back to that same area again.

In the time we were sleeping, the investigators interviewing the suspect had determined that he had buried the three bodies in a pre-dug grave at a location a few miles from the murder scene. Our job now was to search areas for freshly dug graves, which was like finding a needle in a haystack in that remote area of the county. Investigators finally convinced the suspect to show them where the grave was. He did so, and it was so well disguised with leaves and pine straw, it never would have been located without his assistance.

The crime scene techs began the arduous job of conducting a pyramid dig to recover the bodies. A pyramid dig after establishing the location of the grave is that you slowly and carefully dig a trench around the bodies in their buried state. Then the techs slowly begin removing dirt a little at a time, while standing in the trench around the grave, which eventually places the grave at the eye level of the techs digging. The grave is handled very much like an archeological dig and is the best way to preserve evidence when a crime has been committed.

The suspect had dug a deep hole prior to committing the murders, which of course constituted premeditation, so when he left the murder scene, he drove immediately to that location and quickly buried the three victims, then returned the truck to where we had found it. I did not participate in the dig but served as security to keep the news media from entering the area, but I was able to view the site. As you can imagine a triple homicide is news wherever it happens. The techs dug all night, and during the dig, it began to rain, which made their job even more difficult to accomplish.

The suspect was eventually tried and convicted of three counts of murder and sentenced to death in February of 1986. Little did anyone know that this suspect would again be the subject of a manhunt in January of 1988.

***

While working on the SCAT Team, we would often congregate in the parking lot of the 7-11 store across the road from the main gate to the Charleston Navy Base. It was an extremely busy intersection with a bar on one corner, the 7-11 on one corner, a fleabag motel frequented by prostitutes on one corner, and a cemetery on the fourth corner. One night while four of us were parked in a line against the curb in the 7-11 parking lot, taking a quick break and drinking a soda, an intoxicated sailor walked out of the 7-11 and saw four white cruisers parked in a line, which he thought were taxis waiting for fares. The front car in line happened to be that of our K-9 handler Don, with "Sam" sleeping in the backseat. Well, the drunk sailor proceeded to walk to the front cruiser occupied by "Sam" and opened the rear door to get in and was met by "Sam" growling at him and showing every tooth he had! The sailor turned pale white and jumped back, slamming the door. He turned to see the four of us laughing our butts off. We actually gave the guy a ride back to the base and dropped him right at the dock where his ship was berthed. He probably had to get onto the ship to change his pants and shower!

***

I continued to make many drug cases and enjoyed doing so. Making a drug arrest involves about three times more paperwork than any other report because of the evidence submission and chain of custody paperwork required.

One night on my way to work from James Island, I saw a driver in a vehicle acting suspiciously and stopped the car. I did not usually make any stops on the way to work, but something told me to stop this guy. When I made the stop, the driver immediately got out and started walking to me, so I ordered him to get back into his car. His actions sent signals to me that he probably did not want me to see something he had in the car. When he got back into the car, I observed a quantity of marijuana under a towel in the front seat, so I immediately handcuffed the subject and placed him in my backseat. I went back to the car and recovered over 5 lb. of marijuana and some packed in smaller bags for resale. This was definitely a nice drug arrest in 1985.

I had the car towed, and I transported the subject to the METRO office located right downstairs from where we had our nightly roll call. I walked in with 5 lb. of dope and the suspect just as the narcs were having their nightly roll call. When the METRO sergeant, James, saw what I had, he went ballistic, not on me, but on his narcotic investigators sitting at their desks. He yelled to them, while he held the large bag over his head, the sergeant yelled, "Ray got this dope on his way to work, and you shitheads can't find this much while working!" I was very embarrassed about them getting their butts chewed, but it was all a show by the sergeant to get his people motivated for the night. This form of leadership was different, for sure, but one that I filed away in the back of my head for future reference. I ended up working for James on my next assignment.

Around the same period, I chased down a known drug dealer during street sweeps in a neighborhood riddled with drug dealers. He threw the drugs down as I chased him, but I made a mental note of where he dropped the bag. I went back and found a bag with numerous little one-gram bags of cocaine packaged for resale. This arrest pissed off the METRO sergeant too because this was a guy his unit had been trying to arrest for a while. Again, he was not pissed at me. He was pissed at his guys for not getting him. I had decided that I would love to go to METRO at some point to become a narcotics investigator. At least I knew that the right people were noticing my drug arrests.

***

At some point, we were plagued by a series of vehicle break-ins in hotel and bar parking lots in our district. There had been over one hundred such thefts, which drew the attention of the command staff, who wanted something done to stop the rash of crimes. The target of the thefts was mostly radar detectors, which were popular at the time and usually sitting on the dashboard of the cars being broken into.

Our sergeant, Tommy, had arranged for us to get a radar detector from evidence with the permission of the Crime Scene sergeant, the same who chewed my butt over the suicide note my first week on the job. We set up surveillance in the parking lot of a Howard Johnson's Hotel on the strip where all of the thefts had been occurring. We planted the radar detector on the dash of an old, undercover car from METRO we had borrowed and left it unlocked and set ourselves up in a nearby van with Don and his K-9 "Sam" nearby, just inside of the back door of the hotel.

On our second or third night of surveillance, our suspect showed up in the parking lot checking for unlocked doors when he discovered our planted radar detector. He went into our decoy car, took the bait, and started walking away out of the parking lot. We had given the signal to Don to let "Sam" loose, which he did, but "Sam" failed to attack the suspect when ordered by Don. The chase was on as Larry and I chased the suspect on foot as he ran across the busy, four-lane road, almost being hit by several cars. Tommy was waiting across the street in the Hardee's parking lot, and the suspect was running in his direction. Tommy bailed from his car and was within five feet of the suspect as he ran past him at full speed. Tommy chased him through the Hardee's parking lot and around a house as I made it through traffic to him. The suspect came around the house and stopped when he saw me pointing my weapon at him. At that point there was a drainage ditch filled with water between him and me, and he elected to run again. I hopped the ditch and was about eight feet behind him when I fired two shots in the air, hoping it would make him stop. Firing warning shots had the opposite effect because as soon as the shots were fired, he tripled the distance between us and got away. Firing warning shots was prohibited by policy but was still a form of old-school policing that did not seem to die.

Our boss, Tommy, was pissed off at us for letting him get away, but he had let him get away too. We, however, did not say anything to him about that. We usually got off at 3:00 a.m., and it was now about 1:00 a.m. Tommy told us we were staying out until we either found the suspect or found out who he was. We ended up staying out until daylight empty-handed.

We came back in that night and hit the streets, hitting up our informants for the identity of who was doing all of the car break-ins. We also figured that he might be bragging about getting away from the police after shots were fired.

I went to the home of an informant named "Slim," and his mother told me he was sleeping, so I pretty much forced my way into the house and woke his ass up right out of his bed. I stood there while he got dressed then took him to a nearby cemetery to tell him what had happened and what we needed. Within three hours of him hitting the street for information, he found us to tell us he had found out who it was. All he had was a nickname and a physical description, but no real name. The nickname was "Bug Eye," which was enough information for us to get his real name. Once we had a mug shot, we were all able to positively identify the subject and to obtain arrest warrants. I was elected to do the paperwork and managed to place several charges of Breaking Into a Motor Vehicle on "Bug Eye," who we managed to locate and arrest at his home the night we identified him.

Before I went to his bond hearing, I had a conference with the judge, who had a reputation for placing high bonds on subjects appearing before him if you were smart enough to meet with him beforehand. During my meeting with Judge G, I told him that I only had a few charges for now but was working at putting an additional seventy or more on the suspect. When I appeared before the judge with the suspect, he placed a $200,000 bond on "Bug Eye," which was ridiculously high, but I knew that would surely keep him in jail while I got the other warrants prepared. After the hearing, a Charleston PD narc came up to me and wanted to know how in the hell I got such a high bond for three car break-ins when he had a guy for heroin distribution, who only got a $5,000 bond. I smiled and said, "You just have to talk to the judge."

Another amusing incident occurred when we were assigned to shut down a club that was selling bootlegged liquor. The club was in an extremely rural area, and we had to go up a long, dirt road lined with houses close to the road. It was almost impossible to conduct surveillance because of its location, and we needed to see the place to be able to send an informant in to make a purchase with marked money then have a description of the building for the search warrant. We found out that the houses on the dirt road had no running water, and all of the houses used well water in that particular rural area.

Larry and I borrowed a pickup truck from Public Works with county license tags, and we borrowed a surveyor's transom and dressed in civilian clothes with hard hats and went into the area to scope out the club. When people started asking what we were doing, we told them we were surveying for the county because they were going to bring in running water. The residents praised us for our work, never knowing it would be a long time before they ever saw running water, if ever.

We were able to get the information we needed and worked out a plan to get to the club without being seen when the time came to go inside. Being creative was all it took to get the job done, with a little fun along the way.

***

One night the entire team, minus the sergeant, was on its way to a club on the main drag in North Charleston to be there when they closed for the night. This club had a reputation for having problems at closing time. We were driving in a line, and I was last behind Larry, not a mile from the club when all of a sudden a motorcycle driven by a young sailor with a female passenger ran the stop sign from our right and ran right into the right rear quarter panel of Larry's cruiser, throwing both occupants airborne. I had to swerve violently to keep from running over the female passenger, who had landed in the lane of traffic in front of me.

I did a quick U-turn to come back around to protect the lifeless female from being hit by other oncoming traffic. The female died at the scene, and the driver, a sailor, lived to have a Felony DUI charge placed on him.

This incident was unnerving to have happen right before my eyes. The female passenger was at least twenty-five years older than the sailor and was married to the father of a friend of mine. She had been out fooling around with someone young enough to be her son and ended up dead as a result.

***

One Saturday night while on patrol near the Navy Base, we overheard on the scanner a North Charleston officer putting out a Signal 46, which is the radio term for a cop who needs immediate assistance. We were just blocks away and rode up on a fight in progress between a large male and a buddy named Roy, a North Charleston officer. It was obvious that the cop was in bad shape. His uniform was torn, and he was so exhausted he just rolled out of the way when he saw Larry and me jump into the fray. The subject continued to resist us, but we subdued him quickly. While attempting to put handcuffs on him, we saw a small, derringer-type pistol lying under the suspect. Seeing the gun just put the fight into a higher level, and we practically tore the guy's clothes off making sure he had no other weapons. After cuffing and stuffing the subject into the backseat of a North Charleston cruiser, we found out that the gun belonged to Tommy, our sergeant, who had dropped it from his leg holster during the fight. We all wore backup weapons on our leg in our boot. The best part about helping out another agency was that we never had to write a report. We just went where we were needed, did what we had to do, and went on to the next call.

On the main drag in our district was a club called "The Flying Dutchman," which was frequented by military personnel. It held several hundred people and was a definite hot spot for fun and trouble at closing time. In those days the club had a $5 cover charge, and anyone could drink beer on tap until midnight on that cover charge. When midnight came, the all-you-can-drink beer ended, and patrons had to start paying for each individual drink consumed, which usually pissed off the sailors who only had $5 to start with.

Just as we had parked in a line at the 7-11 in a previous story, we parked at the entrance of The Flying Dutchman just before closing time and sat on the hood of the front cruiser waiting for trouble as people exited the club. Drunken sailors were always making smartass comments directed at us, which often led to their arrest.

One night an incident started that ended up with Larry and me chasing two sailors into the parking lot. The lot was full and very hard to exit because people just parked their cars wherever they wanted once it got full. We chased the two into the bed of a waiting pickup truck. The truck started to negotiate through the lot to the exit while Larry and I duked it out with the two sailors we had chased into the bed of the truck. By the time the truck made it to the exit to get out of the lot, we had handcuffed the two, and the driver decided it would be in his best interest to stop. We took the two sailors to jail for Disorderly Conduct.

Another incident with a sailor is also worth noting. I encountered an intoxicated sailor acting suspiciously next to a business across the street from The Flying Dutchman. I got out of my cruiser to investigate, and he became so loud and belligerent that he just had to go to jail. When I put my hands on him, he pulled away and started to resist, so I put him onto the pavement. While I was handcuffing him, a buddy of mine named Kevin drove up to assist. He helped me to complete the handcuffing as the sailor continued to yell and scream loudly.

While I tried to get information from the sailor's military ID, Kevin told the sailor to shut up, but he got even louder and started cursing Kevin.

This prompted Kevin to take his flashlight and stick the end of it into the sailor's mouth, which stopped the screaming for sure. Kevin said, "Hey, Ray, look at this." He pulled the flashlight out, and the screaming began again, so he reinserted the flashlight, and the screaming stopped. I told Kevin that we would need to take this guy to the Naval hospital because he needed to be stitched up for a cut over his eye, sustained when I put him down on the pavement. Kevin said he would follow me there, and he would assist me with him in the emergency room (ER). The ER at the Navy hospital on a Saturday night was just as busy as any other hospital because of the huge military presence of Navy, Air Force, and Marine personnel in the Charleston area. Kevin was about six feet five inches and weighed in at over 300 lb. We both walked the prisoner into the hospital from my cruiser, and his feet never touched the ground until we got inside.

We got to the ER, and the sailor remained as loud as he had been, so the nurse told us to bring him in the back to a treatment room. We had by now handcuffed the sailor to a gurney as he continued to yell, so Kevin did the flashlight thing a few times to the amusement of a few duty Navy corpsmen waiting to treat him. All of a sudden, a female lieutenant commander nurse, who was obviously in charge, walked in and started to berate us for having handcuffed the sailor to the gurney. She told us to take the handcuffs off, and we explained that to do so was a mistake. We finally complied with her insistence, and just as we uncuffed the right wrist, the sailor punched the female lieutenant commander in the mouth. She quickly recovered and said, "Handcuff him. I will stitch him up myself." A corpsman told the nurse about the flashlight trick, and Kevin again demonstrated to her delight. The nurse proceeded to stitch the sailor without the use of a numbing agent—her little way of returning the favor for the punch!

I ended up calling the Shore Patrol to get him at the hospital, deciding not to take him to jail. The Shore Patrol didn't play either and would notify the sailor's command. Another fun night messing with sailors on the mean streets of Charleston County!

***

By now, a year had gone by, and Larry was promoted to sergeant. We were all very happy for him and went to a restaurant at 3:00 a.m. to buy him one last breakfast. Believe it or not, at 3:00 a.m. the restaurant was packed, mostly with people who had been out clubbing and went there when the bars closed.

While the five of us were eating our last breakfast together as a team, there was, of course, some drunk who became loud, boisterous, and rude, necessitating his ultimate arrest. I volunteered to be the one to take him to jail, and he became even louder as I put the cuffs on him. As I walked out of the door with him, everyone in the restaurant began to applaud. While walking him around the building to my car that was parked out back, he bounced against every window we passed—with my assistance. This was how Larry's year on the SCAT Team ended. There were countless nights when this same action became necessary to a point that we hated to set foot into a restaurant that late.

We did sometimes frequent a restaurant that was located in two counties. The front half of the place was in Charleston County, and the back half in Berkeley County. We would go there for breakfast and sit in the back portion where we had no police jurisdiction. If we saw something happen, we would just call the police agency from Berkeley County to handle the matter.

Just after Larry left, we had plans to go to a house out in the East District in a somewhat rural area where bootlegged alcohol was being sold. We did not need nor did we have a search warrant because we knew our presence would cause everyone inside to run out of the house. We approached from the backyard area and immediately encountered several male subjects running out of the back door. Of course, the biggest guy in the group chose me to mess with. He was about six feet one inch and about 240 lb. and had been a high school wrestler. He saw me, and instead of running away as the others did, he charged me and wrapped his arms around me and pushed me down so that I banged the back of my head on an abandoned vehicle in the yard. He was now on top of me, and Tommy ran over and began hitting him on the head with his flashlight until he got off me. While he was doing that, I was doing the same from the ground. His head ended up looking like a beehive with all of the welts he sustained. I ended up in the ER to be treated for a golfball sized bump and laceration behind my ear because of the fall. After finding out about the suspect's experience in wrestling, I realized that he acted on instinct when he attacked. The only problem was that he did it to a cop in uniform.

If you have ever seen *COPS* on TV, you often see a number of cops trying to subdue a small person, especially a small woman. I have always said that if a person does not want to be arrested, his or her size makes no difference at all. If a person does not want to go, it will be hard to restrain anyone.

One Saturday night near the end of my second year with the team, I was on my way home from the jail after a late arrest, and I heard an officer named Dennis check out on the radio at a location with a male suspicious subject. Minutes later, I heard a strange voice come across the radio asking for help for an officer who was down on the ground. The civilian had the presence of mind to get on the officer's car radio. I immediately started heading to Dennis and got there just as Darryl, the guy who replaced Larry on the team, arrived. Dennis was badly beaten with his own metal flashlight and was not very coherent, so I got down on the ground next to him to let him know he would be all right until medical assistance arrived.

We knew that he needed to get to the hospital quickly, since he was in bad shape, so when the Emergency medical services wagon arrived, my buddy Darryl drove the EMS wagon while the two EMS techs feverishly worked on Dennis in the back on the way to the hospital.

We stayed out several hours trying to find the suspect, who was located days later. Dennis, unfortunately, was never the same. He wore a halo to support his neck and head for months and took years to recover to some sort of reasonable normalcy. When he was well enough to work, he transferred to the crime lab, where he remained until his retirement.

At some point in the second year of the team's existence, Chuck was transferred to the Criminal Investigations Division as an investigator. Chuck's prior experience as an investigator at the North Charleston Police Department made the department's decision a no-brainer.

***

It is very easy to see why I looked forward to going to work every night. I have talked to all of my former team members, except for Tommy, who sadly passed away in 1991, a victim of cancer. I was a member of the Honor Guard and honored to be an active participant in his funeral. Larry and I talked after Tommy's premature death, and we were both greatly upset that we had not gone to visit him, although we were unaware how sick he was.

We all agreed that the best time we had in our career was while working on the SCAT Team. Not a lot of people can say that they look forward to going to work every day, but we all could. Whenever Larry and I spoke over the years, we always spoke about the crazy things we did together on the SCAT Team.

I did not intend to end this chapter in this manner, but sadly, in the middle of writing this very chapter, I received notice that Larry had taken his own life. It is indeed ironic that this happened while I was writing this particular chapter. I had known him since I rode with him as a reserve officer in 1982, more than thirty years ago.

Larry loved animals, especially dogs, and spent the last eighteen years of his career as the commander of the K-9 program for the entire sheriff's office. The program included his beloved bloodhounds and tracking dogs. He never took time off, but he went to the kennels seven days a week, even on his scheduled days off, to feed and exercise his dogs. Larry had been retired for three years after a stellar thirty-five-year career in law enforcement. He called me several months ago and told me that he was bored and had nothing to do, and I insisted that he needed to find something and made some suggestions. I had last seen Larry on the day he retired and met him in his office as he packed his desk. We talked on the phone for over an hour and caught up on mutual friends and what was going on at the Sheriff's Office.

Two weeks after our phone conversation, he had a minor stroke and was having difficulties in dealing with the side effects and limitations. I loved him like a brother and emulated many of his traits on the job. He was one of the best street cops I ever ran across, and he was feared on the streets by the criminals who had the misfortune of an encounter with him. Above all, his peers and subordinates and, more importantly, his superiors respected Larry. He was an old-school cop and was sometimes misunderstood by some of the younger cops who had contact with him, but they all respected him—that was for sure.

His family and friends will sorely miss Larry. May God rest his soul.

Lieutenant Larry Eugene Smoak
Born July 12, 1951
Died July 14, 2012

METRO

19

AFTER TWO YEARS ON THE SCAT TEAM, I had an interview for consideration for transfer to the narcotics unit, METRO. The sergeant, the lieutenant, and one of the investigators in the unit, interviewed me. I was selected and transferred and began to do what I had come to love to enforce as a cop—making drug arrests. The work schedule was the same as it had been for the past two years, Tuesday to Saturday, 7:00 p.m. to 3:00 a.m., and off on Sunday and Monday. As far as I was concerned, Sundays and Mondays were great days off because I could go to church with the family and spend quality time together and have a day off during the week.

My new sergeant was James, who I referred to earlier after making a 5 lb. marijuana arrest while on my way to work. James was very much like Tommy—"my way or the highway"—but he knew how to motivate people and, above all, knew how to run a narcotics unit. James had been in the unit for years, had developed numerous informants, and knew every drug dealer in the county by name or nickname.

A lieutenant, Marvin, who later rose to the rank of chief deputy, commanded the unit at the time. Marvin too was highly respected and had been running the unit for quite some time. He was laid back and pretty much let James run the show. He had a way of getting pissed off at James, and we saw that happen on many occasions, but that was the lieutenant's way of getting James motivated in order to get the guys motivated.

There was a second sergeant named Duke who ran the Vice Unit that worked out of our office. Duke had been one of my two patrol sergeants in my first assignment in patrol several years earlier. He had not changed one bit and was about as laid back as anybody I ever ran across.

METRO was an extremely active unit, and each of the dozen investigators always carried a caseload of at least ten to fifteen active cases each. When personnel were needed for certain operations, we had the Vice Unit Investigators available to assist. We went on at least two search warrants nightly, anywhere in the nine hundred-square miles of our jurisdiction.

I was partnered with the only female investigator in the unit, but the best in the unit and the most senior for her time in the unit. Barbara and I hit it off immediately, and I soaked in every bit of information she fed me. She was a wealth of information and most knowledgeable in her field. She taught me that working in narcotics was a form of law enforcement where no one can or should ever be trusted. I quickly found out that every citizen involved in drugs that I dealt with was inherently dishonest, untrustworthy, greedy, undependable, and generally bad people, unlike working in uniform patrol where I was helping people and only occasionally coming into contact with bad people. Now I had to acclimate myself to trust no one and to deal regularly with the dregs of society. I must say that I found this advice to be extremely accurate and right on. Up until now, I thought that I was a pretty good cop, but until now, I had not adopted the premise of distrusting those whom I came in contact with. Once I adopted this trait, I believe I became a better cop and worked that way for the remainder of my career. Not trusting a soul may be scary to think about and is something that I never shared with anyone, except other new investigators who were later partnered with me to train. I got used to reading body language and reading the eyes of people I came in contact with. My only regret was that I didn't have this knowledge sooner in my career. I became attuned to distrusting everyone, even other cops, which was an advantage when sometimes dealing with dishonest or unethical cops. They were few and far between, but they existed.

My initiation to the unit started one of the first nights I worked. In those days, we took all arrestees to the office for processing and possible interviews for information. We strip-searched all arrestees, which is common practice in law enforcement, when arrested for drugs. We had one small, unisex bathroom in our office used to conduct the searches, and the rookie in the unit always conducted them. Little did I know, but the arresting investigator told the arrestee that I was gay. When I went into the bathroom with him and told him to disrobe, he refused. Well, the fight was on, and he began bouncing off the walls of that little bathroom that adjoined the office. When I came out with the prisoner, the entire unit was laughing hysterically, so this was my welcome to the unit!

Around the time of my arrival, the movie *Heartbreak Ridge* was out with Clint Eastwood starring as the foul mouth marine Gunnery Sergeant Highway. The guys all knew I was a former marine and had been a drill instructor and had a foul mouth, so I immediately inherited the nickname "Gunny", which still sticks today more than twenty-eight years later.

As I mentioned earlier, Charleston County was unlike many other areas of the country. We were a county bounded by the ocean on one side, with dozens of barrier islands and marinas ideal for drug smuggling. It was common for an entire boatload of marijuana to be unloaded on an island and quickly picked up and redistributed. The Coast Guard, which has a station in Charleston, regularly found bales of marijuana floating as well as bundles of cocaine packed in kilo-sized packages. Because of the fact that there were many rural farms and undeveloped property there was an abundance of marijuana cultivated in the fields as well as indoor marijuana grow houses too.

Heroin was also a big problem in our jurisdiction and was sold exclusively by black dealers in our area. There were many heroin users of all races, but the blacks controlled the heroin trade. All heroin had a street name that was stamped on the glassine envelope that it was sold in that allowed the buyer to ask for the name specifically. The name stamp signified who was selling it and really made it easier for us to track the source. Stamped heroin also made it easier for us to track down dealers when there was a rash of heroin overdoses in town that killed a few users. It happened to be a bad batch, much stronger than intended. Normal doses of heroin were only about 11 percent pure, the remaining 89 percent was a mixture of a cutting agent used to dilute the strength of the heroin and to increase the volume of the amount purchased. Some of the overdoses were the result of some batches of heroin hitting the street at a higher percentage of purity. The regular heroin addicts who were used to 11 percent overdosed as a result. Cocaine was prevalent and easily available and sold for as little as $10 a hit and up to $28,000 per kilo. Crack cocaine had not yet hit Charleston, but by the time I left the unit, it was beginning to take its hold on the users in the area. Cocaine could be purchased from one-tenth of a gram, to grams, to ounces, to kilos.

We also had the availability of LSD or acid, as some know it. This was prepared in liquid form and with an eyedropper placed on sheets of paper with cartoon imprints separated by squares. Each square on a sheet was $5, and one entire sheet could have as many as one hundred hits. This drug was popular among sailors and Air Force personnel because it was easy to conceal in their lockers on base or on their ship, and they knew that their periodic drug tests did not test for LSD. Because of the presence of the Navy in Charleston, Barbara and I regularly visited different ships on base and lectured the officers and chief petty officers of each ship. We gave identification training to them so they would recognize the various drugs if they came upon anything while inspecting their subordinates' living quarters.

The sale of pills was big in the '80s, especially the prescription medication Dilaudid, which was at the time the most powerful prescription pill manufactured, generally prescribed to cancer patients for pain. At the time, these pills were being sold everywhere for $50 per pill. The availability of this prescription medication resulted in many investigations of nurses in doctors' offices and hospitals who had access to the drug.

Within a week of being assigned to the unit, I developed information through a source that indicated a large marijuana operation working out of a mobile home in a mobile home park in North Charleston. Barbara was off either on vacation or attending class at the time, so I shared my information and gave the case to another investigator named Guy, due to my inexperience. He appreciated the fact that I did not feel comfortable on my own and walked me through the process. We were able to obtain a search warrant and hit the house on Friday night while the dealer and others were present. The dealer had one room devoted entirely to packaging the marijuana on a large table with scales and bags for packing, as well as a fair amount of money that we seized. This turned out to be a major hit in the area, and I learned a lot from watching the process.

I started making my own cases and quickly learned the proper manner in dealing with developing informants. They usually started out as a pissed-off girlfriend wanting to get back at her ex-boyfriend or vice versa. They were also some of the people we arrested for small amounts who were willing to provide us with the information of where to get bigger amounts. A constant merry-go-round never ended because every person arrested had the potential to inform, and there was always someone higher on the totem pole who dealt bigger quantities.

My first or second week in METRO, James called me into the lieutenant's office to counsel me for being too heavy-handed while dealing with informants. Marvin and James were known in the department as being two of the heaviest hands who ever walked the streets, and they were counseling me. It was not an ass-chewing, just a reminder to slow down some. I got the message, and when I went back out into our office, everybody was astounded that they had counseled me about being too rough with informants and arrestees because of their own reputations.

***

On May 2, 1987, we ended up needing to hit an apartment in an adjoining county. Our entire unit met in a police station in that jurisdiction, and we set up a plan for entry. By that time, I had progressed to being the doorman on most all entries on search warrants, meaning I carried the steel battering ram and was the first one in the door. The first one in the door is always supposed to go to the farthest point and detain any persons encountered. I was the first in the door that night to the apartment. There was no rear entrance, so once we entered, there was no place to go to get away. I ran to the master bedroom, encountered the suspect, and located him in a corner with drugs in his hands and no place for him to go. I grabbed him and put him on the floor face down. I slapped the handcuff on him, but because he was struggling and resisting at the time, I slapped one cuff on his left wrist and due to the force I used, the other half of the cuff went through the palm of my right hand and exited above my pinky finger on the top of my hand. I was now literally handcuffed to him, and he was still resisting. Barbara and another guy immediately saw the pain on my face and the cuff protruding from my right hand. Every time he moved, the cuff in my hand rubbed against the bone at the base of my pinky. Barbara uncuffed the suspect from me and put new cuffs on him, brought him out to the living room, and sat him down with the other occupants on the couch in the apartment.

They walked me out to the kitchen where I caught my breath and sat waiting for EMS to arrive. I had to hold the dangling half of the cuffs with my left hand to keep the steel cuffs from rubbing any further against the bone. While sitting there waiting for medical assistance, one of my guys, Eddie, asked me which one of the four on the couch was the one I was handcuffing. I pointed out the one, and two of the guys in my unit took him out of the apartment and took him for a ride somewhere. I never set eyes on him again, until I saw him in court, but I am sure that they had a nice little talk with him.

When the fire department arrived, the EMTs wanted to cut the cuffs off with bolt cutters, but I immediately told them that they were not going to do any such thing and to get the hell away from me. EMS transported me to the hospital for X-rays and visits from about every doctor on duty in the hospital for show and tell. Finally, some numbing agent was shot into my hand as a hand specialist gently backed the handcuff out of my hand. I still have the X-ray with the cuffs in my hand and used it as a training tool for years while teaching officer survival classes to recruits. The doctor later told me that he used to bring that X-ray to hand-specialist conferences and showed it to everyone. He said that no one had ever seen anything like it!

The injury healed quickly, and I was back to full duty in about ten days—lesson learned and another on my list of close calls and, hopefully, my last trip to the hospital. Once recovered, I was happy to be able to resume my job as the doorman on search warrants. We did at least two per night, so in a five-day workweek, we kicked at least ten doors a week. We did not do soft entries, and prosecutors allowed us to make the type of entry we did because of the nature of our business and the possibility of criminals destroying valuable evidence before we made entry.

One night we got a tip that a boatload of marijuana was going to be unloaded at a boat landing in the southernmost part of the county. This tip was considered credible, so we acted accordingly. A crew of us went down there in a van and an undercover vehicle, a trip of almost fifty miles. I spent the night lying in the bushes waiting, and while I waited, a vehicle occupied by two guys pulled into the parking area. We did not know whether they were part of the drug smuggling, so we acted accordingly. I made my way around the wooded area and got behind the car to get a tag number so we could identify who it was registered to, and I determined that the tag was unreadable. As I got closer, I saw that the tags were US government tags obliterated with masking tape. I now knew they were friendlies, but decided to give them a little scare, so I sneaked up on them and stuck my 9 mm pistol into the window and scared the crap out of both of them! These guys were Coast Guard intelligence officers who had received the same tip and decided to investigate for themselves. Unfortunately, they failed to advise us of what they were planning. We all had a good laugh over what happened, and they left the scene. The boat never arrived, and we began to suspect that the tip was a ploy to get us to go to the opposite end of the county where the boat was actually unloaded. The people doing the smuggling were smart people and were not above undertaking such a diversion.

One time I acted on a Crime Stoppers tip of a guy growing marijuana in his yard. I investigated by asking a neighbor for permission to go into her yard and look over the fence. She agreed and there was one well-cultivated marijuana plant in plain view growing in the yard. I prepared a search warrant and went to visit the owner, who turned into one of the best informants I ever worked. He agreed to provide me with information to avoid his arrest, and during my debriefing with him, he admitted that from time to time he received a phone call in the middle of the night to go to a certain location and help off-load bales of marijuana from fishing boats. He provided a gold mine of information and intelligence about the smuggling in the area, and I got it all because he grew just one marijuana plant.

I developed him into an extremely reliable, confidential informant to a point that I kept blank search warrants at home. When he called with information, I just started typing the warrant at home because his word was golden. When I went to his house, it was quite obvious that he had nothing and that as a commercial fisherman, he did not make much money, so once he worked off his manufacturing charge for one plant, his motivation was to be paid for his information.

One night a group of four narcs went out to a local bar to watch the clientele because we had information of major drug use on the premises. We were all in the same vehicle—a surveillance van—and were busy this Saturday night watching people and running license plates over our police radio. While we were sitting in the lot, a group of people got into a white van parked next to us on our right, turned on the interior light, and began to run lines of cocaine off a mirror they were holding. We could not believe that anyone could be this stupid. We quickly devised a plan to exit the van quietly and surround the car and arrest all occupants. Barbara and I immediately recognized the driver as a well-known cocaine dealer in the area, whose nickname was "Rinky." It was "Rinky's" van, and when he saw what was happening, he threw a large bag of packaged cocaine under the van. We arrested all occupants, retrieved the bag of dope, and seized the van.

While "Rinky" was awaiting trial, I developed another case against him, which brought me to his home this time. It was common for drug dealers to continue their business after being arrested, because they always need more money to pay for a lawyer, but they get sloppy and make mistakes. My information allowed me to obtain a search warrant to his upscale condominium unit near the ocean. Once a judge signs a warrant, you have only ten days to serve it before it expires. We ended up hitting the house around December 20, and when we arrived, he and his wife and small children were present. The Christmas tree was up and decorated, and presents were under the tree. A search warrant for drugs allowed us to search anywhere and everywhere in the house along with any vehicles present and any sheds or outbuildings.

During my search, I found a legal-size envelope in a plastic bag hidden under some cushions on the back porch. I opened the envelope and discovered freshly issued Family Court divorce papers signed by an attorney and a judge. I asked "Rinky" if he was getting divorced, and he said, "No, I am happily married," so my question was "Then why are there legal divorce documents here?" Apparently, his wife had filed for divorce, but he had not yet received the papers. What I found on the porch was his wife's copy that she was hiding from him until the original was legally served upon him. Because of my find, his wife had to spill her guts and admit she had filed for divorce. Merry Freak in' Christmas, Rinky!

Months later, I developed information that "Rinky" was still dealing and was doing so out of a rented house on James Island. By now, he had split with his wife and had continued to deal to keep earning to support his family, his habit, and to pay his attorneys. We hit the house one evening, and he had cocaine in his hand when we entered. As we entered he attempted to rip the bag and throw it in the air, which he did, but there was enough to salvage to charge him again with Possession of Cocaine. Then we found some cocaine inside of his hatband.

After we entered and other guys were clearing the rest of the house, we heard a gunshot from the back room. Buddy, one of our guys from the North Charleston Police Department, had accidentally misfired his

.45 automatic into the floor. "Rinky" asked what the noise was, so our sergeant said, "That's just Buddy messing with fireworks again."

"Rinky" was now a three-time loser and ended up being sentenced to twenty-five years in prison for Trafficking in Cocaine and died several years later of a heart attack while incarcerated.

***

One afternoon we had Bill, who was a corporal in our unit from the Charleston Police Department, acting undercover for the sale of 10 lb. of marijuana in a rural area in South District. He was wired, and we were monitoring the conversation between Bill and the dealer. The dealer showed up with what was supposed to be 10 lb. of marijuana, but Bill thought it looked more like 5 or 6 lb. fluffed up to look like 10 lb. in a large dog-food bag, which was a rip-off as far as we were concerned.

The deal went bad, and the dealer dropped the dope and ran from Bill and out of our surveillance and across four lanes of busy Highway 17. He ran past my position, so I bailed from my car and chased on foot, and since we were in a rural area, I fired several shots into the air in an attempt to slow him down. As I fired each shot in slow succession, all I could hear was James from across the four-lane highway yelling at me, "No, Gunny! No, Gunny!" The bad guy got away, but we were able to obtain arrest warrants for him because we now knew who he was. Months later when he was arrested, he told us that he climbed a tree after the cop shot at him and hid there until we left. As in the time two years prior when I fired at the guy who had just broken into a decoy car and stolen our radar detector, I had fired unauthorized warning shots. More fun in the mean streets of Charleston County!

***

One night we were going to execute a search warrant at an apartment in North Charleston within blocks of the Navy Base. When we saw that nobody was home, we decided to come back when the apartment was occupied. While getting ready to leave the area, I saw a sailor come out of an adjoining apartment accompanied by a known prostitute. Around that time, AIDS was beginning to be a hot topic in the news and highly reported on a regular basis. I decided to have some fun with the sailor and the prostitute, who I knew by name as Cynthia. I identified myself to the sailor, and he said his ship just came in, and he came right here to have some fun. I asked him if he ever heard about AIDS, and he replied that he had. I told him that Cynthia had AIDS, and he had better get to the Naval Hospital to be treated right away before his penis fell off! I told him to tell the corpsman there that he just had sex with a girl who had AIDS, and he needs to have his penis cleaned and sanitized right away. I told him if he was treated within an hour of being infected, he would be all right and directed him to the Naval Hospital. He ran all the way, almost two miles.

After the sailor took off running, Cynthia told me that I knew she did not have AIDS, so why did I do that to her. I told her that the alternative was jail for soliciting, so she got off easy. Almost twenty years after messing with sailors while stationed at the Philadelphia Navy Base, I was still messing with them as a cop. Life was still good!

***

One time we had developed information that a serviceman stationed on the local Air Force base was having steroids regularly mailed to him by Federal Express. We did some checking and started flagging his address, and, lo and behold, within a week he had a large box scheduled for delivery. We ran a drug-sniffing dog on the box and confirmed that it contained drugs. The suspect lived in a two-story townhouse not far from the base, so we arranged for the delivery and witnessed the box being delivered. We sent Barbara to the door by herself to sweet talk her way into getting him to open the door. When she started talking, he slammed the door on her foot, but she managed to keep her foot in the door until we got to her. She saw me coming and knew I was going to kick the door, so she wisely moved her body out of the way with her foot still lodged in the door. I kicked the door right into the suspect, splitting his forehead wide open.

The suspect was a major bodybuilder and had been a military policeman on the base. He was also a neat freak and was extremely upset that some of the investigators were smoking in his house and that his blood had gotten all over the carpet. The Air Force wanted to adopt this case from the state for prosecution, and we testified at his court-martial. This was an unusual case and one the few steroid cases we ever made.

After I had been partnered with Barbara for about six to seven months, she was promoted to sergeant and transferred out of the unit. Whenever someone left the unit, we had a party for him or her and ended our party by passing around a bottle of tequila. Tradition dictated that the person being transferred had to finish the bottle and swallow the worm. We were happy for Barb and knew her promotion was well deserved. She left the department a year or so later and went to the Mount Pleasant Police Department as a captain.

John came into the unit to replace Barbara and was eager to learn. John was a good street cop who enjoyed making drug arrests. His assignment to METRO was a little strained on the home front because his wife did not approve of his move to our unit. John and I were paired up as partners, and within two weeks of his coming in the unit, we were scheduled to attend a narcotics investigators class in Jacksonville, Florida. When I met John in the parking lot of a local hotel for the drive to Florida, his wife was still not speaking to him. I tried making small talk with her, and she did not even acknowledge that I was speaking to her. I suppose if she was not speaking to him, why speak to me? He did not seem to mind because he wanted to be a narc in the worst way. On the way to Florida I found a strong radio station signal that was playing nonstop Lynard Skynard, a southern rock band that freely flies the Confederate flag, and my favorite musical group, and John being black , he never once complained. We have joked many times over the years about that trip, and always laugh about it. He and I hit it off and did good things together, and he remains one of my closest friends in law enforcement.

People were being transferred out regularly since the bosses did not like people to stay in one specialized unit for too long. It was time for Guy to make his move, and he was transferred. Guy's replacement was a female named Andi, who was transferred to us from CID where she was a juvenile investigator. She had no drug experience but had experience as an investigator. Andi was assigned to be my partner, and she learned the trade quickly. She was a new face on the street, and we used our new female face in many undercover capacities. Andi and I hit it off and worked together for many years after this assignment, and she too remains a close friend.

Around the same time, our sergeant, James, injured his shoulder, which required major surgery. James left for the surgery and thought he was coming back to the unit after he recovered, but that was not to be. Within a week or two of James's departure for the surgery, the lieutenant ordered that his desk be packed in boxes, and a new sergeant arrived. James taught me a lot. His departure made some people happy and some mad. Above all, James was highly respected, and I must say that I learned much about his style of leadership and drug enforcement by working for and with him. Once James recovered, he left the department for a position in the Berkeley County Sheriff's Office as a captain.

The new sergeant was Jim, another guy with years of investigative experience. He had spent many years working in the Criminal Investigations Division (CID) and had previous narcotic experience. He had been recently promoted to sergeant. He had been a member of the South/West SCAT Team when the teams were originally formed in 1984, and I had worked with him as a peer. Jim was an entirely different kind of leader. He was weak administratively and liked to joke around a lot, but he knew his job, and we respected him for that. His leadership style was unique, to say the least, but he fit in and let us do our job because he knew that we knew what we were doing. He told me that his goal was to get Andi and me promoted to sergeant, which I personally had no problem with.

***

At some point while I was assigned in METRO, some of the drug laws changed somewhat. The state legislature enacted one law, which was Trafficking in Cocaine, which articulated that if a person was convicted of possession of at least one hundred grams of cocaine, he or she would be sentenced to a minimum of twenty-five years in prison. An ounce of cocaine weighs twenty-eight grams, so it took only four ounces of cocaine to exceed the one hundred-gram threshold for trafficking. Well, we started to become creative and began ordering four to six ounces of cocaine when making undercover purchases, which automatically gave the offender twenty-five years in prison when convicted. In cases in which we had previously arrested people who didn't get jail time because it was a first offense or if someone had a pending drug arrest and had not gone to trial yet, we would target those people to ensure that when their trial came, they would be sentenced to some serious time.

One such case was a full-blooded Indian whose nickname was "Cherokee." We had a very hard time hooking up with this guy to purchase five ounces of cocaine. Drug dealers are never on time and are extremely unreliable when it comes to time. We spent many hours waiting for deals to happen and called deals off, so we did not seem too anxious to make the buy. As I said in some earlier examples, officers have to be creative.

The deal with "Cherokee" fell through several times. The day to deal finally arrived, and we arranged for "Cherokee" to meet us in a Taco Bell restaurant on Dorchester Road in North Charleston. We had our undercover narc Melvin inside waiting for him, and we had set up surveillance in the parking lot. There was a shopping center being built in the lot next door, so I climbed up on a trailer of cinder blocks being unloaded by a crane attached to the truck to look as though I were one of the construction workers. The others were spread out around the lot in undercover vehicles.

"Cherokee" arrived but had a female with him, who as I recall may have been his daughter. They went inside, sat with Melvin, talked business, and within a few minutes came out. There was a prearranged signal from Melvin to us to indicate that he had seen the drugs. "Cherokee" showed him the cocaine in the car, Melvin gave his signal, and we all converged on their vehicle. We recovered the marked money that we used to purchase the cocaine and the five ounces of cocaine located in a Pringles potato chip container in the car.

We went to trial, and "Cherokee" was convicted and sentenced to twenty-five years in prison for this sale of 140 grams of cocaine to an undercover police officer. While incarcerated, "Cherokee" became a jailhouse lawyer and several years later sued all of us, including the police department, in civil court. He charged that we had illegally seized his vehicle and money. "Cherokee" lost that case too, and we were exonerated.

Another case involving our purposely ordering over 100 grams of cocaine involved the use of a paid informant. Melvin was again the undercover cop who took the informant to several locations before the deal was made. Melvin owned a Corvette at the time, so I drove his car while Melvin went elsewhere to meet the informant. Once he met the informant and we put a plan together, we hooked back up with him and gave him his car back for the deal.

We had Melvin wired so we could hear all of any conversation he had with the informant and the bad guys when they met up. We started out following Melvin and the informant to a remote area on John's Island, where they went into a mobile home. They met some contact people, and while in there, Melvin told us there was a large quantity of marijuana in plain view in the house. The deal was to purchase six ounces of cocaine, so we were not interested in a little marijuana. They were meeting with a middleman who ended up arranging the deal that ended up hours later in the parking lot of a busy tourist restaurant on the water.

We monitored and taped the conversation, and after killing some time eating dinner, we ended up sitting in the parking lot of a popular restaurant on an inlet creek in the in town of Mount Pleasant. We still did not know who we were getting the cocaine from. All we knew was that his first name was Jerry. After a long time waiting, we finally saw Jerry arrive in an older model Mercedes, when a second accomplice appeared from the restaurant. They met Melvin and the informant in the parking lot, and during the conversation Jerry opened his leather jacket to show a cocked .45 Colt semi-automatic pistol to prove he was armed. The money was given to Jerry, and he left the lot, drove away, and was gone for a short time and returned in less than four minutes. He was followed when he left and came back into the lot, where he showed our people the cocaine. The bust signal was given, and we all converged on the participants in the parking lot. I went right to Jerry because I knew he had the weapon, put him to the ground, and disarmed him. The second accomplice ran toward the nearby restaurant, into the lobby, and into a phone booth, where he too was arrested.

We arrested both for Trafficking in Cocaine and ended up conducting a search warrant later that night on the accomplice Glen's house in an upscale neighborhood in Mount Pleasant. Months later when their trial was set to begin, I noticed an old couple in the audience intently watching the trial and recognized them from my church. During one of the breaks, I approached them in the hallway and asked what they were doing in the courtroom. They told me that Jerry, the guy I arrested in the parking lot with the gun, was their son in-law. I had never put two and two together and felt bad that I was responsible for their son in-law going to prison for a very long time. They understood completely and knew that I was doing my job. Both parties hired very expensive and high-profile attorneys, but both were convicted and sentenced to twenty-five years in prison anyway.

Not long after changing sergeants from James to Jim, our lieutenant was promoted to captain, which meant that he would be leaving. Marvin had been the lieutenant in METRO for quite some time and had worked with the same sergeant, James, for many years. We had figured out that Marvin was the one responsible for firing up James and for him going off on people for not seizing enough drugs or making enough arrests to his satisfaction. Marvin knew exactly what he was doing and knew just how to push James's buttons. We laughed about it after we realized what had been going on. Marvin was promoted while he was away in Texas at a training session, and when his plane arrived back in Charleston around midnight, the entire unit was there to meet and greet him to congratulate him for his promotion. Marvin would end up retiring as a chief deputy after a long and successful career.

I became close to Marvin and worked for him several more times in my career. His replacement was Eddie, who was an entirely different personality and leader. I learned much from him over the years. Eddie knew nothing about drugs and wanted to learn, so he rode with us several hours per night. He went on search warrants and street sweeps with us and quickly learned the trade. He was easy going and by the book, but he knew how to handle people and was particularly adept in the way he handled citizen complaints.

As an example, one day I was on my way in to work a dayshift at 10:00 a.m. Along the way, I stopped a car for driving in the median to avoid waiting in slow-moving traffic. I stopped the vehicle in question, which was occupied by a man in his fifties, his wife, and a male friend in the backseat. He did not appreciate the way I spoke to him, apparently, and the fact that I gave him a four-point ticket. After I arrived in my office, the three of them appeared, wanting to speak to my lieutenant, Eddie. Eddie listened and promised them that he would deal with me. They left, and I spoke to Eddie about the complaint. He explained that he always asks complainants what they want done to the person they are complaining about. He said they usually back off and say they do not want anything done, and he generally satisfies everyone by the time they leave. When the man's court date came, he actually had the nerve to come up to me and ask if I would reduce the charge to a lesser offense and lower the fine. I politely refused.

I saw Eddie use this method several times with other complaints and years later when I worked for him again. I definitely filed this tidbit in my head for later use in dealing with citizen complaints.

Eddie continued to ride with us and learn the ropes and made sure that our arrests made the newspaper. Doing this was an important factor because it spreads the word that we are out there on the streets and actively making arrests and seizing drugs. The local police crime beat reporter made it a point to stop in regularly to see if we had anything to report. It got to a point that there were daily articles about our arrests and seizures in the newspaper.

When we did not have search warrants scheduled for the night, which was rare, we would regularly conduct street sweeps. The sweeps involved going into known drug neighborhoods in multiple cars from different directions to chase those who ran and to arrest accordingly. We took pride in being creative and decided one night to commandeer a taxicab, which was a van. We put Andi in the front seat, with Melvin driving, and two or three of us hid in the back. We would drive through drug neighborhoods and stop while Andi purchased drugs from the passenger window. As the deal was made, we would jump out of the back, grab the dealer, put him in the taxi, and drive away. After going to several places and locking up about five or six, we went in to do the paperwork and gave the cab back to the operator. One hour's work netted six arrests.

At the time the department was switching over from Dodge Diplomats to Ford Crown Victoria's, and I had the idea to take one of the stripped-out white Dodge police cars and have it painted as a taxi. It was painted as METRO Cab Company and we used it very successfully for different deals around the county. We even painted our office telephone number on the car.

There were times when Jim went home early or went on vacation, and in his absence, he would leave me in charge. I had no more rank than anyone else in the unit and was junior to some members, but I had been in the unit by now longer than anyone else. The guys all respected the fact that I had been left in charge, and it worked out well. I appreciated being recognized as a person capable and responsible enough to be in charge.

***

In January of 1988, the convicted triple murderer that I helped to arrest in 1985 was back in court for a hearing regarding his previous sentencing. At the end of the hearing, a family member was allowed to hug the subject and had apparently passed a handcuff key to him.

Not long after the hearing, two Sheriff's Deputies, a male and a female, were transporting the subject back to the jail, when he somehow unlocked his handcuffs and overpowered the two deputies, taking both of their weapons, but he did not harm them. He was now on foot in a familiar area with two weapons. The word was quickly broadcast. Perimeters were set up, and the search began again for this ruthless, convicted triple murderer. We had just come to work and were immediately told to get extra ammo and to suit up in our gear with vests.

Jim immediately opened the weapons locker and handed me the M-16 rifle that was stored there and two loaded magazines. One of the guys in the unit who was on the SWAT Team told Jim that I was not authorized or trained to carry it. Jim, who was also a former marine said, "He knows what to do with that better than anybody in this room." I then proceeded to field strip the rifle, broke it down, and took it apart to show that I did indeed know what do with an M-16.

We were directed to the neighborhood of the escapee's mother, which is where we expected he would head to now that he was on the loose. This was also the neighborhood that the escapee had grown up in, and he knew it and all of the neighbors. We started patrolling the neighborhood by sitting on the tailgate of a pickup truck with shotguns and my M-16. Within minutes, a woman in the neighborhood called 911 to report that the escapee had come to her back door asking for money. The woman knew him by sight from growing up there and confirmed his identity to 911. We were just a block away when the call came out, and when we arrived, the woman said that he had just left less than one minute before our arrival.

The escapee's mother lived only two blocks away, and all units headed for that area. By now, it was about 10:00 p.m., and I was assigned to be a part of the perimeter surrounding the mother's home for the night. Melvin was assigned to be with me. I positioned him about five feet to my right, and I set up in the prone position with my rifle pointing to the side door of the residence. We were set up in a position that allowed me a visual on the side door and entire rear of the house.

Melvin was only about twenty-four, had never been in the military, and had no discipline for lying still or for being quiet. I had to continually kick him or poke at him to get him to be quiet and to stay awake. We were in that position for the entire night until daybreak and were certain that the escapee had not made it to her home. When daylight came, Melvin kept saying that he could not believe that I was able to lie all night and be so quiet. The escapee remained at large for at least two weeks and stayed in the neighborhood the entire time, stealing clothing from clotheslines and eating what he could find in the garbage.

On Super Bowl Sunday, January 31, 1988, I received a telephone call from headquarters as I walked in the door from church ordering me to suit up, come out, and search for the escapee, who had reportedly been sighted in the area. I was really pissed off because the Giants were playing the Broncos, and I was a huge Giants fan. I was out from 1:00 p.m. to about 7:30 p.m., and when I got home, I was tired, wet, and muddy. By the time I got home and cleaned up, it was halftime, but the Giants won forty-two to ten, so it ended well.

So far, this case had made me some serious extra money in the form of overtime pay, but it was getting a little ridiculous now that this guy had been at large since January 19 and had only been seen once since the evening of his escape. We were all puzzled because even though the escapee was an outdoorsman, this was January, and it had been near freezing nightly for two weeks. January is the coldest month of the year in Charleston, and this January was no different.

On February 4, 1988, he was captured after being at large for seventeen days exposed to the weather. He was located hiding under a tarp under a boat in someone's backyard. His capture made world news mostly because he had vowed never to be taken alive. We believed him because we knew that he had the two handguns he had taken from the deputies in his possession. The subject was put back in prison where he belonged and was finally executed on July 19, 1996, more than ten years after he was sentenced to death.

***

Because of the expansive, undeveloped land in Charleston County, many people grew and cultivated marijuana on land that they either owned or leased. It was so prevalent that we had a pilot who flew on a regular basis searching for grow spots. If you know what to look for, it is easy to locate them. Once located, the pilot would notify us and direct us to the location via radio. We were issued snake boots or snake chaps and machetes, which we kept in the trunk of our car. It was often hard to determine who was tending to the plants, but we had good luck in being able to prosecute in many of the manufacturing marijuana cases.

A well-fertilized and well-fed plant can grow to over eight feet tall and at maturity can produce $3,000 to $5,000 per plant. The smaller plants could be pulled out of the ground by hand, but the big ones had to be chopped by machete. If we were unable to locate the owner of the plant, we would drop one of our business cards into each hole left in the ground. This really pissed off the bad guys, which is why we did it, just a little payback time as we were seizing crops valued into six figures. Leaving our cards was very reminiscent of leaving Ace of Spades playing cards on dead bodies in Vietnam.

One marijuana case in particular comes to mind as an amusing incident. It did not involve smuggling, but the dealer we were targeting was moving multiple pounds of marijuana each week and was of particular interest because he was the brother of the municipal judge in North Charleston. We had information that the target liked to frequent a particular prostitute known in the area as "Mattress Mary," who was known to be infected with AIDS. The information also indicated that when he met with the prostitute, he videotaped their activity. Soliciting for prostitution is against the law, but videotaping was not.

We developed enough information to obtain a search warrant and on the night we hit the house, I kicked the door. When I did, my right leg went completely through the old, paneled door, and a large, wooden splinter went into my calf, preventing me from recovering my leg. When the target came to the door, I reached my handgun through the hole in the door and ordered him to unlock the door to allow our entry. This ended up being a truly unusual search warrant. As is customary, before any searching begins, the warrant is read to the occupant of the house. He or she is then seated with the officer assigned to log in all evidence seized.

As teams of investigators searched the house room by room, they began to find evidence and brought it to the kitchen, where the target and an investigator were logging it in. The law requires that the evidence must be logged with the location and by whom it was found. I was searching the master bedroom and found the video equipment, then the videotape I described with "Mattress Mary." The videotapes were full of the target and the prostitute in various stages of undress, and some had the target dressed in Mary's lingerie, which was hilarious. We also located many still photos of the same thing.

We were unable to find much marijuana in the house but observed residue all over the house. We looked into the trash compactor in the kitchen and, bingo, found a lot of marijuana residue there. As a few of us were talking in the kitchen, we heard a loud bang, and, all of a sudden, one of the guys who was searching in the attic fell through the ceiling, clinging to a an entire bale of compacted marijuana. We were laughing so hard we could hardly stand it, and here is Stuart, the narc who fell through the ceiling, full of insulation and plaster dust and clutching a bale of marijuana, laughing hysterically. We located about seven bales in the attic and charged the target with trafficking in marijuana.

We took him back to the office to process the target and the evidence, and while he was sitting handcuffed at my desk, one of the guys put one of the seized videotapes of him and "Mattress Mary" in the VCR, and we all watched it while we processed the evidence.

The next morning I answered my phone at my desk and spoke to a very prominent attorney who I had dealt with before. He was calling on behalf of our target, and while trying to hold back his own laughter, he asked about videotape of his client in women's underwear. I then asked him if he wanted video, Polaroid, or 35 mm stills. That got another laugh, and we ended up returning that evidence.

***

Whenever we do our research and investigation before entering someone's house on a search warrant, we try to gather as much intelligence on that person as possible. We especially want to know about the presence of children, so we can be prepared for dealing with them.

Since I was the door man at least 90 percent of the time, I needed to know about the door, whether there were storm doors, whether the doors were solid or hollow, whether they swing in or out, were on the first floor or higher, and so forth. One night we were out on John's Island in a very rural area, and we had no intelligence about the presence of children, but as we started walking through the yard, I saw children's toys and became apprehensive about kicking the door. I went up to the door, peered into the high windows, and saw children asleep in the floor very near the door. At my direction we made a soft entry and announced or presence. Had I kicked the door, I would have slammed the edge of the door into the upper portion of the child closest to the door, probably resulting in serious injury. It was scary to think of what may have happened, but I felt good knowing that I had made the right decision.

One night we hit a two-story townhouse in Mount Pleasant, and the front door was at the end of a long, cement walkway. Everyone was following me, and while running at full speed, I kicked the door. Instead of the door opening at the hinges, the force of my kick pushed the entire door and frame into the house, leaving me standing there in a cloud of plaster dust like something out of *Star Wars*! We ended up entering the house laughing at our unique entry!

We did another search warrant one night to a mobile home, with intelligence that the occupant was a huge gun collector and always had at least one weapon nearby. We approached the home very quietly because it sat all by itself with only a few nearby businesses. When I got to the door, I could see the suspect sitting in the front room watching TV and saw that the door was a steel security door that swung outward, so I reached through a broken screen and unlocked the deadbolt lock, and we all made entry. He had at least four loaded handguns within arm's reach. The suspect turned out to be a jovial guy but got sick when he found out we were seizing all of his guns.

Another dynamic but funny entry was a second-story apartment over a Chinese restaurant one Saturday night in North Charleston near the Navy Base. I was not the doorman this night, and after climbing the long, metal outside stairwell, we got to the landing and discovered that the door swung out. One of the guys named Eddie was always armed with a pistol-grip, short-stock shotgun, and he ended up breaking the stock of his shotgun banging the doorknob to gain entry. When we got in, we discovered that nobody was home, which wasn't an unusual occurrence. We searched the apartment, logged all of our evidence and left. While going to our vehicles, we heard someone moaning around the backside of the building. When we walked around to investigate, we found the target of our investigation lying in the yard with two broken legs. While we were banging on the door to get in, he was jumping out of the back window. Because it was dark, we did not see him during the search.

Entering mobile homes on search warrants was always troublesome because of their entrance doors. Owners sometimes modified the doors or placed locks and hasps on them because the doorknob had broken or for additional security.

One night we were hitting another mobile home within blocks of the Navy Base, and as we approached the property, we observed that there were a number of people inside. This door also opened outward, and the narc assigned to hit the door was Mike. When he got to the door, it was locked, so he smashed the narrow window with his fist, which was not very smart, and he reached in and unlocked the door. As he was making entry, we could all hear people scattering in the house and running around. Jim, our sergeant, always kept his gun under the seat of his car, and he never wore a holster. He was outside of the bathroom window and when he heard people scattering, he got the bright idea to hit the bathroom window with his .38 snub-nose revolver. When he hit the window, he lost his grip on the gun and it went through the broken glass and into the bathroom. He saw me getting ready to go in the front door and yelled to me, "Gunny, Gunny, I lost my gun! It's in the fucking bathroom!" As soon as I made entry, I ran directly to the bathroom and found his gun lying in the bathtub. The drug dealer was so busy trying to flush his drugs that he never noticed that a gun had been delivered through the window!

***

One night our lieutenant, Eddie, was riding around with Andi, Jim, and me. I was driving. This was the lieutenant's way of learning the drug trade, and he was never too proud to ask one of us a question and rode with us several nights a week.

We rode up near a diner about two blocks from the Navy Base when I saw a well-known drug dealer with whom I had pending drug charges. His name was Earl, and he was a pimp to several low-class prostitutes in the area. He had an old Cadillac and always parked in front of the diner and often went to his car to get drugs when a customer rode up. Well, we sort of caught him with his pants down because as we pulled up, he had the bag in his hand and did not know whether to throw it in the car or run. He decided to leave the bag and to run around the building. Well, I drove my car right around the building after him onto the sidewalk and between a guy wire to a telephone pole, and all we could hear was Eddie yelling, "Get him Gunny! Get him!" Earl was about six feet five inches and about 350 lb., so his run did not last very long. We jumped out, cuffed him, walked back to his car, and seized his stash of cocaine and marijuana.

These charges, along with what was pending, were surely enough to put Earl away in prison for a long time, but my dealings with him were not over yet.

Several weeks later, I received a Crime Stopper Tip, which I always liked to work because these tips were generally very credible. Crime Stoppers is a national organization in hundreds of cities across the country manned by sworn police officers that accepts anonymous tips from citizens with information about crimes being committed. Lo and behold, I got a tip about Earl dealing large quantities of cocaine from an apartment about two blocks from the diner where I last arrested him. Earl had carelessly started to deal in major quantities to pay a lawyer to represent him on all of his pending drug charges. I was able to meet with the Crime Stopper informant, which is unusual since informants are usually anonymous, and interviewed him about his information. He was Hispanic, so I arranged for a Spanish-speaking police officer to go with the informant to buy a kilo of cocaine from Earl. We put the undercover cop in a rented Cadillac, and we busted Earl with the entire kilo. A kilo of cocaine weighs 2.2 lb. and at the time cost $24,000. The street value is much higher because dealers mix smaller quantities with a cutting substance, which weakens the purity of the cocaine. I paid the informant $200, and Crime Stoppers paid him an additional $1,000 for his information.

The county prosecutors decided to have several trials for Earl, which would net him more prison time because as each trial ended, he would have another conviction on his record. By the time three trials were over, Earl had been sentenced to a total of thirty-seven years in prison.

Another Crime Stopper Tip that I worked was a heavy dealer of cocaine in a large mobile home park. We were able to get an informant to make a purchase of cocaine from the dealer whose nickname was "Cocky." We had an informant who was to be paid $200, and we were going to send him into the house with Andi, who would give the signal because this was going to be a Buy–Bust situation. A Buy–Bust is when you know drugs are in the house because of an informant or an undercover officer has seen them, you enter the house, secure it, then wait while a judge signs a search warrant. Then and only then can the search begin.

The paid informant traveled from Columbia, about 110 miles away and arrived too late for us all to meet him face to face at the briefing. We had a general physical description, and Andi was the only cop who had met him. We had all gone to the surrounding area to set up surveillance of the house, and Andi was wired so we could hear and record the conversation inside then hear her signal that she had seen the drugs. We had ordered six ounces of cocaine, so the money involved was considerable. Well, Andi and the informant entered and the normal drug-purchase conversation took place. Then Andi came outside allegedly to get the cash in the car and to give us the signal, leaving the informant inside momentarily. Jim was the supervisor on scene, but this was my case, and I had invested a lot of hard work to make the deal happen. When Andi gave the signal, Jim told us to wait. We were talking on a secure radio channel that only we could monitor, and I didn't want to endanger Andi or mess up my deal, so I said, "Fuck you, Jim, we aren't waiting. We are going in," and I gave the order for everyone to converge and make entry.

We drove in from several different locations, and as we all pulled up, we made entry, and a guy ran to the front room and dived through a window. He dived through the curtain, blinds, inside window, and storm window and out into the street. John and I immediately chased the subject through the mobile home park for about two blocks, where we caught him and began to throw him to the ground and fight with him as we tried to handcuff him. He was cut from the glass and had some road rash from being apprehended. We took him back to the house where all of the other occupants were handcuffed while we waited for the search warrant to be signed. When John and I walked in with this guy covered in blood, someone whispered to me that we had beaten the crap out of the informant. The informant had decided to make the deal as realistic as possible and ended up thanking us, which saved his cover for the time being.

We had carelessly failed to introduce the informant to all of the cops participating in the deal, which was bad on our part, but it all ended well, and "Cocky" was convicted and went to prison.

As for overriding Jim's order to wait and elect to go on my order, that turned out to be the right decision, and I would do it again if I had to. Jim was known for being indecisive and everyone knew I had made the right decision to move in when we did. When conducting drug operations, the procedure is very much like the military. We have our briefings prior to leaving on a particular job, where we draw diagrams of the target location, and show on the chalkboard where each person is assigned. We provide all involved with personal information on the target and a photo if available. We even go so far as to indicate what medical facility we will go to if someone is injured. Our briefing in the previous incident should have included the introduction at the briefing of the informant, but because he had not arrived in town yet, the introduction was deemed unimportant, an obvious mistake.

This procedure is very much like receiving a Five Paragraph Order in the Marine Corps prior to a mission. The acronym SMEAC stands for **S**ituation, **M**ission, **E**xecution, **A**dministration/Logistics, and **C**ommand. Cops who are former military understand this concept to the letter. Even though the case agent to a particular case has no rank, he or she has the authority to prepare the Operations Plan (Ops Plan) in the form of a briefing prior to all planned operations.

I estimate that I have personally participated in excess of one thousand search warrants, which is a lot of kicked doors. More importantly, the experience gained in preparing information and typing a search warrant became second nature to me. If you give me the description of the property to be searched and a little bit of information, I could have a search warrant ready for a judge's signature in twenty minutes. This experience proved to be extremely beneficial in later assignments in my career.

When others were having problems on a case and needed to get into a house, they would sometimes come to me and outline what they had, and I would help them put their investigative information together and dictate the wording for preparing a search warrant for them.

Another part of working narcotics was the debriefing of persons arrested. I loved gathering information from them and began to excel in making deals with them for information. The office that prosecuted our cases approved of our dealing, knowing that the deals needed to be made right after the arrest was made not weeks later after an attorney has made a decision. To me, this was the most rewarding part of working in drug enforcement. We had our own prosecutor assigned to our unit who would come to our office twice a month and review cases with us in preparation for trial.

The nature of the world of drug enforcement is such that it can go from zero to one hundred miles per hour very quickly. There is an abundance of waiting involved in the drug trade, and dealers are notoriously late for their deals. Some dealers are so paranoid that they are overly careful and are always looking over their shoulders.

During my tenure in METRO, I enrolled at the local technical college and studied Criminal Justice. This turned out to be one of the toughest things I ever did because I had been out of school for more than twenty years. I was married with three children, was working 7:00 p.m. to 3:00 a.m. five or six days a week, and called out while off duty at least twice a week, so college was not that easy. There were times that I was even called out of class, but the professors understood.

One of my professors ended up being a former marine who had also been wounded in Vietnam, and after comparing notes, we discovered we were both stationed at Marine Barracks, Philadelphia, at the same time.

One of the biggest drug deals to date that I ever participated in was for 25 kilos of cocaine, which was a deal that we did in conjunction with the local Drug Enforcement Association (DEA) office. They used us for the surveillance and manpower when the bust was to take place. This was in the days before there was a DEA Task Force in Charleston. The cocaine was due to arrive on a motorcycle, which was coming from Florida. The driver was a guy in his mid-forties and had the cocaine packed into the hard shell saddlebags of his big road bike. One of the DEA agents and I were set up near the exit to the interstate that he would be getting off at to get to the hotel, and we were assigned to advise when he exited the interstate and entered the hotel property. He was due to arrive at the hotel in North Charleston at a specific time and for the first time ever, the motorcycle with the cocaine arrived within five minutes from when it was due. We notified the others, and when he pulled up to the room, he was swarmed by DEA and METRO agents and arrested.

At about $25,000 per kilo, the cocaine was worth over $600,000, with a potential to turn into multiple millions of dollars after it was diluted into smaller quantities for resale on the street.

One of the most rewarding cases I was ever involved with was a case that DEA handed to us to work. A DEA agent had received information that a female subject was going to arrive at the airport that evening, and she was supposed to have a large quantity of cocaine in her possession. We had a general description of the female, who was arriving from Florida, and we waited near baggage claim for her after her flight landed. We waited for her to claim her suitcase before we approached her. Once we approached her and identified ourselves, we took her to an office nearby and got consent from the female to search her suitcase. When we searched the suitcase, it contained a wrapped present about the size of a kilo of cocaine. We did not want to disturb the wrapping because we wanted to preserve any fingerprints on the paper and tape that would have been left by the person who wrapped it. We carefully inserted a knife in the corner of the package and pulled out a small sample for testing, which tested positive as high-grade cocaine.

After interviewing the female, she told us that a male subject placed the package in her suitcase before she left Miami, and she was given a telephone number of a guy named "Sam," who she was supposed to call when she arrived. "Sam" knew when the flight was scheduled to arrive, so we had to move fast. We monitored the telephone call to "Sam," and she arranged to meet him in the parking lot of a shopping center not far from the airport. He told her to catch a taxi and to meet him. She told him she had no money for a taxi, so "Sam" assured her he would take care of the taxi fare when he met her. This scenario was playing right into our hand, so we had Melvin quickly go back to our office to get our METRO Cab Company taxi that we used for undercover deals. We got the girl and her suitcase into our taxi, and off we went to the shopping center. "Sam" was doing what all careful drug dealers do—made her wait and never showed at that first location.

Since our cab driver was a cop, we had the control we needed of the female and the kilo of cocaine, and at one point Melvin asked to get on the phone with "Sam" to complain that he needed to pay for the cab fare. This was great since it allowed one of our agents the opportunity to speak directly to "Sam," whom by now we had identified as a major cocaine dealer in the downtown Charleston area.

"Sam" ended up telling Melvin to meet him in the parking lot of a Hardee's restaurant about two miles from the shopping center. Andi and I were in a pickup truck, with me at the wheel, and the others were set up in the area in their undercover vehicles to wait for "Sam" to arrive. After a short wait, a new Lincoln Town Car occupied by three male subjects arrived and pulled into a parking spot next to our METRO cab, occupied by Melvin and our female and her suitcase. As they started to exit the cab to transfer the suitcase, I rolled up in the pickup and blocked the Lincoln in with the passenger side of the truck. As we pulled up, the driver of the Lincoln threw it in reverse and rammed the passenger door of the truck. I bailed out and went right for "Sam." Andi slid over, and out of the driver's side to assist the others in taking all parties, including the female, into custody. We had arranged to arrest the female to protect her cover until the case went to trial.

This case was very rewarding because we had to do a lot of after the arrest work in tracking the dope back to Florida and preserving the wrapping of the cocaine for fingerprints. "Sam" had a very high-priced, high-profile local attorney to represent him. We were able to protect the female, and she testified at trial for the prosecution, and "Sam" was sentenced to twenty-five years in prison for Trafficking in Cocaine. The two subjects who traveled to the Hardee's with "Sam" were also convicted of other charges for helping "Sam."

After the case was adjudicated and all appeals exhausted, I ended up with the cassette tape of the conversation between Melvin and "Sam" when he posed as a taxi driver. It was hilarious to listen to after the fact, and I had it in my possession in my desk for more than twenty-five years. I met Melvin after I retired and handed the cassette tape off to him for posterity. About two months later, he retired as a captain at the North Charleston Police Department.

I mentioned earlier that we always had a briefing prior to going out on an operation, but as you can plainly see, this airport operation left no time but to act on instincts and experience and with available assets to deal with what time and our surroundings allowed us to do.

Another interesting case involving an undercover narc was when Guy was still with us, and we had Guy meet with several people in a local bar one Saturday night. He was wired for sound, and his conversation was monitored in a surveillance van out in the parking lot. It was a very cold night, and the several guys out in the van froze their butts off. I was happy to be inside of the bar with Buddy, and we were there to provide security and to keep an eye on Guy and to go periodically into the men's room to provide him with fresh 9-volt batteries to power his audio transmitter. Once the batteries start getting worn, they get hot and can cause burns to the wearer if not replaced.

The only time we were allowed to consume alcohol while on the job was when we were acting in an undercover capacity. While our buddies were freezing in the van, Buddy and I were drinking draft beer by the pitcher. We were watching Guy, who was also drinking beer, but with three others at his table. When it came time to leave and follow the people Guy had been drinking with, almost three hours had passed. With three hours of beer, a $37 tab, and enough popcorn to sink a ship, we were buzzed.

Guy had arranged for one of the people he was talking with to purchase a kilo of cocaine, and the dealer was supposed to go home, take a shower, and immediately drive to Miami to get the cocaine and drive right back, scheduled to arrive in Charleston the following evening, a twenty-four-hour turnaround. This practice was common in the drug world out of Charleston because dealers are able to stay awake by snorting cocaine during the trip. By having this important intelligence, we were able to sit and wait along the only route from I-95 back into Charleston Sunday night.

We managed to follow the dealers to the house and were driving with the windows down to keep us alert and to take the buzz off from our drinking. The following evening we waited for and intercepted the suspect on Highway 17, almost twenty-four hours to the minute from when he left. We seized the kilo of cocaine and his car, and he went to prison for a long time.

I must make this point that in the mid-'80s, we rarely ran across a drug dealer with a weapon, and it was unusual to seize weapons even from houses when we conducted search warrants. In the course of time, we saw that change as more and more people on the street felt the need to carry a weapon. We were always cognizant of officer safety because of what we did and were extremely careful.

One night we were conducting street sweeps and chased a group of male subjects into a fenced-in yard where they had no way to escape. We put all six to eight of them against the wall of an apartment building and had them assume the position to be patted down for weapons. I was busy talking to someone and did not do any of the patting down, and after they were supposedly all clear, I noticed one guy in particular acting suspiciously and extremely nervous as I was reading his body language. I walked up to him and asked him what his problem was, and as I spoke to him, I touched his shirt and felt something hard. I quickly spun him around, put him against the wall, reached into his shirt, and found that he had a loaded pistol in a shoulder holster concealed under his shirt. I threw him to the ground, ripped his shirt off and his shoulder holster, and handcuffed him. After that, we had a little talk about conducting better searches before someone got hurt.

I had been taught early on by James, my former sergeant, to pat at people's pants pockets and shirts while talking to them. Drug dealers expected officers to be up close and personal and in their faces, so touching while talking was the way to go. If they objected, that usually meant that they had something to hide. This proved to be good advice time and time again.

As crack worked its ugly way into society and into the drug world, we saw an immediate change on the street. Crack was cheaper than marijuana and any other available drug. It was small and easy to conceal, but was highly addictive. It is said that a person would be hooked after smoking crack just one time. The known cocaine dealers were now switching to crack and were using it themselves.

One of those dealers I recall in particular was nicknamed "Buffalo." He had been one of the most feared guys on the street and was feared by everyone. He had made the switch to crack from powder cocaine. We had a search warrant for his apartment, but we had not seen him on the street for quite some time. We hit the apartment, and just prior to our entry "Buffalo" and his friends had cooked a batch of crack and were now smoking it when we arrived. The crack fumes in the apartment were so strong that we had to open the windows and go outside so we would not be overcome ourselves. Inside, our dealer, "Buffalo," was in a stupor and was a shadow of his formerly muscular 250 lb. His eyes were sunken in, and he was down to about 150 lb. The physical transformation he made was unbelievable, and when I realized it was him, I said, "Buffalo, you're gonna die soon," and that scared the crap out of him hearing that from us. I took a Polaroid photo of him that I still have today, and I used to keep it to show others what crack did to people.

***

METRO was definitely the place to be if you wanted to be promoted. The lieutenant's position was a lock for promotion to captain, and now it was time for Eddie to leave when he was promoted. He was transferred to be in charge of the Criminal Investigations Division (CID), just upstairs from our offices. We shamed Eddie by telling him that we were responsible for his promotion because of all of the high-profile drug arrests we had made, and he felt so bad that his wife made him take the entire unit, including Vice, out to dinner just before his departure.

Eddie's replacement was my old road lieutenant, Larry, the one who had responded to my shooting my last weekend in training and my squad commander while in my first uniform assignment. Larry was a great leader who loved to work with the troops and to get his hands dirty. He knew very little about drugs but learned quickly. He was another boss who always stood behind his people, even when they were in the wrong, as long as they did not lie to him. He would never ask anyone to do anything that he had not already done himself or would not do himself.

One of the first deals we did under his command was a deal at a fleabag motel watching a target that ended up sending a major dealer to prison for a long time. Larry and I set up in a room next to a target, and the walls were so thin that we could hear every word of conversation the target had on the room phone. Andi joined us in the room later with some food, and we sat in that hot room for several hours. We could not run the air conditioner because when it ran we could not hear what was going on in the next room. We determined that the target was going to receive a delivery of cocaine very soon, but we did not know who was making the delivery, so we alerted the guys that were set up outside to be on the lookout for whoever showed up and went to the room next to us.

After about three hours, we got word that someone was approaching the lot and parking out front. The person was carrying a canvas bag, knocked on the door, and was allowed entry. By the conversation we could overhear, we determined that the delivery was being made. We relayed this information to the guys outside, and they were ready to snatch him when he exited and went to his car. As the delivery guy left empty-handed and headed toward his vehicle, our people moved in, but the bad guy decided to abandon his vehicle and ran from the area. We now had the cocaine in the room next to us with the target and the supplier on the run with his car parked out front. The lieutenant decided that the circumstances would allow us to make an exigent entry into the room without a search warrant because the target had the ability to destroy the evidence when he heard the commotion outside. I kicked the door and caught the target getting ready to get into the shower. You cannot do too much resisting when you are naked and forced into the shower.

We secured the room and did not search until we were able to get a search warrant signed by a judge. While waiting for the search warrant, I sat down with the target and debriefed him for information. The business of drug enforcement is to always go after a bigger fish, and the bigger fish in this case was on the run. The car was not registered to him, so identifying the deliveryman was paramount. We knew that if a person can handle selling six ounces of cocaine, he probably deals in heavier weight and probably a more major supplier.

The person who escaped was located and arrested later in the evening, and when we brought him to our office, he refused to cooperate. Based on information gathered, we had enough information to prepare a search warrant for his apartment. It was by now almost 3:00 a.m., and I drove to a magistrate's house and woke her up to sign the warrant. We immediately went to execute the warrant and were unable to locate any more cocaine, but we gathered a huge amount of intelligence, such as receipts, phone bills, and packaging material. We charged both parties with Trafficking in Cocaine, which carried the mandatory twenty-five-year penalty that I have previously discussed.

It ended up where we were able to get the original target in the motel to be a witness for the state at the trial of the person who delivered the cocaine to him, who was the bigger fish we wanted. The first initial of the target was "Z," who upheld his end of the bargain at trial, resulting in a conviction for the deliveryman.

We made the case against him with only circumstantial evidence, and when the trial was over, the judge, before a crowded courtroom gave a short synopsis of the great work we did in this case. He echoed the fact that we made the case based on good solid detective work. He went on about what a professional investigation we had conducted and generally praised our hard work. This was great to hear from a well-known, well-respected and admired judge in our circuit and was great for our ego in letting us know that we had done a great job. "Z" was placed on probation for five years in return for his testifying for the state and being instrumental in our identifying the bigger dealer. This, however, was not the last of my dealings with "Z."

***

In mid-1988, I was slated to attend a week-long instructors' course at the police academy in Columbia. Completion of this course would allow me to teach any police subject that had a lesson plan. I was unaware that we were expected to bring a uniform to wear for the last day when we gave our final videotaped, fifteen-minute presentation. Since I was a plainclothes narcotics investigator, I wore to class what I wore to work, which was jeans, loafers with no socks, and a Hawaiian-type shirt worn out of my pants. The chief instructor was a friend and allowed me the privilege of wearing civilian clothes for my testing. Besides I wasn't about to get a haircut or shave my beard for this class.

In October of 1988, I was reluctantly, but temporarily, transferred from METRO to the Training Division and was slated to assist the training staff with a large, incoming Recruit Training Class. I was pissed off at first because I had a load of active cases, and I would have to shave my beard and cut my hair short in order to wear a uniform for this assignment. On top of that, the transfer would cost me extra income since I would lose the benefit of all of the overtime pay I received by virtue of working the long hours I worked in METRO. I was told that the decision to pull me came directly from the chief, so I kept my mouth shut and bit the bullet.

I began to think that the temporary assignment would not be bad since a friend named Paul was the lieutenant of the Training Division. Working directly for him might end up being a bonus.

This recruit class was the largest the county had ever had, since there were fifteen new Charleston County Recruits and fifteen from other area police departments, including Navy personnel. Apparently, my experience as a drill instructor and the fact that I was now a Basic Instructor were the deciding factors in me being chosen.

At the time, the Training Division was housed in the downtown campus of a local technical college. The location was ideal because it was away from the police department, and there were several dedicated classrooms and a gymnasium for physical training. Each day started with a personnel inspection by me, and those who had issues received remedial training, such as physical exercise, just like Marine Corps boot camp. I enjoyed every minute of this training and taught many of the classes in the curriculum, including, of course, Narcotics, Officer Survival, Personal Appearance, Driving, Police Ethics, Courtroom Testimony, and several other subjects. I was surprised at how much I had missed training others, and I fell right back into the role.

There were some Navy personnel in the class who just were not that impressive. One was a chief petty officer who thought because he was a CPO, he was above doing what everybody else in the class did. I treated everyone in the class the same and showed no favorites. We did have one former marine sergeant who was squared away and always had the cleanest weapon and best appearance in uniform. I regularly used him as an example and a motivational tool, which I know, pissed the Navy personnel off, but here I was again messing with the Navy—life remained good.

When the class graduated, I was ready to head back to METRO so I could earn some of the extra overtime pay to help pay for Christmas. That was not to be because there were not enough Field Training Officers (FTOs) in the Patrol Division to accommodate the fifteen graduating county recruits. You guessed it—I was ordered to be a Field Training Officer for an additional eight weeks. One consolation was that I could pick the two recruits out of the class that I wanted to train.

The system dictated that a recruit spend a solid month with his or her FTO, then switch to a second FTO for two weeks, and then return to his or her original FTO for the final two weeks of training. I selected a guy named Chris for the first month and a woman named Beth for the other two weeks.

I was assigned to train Chris on a squad in my old sub-station and worked with many of my old friends in patrol. A buddy of mine named Chuck was on this squad, and he too was assigned a recruit, named Tom. We worked the same shift in the same district and went on all two-man calls together. There were many calls that required that two officers respond, and Chuck and I were considered two officers and the fact that we each had a recruit riding with us did not allow the recruits to be counted as a trained officer for two man calls.

On the very first night, back on the street with a recruit, Chuck and I both responded to a trailer park where a male subject was causing a disturbance. This call was the two recruits' first ever response to a call for service in their career, so they were along for the ride, so to speak. My orders to Chris were to stay by my side and say nothing unless asked. Well, when Chuck and I rolled up, we immediately confronted an intoxicated male subject causing problems in the park. We spoke to him, and he answered us by letting loose with a string of profanities. I immediately put the guy on the ground, and Chuck and I had him cuffed and stuffed in the backseat of his car in about fifteen seconds. We looked up at our recruits, and they both stood there with their eyes about to pop out and their jaws hanging wide open. They later said that they could not believe how fast the situation went from talking to an arrest, and how little time the arrest took, which was part of their learning process.

About two weeks later, Chuck and I responded to a call from a little, old, black lady who was known to be a little crazy and who was complaining of weird, satanic things going on in her house. She had a history of being very religious, but a little out there, so I thought we would have some fun at the expense of our two recruits, Chris and Tom. There we were in her house, four cops in uniform, and she was going on and on, and Chuck and I knew exactly where she was coming from. I then told her that Chris and Tom were part of a new program in the police department where Ordained Ministers traveled with us in uniform, and I introduced Reverend Chris and Tom to her. Chuck and I walked out to let them deal with her. She just loved what I had told her and started praising Jesus as we walked out. Chris and Tom knew that we had done them bad, but they both grinned and played along and made a lonely little woman feel good for the night.

Chris and Tom ended up being outstanding cops and have to date risen to the rank of chief inspector and Tom to the rank of sergeant. Both are exemplary cops, and of course I attribute their success to their fine training as rookies.

After completing my time as an FTO, I returned to METRO, resumed my caseload, and began to hit my cases hard.

In early 1989, the new TV show *COPS* came into existence. It was highly advertised on TV and was probably one of the first reality shows ever. We as a group were upset that the show was on at 8:00 p.m. on Saturday night, easily our busiest night of the week. The first night that it was on we were executing a search warrant in North Charleston and were in the middle of searching a house when someone yelled, "Hey, it's 8:00 p.m.! *COPS* is on. Someone tuned in the TV in the living room of the house we were searching, and we all stopped and sat down in the dealer's living room and watched the first episode. We took the owner of the house into the living room with us, and we all sat and watched this great new show and analyzed the crap out of it.

While we were watching, one of the guys asked the owner of the house if he had any ice cream in the freezer. Somebody went into the kitchen, got a half gallon of ice cream, and came out with a handful of spoons. We all ate ice cream while watching *COPS* with a drug dealer in his living room, while the owner of the house told us we were not such bad guys after all. Just another fun night on the mean streets of Charleston County.

Not long after my return to METRO after being away for three and a half months in early 1989, those of us eligible were preparing for testing for promotion to sergeant.

We had a relatively new chief of police who was not well liked and had been around less than two years. Our old, longtime chief had retired the previous year, and County Council decided to hire a new chief from the outside. Well, they sure did, and he tried to put his stamp of very unconventional leadership beliefs on his staff. He came up with some sort of Life Triangle way of thinking that he had taught to all personnel in mandatory training sessions. The old-timers, especially those on the command staff who were eligible for the position, resented him. The new chief also hired some questionable personnel who had worked for him at his very small former police department upstate.

One of the positive things he did institute the previous year not long after his arrival while I was on the SCAT Team, was to hold an all hands mandatory personnel and equipment inspection. This practice was something that definitely did not go over well with the old-school guys because they had never had any such thing in their entire career, except for the various informal squad inspections held at roll call on a regular basis. The department was separated in half for the inspection. The West District had its inspection in a school parking lot on James Island, while both SCAT Teams answered calls for service for them. The North District had its in front of headquarters in North Charleston. Once the Chief inspected the troops in formation, various assigned staff inspected our assigned vehicles and equipment. Some sergeants and patrolmen were gigged for dirty weapons, dirty brass, or unsigned shoes, after some failed to take the inspection seriously. I received an exemplary appearance comment from the chief after he inspected me.

For many years, the department had a set policy in writing that dictated the promotion process, but the new chief quickly changed that, which I thought was a change for the better because I was not a good test taker, and practical application was to my benefit. He instituted a series of testing all done in one day. The process started out with a written test, then on to a one-hour, in-basket exercise where everyone is given an in-basket of things to do, which had to be prioritized and completed, which included scheduling for special events and operations with obstacles, such as people calling in sick or being unable to work due to injury. After the in-basket exercise, we participated in an assessment center practical application test with role players brought in from the outside, who graded the participants in real-life police issues, which included search warrant and arrest warrant preparation, disaster response, and all aspects of law enforcement. Some of the role players were instructors from the South Carolina Criminal Justice Academy, and some were paid civilian actors.

Our day for the test arrived, and we gathered in an abandoned high school that was used for furniture storage for the school district. There were almost fifty participants eligible for promotion to the rank of sergeant. All participants took the written test, and after a short break given the packet of information for the in-basket exercise. Within minutes of being given the packets, two participants got up and walked out shaking their heads, apparently overwhelmed by the exercise. I was surprised at who they were because I knew that they were smart guys and good knowledgeable cops.

We completed the four-hour process, and after comparing notes with others, I felt pretty good about my chances.

The last part of the process was an interview before the entire command staff of the police department, which consisted of all captains and above. The chief sat in on the interviews, but he was not a voting member in the grading process. The interview before the command staff went well, and I got the word that I had aced the interview grade-wise. Now all we had to do was to sit and wait.

In March of 1989, the promotions were imminent, and one night while working, I got a call to go to the chief's office. First, he was never in his office after hours, so I was not sure what to expect. I went in, and he told me that he was promoting me to sergeant. He told me that I was the first of nine that he would notify, so he asked that I keep quiet until he made all nine notifications. Being called to the chief's office was not something that could be kept secret, so when I got back to my office, the whole unit was there, wanting to know what had happened. Two other investigators in the unit were also promoted that night, and they figured out what was up because Andi then got her call to see the chief, and she came back five minutes later grinning like a Cheshire cat from ear to ear. The third promotion out of the unit was a woman who worked in Vice.

The chief held a formal promotion ceremony at the training facility downtown. Nine of us were promoted that day, and now we were all anxious to find out where we were being transferred.

There was about a week from the date of our promotion to our departure from METRO, so we spent that time closing out our cases and giving them to others to complete. I had been hoping to go to the Patrol Division and be a road sergeant, but when the transfer announcement came out I was very disappointed. I had already received a heads up telephone call from Andi, who had heard before the announcement where we were all going. She had been assigned to the Training Division as the training sergeant, and I was scheduled to take over the Warrants Division. The bright side of the assignment was that we were both now working for the same lieutenant, Paul, who was a great guy to work for. I had known Paul since before I was a cop and knew his family. I was really so happy to make sergeant that I never bitched about my assignment. Paul was a laid-back guy who had been one of the best investigators who ever worked in CID and had spent many years working numerous high-profile homicides. He was a very easy person to work for and just asked that I keep him apprised of what was going on and things would be fine.

FIRST JOB AS A SERGEANT

20

I RELIEVED MY BUDDY J. J. IN WARRANTS who was being transferred to the Vice Unit. He was a happy camper, and it did not take long for me to find out why. He had inherited a mess after the previous sergeant had been unexpectedly relieved. He cleaned up what he could in the time he was there, but it appeared that I had more cleaning to do. I had eight officers and two women civilian employees working for me in the office.

The Warrants Office had, at the time, over 13,000 active arrest warrants on file, with a monthly influx of between 1,000 and 1,200. Each of the eight officers was expected to serve at least 100 warrants each per month, so simple math shows that if we were serving 800 to 1,000 per month and receiving at least 1,000 we would never get ahead. If an officer went too long not serving his or her expected 100 he or she was summarily transferred. Some barely made it, and some served as many as 150 or more.

After working 7:00 p.m. to 3:00 a.m. for more than five years, I now worked 8:00 a.m. to 4:00 p.m. and was home every night. My kids appreciated my presence and it was nice to be home with the family almost every evening. For more than five years, I had made supper and had it waiting on the table when my wife got home from work as a nurse. We had been like two ships passing in the night, and now I was home every evening. Even though I worked nights for that long, I never missed a wrestling match, a football game, a track meet, a Girl Scout meeting, or any other extracurricular activity of any of my three children. I always rearranged my schedule to accommodate their activities. Whenever I was home, my one rule was that we all sit at the table together and eat as a family. It was at our family meals that we discussed school, work, problems, schedules, friends, and the rest of the issues of their world.

In the office, I had immediate issues with a woman employee who was convinced that I was put in the office specifically to get rid of her, and she was very vocal about her feelings. My newfound leadership was soon put to the test because I had no such order.

I quickly figured out that one woman was an extremely hard worker and was good at what she did. The one who thought she was on the way out was lazy and only worked when I was in the office. Others had told me that as soon as I left the office, she immediately got on the phone, making personal calls. On top of that, her productivity was questionable. After about two weeks, I announced that I was leaving for the day, but I went downtown and stayed with Paul, my lieutenant, and killed time in his office. The next day I had a communications supervisor provide a computer printout of all of the telephone calls made on her phone while I was gone. I also had a computer tech supervisor provide me with a printout of how many warrant entries she made in my absence. Records indicated that she did not enter one warrant and had spent all of her time on the phone on personal business.

I confronted her with this information and counseled her about her lack of productivity and personal use of the phone. My counseling did not go over well with her, and she did just enough work to get by and no more. This woman thought she was untouchable because, as rumor had it, she was sleeping with a high-ranking member of the command staff, but I just did what the circumstances dictated.

One day both of my female employees were in the ladies room around the corner from our office, and the lazy one started in verbally with her coworker. Words were exchanged, and the lazy one ended up slapping the other in the face. I kept them both separated and sent the lazy one home for the rest of the day while I decided how to handle the matter. My lieutenant and I met with her the following day, and she was terminated from employment. That quickly ended the issues of productivity in the office. Her laziness had been a morale issue and a cancer in the office, and her departure made noticeable changes in and around the office. The terminated woman was a longtime employee, and word quickly went around that I was a hatchet man, which was not true because everyone knew that a sergeant did not have the authority to have someone terminated.

When I first arrived, I had a meeting of all personnel and told them what was expected of them and what to expect from me. I knew every one of them, so that was not an issue. I had an extreme dislike for one of my guys, but I vowed to be objective, and as his supervisor, I ignored the feelings I had about him. As a result of my giving him a chance, he turned out to be one of my best employees and hardest workers.

Since nine people were promoted to sergeant at one time, the chief had scheduled several classes for us to attend, which proved to be very beneficial. The classes were scheduled so we spent a solid week attending these classes. One of the most beneficial classes was one that taught us how to recognize when subordinates were having personal issues, especially when these issues had an effect on their job performance. We were instructed on the proper procedure for referring an employee to the Employee Assistance Program that offered anonymous counseling to the employee free of charge. The training also explained how and when the counseling could become mandatory. I filed this information into the back of my brain as important information and went back to work.

Upon my arrival in the Warrants Office, I noticed that there were arrest warrants in desk drawers, in boxes, and, when I spot-inspected my officers' vehicles, saw warrants in their trunks. I put out an immediate order that dictated that all warrants once entered into the computer by my girls would then be placed in file drawers. The only other place warrants should be was in the possession of one of the warrant officers who had signed them out for service. This action had an immediate and positive effect on locating warrants when attempting to confirm their existence if a wanted person was stopped out on the road.

Other than dealing with the issue between the two women early on, I had no problems with personnel until one night we had to go to an officer's house to retrieve warrants from his car while he was on vacation and found dozens of warrants he had not signed for. Unfortunately, he was a good guy with over twenty years on the job and was consistently a top producer, but he had violated my order, so I had to take disciplinary action.

I conferred with my lieutenant, Paul, who agreed that he needed to be suspended without pay for at least three days. I prepared this, my first serious form of disciplinary action, against a sworn officer. This disciplinary action was something that had to happen, and I did it. He accepted the punishment and told me he deserved the suspension for violating my order. He did ask that he not be transferred out of the unit, and I told him I had no control over that. The boss decided that he also needed to be transferred, and he was. He knew I had done what I had to do and knew I had no control over his transfer. He ended up working for me years later in two other assignments.

Part of my cleaning-up process in the office was to purge old warrants. Many were fifteen years old or more, and many were for military personnel who were no longer stationed in the Charleston area. I decided to invite myself to a meeting of the Charleston County Magistrates to discuss the purging of these old unservable warrants. I was well received at the meeting, and we came up with criteria for purging old warrants and were able to alleviate several thousand of the stagnant warrants on file. I had a great relationship with many of these magistrates, as I had awakened many of them in the middle of the night to sign search warrants for me when I worked narcotics. Many agreed that they were glad I was no longer in METRO because of my regularity in waking them up to sign warrants. My friendship with many of those magistrates remains to this day. Some have retired, some are ready to retire, and some are still on the job.

In the summer of 1989, my entire family spent a week in a rented house on Folly Beach right on the ocean, which was just five miles from home. During that week I spent some time on the phone with work and shuttled my oldest son to football practice twice a day and to the house to feed the dog. We had an overall great time with the kids and some of their friends who came out to visit.

In the middle of the week, while on the beach I received an alarming telephone call that one of my former coworkers in METRO had sadly committed suicide. Stuart was a good guy who had come over from another local police department, and he had apparently become too involved with a paid informant that he had worked with. It was nothing of a romantic nature but a situation in which he had become too involved in the informant's personal life and was unable to separate the personal part of friendship from the professional relationship of receiving information from the informant. Stuart was the same guy who fell through the kitchen ceiling clutching a bale of marijuana.

There was an internal investigation, and several of his former coworkers were called in, including me, hoping we could come to some sort of reasonable understanding of why he thought he needed to end his young life.

It is unfortunate, but I think I have gone to almost as many funerals of cops or former cops who have committed suicide as those who died in the line of duty. It is a sad commentary for the profession, but I believe it can be compared to the high number of returning soldiers and marines who are presently returning from Iraq and Afghanistan suffering from Post-Traumatic Stress Disorder (PTSD) who eventually end their own lives.

I had wanted so badly to work in the Patrol Division that I worked many Friday and Saturday nights for other sergeants to fill in while they took time off. Doing this was satisfying and kept me sharp in the duties of dealing with service calls as a supervisor and with other personnel I had never worked with before. The extra shifts in an overtime status were a good thing too because my promotion to sergeant did not result in any large raise in pay. I had actually made more working in METRO because of the regular overtime.

I made it a point to reward officers who did good things by writing a letter of appreciation or a letter of commendation when appropriate. I had seen how important it was for officers to be recognized when they went above and beyond, and I quickly saw the positive results of doing so. We had one unmarked police cruiser assigned to the unit, and I made sure that the top warrant server for the month had the use of that car for the following month. To drive an unmarked car was a perk and was appreciated by the guys and was an incentive to serve the most warrants.

***

In September of 1989, Hurricane Hugo devastated the Charleston area. We had ample warning several days out that the storm was coming, and the entire county had a mandatory evacuation. The entire department went on immediate twelve-hour shifts, and I was assigned to work in the district where I lived, which was convenient because it allowed me to come by the house from time to time to check on my kids, who by then were eleven, fifteen, and seventeen. I was at home for the night when the storm hit sometime around midnight. I was working 7:00 a.m. to 7:00 p.m. and tried as hard as I could to sleep, which was nearly impossible. At first light, I took a ladder, went on my roof to survey the damage, and did not have one missing shingle, just some water damage where water had come in under the seams of the windows and few cracked pieces of glass. When I looked out on the neighborhood from the roof, I saw many trees down and heavily damaged homes. We were without power and would be without for over thirty days.

I never made it to work at 7:00 a.m. because I was unable to maneuver my cruiser out of the yard and into the neighborhood because of all of the hurricane debris. I made it to work, but not until about 9:00 a.m. I slowly made my way around, got to the station, and did nothing but help people in distress for days. There was a problem with looters, and we had orders to deal with them in any way we saw fit because we were discouraged from arresting them because the jail was working only on generator power. If we caught people in a damaged house or business, they were dealt with accordingly and then sent on their way. Martial law was in effect, and anyone out after the 7:00 p.m. curfew was fair game. At no time ever again in my police career did this unique situation arise. We had to keep law and order and were allowed to deal with issues, such as looters and thieves, the way we saw fit.

About two days after the hurricane, I was transferred to be one of the daytime supervisors to the North District and worked out of our headquarters. We held morning roll call in the heavily damaged Criminal Investigations Division office, with only a partial roof over our heads. We had about forty officers on the street in our district, and some were in somewhat remote sub districts in the north area. The Salvation Army, the Red Cross, and most other major fast food corporations were providing police and fire departments with food for us and for our families. When food was given to supervisors for distribution, I would fill the backseat of my car with whatever I had or what I could scrounge and made sure my people were fed two times during a twelve-hour shift. I remember when I brought the first batch of pizzas to my people in one remote area, they told me that I was the first supervisor they had seen, and this was the first food they had had delivered to them since twelve-hour shifts began several days before.

It made me feel good to hear that from the troops, but it made me wonder what the other supervisors were doing with the supplies given to them for distribution. I knew who the failing supervisors were and made sure I said something to them when I saw them. The Marine Corps taught me that you always had to take care of your people, and this was second nature to me. When I was able to get foodstuffs that they could take home for their families' use, I did. I delivered loaves of bread, cereal, pet food for those with dogs and cats, canned goods, fruit, milk, and eggs.

We worked for thirty-three straight days on twelve-hour shifts without a day off and were glad when it ended. We were, of course, compensated in the form of overtime pay, which was subsidized by FEMA, but so many people had such major damage to their homes that extra money really did not matter. One close friend, Jimmy, lost his entire home and his pets that washed away in the storm surge that hit his area. His dad was a retired major with our department, and all of his police memorabilia, such as guns, badges, plaques, and uniforms, was gone forever. By mid-October, we were back to our normal work schedules, but it took many months to get our facilities back to some state of normalcy.

In November of 1989, I had to fire my duty weapon for requalification, so in the middle of the day, I decided to go home and change into clothing suitable for the shooting range. Well, on the way home, I happened to see my family van going in the opposite direction, driven by an unknown male with my wife sitting in the front passenger seat. She saw me and ducked down, so I turned around, caught up to my car, and stopped it. I made the unknown driver exit my car and had him sit on the curb in the rain, while I attempted to find out what was going on. To make a long story short, that was the last day that my wife ever lived in my house, which was her choice.

My children all understood what was happening, and all three decided that they wanted to stay with me. I was the stability in their lives, and they knew that. I do not think I have ever let them down and have always put their interests first and foremost. They were aware that I was the one who got them up, made their lunches for school, cooked their dinner every night, and attended all of their school activities. I do not think they have ever regretted their decision to stay with me, and I remain close to all of them to this day.

One helpful and enlightening factor to my family life in that same period was that my mother had decided to relocate to Charleston after selling the house in New Jersey, where I grew up. She purchased a house just five minutes away from mine, and her presence was especially helpful to my children. My grandmother was also coming with her, so the kids would be able to spend quality time with their grandmother and great-grandmother.

Unfortunately, the split was right before the Thanksgiving and Christmas holidays. One day not long before Christmas, I was in the local K-Mart picking up stocking stuffers for the kids for Christmas and had a full cart of merchandise and saw that everyone in the store was in the holiday spirit, with Christmas music playing loudly. Happy people smiling and laughing surrounded me, and all of a sudden I felt as though the walls were closing in around me. I left my cart, walked out of the store, got in my car, and went home empty-handed. I had figured out that I was probably in a state of depression and needed some help in the form of counseling.

I had received training when I was promoted about how to recognize behavior brought on by family issues, and I had identified myself as being in that category. The next morning I referred myself to the Charleston County Employee Assistance Program free counseling. I was immediately given an appointment for that afternoon and attended four sessions. The counseling was great and snapped me out of my funk, and I again felt somewhat normal. That Christmas was a rough one emotionally, but my children helped me through it.

I was the first employee that I ever referred to counseling, but I did end up sending quite a few others over the next several years, some voluntarily and some mandatory.

About five months after our split, I made contact with the girl that I dated in 1979 when I was divorced for about eight months. Her name was Paula, and she was also from New Jersey and lived not far from where I grew up. My little sister had her as a teacher at the time in my old high school and had introduced me to her. By now, eleven years later, Paula had left teaching and had entered the private sector and was now an office manager for ESPN in New York. She ran offices in Denver, Detroit, and Beverly Hills. She and I reconnected and began a long distance relationship. We were engaged later in the year. She visited me here in Charleston, and I drove there on a monthly basis and once met her in California while she was there on a business trip. We spoke to each other on a daily basis because she had the ability to call me from work at no cost.

In the spring of 1990, I became involved in a major incident within the department. A male burglary suspect was arrested and brought to my old sub-station for questioning and completion of paperwork. A seasoned female lieutenant who was the shift supervisor for the day had mishandled the situation from the beginning. The lieutenant unhandcuffed the suspect for questioning, then inadvertently left the suspect with a rookie female officer with little to no experience in handling arrestees. While the arresting officer was in another room, the suspect overpowered the rookie female and ran out of the door and across the street into a wooded area. The rookie and the lieutenant never pursued him and left a third female officer on her own to chase the suspect into the wooded area, where the suspect overpowered her, took her gun, and shot her in the leg.

A huge perimeter was set up around the wooded area. Paula was in town visiting me at the time, and I was off for the week, so I did not respond. The situation ended when one of our sergeants got a good shot at the suspect while he was holding the bleeding officer captive and killed him with a single slug from his shotgun. At least two other officers also fired their weapons simultaneously.

When I returned from my short break, I was appointed to be a member of a Peer Review Board, consisting of four sergeants, to review the incident in its entirety along with three other sergeants. We were tasked with making the determination of whether the sergeant who shot and killed the suspect did so within policy and procedure. The Board was provided with all of the facts of the incident, including tapes of the radio communications, statements, reports, supplements, reports of other incidents involving participants, and anything else we needed to complete our assignment. We were also allowed to interview the injured officer, the rookie officer, two other officers who fired at the suspect, and several civilian witnesses.

We meticulously conducted our investigation and used our investigative skills to conduct the process professionally, concisely, and accurately. Andi, who worked in the same bureau that I did, was also a member of the board, and we worked together to compose the report for submission at the completion of the investigation.

We overwhelmingly found that the sergeant acted properly when he was forced to shoot the suspect and was cleared of any wrongdoing. We recommended that the rookie officer should no longer be an officer, and she was transferred to be a dispatcher, which was a nonsworn civilian position.

The female lieutenant who was the supervisor that day was an entirely different story. Our investigation found her at fault and responsible for allowing the situation to escalate, which resulted in the severe gunshot wound to the officer. She had unhandcuffed the suspect, which allowed his escape and caused the situation to further escalate. We had information that in 1983 she was the sergeant at the scene of a domestic dispute that resulted in a suspect being shot and killed by an officer because she left the officer alone in the residence. The findings from that investigation laid fault in her lap for that incident as well.

Our findings were limited, however, only to the sergeant who shot the suspect, but we made scathing recommendations for the lieutenant's removal from any future supervisory responsibilities. I do not think she ever commanded another sworn officer for the remainder of her career in an administrative capacity.

While we were conducting our Peer Review Board, a group of lieutenants was holding a similar peer board to investigate the actions of the lieutenant in question. We met with them at the end of each day of hearings and compared notes, but Andi and I composed the six-page report without any outside influence or intervention. Our report was a hot topic in and around the police department when word got around that we did not have much nice to say on behalf of the lieutenant. Unfortunately, she had a history of making bad decisions, and, as a result, was not very well respected by others as a decisive leader.

Once the written findings of both peer review boards were published, I had other lieutenants and captains approach me wanting to know who wrote the report for us. I said to each person who asked that Andi and I composed and prepared the entire report. I believe that our skills exhibited in this investigation due to our investigative experience resulted in our future assignments.

By now, I had been in charge of the Warrants Unit for about a year and had cleaned the office to a point where the warrants were now properly filed, and we were managing the influx of new warrants by repeatedly serving more than we were taking in. By meeting regularly with the magistrates at their quarterly meetings, we had also tightened up on the criteria for obtaining a warrant and, more importantly, stopped the practice of obtaining an arrest warrant for traffic charges when someone failed to appear for a minor infraction. I encouraged them to use the traffic tickets themselves and the department of motor vehicle laws to suspend a driver's license for failure to appear in court rather than producing a warrant.

It was now decided that we were going to conduct an audit of our warrants, which was to be administered by an auditor from Charleston County Government. The audit began with the approval of my chain of command, including the chief. This was the first audit conducted in many years, and no one could remember when it had been done last. I received the results of the audit, which reflected 1,343 unaccounted warrants, which was about 10 percent of my entire inventory. I immediately reported to Paul, my lieutenant, and he, in turn, notified Carroll (male name) our captain. We expected there to be missing warrants but had no idea how many there would be, as there had been literally dozens of officers working out of the office over the years and no accounting for at least the last fifteen years.

We were scheduled for a meeting with the chief in the conference room at headquarters, attended by Paul, my lieutenant; Carroll, my captain; the chief; and me. The chief asked for the results, and I read from the written audit and came out with the magic number 1,343. You could see the color go out of the chief's face, and he appeared angry. Then he sat back in his chair holding the report to his head as we sat there waiting for him to speak.

The chief then leaned forward and said, "Now, I'm going to get up and walk out of here, and I am going to give the three of you one hour to come up with a plan to make those 1,343 warrants go away." As he was speaking, he was shaking the audit in front of his face. The chief then got up and walked out, leaving the three of us sitting there behind closed doors to discuss the matter.

The captain looked at both of us, and we all agreed that the chief had just asked us to do something completely unethical, as well as against the law. With God as my witness, the three of us sat there for one hour, shot the bull, and joked around. We did all agree, however, that word had to get to the outside so someone would know what the chief had ordered us to do. The chief had been there approximately two years and had a rocky relationship with the county council already, not to mention the old-timers who still resented his being hired over more qualified staff. The chief came back in after an hour had elapsed, and the captain told him we had come up with a plan. It was a good thing he did not ask what it was; there was no plan.

At the time, a police commission with a county administrator and two deputy administrators, one of which was also the public safety director, controlled the police department. The administrators answered directly to the county council. I knew the director personally and had attended several social events where we had become acquainted. The captain got word to the public safety director, and within days the three of us were called individually to his office downtown to answer questions as he completed his investigation.

Almost immediately—because of this incident and a compilation of other issues—the chief was terminated. The department was jubilant, the ranking major of operations was placed in the position as interim chief, and my captain, Carroll, was promoted into his position as major.

After the chief's termination, someone who was a close friend to the director of public safety told me that he had made his final decision after hearing what I had said during my interview with him. Several people had told him about my work ethic and how honest I was. This made me feel good in a way, but I questioned my own loyalty for a minute because loyalty is one of the lifelong traits I had learned from the Marine Corps. Another of those traits is trust, however, so after thinking it over I felt better knowing that I had, in fact, done the right thing. I had also put to use the traits of discipline, responsibility, and respect. I mentioned earlier that you sometimes come across leaders that you *have to* respect because of their rank but have a hard time respecting them as people. That said, I have to recognize that he did do one good thing as chief: he promoted me to sergeant.

The new interim chief was a good guy who always looked out for his people, and he had a good reputation as a leader. He actually inherited the position because he was the highest ranking officer below the chief. He was very approachable and someone you could easily sit and talk with. He was an old-school cop with twenty-five years on the job with Charleston County. He had a habit of walking around headquarters and stopping in at each office to check on people and was, above all, well respected.

After I had been in the Warrants Unit for about eighteen months, I expressed an interest in going to the Criminal Investigations Division (CID) to replace a sergeant there who was rumored to be transferring soon.

One day in late August, my old METRO lieutenant, Eddie, who was now a captain and who had been the commanding officer of CID approached me and asked if I was ready to come upstairs. CID was referred to as "upstairs" (and still is) because it is the only unit on the second floor of the headquarters building. I told him that I was extremely eager to work for him again. He told me the move would happen within the next week to ten days. I was ecstatic and immediately called Paula in New York to tell her the good news. Our wedding was planned for the following March, and everything now seemed to be falling back into place for me.

 I called Paul, my lieutenant, and advised him that the change would be forthcoming since he needed time to figure out who my replacement would be. He had been a great guy to work for, and I had learned a lot. The last eighteen months in what was essentially a desk position served as a great foundation administratively to my career in law enforcement.

CRIMINAL INVESTIGATIONS

21

IN EARLY SEPTEMBER, I WAS TRANSFERRED UPSTAIRS AND assigned as the property crimes sergeant. I was now responsible for ten investigators and three civilians for administrative support. The Person Crime Unit was across the hall and had six investigators as well as two Juvenile crime investigators. A persons crime is any crime against a person such as, rape, assault, stabbing, shooting, or homicide. As a collective group, "upstairs" had sixteen investigators, two sergeants, a lieutenant, and a captain.

The other sergeant was a friend named John who had been in CID for quite a few years and who was known as a top-notch investigator and supervisor. He and I would take turns every other month "taking call," which meant that for any issue that arose after 10:00 p.m., we were called at home to take appropriate action and, when necessary, to respond to a crime scene ourselves.

We worked alternating shifts: one shift ran from 8:00 a.m. to 4:00 p.m., the other from 2:00 p.m. to 10:00 p.m., so we overlapped for two hours from 2:00 p.m. to 4:00 p.m. John and I got along well, which was paramount for the entire office to run smoothly.

My new lieutenant, Ernie, was an old-school guy and a stickler for detail and punctuality. He wanted all of his eight-to-four investigators at their desks at eight and not a minute later. Ernie was highly respected and had paid his dues with many years on the job. He was the Crime Scene sergeant who had chewed on my butt my first week on the job when he found out there was a suicide note and that it had been removed. His upward mobility had been hampered, most believed, because he was so effective in running the crime lab that he was passed over for promotion because bosses did not want him to leave. Ernie had been an artillery marine in Vietnam and was now a senior staff NCO in the Army Reserves, so he was as deaf as I was, a fact we often joked about.

The captain was Eddie, who I had worked for in METRO. Both the lieutenant and the captain wanted to be apprised only about after-hours developments or when major crimes occurred. Unless an incident was a major event, neither of them generally responded to crime scenes, though that would soon change. They both knew they had a good crew and let us do what we had to do without too much oversight or input.

The office had three secretaries, and two were the best I had ever seen. They could both easily type eighty to over one hundred words per minute, transcribe with the best, and, most importantly, multitask. Carol was married to the chief of a local police department, and Avie was married to the major of another local department. I had known Carol for several years because she worked for a magistrate where I used to set cases. Avie was a very quiet girl who had lost her first husband in the late 1970s to an in-the-line-of-duty police death. The third secretary was probably working at a level way above her competence. It took me some time to properly deal with her shortcomings and to deal eventually with her issues.

I was assigned to property crimes, but that did not mean that I was limited to supervising only property crimes. If a "person's crime" occurred on your shift, it was yours to work. A property crime is a crime against property, such as a burglary, any type of larceny or theft, vandalism, white-collar crime, fraudulent checks, and stolen vehicles.

It was the duty of the 8:00 a.m. sergeant to read all paperwork generated by all officers in the department on a daily basis. It was from those reports that cases were assigned to investigators.

I quickly found out that case management was a high priority, and the previous sergeant had let the management of property-crime cases deteriorate. With ten investigators and a caseload for each one at approximately twenty-five to thirty cases each, keeping track was of utmost importance. Case management involved having individual investigators bring their cases to me to check on the progress of their cases, available leads, and the existence or non-existence of evidence. The decision to continue or close a case depended on whether additional leads were available or the leads had all been exhausted.

Not long after my arrival, I found a piece of evidence in a file that should have been entered and placed into evidence. It was a shell casing from a shooting, and its omission from the file was a major breech of policy and procedure on the part of the investigator. I had no alternative but to suspend the employee without pay for two days, which had a positive effect on the others of ensuring that I did not catch any other violations while checking case files. It also sort of put people on notice that I was serious. By no means did I come into the unit to prove anything, but this was something that I could not ignore.

With all of my investigative experience being in drug enforcement, I thought I would be at a disadvantage in property crimes, but when I started reading the names on reports and following trends in different neighborhoods where drug sales were prevalent, I quickly saw a connection: the same scumbag users and dealers I had been dealing with for years were committing property crimes to get the cash to buy and sell drugs. To understand what was happening was to know the people in certain areas of the county. Since I had been used to working all districts in Charleston County while working in METRO, I knew most of the players in the various neighborhoods, which made it easier to give specific instructions to whatever investigator I assigned to work a particular case.

In South Carolina, cases were officially "cleared" by categorizing a case in one of several ways. Cases could be categorized, for instance, as "cleared by arrest" (CBA) or "unfounded" (U). The latter meant the investigation proved that the crime was erroneously categorized or had never happened (for instance, many times a report was titled a burglary, when it was only a trespassing or vandalism). A third category was "inactivate" (I), which meant putting the case on the "back burner" until more leads were generated. The last category of clearance was "exceptionally cleared" (EX/C), which meant that you determined who the suspect was by name and had enough information to identify a suspect to make an arrest, but for whatever reason did not charge that particular person.

A great example of an EX/C situation occurred when there was a rash of burglaries in several neighborhoods on James Island, and my guys had not been unable to develop a suspect. One night, they responded to an attempted robbery of a bar on James Island, where a guy pulled a gun on the bar owner and his wife as they were leaving with the night's receipts. Well, Mr. Crook never counted on the fact that the owner may have been armed with a weapon. When the guy pulled his gun, the owner pulled his own gun from his back pocket and shot the crook dead right where he stood. When my guys responded to investigate, the first thing they did was to run the serial number of the suspect's weapon. Our computer check indicated that it had been stolen during one of the recent local unsolved burglaries. Even though the burglary suspect was now dead, we concluded that he was probably the person who had committed the burglaries, so we "exceptionally cleared" them to the suspect, even though he was now dead.

I was proud of the fact that although the national clearance rate of crimes in the United States is usually in the 60 to 65 percent range, we consistently cleared about 70 percent or more of our cases.

My investigators were assigned districts of the county to work crimes committed in specific areas, and I immediately recognized that the thieves did not work within geographical boundaries. Because of the existing arrangement, multiple investigators may be working crimes committed by the same person(s). I quickly campaigned to change this arrangement and to allow my guys to work anywhere in the county they needed to. This strategy showed immediate success.

The new sergeant of the crime lab was an older cop named Lenny. He had risen to the rank of captain and had been forced to retire as a result of heart surgery. He fully recovered from his heart issues, re-applied to the department several years later as a police officer, and was rapidly promoted to the rank of sergeant. A lot had changed while Lenny was a civilian, so he knew he needed to ask advice from some who may have previously worked for him and who were now his peers or superiors. Lenny was highly respected and ran a tight ship. He was as hard a worker as anyone I have ever seen who was half his age. Not long after my arrival, his son Kenny started working for me as an investigator in property crimes.

I quickly recognized that there was a lot of stolen property to be recovered. I began to teach my guys how easy it was to prepare a search warrant and to seize property that had obviously been stolen but where or whom it was stolen from was unknown. It was much easier to research stolen property when you were not rushed to find the owner than when you knew who it had been stolen from. It did not take but a few months of search warrants and seized property before Lenny came to me bitching about all of the property that was filling his evidence bins and warehouse. His own son, Kenny, had become one of the biggest reasons for the influx of evidence—he was doing a first-rate job of locking up thieves and seizing stolen property.

On September 21, 1990, within a few weeks of my arrival in the office, we had a homicide. An arrest followed quickly. When a homicide occurs, all available people are called out, less one or two to handle normal issues that arise. Anyone familiar with the TV show *The First 48* knows how important it is for investigators to work any lead and to stay hard on the case for at least the first two days after the crime has been committed. The first forty-eight hours are especially important because the chances of solving a murder declines drastically as time goes by.

Our process worked like this: once a case agent was assigned a homicide to investigate, he was in charge of his case from that minute forward. Many times he would spend time at his desk and supervise what he needed to have done by troops as information developed. All information in a case was run past that case agent for input and/or rejection. Many times ideas were passed around as a group working a case bounced ideas out for discussion. We knew that the more brains we had providing input, the better. I cannot count how many times cases were solved on hunches thrown out to a group of investigators over a cup of coffee.

Speaking of coffee, we had a coffee fund that we contributed to each payday, and we put Carol in charge of that. The money was kept under lock and key, and she purchased supplies such coffee, cream, sugar, etc. One dollar of our contribution went to a flower fund, which was for flowers when an immediate family member was hospitalized or died. Well, Carol took her job seriously because, if one of the guys did not pay his three dollars each payday, she would repossess his coffee cup and hold it for ransom until he paid up.

***

HOMICIDES

Over my entire law enforcement career, the arrest of someone responsible for taking another's life was the most rewarding feeling of accomplishment we could have. To kill someone is the ultimate violation of our civilized society, and I always slept well after participating in a case that took a killer off the street.

We had a great group of investigators and had many young prospects champing at the bit, waiting for someone either to be promoted out of the unit or transferred. An officer had to have at least eighteen months on the job before he or she was eligible to go into a specialized unit. In time, we ended up with a crew of young hard chargers who were never afraid to put in the necessary hours to get the job done. I sometimes had to tell them to go home so they would not get burned out.

In November of 1990, there was a referendum vote before the citizens of Charleston County to decide whether our police department should be merged with the Charleston County Sheriff's Office. The referendum was worded in a confusing manner, and to everyone's surprise, the referendum went in favor of the merge. On that day, John and I were in Florida attending a week-long class on Commanding a Detective Office. We were both extremely surprised to hear the voting results and did not know what to expect when the merge took place in January of 1991.

The Sheriff's Office was presently responsible for the management of the county jail and had only thirty-seven sworn deputies who worked on the street. The sheriff, however, was a career law enforcement officer who had paid his dues. He started with the soon-to-be gone Charleston County Police Department, then went to the North Charleston Police Department, and rose to the rank of lieutenant. He then decided to go to law school and returned in 1984 as the chief of the North Charleston Police Department until 1987. He was elected sheriff in 1988 and had been the sheriff ever since. He was and remains a highly respected career law enforcement officer, and we were all anxious to see what would happen to us.

December ended with two homicides, one on the nineteenth with a quick arrest and clearance, and another on the thirtieth, which was not discovered until January 1—also the first day with both departments coming together as a unified sheriff's office. A daughter and her husband found her mother in her bed deceased. This case started out as a "whodunit" case because the deceased was discovered at least two days after her death. The forty-seven-year-old victim had been stabbed, and her eighty-three-year-old mother was in the house for two days, not realizing that her daughter was dead. This last homicide was listed as a 1990 case since the date of death was estimated to have occurred on December 30. We ended 1990 with nine homicides for the year, which was the norm.

Since this was technically the first homicide for the sheriff's office, several members of the sheriff's staff, as well as the sheriff himself, responded. Their presence was well intended, but they definitely got in the way and caused some issues for investigators. We were fortunate to be finally able to develop a suspect and make an arrest.

Many people do not understand that even though the police make an arrest, there is much more work involved in a homicide investigation after the arrest. A motive for the crime must be established, and all evidence must be precisely documented and analyzed because preparation for trial is of the utmost importance.

January 1991 began just as 1990 ended, with homicides: one each on January 14, 19, and 25. The first month of the year had produced one-third of the entire previous year's totals.

The January 14 case was a common type of occurrence in a club after a verbal dispute over a girl. This incident resulted in an immediate arrest and closure.

The January 19 case was a female cab driver found shot to death in her cab on the edge of a neighborhood known for drug dealers and prostitutes within blocks of the Navy Base. The responding officer found the cab unattended and running, with three spent shell casings in the backseat floorboard, which meant she was probably shot by someone from the backseat.

While investigators were at the scene to process the evidence, it began to rain very hard, and we had to try to preserve what we could of the crime scene. We were now two weeks into being under the auspices of the Sheriff's Office, and again the sheriff, the chief deputy, the major, the captain, and the lieutenant all responded. Before the merger, the brass almost never responded to a crime scene unless it was major, but now they knew that the sheriff and his chief deputy were coming out for everything, so everybody else felt they needed to respond as well, even though no one else was really needed. The brass from the old department did not want to be outdone by their new bosses.

One good thing that did occur by all of the new response from the brass was that we began to get equipment that we never had before. The old department ran a very tight budget, and it was hard to get things unless it was in the budget. A quick result of the merge was that the day after the taxicab murder, every investigator was issued a tarpaulin to keep in our trunk to protect our crime scenes if it rained. Another homicide response was on a bitterly cold night and the chief deputy saw to it that we all had new winter jackets within a week. We were now seeing the benefits of the merge in departments, and when you give cops good equipment, they quit bitching. The same thing proved to be true in the military because marines were used to hand-me-down antiquated equipment, but when they got something new, they too quit bitching. The old saying "A bitching marine is a happy marine" translated well to law enforcement. It was very evident that the sheriff had more discretion in spending his money the way he saw fit, which was a definite plus to the troops.

Unfortunately, we never made an arrest of the taxicab murderer, and it was the only murder not cleared by arrest in my entire tenure in Criminal Investigations.

The homicide on the twenty-fifth was another in a club that started out as verbal altercation and ended with the victim being shot in the face. The weapon was recovered, and an arrest was made very quickly.

I spent the entire month of January 1991 attending the prestigious Medical Examiners School at the Medical University of South Carolina in downtown Charleston. This was a much-sought-after training class offered to one investigator per month to a law enforcement agency in the area. Although I did not participate in the investigations of the three homicides I just described, I was present at all three autopsies of the victims in these cases and was very familiar with each case.

This was a hands-on class in which I was assigned to respond with the county coroner or his deputy to any questionable death during the month of January. We also participated in all autopsies performed during the month. During the month, I attended and participated in approximately forty-five to fifty autopsies, and the unique learning experience was that it was completely narrated and explained by the doctor performing the procedure. This knowledge made future cases easier to investigate and understand. I participated in autopsies of burn victims, gunshot and stabbing victims, drowning victims, and at least two infant deaths. By the end of the month, I was ready to get back to work, but I enjoyed my month of death immensely. More importantly, I got to work hand in hand with two great and very well respected forensic pathologists, Dr. Sandra Conradi and Dr. Clay Nichols.

My return on February 1 brought me right back to the usual caseload of my guys and catching up with things. I had been going into the office after being at the hospital each day for about an hour so I would not fall behind in case management. I was going to get married on March 10 in New Jersey and then take a week-long vacation in Mexico, so I had six weeks to catch up and leave again for the wedding and honeymoon.

Almost as soon as I got back from the month-long Medical Examiners School, I was bombarded by complaints from some of my guys regarding the third secretary who had issues because she was not proficient in spelling and failing to properly proofread her work. We were working from IBM electric typewriters, just before the switch to computers. When one of my guys had a case for which he or she needed a warrant affidavit typed, he or she gave it to her in handwritten form, and she typed it so the investigator could take it to a judge for the actual arrest warrant for an impending arrest. My guys complained that she was transposing dates, misspelling words, and, in some cases, putting the wrong statute of law next to the charge.

My solution to this was to bring me all work that this secretary did for them, and I would proof the work with a red pen, document the mistakes, and counsel her accordingly. She was a longtime employee, and proper procedure had to be followed in order to take progressive disciplinary steps and to give her the opportunity to improve. She was working at a position way over her competence, and I, for the life of me, could not figure out how she was ever selected for this, a very vital position in CID.

So far, as a sergeant I had to deal with the female employee who assaulted her coworker in the ladies room. I now had to deal with a female employee who bordered on incompetence and had to take the necessary steps to have her transferred. As a sergeant in the Marine Corps, I never had to deal with female employees because I never had any. Now as a police sergeant, I was being tested in the delicate handling of female employee issues. This was only the beginning.

Unbelievably, I had to counsel this same employee for not wearing shoes in the office. She was in a position where she regularly met citizens and attorneys who came into the office to meet various investigators. She was from the country and thought that it was fine to go barefoot in the office. This practice was very unprofessional and improper, so I counseled her accordingly. Never in my wildest dreams did I ever think that being a supervisor would involve the issues that I was forced to deal with.

Another ticklish and delicate issue involved another female employee. I received regular complaints from coworkers that the female in question, who was an investigator, and a good one I might add, offended them because of her extreme issue with body odor. It was hard to miss if you came closer than five feet away and was especially bad in the winter when she wore sweaters. I counseled her and gave her the opportunity to go home to shower and to change her clothes. I think I handled this matter as professionally and delicately as possible with positive results.

My idea to proofread every document the secretary produced proved to be her demise. I was able to place her on probation with subpar performance evaluations and eventually had her laterally transferred to another position within the police department, thus, saving her job. Once she was transferred, morale in the office immediately improved, and we were able to replace her with an employee who knew how to produce quality work.

So much for dealing with subordinate employees. John, the other sergeant, laughed when I told him what I was dealing with, and he repeatedly stated he was glad that the problems stayed on my side of the hallway.

March came and I loaded my entire family of three kids, my daughter's boyfriend and future husband, my mother, and grandmother into a rented fifteen-passenger van for my wedding in New Jersey. The wedding went off without any issues, and we left the following day for our honeymoon in Mexico. My oldest son, Doug, was my best man and was responsible for driving the family back to Charleston and for the children to resume their high school classes. We enjoyed our week alone—no phones, no pagers, no middle of the night calls and callouts. When we returned from Mexico, we loaded my wife's car and made the eight hundred-mile drive south to Charleston.

***

I returned to work on or about March 20 and missed only one homicide while I was gone, which was solved quickly with an arrest. There was another on May 21 that was also cleared quickly by arrest. We had now had five homicides in as many months and were on track to break the record for homicides in a single year, an unwanted record for sure.

By early May, we received the great news from our doctor that Paula was pregnant, which was, of course, her first child and my fourth. We broke the news to my children and were met with a mixed response. My oldest, Christy, was graduating from high school that month and had planned to go out on her own, eventually sharing an apartment for a short time with her mother. My wife was still adjusting to her new life as a married woman eight hundred miles from home, with an instant family, and now pregnant. She had the added issues of being accepted by my boys, who did manage to test her as often as possible. They all grew to love my new wife and to accept her as the person I chose to spend the rest of my life with. More importantly, they accepted their new brother when he arrived.

Paula was extremely understanding of my weird hours and being called out in the middle of the night and never once complained. I tried never to bring my work home with me and kept quiet about some of the morbid and unusual things I had to deal with on the job, but both of my boys pumped me with questions because of their extreme interest in what I did.

My two boys were fourteen and sixteen and had been involved in the Charleston County Police Explorer program, which was a form of scouting and a great venue for kids interested in law enforcement to participate in. The Police Explorer program was open to boys and girls, and the sheriff's office had a very active group with about twenty to twenty-five members. Their advisors were the traffic squad lieutenant and one of his deputies. The lieutenant had asked me to assist since my two boys were involved, and I agreed. I quickly saw that they needed better quality training since the one advisor was very weak. I jumped in with both feet and began to attend weekly meetings. I then began teaching the cadets the same subjects taught to all deputies in training.

The Explorers had a rank structure from sergeant to lieutenant to captain to major, which was the ranking officer in the unit. Prior to my arrival, my son Doug was promoted to the rank of major—he ran the meetings in the absence of an adult advisor. We trained hard, and I quickly saw the kids thrive and become more confident with every class completed. There were other cadet posts within the area, and from what I saw at some of the competitions, we were far better than the others.

They all attend a yearly statewide competition called SCALES, which stands for South Carolina Association of Law Enforcement Explorers. The competition lasts an entire week at a different city in South Carolina each summer. The explorers compete from morning until evening daily, with nightly activities to keep them busy. I went with the group to the week-long competition held in Pickens County in the upstate of South Carolina. My cadets did well and took first place trophies in several categories. My oldest son, had been nominated to be considered for Cadet of the Year. He competed against many other candidates with independent judges and received the award as 1991 Police Cadet of the Year in the state of South Carolina. He won it again in 1993 as well as the J. Edgar Hoover FBI Scholarship Award upon his graduation from high school.

***

On Friday June 14, the day shift was getting ready to go for the day and to start our weekend off. I got a phone call at about 4:30 p.m. from the captain of another local police department who had received a tip that there may be a dead body in a mobile home in our jurisdiction. I grabbed the only guy left in the office, Kenny, and told him to follow me to the mobile home park located in North Charleston.

We arrived and found the door locked, but there were some open windows. I recall that there was an orange extension cord running from an adjoining mobile home, which was the source of power to the home. Kenny and I crawled into a window and slowly cleared the house (searched), which was a mess, not because it had been ransacked but because the homeowner was extremely messy. Dirty dishes were piled in the sink, the cabinets were almost empty, and roaches were running all over. I entered the master bedroom and saw that it was clear, but when I slid the closet door open and looked into the closet, I saw what appeared to be a female body rolled up in a small area rug. I took her pulse, but she was cold to the touch. Her wrists were bound by rope, and a rope was around her neck. We immediately backed out of the house to secure it and to make the appropriate notifications, i.e., crime scene techs, additional investigators, the coroner, and my superiors.

Within minutes of calling the homicide in on my cell phone, there were the five investigators that I had requested, my lieutenant, my captain, a major, two chiefs, and the sheriff, as well as a newspaper reporter. Six months after the merge of departments, we were still having issues with too many of the brass showing up at crime scenes. The new hierarchy had not yet figured out that they were not needed at these scenes, but they persisted.

The newspaper reporter was there because the reporters had figured out that handheld scanners with the proper frequencies could monitor cell-phone conversations, which tied our hands somewhat when trying to communicate via cell phone to avoid giving away our positions on the police radio. When I saw all of the brass on scene, I knew we had potential problems. I assigned the case agent who would be working the case and gave out assignments to my guys verbally on scene to avoid using the cell phone.

Ernie, my lieutenant, knew we knew what we were doing and came to me and asked me what I needed. My response was "Keep that fucking brass away from this trailer," and his response was "You got it." He was well aware of the problems we were having and did exactly what he said he would—he kept them all away. One of the chiefs from the old sheriff's office had already come to the front door wanting me to show him the body, but I politely turned him down. While the brass was all outside we had a torrential downpour, which served its purpose, it made them go to their cars and/or leave. Mission accomplished.

We very quickly developed a lead in the form of a suspect. The victim was a twenty-three-year-old girl married to a sailor who was out to sea. She had apparently gotten pregnant by another sailor, the suspect, while her husband was out to sea, and the suspect killed her to remove his problem. He then made the mistake of telling someone what he had done, which generated the tip to the other police department.

We were able to obtain video of some ATM transactions made after the victim's estimated time of death with her ATM card. We knew who to look for and within three hours of finding the body, my guys located him in a convenience store about four miles away. He was in the Navy and immediately invoked his constitutional rights to refuse to talk to investigators without an attorney present. We developed tons of evidence, made our case, and prepared for trial. The suspect was convicted and subsequently sentenced to life in prison, where he remains.

Just two weeks later, on June 29, we had our seventh homicide of the year. This was a stabbing death, and the victim and suspect were both migrant farm workers. The incident was the result of a long night of alcohol consumption that ended in a fistfight that escalated into the suspect pulling a knife and fatally stabbing the victim. Fortunately, for us, the patrol sergeant on duty that day was a Hispanic male and a former investigator who managed to translate much information from several witnesses of the incident. We allowed him to take all of the written statements for us, which was a great help.

Just 15 days later, on July 14, we responded to our eighth homicide, which was, fortunately, a very easy one to solve, with an arrest within hours of our notification.

One night at about 9:30 p.m., while getting ready to leave the office for the night on the two to ten shift, I received a call from the local Crime Stoppers office that it had received a reliable tip. The tip was that a local fugitive "Jimmy B," with an outstanding arrest warrant for Assault and Battery With the Intent to Kill, was presently at his mother's house. He was well known to local cops and wanted for a shooting at a local football game the previous year that wounded an innocent student leaving the game. I had previous dealings with him and knew him by sight. He had been shot in the leg several years prior and walked with the aid of a wooden cane.

I grabbed Kenny and Jerry, and the three of us went to the house in question, and due to the nature of the felony charge, we went into the house to look for him. I found him hiding under his mother's bed in the master bedroom after she, of course, told me that he was not there. When I checked his pockets, I found a large quantity of cash—seven or eight hundred dollars—which I took and threw on the bed because he would not need the cash in the jail.

We took him to jail and gladly lodged him, which eventually resulted in a conviction and prison time for the charge we arrested him on. While at the jail, I got a call on my cell phone from my old partner John in METRO who asked if we were just at "Jimmy B's" house. I told him that we had been, and we just arrested him for an outstanding warrant. He proceeded to tell me that he and his guys had just made a purchase of a large quantity of cocaine from "Jimmy B" minutes before our arrival. John asked if I had seen any money while we were there, and I told him that I had taken seven or eight hundred dollars out of his pockets. John sounded relieved until he asked where the money was. When I told him I left it all sitting on the bed, he sighed and could not believe what I had done. He said that their "buy money" was part of that money and was of, course, cash that they had made copies of before the buy. Well, that shot their drug buy all to hell, but the important thing was that he was eventually going to prison, where he belonged. I did not know it at the time, but I would deal with "Jimmy B" again in the summer of 2000.

***

On September 15, we investigated the sad death of an infant who had died at the hands of his eighteen-year-old mother. One of my guys attended the autopsy, where the medical examiner ruled it to be a homicide. Working these type of cases was sad and depressing, but nonetheless, a homicide. This case was investigated by one of the juvenile investigators and did not sap any manpower to work because one investigator worked the whole thing.

Just four days later on September 19, we had our tenth homicide of the year. Two female roommates, aged thirty-three and thirty-seven, had apparently gotten into a verbal argument in their home that escalated to a point where a gun was introduced into the argument. The girl who answered the door to deputies who responded was covered in blood and immediately told the deputies that she shot her roommate. The deputies found the victim in the master bedroom with a gunshot wound to the upper chest. Every room from the front door to the victim was covered in blood, which indicated that they continued to argue after the fatal shot was fired. The suspect was charged with Murder and found guilty of the lesser charge of Manslaughter but still received a lengthy prison sentence.

The next homicide we handled was on October 22, when a group of male subjects jumped a nineteen-year-old kid who was on his way to work at a local chain grocery store. The problem with this case was that there were six suspects. The incident occurred in an old, pre-WWII neighborhood that used to be housing for Navy Yard workers and was almost now totally rental homes occupied by low-income citizens.

I was the first investigator to arrive at the crime scene and observed the victim lying in a semi- fetal position in a drainage ditch on the side of the road. I quickly made the determination after gathering information, without a doubt in my mind, that this was a racially motivated hate crime committed by six black, male subjects against a white, male victim. This was a fact that we would never let on to the press because the press had a habit of often making matters worse by irresponsible reporting. In those days, the Sheriff's Office did not have a public information officer, and CID supervisors regularly gave statements to the press, which John and I did regularly. Whoever worked the day shift was regularly called by radio, television, and newspaper reporters when they knew something had happened or if news was slow, and they were hunting for a story.

Although I participated heavily in the investigation, John directly supervised this case because it happened on his shift before I went home for the day. We had all personnel out on this case because we knew we had six suspects to round up as quickly as possible. The victim had managed to cut one of his assailants deeply on the leg with a box cutter while he was down on the ground being severely beaten. We sent an investigator to the hospital to take that wounded suspect into custody once released from the hospital. It was from our interviews with that suspect that we were able to identify all of the suspects. We responded to the scene at approximately 4:30 p.m. and were out until the early morning hours banging on doors and stopping cars, following up on leads. We arrested at least three the first night, and within two days, we had arrested all participants, ranging in age from fifteen to twenty.

A local newspaper reporter interviewed John the evening of the murder, from which he was quoted as stating that the crime was a racially motivated hate crime, which was, as predicted, sensationalized on the front page of the paper the following morning. John told it just like it was, and what he said was the truth, which I emphatically agreed with.

Of course, this quote now brought the TV media back the following day to try to get someone else to echo the same type of statement. The following morning, my captain called me into his office and told me to tell any media reporter making inquiries that the crime was *not* racially motivated and was *not* a hate crime. Of course, I disagreed and told the captain so, but he said that he was ordered to defuse the situation, which now pitted me against one of my best friends and coworker, John. I reluctantly complied, which actually caused more issues because I refuted what another supervisor had said.

All six went to trial, and five were convicted. Unfortunately, one juvenile who was being charged as an adult for Murder was found not guilty, a verdict for which I accept total responsibility. This one juvenile and one of the instigators was being interviewed with his father present because he was a juvenile, and he refused to cooperate with the investigator. I spoke to his dad who was mad because he was not cooperating, and he gave me permission to get into his ass to try to scare him into doing the right thing. I went in with the other investigator and asked the juvenile if he knew he could spend the rest of his life in prison. He said no and ended up cooperating and providing crucial information in the case, and he provided a full confession.

The trial was held before a jury brought in from the upper part of the state because his court-appointed attorneys said he would not get a fair trial unless a jury was brought in from the outside. The defendant was extremely lucky in that his court-appointed attorneys were experienced in representing murder suspects. The defense attorney brought out the fact that I told the juvenile he could spend the rest of his life in prison, which is not true for a juvenile, even one being charged as an adult. My threat was intended to scare him into talking, which he did. That technicality ended up being a major point of the interview, and the jury eventually found him not guilty. The attorney had made the right move by asking for an outside jury because everyone in our area clearly remembered this brutal and senseless murder. Five out of six was not bad, but I took his verdict personally for a long time.

Sometime in 1991, the lieutenant in charge of investigations for the North Charleston Police Department came to see me to inquire whether we had been having any unsolved rapes. She told me that they had a rash of them with the same method of operation, and they were beginning to think that there was a serial rapist on the loose.

Not long after our conversation, North Charleston Police determined that they did have a probable serial rapist on the loose, and by then our agency had similar cases. A Task Force was established, paying particular attention to apartment complexes, which is where the majority of the crimes were occurring. The joint investigation had determined that the unsolved rapes had dated back to 1990 and now into late 1991. Our agency provided continuous manpower of investigators to the Task

Force, which was assigned for thirty days at a time. As time progressed, there were other rapes committed in nearby Summerville, then in downtown Charleston.

To date, all but two of his victims had been in an apartment complex. In one particular case, he entered a residence and forced a fourteen year-old to perform oral sex on him and returned four months later and sexually assaulted her mother.

Once the local press found out about the existence of a Task Force, they sensationalized the cases to a point where the press jeopardized the investigation. Unfortunately, the press became aware of the situation when a nosy, female TV reporter read a work schedule for Task Force members on a bulletin board in our own office. We continued to provide manpower to the task force until the case culminated more than a year later.

***

We had a homicide on November 11 out in rural McClellanville, about forty miles north of Charleston, and we were able to quickly solve the case with an arrest. The victim's own son killed the victim over money, which is often the case.

Just a week later on November 18, we had yet another homicide—our thirteenth of the year. We were already several cases beyond our yearly average of nine or ten. I got the call shortly after 3:00 a.m. when my buddy Sam, the patrol supervisor, called to advise me of a victim being shot in front of an apartment complex in an area known for dealing illegal narcotics. I called headquarters to have at least six investigators to respond and to meet me at the crime scene.

Whenever we have a homicide in a neighborhood, crowds gathered automatically. Many times the crowd is responsible for hindering our efforts in working a crime scene, and many times the person responsible for the murder is in the crowd looking to see what is going on and to throw off others about his possible involvement. I cannot remember how many times I have instructed an investigator to take a camera and start shooting pictures of the crowd, even if there was no film in the camera. Almost every time we did this, for whatever reason, the entire crowd would disperse. This was especially true in African-American neighborhoods, where, for whatever reason, blacks hated having their picture taken. There were several instances in which we took a surveillance van to the funeral of a murder victim and took pictures of those in attendance, searching for leads.

Even though it was 4:00 a.m., I recall a large crowd had gathered, and the crowd was quiet and fine until the time came to remove the body from the scene. As soon as the crowd saw the transport vehicle arrive, they began to wail. When the body was placed on a gurney and covered, their wailing came to a fever pitch, which escalated to screams and outright hollering and fainting by some. I had come to learn that this was the way that blacks dealt with death. I had often seen the same thing happen, even when there was a simple neighborhood death of natural causes of an elderly person.

Just five days later on Saturday, November 23, I received a call at 6:30 a.m.—at least I slept the entire night this time. This was our fourteenth murder in eleven months. When I arrived at the crime scene, I saw that the victim was a sixty-six-year-old male who had been stabbed multiple times and had been left in a sitting position with his back against the fence. The fact that he was stabbed so many times indicated a crime of passion, which often happens in homicides involving family members or between lovers while arguing. A crime of passion is generally not a premeditated act and occurs because of sudden rage.

The victim had apparently been arguing in the backyard over the fact that his son was not going to work that day, which resulted in the son fatally stabbing his dad. Because he was sitting against the fence, his son probably placed him there after the act was committed. The suspect was quickly identified and was the same person I had arrested several years prior as he was getting into the shower in a motel room we had under surveillance. His nickname was "Z," and he had ended up testifying for the state and helped to convict our supplier. We quickly prepared an arrest warrant for Murder for "Z" and spent all day looking for him. "Z" was still on probation for the drug charge that I had previously arrested him for. He had been, by all indications, a model citizen since.

After about twelve hours, I went home to shower and shave, and as I was getting out of the shower, I got a call that my guys had "Z" in custody, but he would not talk to any of them and was asking for me specifically. His family knew that I had given him a break in life for his drug arrest, and his family convinced him to turn himself in. He told my guys that he would talk to me and only me. I immediately went back to the office and was briefed while "Z" was waiting in an interview room. Danny and I went into the room, and when "Z" saw me, he immediately blurted out, "Gunny, I killed him, man! I don't know why, but I killed him!" I was amazed at how quickly he spoke without provocation. He knew me by my nickname given to me in METRO, and he knew that I had been honest with him when he was arrested on the drug charge and had been given a second chance, and, most of all, he still trusted me. "Z" had blown it all in a momentary fit of rage and went to prison after his conviction and remains where he probably belongs and where he can no longer harm anyone.

On December 10, we had our fifteenth homicide of the year, which started out as a whodunit with absolutely nothing to go on. Deputies responded to a nicely kept mobile-home park to a trailer where a neighbor had asked to check on her friend. When the deputies entered the house, they discovered a deceased twenty-year-old female in her bedroom, lying on the floor naked, and she appeared to have been sexually assaulted. The victim was a student at a local college and was married to a sailor. She had been killed while her husband was standing a twenty-four-hour tour of duty at the Navy Base.

Because this homicide happened in the middle of a series of other unsolved rapes being investigated by the previously mentioned task force, this case drew much attention. We all thought that this may have been the work of the serial rapist, and he just may have gone too far this time and also committed a murder. Because of this fact, the State Law Enforcement Division (SLED) responded to assist in the processing of the crime scene. It appeared that the victim had been brutally assaulted and strangled by an electrical cord found at the scene. Dr. Nichols, one of the forensic pathologists that I trained with during Medical Examiners School also responded so he could inspect the body in the exact state it was discovered prior to doing the autopsy.

We worked this case nonstop for twenty-four hours and finally managed to establish a suspect, who happened to be a neighbor living across the street. When police were at the scene processing the house, the suspect was out in the street with neighbors talking about the crime. He, of course, knew that the victim's husband was away for periods of time standing duty, and when first questioned early on, he had made several inconsistent statements. He was taken into custody and placed in the backseat of my car with Jerry and Kenny, two of my guys, on either side of him. I was driving and had a brand-new investigator sitting up front with me.

Quite often when you have a suspect and a long ride back to the office, it is common to obtain a confession from a suspect before you ever get to an interview room. Suspects often feel comfortable enough that their personal ordeal is over that they begin to blurt out incriminating information. Well, Jerry and Kenny had primed the suspect well, and he was feeling very comfortable and talking freely, so hearing this I was not rushing and took a circuitous route back to the office. The suspect was primed and ready to spill his guts, and just before he gave it all up, he said something to the effect of "Do you think I need an attorney?" He had already been given his Miranda Warning advising him of his constitutional rights, so that was not an issue. When the suspect made that statement, the college-educated rookie investigator up front with me turned around and started to say he had asked for an attorney. Before he got half of his statement out, I reached over and, with my fist, backhanded the rookie in his stomach, knocking the wind out of him. He never said another word. The suspect proceeded to spill his guts and confessed in detail to killing his neighbor.

The suspect never said, "I want an attorney and will no longer talk to you." He asked us a question: "Do you think I need an attorney?" We had not violated his rights and knew how to get around that question. The rookie in the front seat had not been involved in many, if any, criminal interviews and had a lot to learn.

The next day when I came in to work, Ernie, my lieutenant, called me into his office and asked if I had denied the murder suspect his constitutional rights last night. I told him that I did not and proceeded to explain exactly what happened. Getting someone to confess to a murder, the most serious of all crimes in our society, is an art form that takes a long time to develop as an investigator. I would urge those of you who are not familiar with the popular cable show *The First 48* to watch the investigators' interviews with their suspects. They are looking for signals sent out by the suspect that are deceitful and work to those weaknesses. You will notice that when the cop knows his suspect is ready to talk, he moves in closer and touches his suspect to convey the closeness and to be his or her friend who is ready to sit and listen. A good investigator also has to know how to read body language.

This homicide was particularly brutal, and the suspect who confessed was sentenced to life in prison. He had cut the telephone line while the victim was sleeping and forced his way into the front door. He actually got in the bed with her and had repeated sex before strangling her and hitting her in the head with a blunt object at least twice. We executed a search warrant at his house the day of his arrest and located a vacuum cleaner with a cut electrical cord that matched the one used to strangle the victim, as well as much other incriminating evidence. The task force was somewhat upset to know that our arrest was not their suspect, so the task force continued with their nightly assignments.

We were blessed with our last homicide of the year on Saturday, December 14. I got the call about 7:30 a.m., so the homicide gods allowed me a full night of sleep again. I responded and was briefed by patrol officers, and we determined that the thirty-four-year-old white, male victim had driven his pickup truck into a black neighborhood to purchase drugs. The drug deal went bad, and he was shot in the chest while attempting to make the purchase. He then drove away and crashed into a telephone pole. We were able to make a very quick arrest the same day, and our year ended with a record sixteen homicides.

We all got together for a party a few days before Christmas, and we all had a good time. Tom's wife was very pregnant with her second, and Paula was eight months pregnant, so there was not much dancing going on. We were usually so busy that we did not have much spare time to socialize or party in between cases, so Christmas was it for us, which was generally a slower time of the year.

Christmas 1991 came, and I had to call Tom out on Christmas day for a suicide. I hated to do it because he had a small child at home, and his wife was pregnant. He was not out very long, but this was a call that required an investigator. Unfortunately, suicides escalate during the holidays for obvious reasons. There were also more armed robberies committed between mid- November and New Year's, also for obvious reasons. When people need money for the holidays, they tend to take matters into their own hands and steal rather than work.

In this time period, Ernie was transferred out of CID and a short time later promoted to captain. I had gotten along great with Ernie and appreciated his support along the way. We had a lot in common and I enjoyed working for him. I would again have the opportunity to work for him.

His only mandate that I disagreed with was one of the changes I made when he left, with the captain's blessing, of course. We did away with the requirement that the investigators be at their desks at 8:00 a.m. just to be seen then go out to follow their leads. I thought it was more advantageous for investigators to go directly from home to where they had to be, which made them more efficient. This change also forced the guys to arrange their appointments and schedule the day before, which also proved to be more efficient. My only requirement was that they call me at 8:00 a.m. to tell me where they were. This arrangement worked out great and probably saved the county a lot of gas and needless man-hours.

It was also around this time that John was placed on a special assignment with Tom, working an unsolved police homicide from the '70s. They were both gone for nine months, so I supervised both units during their absence. When Ernie, my lieutenant, was transferred, he wasn't replaced, so it was just the captain and me for nine months.

We did not have too much time off from working homicides when we had our first of the year on January 4. I got the call just before 3:00 a.m. and responded with a crew of investigators to a club where a male subject was sitting with some relatives when all a sudden a lone gunman let loose with five or six shots, resulting in the victim's death. The crime lab responded, and I recall that they were able to recover all unaccounted for bullet projectiles. A suspect was quickly developed and located, resulting in his arrest. Both the suspect and victim were only twenty-eight years old.

We did not have to wait too long for the second of the year. On January 16 we responded to the southern part of Charleston County, where a victim had been shot with a sawed-off shotgun. Fortunately, the shooting occurred at four thirty in the afternoon, and there were several witnesses. The thirty-year-old victim was approached by three male subjects in his yard. The victim called inside for a family member to come out, and as the family member was making his way outside, he heard a shotgun blast and ran out to find the victim with a severe and fatal wound to the chest.

A witness standing across the street saw a male subject come from behind the house with a sawed-off shotgun in his hand after he heard the blast, followed by two other guys, who all got into a car and quickly drove away. Believe it or not, all three suspects were teenagers, ranging in age from fourteen to sixteen, who were all quickly identified and taken into custody before the end of the night.

I was on the two to ten shift for the month of January, and one night decided to go to an adjoining county to see my oldest son, Doug, compete in a wrestling match. We are not supposed to leave the county while working unless we were on official business. I got to the gym early enough to see the lower-weight class wrestlers compete, then saw my son's match in the 170 lb. weight class. I was sitting with one or two others across the gym from the bleachers where most of the fans were, and all of a sudden two guys began fighting with someone else in the stands where all of the fans were. The two started walking quickly toward the exit, which was right next to where I was sitting. I was wearing a sport jacket, shirt, and tie and wore my weapon and handcuffs. I identified myself to them and had an arm around each of them, and after some words, ended up putting each one of them in a headlock and was prepared to take them out into the lobby. As I was detaining them, some unknown fan threw a chair that flew across the gym and hit me in the head. I never lost a beat or my grip on my two fighters. I took both outside and handcuffed them to each other around a door handle.

Someone had called the police, and I had the two placed on trespass notice after explaining what had happened. I took my handcuffs back, went back inside, and enjoyed the rest of the matches. Someone managed to videotape the incident, and we all had a good laugh later that night. Remember I mentioned earlier that I never missed a match or a game.

On January 23, my wife had an appointment with her OB/GYN doctor for her normal bi-monthly checkup. When they took her blood pressure, it was dangerously high, and the doctor decided to admit her to the hospital immediately. The doctor was a great guy, and his daughter was engaged to one of my investigators, Billy. Billy and his family were members of my church, and I had known him since he was a teenager.

I got the phone call from the doctor's office and advised Carol, our secretary, that our baby would probably be here before the end of the day. She too was very pregnant and made me promise to keep her posted with details.

Because of the issue with Paula's blood pressure, Dr. P decided to deliver the baby right away, which would be by cesarean section. Our son, Joseph Raymond Wright, was born that afternoon, January 23, 1992, and we were ecstatic. We knew he was going to be a boy but had kept it quiet. The other three kids too were delighted to have a new little brother.

Immediately after Joe was born, my wife developed what is known as HELLP Syndrome, which is a serious condition that can be fatal. In her case, her kidneys began to shut down, and nurses had to monitor her closely and check on her every fifteen minutes for more than forty-eight hours. We were not aware of the seriousness of her condition at the time, but within three days post-birth, she had improved dramatically.

By now, my daughter had just moved out on her own to an apartment nearby, which she shared briefly with her mother. The kids were enamored of the new addition to the family and were very protective and helpful to us. My middle son, Pete, was fourteen when Joe was born, and he remains closest to him to this day because they are closest in age and can talk sports together for hours.

As soon as Paula came home, which I recall was in about a week, I went back to work. Her mom came down from New Jersey, so she was in left good hands while I was gone.

The year had begun just like the previous one had ended, and we were busy on all fronts. The serial rapist was still at work in the county, and by now had committed more than twenty such crimes. The Task Force was working furiously and putting in many hours of investigation. They were working seven days a week and had about every apartment complex in the county under surveillance. Our helicopter was airborne almost every night too using night-vision capabilities.

Women were in genuine fear—and rightly so—and the local press media did not let up with their coverage, which in my opinion added to their fear. The sale of firearms was up in the area, and women were panicking.

***

At some point early in the year, one of my guys was working some vehicle thefts and car break-ins, which led them to a sailor stationed on a ship at the Navy Base. Their investigation also involved some insurance fraud they linked to a senior chief petty officer with over twenty years in the Navy. He had allegedly paid a sailor on his ship to steal his car and to burn it so the chief could be reimbursed for his loss because he could not keep up with the payments. We had also identified at least four sailors on the same ship who were culpable in connected thefts on and off the Navy Base.

Whenever military personnel are involved in a crime or an investigation, we notify the investigative branch of their particular service. In this case, we notified Naval Investigative Service (NIS), now known as Naval Criminal Investigative Service or (NCIS). When we briefed NIS of our findings, it, of course, had to notify the base commander and the commanding officer of the ship in question. Coordinating the arrests was a huge undertaking because the ship was due to go out to sea in the next several days, so we were pressed to take action.

The date of arrest was arranged, and along with NIS Agents, we boarded the ship after first taking the senior chief petty officer down as he exited his vehicle in the parking lot. We gave the executive officer (XO) of the ship the names of the sailors we needed to interview, and he was visibly livid about what his sailors had been accused of doing. I walked behind the XO down a long, narrow passageway as we followed one of the accused to the officers' mess, where we were to interview him. As we walked, the XO actually kicked the sailor in the ass and let loose with a string of profanities describing what would happen if this investigation caused their ship not to sail on the prescribed date of departure.

Several of us interviewed the suspect sailors, and we ended up at an apartment on James Island, where we recovered a truckload of stolen property.

The beauty of dealing with the military is that officers will bend over backward to help you with your case and conduct follow-up, which often results in a court-martial and/or less-than-honorable discharge form their branch of service.

***

It was about this time that Eddie, my captain, was promoted to major and transferred to the Patrol Division. He was one of the best bosses I ever had, but we were all happy he was promoted. He ended his career as a chief deputy and retired in 1999.

Eddie's replacement was my old lieutenant, Paul, who I worked for when I first made sergeant. He had been promoted to captain and was returning to CID, now as the commanding officer.

For a police agency with more than 240 sworn deputies, it seemed as though the same three or four bosses continually supervised my career. I had been very fortunate to this point in my career that all of my bosses had been great guys to work with. Another consideration for repeatedly working for the same bosses was that if they liked your work they quite often recruited you to work for them again. The bosses were aware that good, productive, and proactive subordinates tended to make them look good to their superiors.

Paul was another great boss who had spent many years in CID as a slick sleeve (no rank) investigator, a corporal, and as a sergeant. He had worked many homicides himself and had a wealth of experience that I picked from his brain.

On March 13, we responded to our third homicide of the year after deputies had initially responded to check on the welfare of a nonresponsive male in his bedroom. The deputies found his lifeless body lying naked in the corner of his bedroom with welts and bruises all over his body. We determined that an unknown assailant had beaten him to death. While working the crime scene, an investigator from the town we were in told us that we were in Mount Pleasant, and its department would take over the investigation. I politely told him that the crime scene was in Charleston County, and his town was in our county. They were pissed off but that did not much matter to me. That was the beauty of working for a county agency; there were no boundaries when in other incorporated areas of the county.

We identified the suspect and a vehicle that he was driving and were able to obtain an arrest warrant for Murder. He had apparently stopped at a rest area on the interstate and ditched the car he was driving and car-jacked someone out of their car and at a rest area before he ever left Charleston County. That vehicle was located in Johnson City, Tennessee, and recovered. The suspect was charged with Murder, Kidnapping, and the Theft of a Motor Vehicle and was sentenced to life in prison, where he remains.

On March 21, we responded to yet another homicide, already the fourth of the short year. It was an easy case to work and quickly cleared by arrest. By now, everyone in the Person Crime Unit had each worked a homicide this year and were all tying up loose ends and preparing the previous cases for trial.

On Saturday March 28, I was busy painting the outside of my house and had received several phone calls during the day regarding various incidents within the county, which included a car found abandoned just out of our county with the body of a female in the backseat. I was glad that it was not in our jurisdiction and continued painting. After yet another call, I ended up sending Tom up there to investigate and see whether he could make the determination as to where the murder had occurred. Tom called back after a while and stated that there were a total of three victims. One female victim was dead in the backseat, and two male subjects were found in the trunk of the car rolled up into carpeting. Tom said that it appeared that the homicides had occurred in a house in our jurisdiction, and it was ours to work. I immediately called out everyone to respond to work the case. Because it took about eight hours before the determination was made where the murders occurred, we were a little behind the eight ball, so to speak.

Before the end of the day, we had gathered enough information to obtain arrest warrants for three counts of Murder for the suspect. The suspect ran an illegal tattoo parlor in a building on his property and was known as "Tattoo" to his friends. At that time tattoo parlors were illegal but have since been legalized.

When we worked the crime scene, we immediately saw blood spatter on the baseboards in the living room, missing carpeting where it appeared to have been quickly cut with a knife to remove bloodstains. The missing carpet matched what was found in the trunk of the car with the bodies. Shell casings were also located in the front yard of the residence.

We all ran the leads we had and entered several bars in the area that the suspect was known to frequent. We located the common-law wife of the suspect, and after interviewing her, we determined that she was an eyewitness to the three murders and was scared for her personal safety because of threats made by "Tattoo." After gathering much intelligence from her, we determined that she was with the suspect when he got rid of the murder weapon. By about 4:00 a.m., we all went home to get a few hours of sleep and were back at it early Sunday.

On Sunday, I picked up the common-law wife so she could direct me to where "Tattoo" had discarded the weapon. She took me to a small lake behind a residential neighborhood, about five miles from the murder scene. She described how "Tattoo" had gotten out of the car, stood on a large rock, and tossed the weapon underhand out into the body of water. I had her demonstrate exactly how he did it and how hard he threw it. I immediately arranged for a Dive Team to respond to the area later in the day, and when they arrived, I briefed them and described just how the witness had described tossing the weapon. I recall the head diver asking me how sure I was that the weapon was disposed of here, and my reply was "I'll bet my paycheck on it."

Within thirty minutes of getting into the water, one of our divers retrieved the weapon. When cops dive for evidence they work in grids and methodically search specific squares of assigned area. The weapon was recovered and immediately placed in a sealed container. The weapon, which was a long-barreled .357 magnum, Smith & Wesson revolver, was driven right to the SLED lab in Columbia, some 110 miles away.

The murders happened late Friday night or early Saturday morning, and "Tattoo" had a head start. He had family in Rock Hill, South Carolina, about two hundred miles away and very close to Charlotte, North Carolina. Knowing this we were in constant contact with the Charlotte Mecklenburg Police Department and law enforcement in the Rock Hill area. Because of the news coverage, we were receiving many leads regarding possible sightings of "Tattoo." We flew two guys, Tim and Tom up to Charlotte in the county aircraft, and they worked closely with investigators for at least two days. The two guys we sent were on a mission and were so wrapped up into the case that they never even called their wives to check in with them. Consequently, we had two pissed off wives regularly calling us wanting their husbands to call them. Hell, they were not even calling us to check in!

Six days after the murders took place, "Tattoo" was taken into custody and extradited back to South Carolina to await his trial. We sent two more investigators up to Charlotte to assist the two already there and to transport "Tattoo" back to the State of South Carolina, where he is currently serving three life sentences.

A day or so after the arrest of "Tattoo" in North Carolina, we had our eighth homicide of the year. On April 6, Tom responded to the Magnolia Cemetery in the City of Charleston. The Charleston police department had responded and called us to investigate. There was a body of a thirty-five-year-old female, clad only in a nightgown with an apparent gunshot wound to the head. Charleston PD called us because it was obvious that the victim was killed elsewhere and dumped in the cemetery. The cemetery is an old one, dating back to the late 1700s, and contains scores of victims from the Civil War. One could easily spend the day there just reading interesting tombstones.

The suspect in the murder was the victim's husband, who was present at the couple's home when Tom arrived. He was in an obvious state of intoxication and became extremely belligerent with the officers present. The couple apparently had a violent domestic dispute at their home, which somehow ended up in their car, where she was shot in the head. Tom took the husband into custody and charged him with Murder.

All of the guys in the office were hard workers, and all had families or were about to either get married or have children. Around this time, several of my guys worked off duty to provide contracted security Kiawah Island Resort, which was in our jurisdiction. There are two golf courses on Kiawah, and one , the Ocean Course, is famous as the hardest course in the country. While some of my guys were working there , they established contacts at the golf courses and quickly found out they could play there regularly for free.

None of these guys would ever turn down an hour of overtime , but as soon as there was a budget crunch at the sheriff's office, a mandate was issued that employees had to take COMP time (compensatory time)in lieu of overtime, which meant the extra hours they worked had to be taken in the form of time off. All of a sudden, I had a squad of professional golfers, who would come to me asking to take three or four hours of comp time off. I quickly found out that the guys were all going straight to Kiawah Island to play golf on some of the best golf courses around. If I held a vehicle inspection , I would bet that four or five guys had golf clubs in the trunk of their police vehicles. As soon as the budget crunch was over , they all worked as hard as before, and never asked for time off again.

Just a week later on April 13, my guys responded to a bar on Folly Road on James Island, where a couple was in the process of leaving their business for the night after cleaning up. At 5:00 a.m., a male subject approached them at gunpoint to rob them of their night deposit bag containing a large amount of cash. The robber had no idea that the owner of the bar was armed and was surprised, to say the least, when the owner pulled out his own weapon and shot the suspect where he stood.

I used this case as an example earlier while explaining how to exceptionally clear a case. The investigators ran the serial number of the weapon used by the robber and discovered it had been recently stolen in a neighborhood burglary. There was an ongoing issue with unsolved burglaries in the same neighborhood the robber lived in. As a result, we were able to exceptionally clear all of those unsolved cases to our dead robber. If he had not used the stolen weapon, those burglaries would still be unsolved today. Nobody ever said that criminals were very smart. If someone pulls out a gun in the commission of a robbery, he or she should be mindful of the fact that the person he or she is robbing just may be armed.

***

Weird things can happen when people die unexpectedly, and I recall a suicide that once took an odd turn. We responded in the middle of the day to the report of a possible suicide in an old, well-kept neighborhood not too far from headquarters. When we arrived, we found an elderly male subject deceased in the driver's seat of his car parked in the carport. He had a bullet hole to the head, but the strange thing was there was no weapon that we could see.

We went into the house and found a long letter in the form of a good-bye letter to his family, so we had evidence that he intended to commit suicide and more than likely did. We looked around the house and discovered that the deceased had an extensive collection of handguns, some dating back to WWII.

While responding to the residence, one of the guys happened to notice a well-known street thug walking from the area of the house where we had responded. His appearance was very distinctive since he was bow-legged and known as "Keith" by about every cop in the area. We thought it odd that he was in this area and not the usual drug-infested neighborhood he was known to frequent. Once we realized we had a missing weapon, we set out to locate Keith. Once he was located, a couple of my investigators got him to admit that he had seized the opportunity when he heard the gunshot. He found the old guy dead and stole the gun. We recovered the gun and charged Keith with larceny of the weapon. As I have mentioned before more than once, nobody ever said that the street criminals were very smart.

***

On April 29, 1992, the day that the Rodney King verdict came out, police agencies nationwide had been preparing for the worst, just in case the verdict went the wrong way—according to the citizens out in the street. We were prepared and were on the street in force in the event that there was any rioting.

The Rodney King case out in Los Angeles was one of the worst things to happen to the profession of law enforcement since the 1960s. A few cops with no self-control and who had anger-management issues just about ruined the trust that citizens had for cops on the street.

***

Sometime in 1992, there had been a rash of armed robberies of mostly convenience stores, which we refer to as "stop-and-robs." To date there had been at least six unsolved robberies. One night while working the two to ten shift, I was returning to the office after coming home to eat dinner. On my trip back to the office, a call went out over the radio that an armed robbery had just taken place at the 7-11 nearby. I happened to be the closest officer and arrived at the scene first. While questioning the clerk for a physical description of the suspect so it could be broadcast over the radio, I looked down on the floor and picked up a South Carolina driver's license and held it up to the clerk and asked, "Is this him?" The clerk responded, "Yeah, that's him." I was fortunately able to broadcast the suspect's exact name and personal information. As I said, nobody ever said that crooks were smart. When he pulled the handgun out of his right front pocket, his license fell out on the floor.

I immediately went back to the office and prepared an arrest warrant for Armed Robbery, and we spent the rest of the night chasing the subject from place to place. The night culminated with another robbery at a convenience store, where the same suspect ended up shooting the clerk. We were able to arrest him later that day, and our rash of robberies ended.

***

The day after the bar shooting on April 14, we responded to the southern end of the county just after 1:00 a.m., where a subject had shot one of two subjects trying to burglarize his father's house. The first responding deputy met with the shooter, who had the second burglar in custody. It was determined that the burglars were brothers, and while in the process of breaking in, they were surprised by the homeowner, who shot and killed one of the brothers.

Without a break on April 16, we had our eleventh homicide of the year, and our eighth in thirty-two days. Just after 3:00 a.m., we got a call that a male subject was found shot to death in the roadway. The victim was just eighteen years old and his death was the result of a drug deal that went bad. The suspect was quickly identified, arrested, and charged with Murder.

***

Around this time, the State Law Enforcement Division (SLED) had put together a task force of its agents. The task force was called The Governor's Task Force that targeted drug enforcement. They would travel around the state, and as they went into specific areas, they would get police agencies from that particular area to add to their manpower and would target known drug areas. When they came to Charleston in 1992, they came with about forty agents, and when all agencies kicked in their respective manpower, the force was well over two hundred cops hitting a specific area at one time. We met for a briefing in a courtroom and were given assignments, making sure to partner SLED agents with the local cops who knew the area.

I participated and brought most of the guys from my office, and after our briefing, we headed to neighborhoods in the north area of Charleston County. We were quickly filling paddy wagons of arrestees, but one unlucky criminal in particular picked the wrong night to commit a crime. An off-duty North Charleston Police Department Detective was at a putt-putt range with family members and was enjoying time off with them, when all of a sudden, a criminal approached the off-duty cop and pointed a gun in his face, demanding all of his money. The off-duty cop was unarmed, but before he could respond verbally to the command of the would-be thief, the thief pulled the trigger on the gun pointed at the cop, but the gun misfired. As soon as the word went out over the radio, there were more than two hundred cops in the area. We chased the suspect into an apartment complex and took him into custody and recovered the weapon. He just picked the wrong night indeed to commit a crime.

On May 18, we had our twelfth homicide of the year. We responded to a low-income neighborhood in the northern part of the county where a twenty-five-year-old male was killed one block from his house. We were fortunate in that the murder happened during the daytime, and citizens in the neighborhood assisted us in identifying those responsible. There were three arrests in this case, which was the result of another drug deal gone bad.

On Thursday, June 6, we received information that a fugitive wanted by our agency was in a hotel in Myrtle Beach, South Carolina, approximately one hundred miles up the coast from Charleston. I was with one of my guys, and we were about forty miles north when it was suggested that our helicopter pick me up from the side of the highway and fly me to Myrtle Beach, which would save about an hour. Traffic was stopped, and I jumped in the chopper with our pilot, Buddy. Buddy made sergeant the same day that I did, and I had known him for over ten years. He had been a fixed-wing pilot for more than twenty years but in the past year had become a certified helicopter pilot. The chopper he picked me up in was not our regular chopper, and I found out while making the flight that it was a loaner since ours was in the shop. We landed within minutes at the Myrtle Beach Police Department and two of their investigators drove me to the hotel in question. It took only ten minutes to figure out that we had just missed our fugitive, but we did confirm that he had been there.

I spent a total of approximately twenty minutes on the ground in Myrtle Beach and jumped back into the chopper with Buddy for the trip back to the Charleston Airport. We talked back and forth on the headsets talking about landmarks we were passing, small talk, and generally catching up. We landed and he drove me to headquarters so I could get back to my car. I thanked him for the lift and told him I had not been in a helicopter since I was in Vietnam. Little did I know that I would be in charge of the Honor Guard and be a pallbearer at his funeral in just a few days!

By now the Serial Rape Task Force had been working every day since the previous year and had to date identified twenty-nine rapes committed by the still-unknown suspect. As stated earlier, our helicopter was airborne every night, and Buddy was getting plenty of flight time. He had various deputies trained as observers to fly with him each night.

Just two days after I flew with Buddy, he was on the Task Force mission with Bill as his observer. Bill had been a helicopter mechanic in the military and flew with Buddy most often. Buddy and Bill began their shift at midnight Saturday and were scheduled to work until 8:00 a.m. Sunday. They had just completed installing their infrared heat-sensing device that had been removed while the chopper was in the shop having its engine overhauled, which is why Buddy and I had flown in the loaner that I mentioned previously.

Buddy and Bill spent most of their shift reinstalling the equipment and, when finished, called his captain to report that they were getting ready to take off and fly to their base at the Charleston Airport. Buddy mentioned that it was foggy where they were, and the captain advised that it was clear in Charleston. They were only about twenty-five miles away, so when thirty or so minutes passed without their arrival, the captain began to page them and call them on every radio frequency available. The captain then drove to the Dorchester County Airport and located both of his deputies' cruisers, but no helicopter.

An immediate search was organized, consisting of hundreds and hundreds of law enforcement personnel. My two sons who were members of the Law Enforcement Explorer Post even participated. John was away on vacation, and my captain ordered me to stay in the office while he assisted in the organization of the extensive search. I knew that Bill and John were good friends, and I tried repeatedly to get in touch with John to notify him of Buddy's and Bill's missing status.

John finally responded to my pages and calls late Sunday evening after his return from vacation. When I advised John of the sequence of events, as we knew them, he was extremely upset and told me he would be at the airport Monday morning to participate in the search himself. John too was a fixed-wing pilot and had his own airplane stored at that same airport.

The search lasted all day Sunday, Monday, and Tuesday, consisting of fixed-wing aircraft, helicopters, and four-wheel drive vehicles. The area around the airport was heavily wooded with wet and marshy land in much of the woods.

The crash site was finally located when one of the searchers saw the telltale sign of buzzards flying over a certain area not far from the airport itself. When searchers got to the site, they found the burned wreckage of the helicopter and the gruesome charred remains of both deputies. It appeared that Buddy was thrown from the chopper on impact, and Bill was found very close to the wreckage.

These were the first line-of-duty officer deaths dating back to 1982, almost ten years prior. Since I was a supervisory member of the Honor Guard, I immediately began planning for crews to preside over the wakes and subsequent funerals of Buddy and Bill. Buddy, forty-nine, was divorced and had lived with his mother in an old house not far from headquarters. Bill was thirty-two and lived with his mom. Many hundreds of concerned friends and fellow cops attended their wakes. Their funeral service was in a joint service at a very large church in North Charleston, the only one available large enough to accommodate the huge crowd that attended. There were more than five hundred officers outside when I gave the command "Officers, *attention*." As a drill instructor, I had given the same command thousands of times to thousands of recruits but none as meaningful and chilling as at that moment.

The truest act of respect that can be shown, in my opinion, to military and law enforcement is to honor their dead, and Buddy and Bill were honored accordingly.

After all, of the dozens and dozens of flights that Buddy made while attached to the Serial Rape Task Force, he would have been pleased as hell to know that the rapist was captured just a week after his funeral.

On Friday morning, June 19, 1992, I was in the office and received a phone call from one of my investigators serving his thirty-day tour on the Task Force. Ronnie told me that they now knew who the rapist was, which was established by the suspect's estranged wife on a hunch after she found some unknown women's belongings in her home. She had guessed that her husband, Duncan Proctor, was more than likely the rapist and called Crime Stoppers, which generated an immediate surveillance of the suspect. Ronnie was calling me from the surveillance and while filling me in told me that he had to go because Proctor was leaving the house and getting into his car. Ronnie told me which radio channel to monitor so I could hear what was going on in real time.

Once Proctor got into his car, surveillance vehicles moved into position waiting for Proctor to get out of his neighborhood to be stopped in a safe place. When the flashing lights were activated to stop him, the chase was on. Proctor drove to the interstate and headed westbound on Interstate 26 at high speeds, which ended about eight miles west when his vehicle left the roadway and crashed into trees in the median of the highway. The chase and the rapes were now over, two years, three months, and eleven days after the first reported rape. Proctor, because of the wreck, sustained a severe brain injury and paralysis of both legs and one arm.

As you can well imagine, a wreck of this magnitude and the identity of the victim generated dozens and dozens of law enforcement and rescue personnel and emergency vehicles to the scene, resulting in the closure of the entire interstate in both directions. My daughter, Christy, was getting married the next day, and all of our relatives traveling from out of state to attend were caught in this major highway closure for several hours.

The subsequent follow-up investigation resulted in a weapon and victims' clothing being located in Proctor's house. Because of his injuries, however, a circuit court judge, the following year, ruled him to be mentally incompetent. Little did I know that in 1998 I would have future, extended contact with Mr. Proctor.

I got Christy married, and we had a great weekend of reuniting with my immediate family as well as extended family. They all traveled to Charleston the weekend of Christy's wedding also to celebrate my grandmother's ninetieth birthday. One of my investigators, Danny, was a DJ on the side for extra money. I had hired him to play for Christy's reception, and on Monday, when we returned to work, he told me he never saw a family party as hard as ours. I told him that if my family is going to travel eight hundred miles for a wedding, they are going to party. They are definitely not going to waste the opportunity.

***

On July 6, I responded to our thirteenth homicide of the year way in the northern corner of the county. I was the first to arrive and was escorted inside by the first responding officer and observed a thirty-two-year-old female, dead on the living room couch with her upper body face down on the couch with her knees on the floor. She had a small amount of blood under her head and appeared to have been dead for at least several hours. Nearby was a couch pillow that appeared to be damaged and possibly used to muffle the muzzle of the weapon to contain the sound when it was being discharged. As I was looking around, I found a driver's license lying on the floor. It belonged to the established suspect in this murder. He was identified as the boyfriend of the deceased and had been involved in an ongoing domestic conflict with the victim.

I went outside of the residence and waited for investigators to respond, and while I was waiting, I ran the name on the driver's license I had found and made several cell phone calls to pass on information to my superiors. Once the guys got on scene, I would assign the case to Mark, who was next up in the barrel. While waiting, an astute, young, female reporter working for a local TV station approached me, wanting to be briefed. I politely told her that I would brief all three TV stations a little later on. She then proceeded to ask me if the license I had in my shirt pocket belonged to the suspect. I told her something to the effect of "If it did, I am not going to tell you." As God is my witness she then said, "If you give me the information on that driver's license in your pocket, I will give you a blowjob." My response was an emphatic, "No!" and she promptly went back to her news truck. I was not about to risk my career, my family, or my reputation over a moment of stupidity on my part. She was the same reporter who had reported the existence of a Serial Crime Task Force after reading the schedule hanging on the bulletin board in our own office.

When Mark arrived and I was briefing him, I handed him the license and told him what I was just offered for this license and handed it to him. When I explained, his only response was "Holy shit," and he dropped it as though it had burned his fingers. We both laughed.

By the end of the day, we had located and arrested the suspect and charged him with Murder. He had used a sawed-off shotgun to shoot his estranged girlfriend in the chest and had used the pillow to muffle the blast, as we had suspected, then had turned her face down onto the couch.

About ten days later the operations major and my old lieutenant from METRO, Marvin, had asked me to go downtown with him to the Medical University Hospital of South Carolina (MUSC) to assist in working out arrangements to provide law enforcement security to Duncan Proctor who was recovering and due to be transferred from ICU to a private room there. Because he had been charged, he had to be guarded 24/7. The major and I met with the chief of the MUSC Public Safety Office, and after making all of our arrangements, the major was ready for me to drive him back to headquarters.

While in the car on the way back, a hot call went out over the radio of a shootout that was in progress on Sycamore Avenue, less than a mile from where we were. We responded and were the first cops on scene, and our crime scene consisted of an empty corner lot used as a hangout for neighborhood troublemakers. There were discarded refrigerators and deli cases discarded from a bar on the opposite corner as well as milk crates and makeshift tables used to sit and play cards and drink alcohol.

This was a neighborhood known for its high level of drug activity, and our patrol cars regularly swept through the area to keep loiterers moving and to discourage standing or hanging on this very corner. As we arrived, I immediately observed the body of a male subject with a handgun still clutched in his hand slumped over one of the discarded deli cases, with his feet still on the ground. It appeared that while involved in a gun battle with another subject he sustained a gunshot wound to the head just above his left ear. This was to be our fourteenth homicide in seven months. Because the entire lot was a crime scene, I immediately ordered arriving patrol officers to establish a perimeter and to place crime scene tape around the entire lot. It is amazing how quickly bad news travels, and within minutes, all three TV stations had film crews on scene.

Fortunately, there were witnesses to this incident, and we were able to identify the suspect, who had apparently driven up in a pickup truck, gotten out, and started walking toward the victim with a gun in his hand. An exchange of gunfire resulted in the victim receiving the fatal bullet wound. The suspect drove away but was later arrested and charged with Murder.

Just four days later on July 20, we responded to the fifteenth murder of the year about eight blocks from headquarters. A male subject had been standing on his front porch when all of a sudden a car pulled up, a subject exited the vehicle, walked right up to the porch, and started to yell at the subject. An intense argument quickly escalated to an exchange of gunfire, during which the victim sustained a fatal wound to his upper chest area. Hosts of known gangsters in the neighborhood were known to be involved, but we were able to determine the shooter and made a quick arrest.

Sometime during the summer, I got a call at home that there had just been a burglary, kidnapping, and sexual assault in a quiet neighborhood not a mile from my own home. I told headquarters to call out at least three investigators, and I was at the crime scene within a few minutes. The victim was a woman in her seventies who thought she knew her assailant as a young man who had previously done yard work for her. He had apparently forced his way into the house after dark and proceeded to pull the phone lines out of the wall and used them to tie the victim up, where he then proceeded to sexually assault her. Once I got the name of the suspect, I grabbed two of my guys and went to a house and saw the suspect from outside of an open window lying on his bed watching television. We boosted Kenny into the open window as I held my handgun on him. Then somebody else boosted me into the window as well.

Minutes after I began questioning the suspect outside, he confessed to the entire incident. He was charged accordingly but due to psychiatric problems, he never went to prison, but spent many years in an institution.

Just before 11:00 p.m. on August 7, 1992, investigators responded to the area of a club where a male subject was severely wounded by a shotgun. Witnesses were able to tell us that the shotgun blast came from an SUV that had stopped for the driver to speak with the victim on the side of the road.

While we were still processing the crime scene and speaking to witnesses, the suspect walked into the front door of headquarters and turned himself in, not knowing that the victim had already died. This, our sixteenth of the year, was the last that I was involved with or participated in as a supervisor in CID.

***

Earlier in the year, I had participated in another promotion process and had made the list of eligible sergeants for promotion to lieutenant. There had been an opening for only one lieutenant, and the word was out that the sheriff would be making promotions soon.

The first Friday in September, I was at the bank making a deposit in the drive-through and got a call from the sheriff's secretary, who told me that the sheriff wanted to see me right away. I told her I would be there in ten minutes. When I got to her office to let her know I was there, Marvin, now the chief deputy of patrol, who was in my chain of command, met me. My buddy Keith was also there to see the sheriff too. We were both sergeants and had worked together many times. The chief, Keith, and I were summoned and told that the sheriff was ready to see us, and we all walked in. The sheriff told us all to be seated, and he leaned back, smoking his ever-present cigarette then leaned forward and threw two lieutenant's badges across his desk at us. We each took one, and Keith and I looked at each other momentarily, knowing that there was only one available slot, as far as we knew. Keith and I both said simultaneously, "I thought there was only one position." The sheriff told us not to worry about that and reiterated that we were both promoted to lieutenant. The sheriff and chief both shook our hands, and we were out of there, smiling from ear to ear.

The promotion from investigator to sergeant, salary-wise, was very small, but the jump in pay to the rank of lieutenant was more significant and certainly appreciated with a new mouth to feed. Some friends were promoted to sergeant that same day, as well as the incompetent female lieutenant who had been ruled responsible in the officer-involved shooting of the escaped burglary suspect who had shot the female officer. She was promoted to the rank of captain but was, fortunately, in charge of no sworn personnel of any significance. She was now in an administrative position where she could no longer get someone hurt or killed. I was always cordial and respectful, but I never referred to her by her rank. Because of her incompetence, many others felt the same way I did, as others silently rebelled by doing the same.

When I was promoted, my captain, Paul, was out of work with a severely broken arm. He fell from a tree while trimming branches in his yard. One of the guys promoted to sergeant was an investigator in the unit and would be taking my place, so Paul told me to move into his office and let Wade, the new sergeant, have my desk. I was going to be assigned to the Patrol Division and had a week to fill in Wade on what was expected of him in Investigations.

My promotion was bittersweet because I had been expecting that my partner, John, was a sure bet for promotion. He was senior to me and had been in CID much longer. I felt bad for him and told him so. Little did I know he had been interviewing for a position in the South Carolina Law Enforcement Division (SLED) and was hired as a special agent not long after I transferred out of the unit.

PATROL SQUAD COMMANDER

22

I WAS ASSIGNED TO THE WEST DISTRICT, WHERE I had begun as a patrol officer almost ten years prior. In West District, three, ten-man squads worked eight-hour shifts. North District too had three, ten-man squads and the two smaller districts, South and East, each had three, three-man squads.

A captain, whose office was in the substation, commanded us. I was now one of three patrol squad commanders. Each lieutenant had one sergeant per squad, which had been changed since I had last worked in Patrol.

When we worked the 7:00 a.m. to 3:00 p.m. shifts, we did so for twenty-eight days. On the twenty-ninth day, we went back to the 11:00 p.m. to 7:00 a.m. shifts, then back to 3:00 p.m. to 11:00 p.m., and so on. The day shift was the shift when we were most bothered by brass from headquarters. The three to eleven was the busiest and the one I liked the best because it was so busy.

On my first day as a road lieutenant, I met with all of my guys. My sergeant was Jimmy, who I had worked with in METRO several years prior. I had a great group of guys and already knew every one of them. Only one had worked for me before, and he happened to be the first person I ever suspended without pay for disciplinary reasons. He and I were good to go with no hard feelings. He was a graduate of The Citadel, a military college located right in Charleston, as well as another deputy, who was also a captain in the Marine Corps Reserves. I had another guy who was a lieutenant in the Army Reserves, and they were two of my best guys. They both loved to go after drug dealers, and I made sure they were both assigned to districts that had drug problems.

I had some that loved to do traffic enforcement and would rather write a traffic ticket or handle an accident than anything. I made sure that they too were assigned to areas where there were a lot of accidents and traffic.

I told my guys, which included two females, what I expected of them and what to expect from me. From day one, they knew what I wanted and expected.

After a month or so, I decided to start a little competition between squads. There were three squads: north, south and east, as well as the other two in my own district. I told my guys that I would give the person who made the most arrests for the month a day off each month. I also told them that I would also give a day off to whoever wrote the most tickets. This was friendly competition that added to morale in the unit and encouraged good sportsmanship between other squads in the Sheriff's Office.

In those days, the lieutenant was off on Saturday and Sunday, and the sergeant was off on Thursday and Friday. I understood that my sergeant would want or need some weekend days off from time to time, so when he needed off I just adjusted my schedule accordingly, rather than pay another sergeant overtime to fill in for him.

I had now been with Charleston County for over ten years and had never worked a Christmas Eve or a Christmas, not because I avoided it in any way, but that is just how my schedule worked out at the time. Well, Christmas Eve and Christmas of 1992 were on a Thursday and Friday, respectively, which were my sergeant's regular days off, so I ended up working my very first Christmas on the job.

We ended up working our butts off because we were busy running from call to call. My wife never complained once, and I always appreciated that about her. After spending the last two years being awakened nearly every night by telephone calls and watching me go out many times in the middle of the night, she never once complained. Now here I was, working Christmas Eve and Christmas.

Since being promoted to sergeant, I never asked anyone to do anything that I would not do myself or had not already done. Most road lieutenants used their position of authority to lay back and supervise and never answer a call for service, never stop a car, never write a ticket, never make an arrest, and generally thought that they were better than anyone else and exempt from doing those things I described. I was a working supervisor and loved going on service calls. I went with the guys into drug areas and responded to hot calls as they were dispatched. The only thing that I was not a big fan of was conducting traffic stops. Unless drivers cut me off or were so blatant in their driving that they forced me to stop them, I almost never stopped cars. I told my people that if they heard me stop a car and run a driver's license over the radio that somebody better be on his or her way to my location to transport the driver I was getting ready to arrest.

There was only one other road lieutenant who thought the way I did, and for three solid years, he worked the shift that relieved mine. His squad too was the one and only squad that ever came close to being the most productive squad, a competition we won each month for the three years I served as a road lieutenant. The difference between Mike and me was that he loved to conduct traffic stops and was the only lieutenant with a car that was radar-equipped. He would relieve my squad for three years, and I would brief him on what had happened on my shift and what issues might come up again on his shift. When I heard him check in on the radio, I would automatically make a new pot of coffee. Mike and I would usually end up talking right into his roll call, just catching up on things. Mike rose to the rank of major and ended up commanding the entire Patrol Division before his retirement.

The lieutenant I relieved was a different story. For the three years that I relieved his squad, he almost never had any information to pass on to me regarding what had happened during his eight-hour shift. His sergeant, Al, who had worked the same eight-hour shift with the lieutenant would call me from his cell phone, however, and fill me in on all of the activity from his shift and any incident that may affect our shift.

This particular lieutenant had a poor attitude, and it was believed that he was socially promoted because of his race, certainly not for his accomplishments or knowledge. He had filed a racial discrimination lawsuit in US District Court against the old police department in 1988, stating he had been passed over for promotion due to his race. He was promoted to sergeant the same day I was in March of 1989.

For three years, I would try to make conversation at shift change to get him to talk, even trying to discuss his son's basketball skills while playing for the high school that my kids attended. I could never figure out this unusual individual and never understood why he acted the way he did. On top of these issues, he was also considered by most to be a racist. Everyone in the entire Sheriff's Office was surprised when he was again promoted to the rank of captain and placed in the highest profile position and the most prestigious position in the entire Sheriff's Office as the captain of the Criminal Investigations Division. I have always subscribed to the old adage *"what goes around comes around,"* which was proven again, when he was suddenly no longer employed by the Charleston County Sheriff's Office a few short years later.

***

When you have ten people working for you, there are always personnel issues that arise forcing me to take disciplinary action. While in CID, I was put in the position on numerous occasions of taking progressive disciplinary action on quite a few employees. Some were in the form of Letters of Reprimand, Letters of Caution, suspension without pay, and recommendations to higher-ranking officers for the ultimate disciplinary action—termination from employment.

The very first disciplinary action I took as a patrol lieutenant was against one of my female deputies. I suspended her for Unsatisfactory Performance and Insubordination. She had failed, after being warned, to follow a supervisor's lawful order to retrieve paper bonds in a timely manner for arrests she had made. This was a second offense for the same type of situation. I never enjoyed taking money out of someone's pocket, but she left me no alternative. This action, of course, was not popular with her and she cried when given the Letter of Suspension, which really bothered me because two other female employees had done the same thing when I disciplined them. Another female employee cried when I spoke to her about a particular issue, which wasn't even disciplinary in nature.

I had worked with some great female cops over the years, and some I would put up against any other male cop in any situation. The reason I mention the crying issue is that I feel if a woman wants to work in a traditionally male-dominated occupation, she must not show weakness by crying or becoming emotional over something as trivial as being spoken to about an issue or receiving a Letter of Reprimand or a suspension for whatever reason. Sure, cops male and female have cried at a funeral or shown emotion at the scene of a cop who has been severely injured or killed, but to cry over being disciplined, I find totally unacceptable and a sign of extreme weakness. People who know me know that I treat male and female employees the same and show no favorites due to gender.

I must note that I believe that a female cop in the male-dominated profession of law enforcement must work harder than her male counterparts to get ahead. Many of the old bosses resented females in law enforcement and have at times purposely made their jobs more difficult by not being fair in their treatment of females. I have seen some of these old bosses deliberately treat great female cops like crap just because they were a female who had invaded their hallowed profession of law enforcement. This treatment, of course, was not fair, and I often commiserated with some of these mistreated women. It is because of this that I feel so strongly about female employees crying on the job. I believe it is a weakness that should be overcome and is totally unacceptable.

As I mentioned, I have worked with some of the best females that I ever encountered in law enforcement, who actually earned whatever rank they attained. I have also encountered female cops who thought that sleeping with as many superiors as possible was the way to advancement. In most cases, doing so never resulted in advancement, and I have seen many marriages and relationships ruined as a result of their stupidity.

My little system of incentives for productivity was put to the test after about six months. High producers in the squad were consistently getting a free day off each month because the proactive guys on the squad were regularly the top producers of arrests and tickets each month.

In April of 1993, we were working the day shift, and as I was monitoring the police radio, I kept hearing one deputy in particular conducting many traffic stops. He would call the stop in and write a ticket and just minutes later he would advise the dispatcher that he had written two or three tickets, which was virtually impossible in the time frame that the vehicle had been stopped. I immediately went to headquarters and had the dispatch supervisor provide me with a productivity printout of that particular deputy for the month. I then waited until I heard that deputy make another stop, then call in his action taken to dispatch.

I then called him on the radio and had him meet me at a location in his district, where I ordered him to produce his ticket books, which should have carbon copies of all tickets he had actually written. I already knew the answers to the questions I asked him and told him to report to me the following morning at 7:00 a.m., his day off. He had been reporting more tickets over the radio that he actually wrote, thus, padding his productivity. When he reported to me the following morning, I suspended him without pay for four days, charging him with Unbecoming Conduct and Untruthfulness. Being untruthful by itself was an offense that generally resulted in termination. When I spoke to him, I advised him that he had the right to appeal my action, but to think before he did so, since my captain, Larry, had already told me that if he appealed, he would probably double the suspension to eight or ten days.

This deputy learned a lesson and was grateful that I did not recommend termination because he had essentially lied. Because of this deputy's actions, I was forced to discontinue my incentive program. Believe me, the rest of the squad was relentless in their displeasure over what the deputy had done and made him pay verbally for many months to come. Even though I discontinued the incentive, my squad remained the top producer of all eight squads for thirty-six straight months.

We worked on the honor system, no time clocks and no sign-ins, which was maintained by each squad's sergeant and lieutenant. If someone had extra time, we had the discretion to send someone home early or to allow him or her to come in late if the person had a school event with a child or some other family event. As a lieutenant, I was now a salaried employee, so I was no longer eligible for overtime pay, so if I worked over in any capacity I would take my time in the form of compensation or comp time. I generally saved my comp time for when we were on the night shift and would often go home early using my time or take a day off on the middle of the week.

As a patrol commander, I was now in a position to have deputies regularly exhibit actions that warranted recognition. When in CID, my investigators were busy conducting investigations and rarely exhibited actions that would cause me to write them up for a commendation. In the Patrol Division, the deputies were out dealing directly with the public, pulling injured people out of a burning car, rescuing someone in distress, making an exemplary arrest and so forth. Some supervisors were lazy in this regard and never recognized their subordinates, which was reflected in their subordinates' morale.

I knew that writing someone up for Deputy of the Month, or a Letter of Commendation required the attention of the sheriff. My letter went through our entire chain of command, captain, major, chief deputy, and then the sheriff, who in turn sent an endorsement letter back with the award. This recognition was greatly appreciated by the rank and file and was made a permanent part of their personnel files.

Although disciplinary action was a necessary part of dealing with subordinates, the award system was rewarding and went a long way in keeping the troops content.

My old lieutenant from my METRO days, Marvin was now a chief deputy and the last person in my present chain of command before the sheriff. He knew of my long interest in drug enforcement and from time to time would ask me to put together a small task force of about six to eight guys to target bad drug areas around the county. He arranged for me to have the people I wanted, and we planned one on one where he wanted us to go. These little assignments only lasted two to three days at a time, but we made many arrests and seized a lot of drugs.

Our policy and procedure did not allow for more than two police vehicles to be at a restaurant at any one time. For one thing, it did not look good to the public, and more importantly, it concentrated visible manpower off the street. One Friday night shift, at about 4:30 a.m.,

I got a call over the radio from one of my guys stating that he needed to meet with me as soon as possible. I told him to call my cell phone, but he said he needed to see me. This was an unusual request for so early in the morning, so I agreed to meet him at a local twenty-four-hour waffle restaurant. When I arrived, three of my guys looked guilty as hell, as though they had done something wrong. Not knowing what my reaction would be for there being a third unauthorized deputy out at a restaurant, they walked me outside to the back parking lot where their three marked cruisers were parked. Between the three cars, there were six flat tires.

There had apparently been some loud and boisterous people in the restaurant, who had to be spoken to by one of the deputies. When they left, they had apparently slashed six tires, two on each car. My guys had only three spare tires between them, so that left the problem of finding three more spare tires so they could remedy the situation. They knew I was pissed off, and they worried, I am sure, about whether I would write them up, but my first concern was getting three police vehicles back into service as quickly as possible.

I told them to start changing tires out, and I would find tires, which was an issue because two were Fords and one was a Dodge, which had a different size tire and rim. After about forty-five minutes, I came back with three tires, and my three guys were just finishing putting a spare on each car. By now it was starting to rain. The end of shift was closing in, it was getting light, and they were a sight—dirty, wet, and disheveled. To break the ice, I pulled up and rolled my window down, and they all stopped to hear what I would say. I said, "Can you all rotate my tires?" which resulted in a good laugh by all four of us. I had them take the three tires and told them how to write the report that would have to accompany the vandalism, making sure there was no mention that three cars were parked at the same restaurant. They appreciated that I never took action against the third officer to arrive and knew that I would never mention it to any of my superiors. They had definitely learned their lesson.

My sheriff was one who liked to volunteer manpower and equipment to other agencies, and he encouraged his staff to offer assistance whenever a situation arose. The sheriff was out and about whenever you least expected him to be. He monitored all radio frequencies in the county and often pulled up on a traffic stop as a back-up officer whenever he saw someone on a stop, no matter what agency it was. When hurricanes hit in other areas or in other states, he quickly activated crews of manpower and equipment in that direction. He authorized any patrol lieutenant to offer any assistance other agencies needed.

Part of the duties of a lieutenant were that about every third month or so, we stood duty as the Command Duty Officer, which was from the end of business on Friday afternoon until the start of business on Monday morning. This duty required that we be out and about, especially during the evening to early morning hours. We were essentially the ranking officer of the Sheriff's Office for the weekend. It was our responsibility to make appropriate notifications to higher levels of authority when serious incidents occurred. This responsibility was instituted because sergeants were the ranking supervisors on weekends and the Command Staff felt it necessary to have someone of a higher rank available to make decisions. I think this came about because there had been several incidents in which no notification was made up the chain of command.

***

Family Update

In this time frame, my oldest son, Doug, had graduated from high school, and, as I mentioned before, had enlisted in the Marine Corps Reserves. He went to boot camp just seventy miles away at Parris Island

and ended up in F Company, Second Recruit Training Battalion, the very same company I served in as a drill instructor in 1970–1971. He knew exactly what to expect and excelled through his training. He actually liked boot camp and graduated as a PFC and squad leader and managed to qualify as an EXPERT rifleman. Watching him graduate from Parris Island was a very proud day for me, although I was a little disappointed in the fact that he graduated from a different parade deck from the one I did, and the one that I used as a drill instructor twenty years prior. The old parade deck was in the process of being remodeled and repaved.

While Doug served his six-month active duty obligation to the Marine Corps, my son Pete remained active in the Law Enforcement Explorer program and became the ranking officer in the unit, previously held by his brother. He had enrolled in the Air Force ROTC program when it started his freshman year and was actively working his way through the ranks there too.

My daughter Christy was a store manager for a large clothing chain and had relocated to North Carolina to take over as manager there. She had worked in this chain since she was in high school and had worked her way to becoming a manager.

Several days after Doug's graduation, he was riding with an officer on my squad, which is allowed as long as the supervisor signs a Ride-Along Form. Doug was just home from boot camp that week and on leave before returning to Camp Lejeune and had ridden with officers dozens of times as a police cadet.

There was a hot domestic dispute call at a house we were all familiar with, and we regularly responded there for problems, mainly arguments between husband and wife. I was the first in the door, and I had two other officers there, along with Doug, who was riding with one of those officers. The husband and wife were hollering and screaming, and it became apparent that we were going to end up arresting the husband and probably take into emergency protective custody an infant child who was in a bassinet in the corner of the living room. I got between the father and the baby and was getting ready to announce our intent and to make my move to grab the infant. My guys all knew my intent based on body language and eye contact between us. As I made my move to get between the infant and the father, he saw what I was doing and the fight was on. Once he started fighting, I had the child in my left arm and pushed the father away with my right arm as my guys attempted to place him under arrest. It took both of the two other officers, Lew and Sam, with a little assistance from Doug, who was observing, to subdue the father.

We backed our way out of the house and subdued the father in an approved chokehold, which caused him to pass out momentarily. Lew told me outside what happened, and because of the commotion among all of the other family members that were present, I told Lew to drive around the corner then call EMS to respond to treat his unruly prisoner. That unruly prisoner ended up killing his wife several years later, so you can see that we were dealing with a real fine piece of human crap.

***

One Friday night not long before Christmas of 1993, I was working the three to eleven shift and had a barricaded subject in a house with a handgun and others in the house. I was negotiating with the depressed, male subject who was threatening suicide. I had already notified Mobile Crisis to respond, but they were slow in coming because of the Friday rush hour. While in the middle of negotiating with the suicidal subject, my cell phone rang, and it was the sheriff. He was hosting the annual Sheriff's Office Christmas Party and was notified of the situation that I was working. He offered his assistance and wanted to know what I needed. I assured him that I was close to convincing the subject out of the house, which I did just minutes after the phone call. This is just the kind of person and boss the sheriff was—always aware of what was going on and available to provide assistance when necessary.

***

One night on midnight shift, we had a car chase that ended when the vehicle became bogged down in soft dirt off an exit to a busy highway. I arrived at the scene within minutes, and when I got out of the car, I could immediately detect the odor of fresh gunpowder in the air, so I knew someone had fired a weapon. John met me and briefed me on what happened. Because I could smell fresh gunpowder, I then asked the big question: "Who popped some caps here?" John then hung his head and said, "I did boss." I then did what my lieutenant did for me more than thirteen years before. I told him to get rid of the spent casings and to quickly replace them, and clean his weapon as soon as possible. He was not justified in discharging his weapon, but I did not want to jam him up for his actions. He was a great street cop and eligible for retirement.

***

On May 18, 1994, I went to the house to have dinner and was just finishing when a call came over the radio about a shooting in the southern part of the county. I drove down there with lights and sirens and arrived to find that an elderly couple had been shot and killed in their own home. I notified headquarters to have a CID supervisor make immediate contact with me so I could advise him what he had on scene. Within thirty minutes, there were a dozen investigators on scene.

We quickly determined that the shooter was an ex-boyfriend of the murdered couple's daughter. The shooter, James Earl Reed, had just completed thirty-seven months of incarceration in a federal penitentiary in Kentucky. He had been issued a bus ticket to a halfway house but, instead, hitchhiked to Charleston with the apparent intent to kill his ex-girlfriend. He hid in the backyard and entered the house, wanting to know where his ex was. When the elderly couple told him she was not there, he shot and killed them both. His identity was immediately broadcast, and he was located and arrested within hours of the murders. He was charged with two counts of Capital Murder and was facing the death penalty, if convicted, for his actions.

I had now been a patrol commander for almost three years, and I had not spent more than three years anywhere to date in my career. I started keeping my ears open for available lieutenants' positions and had spoken to my old CID lieutenant, Ernie, who was now a captain in Judicial Operations. He seemed surprised that I was interested and said he would keep me in mind when a position became available. I had ulterior motives in asking for the transfer because my two-and-a-half-year-old son, Joe, had recently been diagnosed as being autistic. The transfer would allow me the luxury of being home every evening and off on weekends. Paula and I were still exploring his diagnosis and closely working with medical professionals to get answers about his particular form of autism, later diagnosed as Asperger' Syndrome. This was devastating news to us, but we were finally able to determine how to deal with Joe's particular physical issues, which turned out to be a very long journey.

For the past two years, I had become affiliated with an Italian deli downtown where my wife, Paula, had cooked part time after the birth of our son, Joe. She is Italian and a great cook, and they paid her well for her time, allowing her to come in when she was available. I had begun to work there part time on the side and ended up becoming the bookkeeper and part-time manager of the store. The owner was an absentee owner and spent much of his time out of state, relying on me to do payroll and to hire and fire and purchase merchandise.

Since jobs comparable the one Paula had in New York were not available in Charleston, she decided to go back to teaching, which paid more closely to what she was used to making up north. She began by teaching part time and cooking part time and was eventually hired full time at a local high school in the business department. Now that she was teaching full time and still cooking two afternoons a week and on Saturday mornings along with my part-time management of the deli, we were able to save enough extra money to move to a larger home in the same general neighborhood. We were now in a two-story brick home with four bedrooms, a large yard, and an in-ground pool, which was a big hit with the kids and their friends.

Not long after moving into our new house, I was on my way home for dinner one evening and responded to a call at a mom-and-pop grocery store not too far from the house. The store was on the corner near the high school and was run by an old couple who had been there for more than twenty-five years. The call went out as an armed robbery, and I was there within a minute. When I arrived, I found the male owner standing behind the counter with a gunshot wound to his arm. His wife was also present but was too excited to talk. He was able to provide a good description of the suspect, who, as it turned out, was a teenager who lived on my street about seven houses away. We tracked him down and were able take him into custody before the end of the night. He went to prison, and the old couple eventually sold the property, which is now a restaurant.

Two of my guys, Kevin and Greg, were big into making drug arrests, and my interest and experience in drug enforcement allowed them to work together and regularly be proactive in areas where drugs were sold. There was one place in particular that I recall on John's Island in our district called "The Hill." We made it a point to make at least two swings through there per shift to keep the drug dealers on their toes. One night I went in with Kevin and Greg. I had three other cars go in with me, and as we went in, I saw one known dealer jump off of a bicycle and run into the woods with the others who had been standing next to an open fire pit. I left my guys there to look for those who ran, and as I was leaving, I saw the bike lying on the side of the dirt road. I knew we did not catch the one who was on the bike. I then told my guys over the radio to tell him if they saw him that he had a flat tire on his bike. I then proceeded to drive over the bike, crushing the bike to pieces and into a mangled mess. There are ways to get back at the bad guys, and this definitely pissed one of them off, for sure.

***

In August of 1995 we were plagued with a rash of car break-ins all over James Island. At the time, there had been over fifty cars broken into as they sat in the driveways of their owners. The group of thugs who had been committing these thefts had been hitting cars every night, and the brass was putting pressure on the Patrol Division to catch them and to make arrests.

On a Friday midnight shift, I was fortunate to have a full squad of deputies working, and sometime right after midnight we met to brief the guys working that area to patrol specific neighborhoods and to be watchful for anything suspicious. Just as we ended our little briefing, a call went out from a nearby subdivision that a car was being broken into, and a description of the suspects' vehicle was broadcast over the radio. Since my mother lived in that very same neighborhood, I knew it like the back of my hand and knew that there was only one way out back to the main road. We swarmed the neighborhood, and Ron immediately engaged the suspect vehicle in a chase through the neighborhood, while we sealed off the only exit. The chase ended when the suspect vehicle, loaded with five suspects, ran up onto someone's lawn and crashed into a large clump of bushes against a tree. Ron immediately apprehended one and placed him in the backseat of his cruiser. One came running right at me, and as he got close, I was able to hit him in the head with my flashlight, which did not affect him one bit as he kept running on by and into the neighborhood. There were now four suspects on the loose in the neighborhood, and we had them contained. This particular neighborhood was surrounded on three sides by salt-water marsh, and the only street out was blocked.

I immediately set up a tight perimeter that contained the four remaining suspects and called for my buddy Larry who was out with his dog team and already on the way since he was monitoring the radio traffic. While waiting for his team to arrive, I went to the police vehicle that had the one suspect we had in custody, and he appeared to be a big guy, about six feet one inch and about 190 lb. As he sat in the backseat, I asked him a question, and he immediately responded with a smartass answer. We had just been involved in a vehicle chase, then a foot pursuit with four suspects, and tempers were heated, including mine. When the suspect in custody let loose with his smartass, profane answer to me, I stupidly responded by striking him with a blow to the side of his head. As soon as I did it, I knew I had made a major and possibly career-ending mistake and immediately exited the backseat of the cruiser.

I had been a cop for thirteen years and had been a lieutenant for three of those years. I had made hundreds of arrests and had contact with many hundreds more and had never struck a handcuffed suspect before that night. I had violated his rights and knew that I would answer for my actions once this ongoing incident was resolved.

Larry and his dog team arrived, and I met with him to show him the direction that the suspects had fled and assured him that we had not contaminated the area, which was information I knew he wanted to know. Larry put one of his bloodhounds out with two of his team members tracking. Within an hour we had located and apprehended all four remaining suspects, who were hiding in four separate locations in the neighborhood.

We transported all five suspects to the station and processed them for the car they had broken into that night, and the Criminal Investigations Division later charged them with additional counts, thus solving the rash of auto break-ins in our district.

In all of the confusion of the incident and chasing suspects around the neighborhood, I had ignored the fact that my right hand was swelling and quickly turning black and blue, so I went to the hospital and had an X-ray taken. The doctors determined that I had broken my hand when I struck the suspect. I had to wait until Monday to see a hand specialist, and when I did, he told me that I had broken my hand in five places and would need surgery to repair the injury.

Since I was injured, I was now considered to be on light duty and was unable to work the road. After seeing the doctor Monday, I went to my captain and told him what had caused the injury, and my major and did the same with his superior. I worked the remainder of the week in the Training Office and had my surgery that Friday. The surgeons ended up putting five pins in my hand to repair the five breaks. As soon as I found out that there had been a formal complaint, I made sure I told my guys who were with me that night that if they were approached by Internal Affairs Investigators that they should tell them exactly what they saw, and I had better not find out that anyone lied in order to help my situation. I told them all that I had made a mistake, and I expected to pay for what I did.

In that same time frame, I was summoned to Internal Affairs to answer the excessive force complaint made by the parents of the suspect

I had assaulted. I gave my version of the story, which was exactly what had happened.

I remained on light duty in training for about a month and until the pins were removed. I now also had to go through at least another month of physical therapy. As soon as the pins were removed from my hand, the transfer that I had previously requested came through, and I had orders to go to Judicial Operations, where I now worked directly for my old lieutenant Ernie, who was now a captain.

JUDICIAL OPERATIONS
23

ABOUT TWO WEEKS AFTER BEING TRANSFERRED TO JUDICIAL Operations, my captain advised me that he had been told to take me to report to the Chief of Operations. This chief was my old captain when I was the sergeant of the Warrants Unit. I had worked for him as a captain, major, and most recently as chief, and we had always gotten along well. When I met him, he advised me that due to the investigation into the citizen complaint, he was compelled to suspend me without pay for a period of fifteen days. I had no issue with his actions and felt that the fact that I was a lieutenant, in a position of authority, I should have had the restraint and maturity not to lose my temper to do what I did.

I did my time and was ready to get back to work, particularly because I never had that many days off in succession in my life. My front and backyard in those three weeks could have easily won an award in *Better Homes and Gardens* magazine because I spent the entire time off doing yard work. I was aware that even though I had to this point had an exemplary career, I was smart enough to understand that I had indeed probably hindered my chances to advance further, at least in the near future. I knew that when the rare opportunity came along for a captain's opening, I would be skipped, at least until a few more years had passed.

I had spent almost six years in the Marine Corps, and except when I was in boot camp, had never been so much as chewed out for any infraction. I had now been a cop for thirteen years and never had any form of disciplinary action taken against me. I had screwed up, and I would pay whatever the price would be.

Being the lieutenant in Judicial Operations was not exactly a pie job. I was now responsible for thirty-seven employees, more than many police departments in the entire state of South Carolina. I was responsible for the security of all courtrooms in the building and for all of the prisoners that had to be brought from the jail to be present for their trial or hearing. My guys were responsible for transporting more than three thousand prisoners a year between the jail and the courthouse. They were also responsible for traveling to various state prisons around the state to pick up prisoners for trials. These same guys sat through trials and hearings and were the only armed deputy between the prisoner and the public. This job required that they be dressed in a suit or sport coat, and they wore the same equipment on their persons under their coats that they would wear if they were in uniform.

I was responsible for a second courtroom facility downtown, which was approximately six miles away, that housed Family Court. This court handled all juvenile cases and all divorce or separation trials or hearings. I tried to get there at least twice a week. I trusted the sergeant in charge, and knew him well since he was at one time one of my patrol sergeants.

I had fifteen jailers who were uniformed personnel, who had all come from the jail and earned the privilege through application and interview to be able to transfer to court security. These positions were sought after since officers worked Monday to Friday with weekends off. There were two holding facilities adjacent to my office that housed fifteen prisoners at a time as they awaited their hearing or trial before a judge.

Each morning and afternoon, the prisoners were escorted in leg irons and waist chains into the short hallway to the holding facility. I regularly sat at my desk and saw each and every prisoner pass by my door. Several times a week I would see someone who I had previously arrested, usually for drug violations, and the prisoner was always surprised to see me sitting there at my desk in a shirt and tie watching over them. Many of the comments from the prisoners were favorable and a reunion of sorts, and in some cases not, since I was often the one responsible for their incarceration.

I was also in charge of all Bailiffs, who were all retired law enforcement officers. They wore a suit or sport coat and were armed, and they were extremely helpful manpower-wise when we were shorthanded. They were all seasoned, veteran cops and supplemented their retirement by working up to forty hours per week.

I don't know how this unit fell under my command, but I was also in charge of the DARE (Drug Abuse Resistance Education), which was a nationally known program that taught children in local schools how to "Just Say No" to drugs from an early age. A female sergeant and four deputies manned that unit.

The chief was a great guy and commanded the bureau, called Special Operations, where I now worked. He was a retired ATF (Alcohol, Tobacco, and Firearms) agent and a colonel in the Marine Corps Reserve. The chief's only drawback was the fact that he was a micromanager.

The captain, Ernie, had always been a great guy to work for. He knew what he was getting from me, and vice versa. I knew exactly what to expect from his leadership and respected him without question.

I was one of two lieutenants in the division, and the other was now my old partner Andi, who I had worked with several times before. We had been partners in METRO and were promoted to sergeant on the same day in March of 1989. We then worked together for the same lieutenant in our next assignment. She was now in charge of Warrants, Transport, Civil Process, and Animal Control. One of us was required to be in the building at all times, so we worked together in making that happen.

Having thirty-seven employees working for me, more than any other lieutenant in the Sheriff's Office, meant that I was usually dealing with a sergeant who had a problem with one of his or her employees. The responsibility of so many employees was never a challenge, but it ensured that I was always busy, especially since I had one-third of my subordinates at another location.

One advantage in this position meant that I had the opportunity to sit in on any trial of my choosing. Since the jail was full of accused murderers awaiting trial, there was an abundance of murder trials to sit and watch, and I was able to watch some of the attorneys in action whom I had known for years. I observed the good ones, and, of course, there were some bad ones. The bad ones were often embarrassing to watch, and I often felt sorry for the defendants who had paid good money for a professional defense, hoping through promises made by some of these incompetent attorneys that they would win their case and their client was not going to prison.

On June 12, 1994, the brutal murder of Nicole Brown Simpson, the estranged wife of retired NFL (National Football League) football player and actor O. J. Simpson, and an acquaintance, Mr. Ronald Goldman in Los Angeles made the front page of every newspaper in the country because O. J. Simpson himself was the accused. His high-profile arrest, car chase, and subsequent ten-month-long trial with overpaid, agenda-oriented attorneys captivated the entire country. I too was caught up and watched as much of the trial as possible.

O. J.'s trial started in January 1995 and went on and on until the unpopular verdict was rendered on October 3, 1995.

I had previously thought that the Rodney King case in Los Angeles in 1992 was the worst thing to happen to law enforcement since the '60s. I was wrong because the O. J. Simpson case, in my estimation, had the most devastating impact on law enforcement ever. Never before had attorneys made a police officer on a case come across as a person not to be believed or that he was a racist who could never be trusted. When Johnny Cochran turned the case into a circus, which he was paid handsomely to do, all he had to do was cloud the issues of the case for one juror, thus insuring a favorable verdict for his client.

That investigation was handled professionally and by the book, as had so many others by LAPD, which regularly handled death investigations with celebrity involvement. The department had crossed its *T*s and dotted it's *I*s, but it did not matter once Cochran discredited the reputation of one of the detectives on the case, Detective Mark Furhman. When the time came in the trial for the moment of truth, when O. J. attempted to try the glove on, even that was tainted by Cochran because who tries on a leather glove wearing an oversized rubber glove? It is impossible. Try it sometime.

The antics used by O. J. Simpson's attorneys now made it possible for local mediocre attorneys to try their hand at using the same tricks on juries by attempting to taint the reputation of an unsuspecting law enforcement officer on the stand at trial. As a result, cops were no longer believable on the witness stand because if an attorney painted a picture to the jurors, and they believed it, obtaining a conviction became more difficult for previously slam-dunk cases.

I have testified numerous times in court in several high profile cases and have never felt the need to be untruthful. There is absolutely no reason for a cop to lie on the stand. If you did not make a good case in the first place, the case would not be in court for prosecution. Prosecutors will never try a badly investigated case or a case in which the evidence at hand is overwhelming, so there is never a need to be untruthful. In more than twenty-nine years of law enforcement, I never stated anything to the court except the God's honest truth.

***

Friday morning was the biggest day of court in the courthouse because we held Bond Reduction Hearings. These hearings were for defendants who had been in jail and had not yet had been able to post the bond that had been set or on cases where there was no bond, such as murder or kidnapping.

It was common for there to be 100 to 150 spectators in the audience at these hearings. Many of those present were often relatives of a murdered victim. There was a wooden railing separating the spectators and the area where the hearings were heard by the presiding judge. Each individual prisoner would be walked in from a side anteroom. He or she was always in waist chains and leg irons to ensure that he or she could not escape.

One particular Friday I was in the courtroom standing near the door where the prisoner incarcerated for murder entered the courtroom. I had ample manpower on either side of the rail and someone standing next to the defendant and his attorney. There were family members of the person who had been murdered, and they were standing in the front row on the other side of the railing so they could represent their family and speak if allowed by the judge.

As the hearing began, I saw a large, male subject, who was about six feet four inches and about 275 lb. quickly jump the rail and run past several bailiffs in the court and right at the accused prisoner. I was about as far away as he was from the accused, and I knew what he had on his mind. As he got to the accused, he got in several punches with his fist to the back of the accused before I was able to drag the suspect away. I fought this guy to the ground, handcuffed him immediately, and pushed him into the side anteroom. This incident could have been much more serious if this guy had had a weapon. The prisoner was taken to another room for his safety, and other family members had to be removed from the courtroom. I escorted the guy who attacked the accused before the judge, and he immediately sentenced him to jail for contempt of court.

Up until then there had been no X-ray machines in the courthouse. The only check of persons entering the building was by a cursory hand-held scanner as each person entered the courthouse. There was a cursory inspection of briefcases and purses, but up until then security was not maximized. It took an incident such as the one I described to cause us to reevaluate security at the entrances to the building as well as more strict security in each individual courtroom. We had to have the cooperation of the chief judge so he could ensure that *all* judges who worked in the building were on board with our new security requirements throughout the building.

There were upset family members of those who were having trials and hearings because of the fact that they were no longer allowed to bring their whole family before the judge to show support for their family member. There was no funding available to purchase more advanced X-ray equipment for the two entrances to the building, so I went to the Federal Courthouse downtown to see if it had any old machines it could spare. I was in luck because they had just purchased new equipment, and they transferred ownership of their old machines to the Sheriff's Office for our use in our main courthouse. I borrowed a county truck myself and went downtown to get the machines. I set up the largest machine in the lobby of the main entrance after hours and positioned it where I wanted it and planned to meet with the morning shift personnel the first thing the next morning in order to instruct them on how to use the equipment and what procedure we would now use for persons entering the building.

I made sure I was in the building earlier than usual the next morning, and I immediately went to the newly acquired X-ray machine in the lobby at the front entrance to meet with my personnel before the building was opened for business. When I looked at the machine, I saw that it had been moved and was now inoperable. When I checked the connections to the machine, I discovered that the power cord had been cut, rendering it powerless. I asked who had moved the machine, and one of my guys told me who it was. I was livid because after all of the trouble I had gone through, the machine was now unusable. When it was moved, the power cord was cut, and I then did something that I have never done in front of subordinates before. I lost my cool and began to chew the man responsible for moving the machine in front of other subordinates. I told him to go upstairs to my office and continued to chew his butt all the way up the stairwell until my captain, who had heard the commotion, stood at the top of the stairwell and said, "At ease, Lieutenant." I realized then that I was out of line.

I went to my office and sat with the employee responsible, and he was unable to give me an acceptable explanation as to why he took it upon himself to move the X-ray machine. The machine, I might add, was as big as a dining room table and about five feet tall. I ended up sending him home and suspended him without pay for three days, and that was the end of that issue.

I realized that I had indeed failed to follow my own core beliefs of leadership and sat back when it was over and reassessed what I had done and reassured myself that I would never deal with a subordinate again in the presence of others. Another lesson in life learned. Chewing someone out as a drill instructor, in front of an entire platoon of his peers, was a different story altogether.

***

Incidents in the courthouse were not common, but we always had to be ready for the unexpected, just as though we were working the street.

There were long hallways in the courthouse that we had to use to escort prisoners from the holding facility to their respective courtrooms. While escorting prisoners, we would first clear the hall and alert those in offices in the hallway that we were escorting prisoners. We did not want an employee to walk out of an office and to be between a deputy and a prisoner. One day we had an unruly prisoner who caused a disturbance in one of the hallways, and while one of the deputies was struggling on the floor to control the prisoner, he had the tip of one of his fingers bitten off in the altercation. Many of the prisoners that were in the facility knew that this was their last stop before lengthy prison terms and really did not care about what they did to a deputy.

Around this time frame, my daughter Christy and her husband Timmy had returned to Charleston after working in Gastonia, North Carolina, for the past two years. Their first child, Jeremy, was less than two years old, and they had missed their family in Charleston. She quickly found employment in the retail business as a store manager and he as a route driver for a local dairy. One day he surprised the entire family by announcing that he had applied to and was hired by the North Charleston Police Department. He never let on to anyone in the family that he was even interested in becoming a cop, and this decision caught us completely off guard.

***

Remember the double-murder case that I mentioned in the previous chapter where an ex-boyfriend looking for his ex-girlfriend ended up murdering her parents on my shift. James Earl Reed's case was coming to trial in the near future, and he was brought over to the courthouse for a pretrial hearing one day. While walking up the hallway to the courtroom, a female family member of the murder victims lunged at Reed as we were escorting him to the hearing. The family member was a daughter of the victims and intended to strike Reed, which she was unable to do because I pushed her out of the way. I came back out of the courtroom and banned her from being present for the hearing. The family complained about my decision, but after I spoke with the judge, he agreed with my decision.

More than a year after the crime was committed, his case went to trial the week of June 10, 1996. James Earl Reed had made the ridiculous decision to represent himself after he fired his public defender (PD). The PD was one of the best attorneys in the PD's office, and Reed should have recognized that because he was being tried for capital murder and faced execution if convicted.

Reed was allowed to wear a suit in court and was admonished by the judge to stay within a few feet of the table assigned for defendants and counsel in the courtroom. Because he was representing himself, we decided to make him wear knee immobilizers, which is a device worn under the pants that locks the knees if he tries to walk too far too fast.

I sat behind Reed through most of the slow-moving trial, which began with jury selection on Monday morning. Selecting a capital murder jury is much harder than for a normal criminal case. Jurors had to be interviewed to determine whether they were capable of making the ultimate decision to execute the defendant. Many were released for either personal or religious convictions.

Because of the publicity in this case, the jurors were sequestered to keep them from seeing the local news and newspapers regarding the trial. We were also in charge of the well-being of the jurors from the time they left the courthouse until the following morning when they returned.

It came to a point in the trial when witnesses began testimony and the medical examiner was called to the witness stand to testify about the autopsies that she had performed on the two murder victims. Prior to her testimony the prosecutor planned to have the judge rule that the doctor was an expert witness, and to do so required that many questions were asked regarding her background, which stretched over thirty years. When the doctor testified that she had personally performed more than 13,000 autopsies and recited her credentials, Reed turned around to me and said, "Damn, she's good. I think I'm fucked." I think it was at this point that he realized that his decision to represent himself was very real.

I always enjoyed listening to Dr. Conradi's testimony on the stand because she was one of the most interesting persons I ever met. I am honored to have worked with her while attending the month long Medical Examiners School in January of 1991. She was only about four feet eleven inches tall and stood on a small wooden stool to perform her autopsies. Often she had to climb up on the table with the body to get a closer look at what she was doing.

The trial moved more slowly than normal because the judge constantly had to remind Reed when legal responses were required on his behalf. It was clear that Reed was doomed when evidence of his confession came out and the three witnesses who saw him leave the house immediately after the shooting testified. He was found guilty after a short deliberation, but in South Carolina, the law required a waiting period of at least 24 hours after the verdict before the second, shorter trial—in which the jurors would determine whether Reed would get life or be sentenced to death—could begin.

Reed wisely allowed the public defender he had originally fired to assist him in the death penalty phase of the trial, which lasted a whole day. In this phase, both sides are allowed to present character witnesses to tell the jury either about their loss or what a great person the defendant is. The original trial ended on a Friday; to allow for the mandatory waiting period between trials, the penalty phase convened on Sunday morning and lasted into the afternoon. The jury was presented with all they needed to make a determination, and it took just thirty minutes for them to deliberate and reach a conclusion. They returned to the courtroom, and the jury foreman read the verdict: death!.

James Earl Reed showed no emotion when he was sentenced to death by the presiding judge, and he spoke only a few words in the car as we drove him to the county jail for eventual transfer to the South Carolina Department of Corrections death row. Reed was executed on June 20, 2008—fourteen years, one month, and two days after he committed our society's ultimate crime, murder.

At the time, my son Pete had just graduated from high school and was about to enter the Marine Corps. He too wanted to be a cop, but he was only eighteen, so off he went. He was medically discharged after thirty-three days at Parris Island, however, because of a back injury he did not even realize he had—apparently, he had been hurt in a motorcycle mishap long since past. Disappointed, he now had to kill time until he was age-eligible to become a cop. He ended up taking a job as a police dispatcher at the same department in which his older brother, Doug, worked. He excelled in this new endeavor, and he was quickly promoted to be the supervisor of his shift.

Pete had also been active as a police cadet and had spent all four years of high school as an ROTC cadet. By his senior year, he had risen to the rank of ROTC colonel and was the cadet commander of his school's cadet program. I believe that his background as a leader of police cadets and ROTC gave him valuable leadership skills that had a great influence on his advancement to become a supervisor before he was twenty years old.

By now, I had been in judicial operations for more than a year and a half. In the time since I was first assigned, the chief deputy had been my patrol captain, my captain while assigned to the warrants division, and most recently the chief deputy of patrol. One of the first black officers hired by the old police department, he had attained the highest rank of any other black officer. Now in his late fifties, he had some health issues. He had recently retired, but arranged with the administration to become one of the retired police officer bailiffs assigned to my unit.

As I mentioned earlier, the only time I was ever in any trouble in my entire career was when I assaulted the suspect we had under arrest. I took my time without pay for my wrongdoing and went on to work hard to regain my reputation. Sometime after serving the time off I learned that the person I had assaulted had sued the sheriff's office. It ended up being settled for the ridiculously low amount of $500, but more interesting and questionable was the fact that the ambulance-chasing attorney was the nephew of the retired chief deputy—was suing my employer. In that time frame, I learned of several other lawsuits filed by the same attorney against my employer after citizen complaints ended up on the chief deputy's desk.

After speaking to several of the deputies who were the subject of the complaints, we all concluded that this particular attorney was probably being provided inside information from his uncle. With these facts, I lost all respect for this former retired chief.

That retired chief deputy was now working for me, which was a ticklish situation. He was chronically late for work and regularly fell asleep in the courtroom during trials. My sergeant and my other crew of courtroom deputies all complained to me about this former chief. My only alternative was to speak to him myself, which ended up being a waste of time. I then went to my captain and asked him to sit in on some trials to see for himself. Once the problem was confirmed, the captain and I went to see our chief and dropped the problem in his lap. My chief met with the problem child, and the situation improved somewhat. Not long after this issue, he was hospitalized and deemed unable to work.

He eventually died, and I think I was the only ranking officer who did not attend his funeral.

Serial Rape Trial

Duncan Proctor—who had terrorized the women of the Charleston area for many months during a string of at least thirty reported rapes in several jurisdictions in the Charleston area—was under surveillance on the morning of June 19, 1992. As investigators attempted to stop him, he took pursuing cops on a high-speed chase onto Interstate 26, which connects to Interstate 95 north of Charleston. When he wrecked, he suffered serious head injuries, and in 1993, he was determined to be mentally incompetent and was sent to a state mental facility.

There came a time when the prosecutors in the case were made aware that Proctor was selling cigarettes and loaning money to fellow inmates. Additional hearings were heard and in 1997, he was now ruled competent to stand trial. His court-appointed defense attorneys, two highly capable females, were tasked with representing him. They successfully obtained a court ruling that he could not be tried in Charleston due to the amount of publicity involved in all of the rapes he was accused of committing and consequently would never be able to get a fair trial in Charleston.

It was decided that Duncan Proctor's trial would be held beginning March 1, 1998, in Walhalla, South Carolina, way up in Oconee County, 260 miles from Charleston. Since the crime occurred in Charleston County, our agency was tasked with providing security for Proctor while at trial. The Oconee County Courthouse was small and old, but adequate in size to accommodate the trial.

Three of my deputies and I escorted Proctor from a prison in Anderson, South Carolina, daily, where he was being temporarily housed, and each morning of the trial transported him to Oconee in a van because he was wheelchair bound.

We were very experienced in transporting prisoners and had a police vehicle in front and to the rear of the van, and I followed in a third vehicle to keep vehicles from driving next to the van transporting Proctor. The very first morning of trial, I was forced to block several Charleston news vehicles that tried to get next to the van as reporters attempted to take photographs, one of the reasons the trial was moved away from Charleston.

The trial was uneventful but extremely interesting to me because of my interest and experience in investigations. After a five-day trial, Proctor was convicted for the best case of the thirty rapes he committed. He was sentenced to life for one count of first degree burglary, one consecutive thirty-year sentence for Criminal Sexual Conduct, one consecutive five-year sentence for Assault and Battery with the Intent to Kill, and one consecutive one-year term for possession of a firearm.

A second trial was held later, with little to no fanfare, in which he was sentenced to similar time for another rape in order to ensure that Duncan Proctor never, ever saw the light of day again in his lifetime. Justice had ultimately prevailed, and we were done dealing with him forever.

Had he had never committed the crimes, there would certainly be two fine sheriff's deputies alive and well today. Sergeant Buddy Lloyd and Deputy William Nalley died needlessly in the helicopter crash in support of the Serial Crime Task Force.

Sergeant Hubert C. (Buddy) Lloyd
Deputy William Nalley
End of Watch, Sunday, June 7, 1992

Since first becoming a supervisor in March of 1989, I administered numerous forms of disciplinary action against subordinates. I do not think I was ever unfair in any way and never had any actions appealed for any grounds, which sends a message that the subordinates either agreed with the punishment or understood that an appeal could result in additional or more severe punishment. The fact that I had been the recipient of disciplinary action myself actually had a positive effect on my later decisions to suspend someone without pay. I think that it made me a little more understanding with others since I had been in their shoes. Thereafter, any disciplinary action given by me was done so with much more deliberation on my part than in the past.

I had a great guy as my courtroom security sergeant who had been with the Sheriff's Office since before the merge, and he knew his job well and was an exemplary employee. I knew as most of those close to him that he had been having some trouble at home with his wife, which I knew included some of his wife's blood relatives.

One day this particular sergeant came to work with a distinct odor of alcohol on his breath. I could have made a big deal about it and could have easily ended his career in law enforcement. Because of the fact that I was aware of his personal problems at home, I decided to send him home and admonished him not to ever return to work with the smell of alcohol on his person again, and I told him to use the day off as sick leave. So far, his actions had never affected his quality of work performance, but I now knew that I had to keep a closer eye on him. He was extremely grateful for the lenience I showed with his situation and never let me down again. I was obligated, however, to notify my captain and make him aware of the situation, and he concurred with my decision.

I had another sergeant, a female, who did a great job in her assignment, but she would come to me every time someone other than she was promoted to the rank of lieutenant. Her trips to me about why she was not being promoted always ended with her in tears, which I have mentioned previously was a huge turnoff and a distinct sign of weakness to me. I did everything I could to facilitate her promotion by nominating her for awards and by providing stellar performance evaluations. After my departure, her position was reclassified to lieutenant, which solved her issue of not being promoted on her merit. She later attained higher rank and thumbed her nose at others after her advancement. She retired as a bitter and unhappy person and was one of those who slept her way through her career.

***

My hours while working in Judicial Operations allowed me the luxury of being able to continue my management of the deli downtown, which never caused me any lost time to the job. My youngest son was now almost six years old, and we had made great strides with Joe's treatment for his shortcomings caused by his autism by arranging for physical therapy, speech therapy, and the assistance he needed in school. He was and remains an amazing person and never ceases to surprise us with his wit and accomplishments.

I had been regularly speaking to an old friend of mine, Keith, who had been promoted to lieutenant when I was. He was now a captain and in charge of METRO, my old stomping ground. He ended up getting married to Avie, one of my old secretaries from CID. Sadly, Avie developed cancer shortly after their marriage, and Keith did not have very much quality time with her before her untimely passing. One of the saddest things I ever did was make funeral arrangements for her, which I did because she certainly deserved a law enforcement funeral as a longtime employee of the Charleston County Police Department and later the Sheriff's Office.

Keith told me that he was contemplating transferring one of his lieutenants and wanted to know if I was interested. By now, I had been in Judicial Operations for right at three years, and I was ready to make the move. The job I was offered was to be the ranking member of the Sheriff's Office in the local Drug Enforcement Task Force

I would be switching positions with J. J. my old friend and teammate from my patrol days. I had replaced him in 1989 when I took over the Warrants Division, and he had been working in narcotics ever since. The orders were published, and the transition for the transfer was arranged.

Upon my departure, I received a Letter of Appreciation written by my captain, and endorsed by my chief deputy and the sheriff, which recognized me for my hard work and dedication to duty.

My August 1984 wreck while responding to an armed robbery of a liquor store.

My official METRO ID photo.

Me while conducting a search warrant in 1986 or 1987.

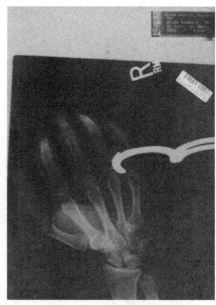
The X-ray of my right hand, May 1987.

In the METRO office, John in foreground, Buddy on right, and me standing in front of my desk.

The Charleston County Recruit Class that I helped to train in 1988.

Being promoted to Sergeant in March 1989. Buddy Lloyd, the helicopter pilot killed in June of 1992, is in front of me.

Our Charleston County Police Cadets after winning first place in 1991. Front row left is my son Doug, and third from right, front row is my son Pete.

My son Pete doing pushups just prior to his graduation from the police academy.

The four cops in our family, L to R, son-in-law, Timmy, son Doug, me, and Pete.

At Pete's graduation, me and my four children, Christy, Doug, Pete, and Joe.

The fifth member of our police family, William Boland Bell, killed in the line of duty in November 2002.

My retirement luncheon, April 1, 2011, with my boss, Chief Tom Buckhannon and my wife, Paula.

Paula and me at a family birthday party in 2009.

Paula, Joe, and me on April 3, 2011.

My entire clan of sixteen, taken on April 3, 2011.

DEA TASK FORCE

24

J. J. AND I WORKED OUT OUR SCHEDULE so that I would spend time with him, bringing him up to speed on his new job responsibilities. After approximately a week, he spent several days with me, and I showed him what was expected of him in Judicial Operations. I think he was ready for a position in which he could again be home at night with his wife and kids.

The Drug Enforcement Task Force was located in a four-story bank building and occupied the entire floor. The Charleston office of the Drug Enforcement Administration had collaborated with my sheriff in 1991, and he provided manpower in the form of a lieutenant, a sergeant, and three investigators. He also provided a civilian clerical employee to assist with Drug Enforcement Administration (DEA) civilian personnel. There were investigators from every local law enforcement agency in the tri-county area so when all of the task force manpower was assembled, there were between twenty to twenty-five agents who all worked cases within the geographical area that the Charleston office was responsible for. The task force was represented by nine federal, state, and local law-enforcement agencies.

When assets were seized, they were shared by the amount of manpower that each participating agency provided. We had six, including the civilian office worker, so my agency received six pieces of pie, so to speak, when assets were shared.

I knew most of the task force members when I reported in because most of them came from local narcotics units I had worked with in the past. Members of the task force who were not already DEA agents were sworn in as Task Force Agents and received federal identification and a badge because, as a member of the unit, agents now had law-enforcement jurisdiction anywhere in the United States.

My sergeant was Jim, who was my sergeant when I was in METRO in the mid- to late-'80s. He stayed in METRO for several years and had been a member of the task force since its inception. Jim was nearing retirement but worked as hard as anyone else half his age. As far as rank was concerned, it is not often that roles are reversed like this. He worked as hard for me as I had worked for him, without question. Jim ran the Transportation Unit within the task force and was responsible for drug interdiction on the interstate highways, train stations, and airports. He facilitated the currency seizures, making sure that it was properly seized, counted, and deposited into a designated bank account.

The other three Task Force Agents (TFAs) were good guys. Larry, a former marine had worked for me when he was in patrol. We gave him the nickname "Lunch" because he always wanted to go to lunch. Kevin was a graduate of The Citadel and had been a cop for several years. Buddy was the most experienced of the group and had been in the unit since its inception.

The DEA bosses were great guys to work for, made me feel at home, and included me in personnel matters and other issues that arose. Ed was the Resident Agent in Charge (RAC) and was a former homicide detective in the city of Baltimore before joining the DEA. Phil was the Group Supervisor (GS), who, as second in command, was the hands-on boss of the task force. Both of them were transferred to their headquarters in

Washington, DC, after this assignment to higher supervisory positions with greater responsibility.

Part of my responsibilities, other than personnel, was that I was the Evidence Custodian for the task force and responsible for the management of a six-figure cash account of funds used to purchase what was needed for the unit, other than what was budgeted. I also provided "buy money" to agents for undercover narcotic purchases and whatever other needs arose.

My computer experience prior to arriving in the task force had been limited to typing memos and minor letter writing, but I was now in a position where I was forced to learn the computer system because I now had to manage my employees' overtime that was submitted bimonthly to DEA Headquarters for reimbursement to Charleston County. The federal government subsidized our overtime up to a certain amount, and when that money was exhausted, the overtime that my guys earned was then compensated by Charleston County. Not only was overtime plentiful, it was encouraged, and my guys had no problem staying out. I had been a salaried employee since becoming a lieutenant in 1992, but now I was in a position to be reimbursed for my hours beyond my scheduled forty-hour week.

Throughout my entire police career, I had fired my duty weapon for qualification twice a year. Policy required that an officer must qualify with his or her assigned weapons, duty and off duty and any personally owned weapons that a person chose to carry off duty. The federal policy, as a member of the task force, required that we shoot for qualification every three months. This was not a problem for me because I enjoyed shooting, and the ammo was free. There were some, however, who did not enjoy shooting, mainly because they were bad shots or simply did not care.

One of the biggest sources of cash for the sheriff's office and all other agencies involved in the task force was money seized during operations.

We regularly seized large quantities of money, and we received our share once the legal process involved with seized currency was complete. It was common for us to seize from between $200,000 to $800,000 at a time, so after administrative fees were subtracted, my agency in particular reaped many hundreds of thousands of dollars that the sheriff was able to redistribute wherever needed. As a result, we always had state-of-the-art equipment and were rarely denied anything we requested.

Without giving too much away in the form of procedure and particulars, members of the unit targeted people traveling southbound on Interstate 95, the main corridor highway from Boston to Florida. We targeted southbound vehicles because those traveling in that direction were heading either to Florida or Atlanta with large sums of cash to purchase large amounts of illegal narcotics, mainly cocaine. Cars with suspicious occupants were interdicted and stopped by uniformed officers trained in the art of identifying these so-called "drug mules." Once the interdiction cops made the stop and located the currency and/or drugs, they would contact our office, and we would assume seizure proceedings for their particular agency. Jim, Kevin and "Lunch" spent most of their nights traveling between Charleston and I-95 to assist when stops and seizures were made.

Similarly, to keep the bad guys off balance, we often switched our efforts to vehicles traveling northbound, which generally resulted in seizures of drugs that they had just purchased in either the Miami or Atlanta area. The theory was that if we missed them traveling south with money, we would get them traveling north with the drugs. The interdiction officers used the same basis for their stops, no matter which direction the bad guys were traveling. It was also common for the bad guys to travel in more than one car in order to provide backup or protection of the target vehicle. Drug smugglers used sophisticated methods to keep secret their money and drugs, sometimes by building electronically released hidden compartments or by hiding them in spare tires. They also altered gas tanks, panels, dashboards, and compartments in the floorboard.

The drug smugglers had millions of dollars in drugs and/or cash seized by our office, and it got so bad for them they would often change their methods and sometimes travel on Amtrak. We often met the Amtrak train at the North Charleston terminal and used the same means of interdiction used on the highway, only these encounters were more "up close and personal." Many times we drove seventy-five miles north, in Kingstree SC, boarded the train, and walked through the train checking out suspicious people until the train arrived in town.

As word went around the drug enforcement community, other units north of Charleston began to use our methods and seized drug money before it passed through our jurisdiction. No matter who got the seizure, these operations definitely put a large hurt on the drug pipeline along the east coast.

My sheriff got together with the sheriff of the adjoining county between Charleston and I-95 and formed a team of drug interdiction officers that included trained drug-sniffing dogs. The team seized not only currency and drugs, but also often ran across fugitives from justice, escapees from other states, and people driving stolen vehicles. It was common for them to become involved in high-speed chases that lasted for miles. All the guys who worked the interstate were highly trained. I often watched videotapes of their stops and chases.

Early on, I decided to send all of my task force agents (TFAs), including me, to a drug-interdiction training class that was to be held in Charleston. It was one of the best classes I ever attended, and I wished I would have had the information earlier in my career.

By now, my oldest son, Doug, had been a cop himself for a few years and quickly became interested in drug enforcement. He ended up becoming a member of the interdiction team my sheriff was responsible for forming. He was on that team for quite a few years until his impending promotion to lieutenant required that he return to his home department.

My son Pete had by now turned twenty-one and was sworn in as a police officer for the department where he had been dispatching. It was truly a proud moment when I went to his academy graduation and was able to have a picture taken together with my two oldest sons, Doug and Pete, and my son in-law, Timmy. By now, Timmy had left the department where he was first hired, and all three of them were now working for the same police department, where I knew they would all look out for each other. One of the instructors at the police academy was a friend of mine, and when I went outside I saw that my buddy would be marching the class into the auditorium. I had a little talk with him, and he pulled Pete out of formation and had him do pushups in his dress uniform, which we all thoroughly enjoyed.

The beauty of working the task force was that you were never rushed to make a case and could take as long as necessary to complete your investigation.

I inherited a marijuana-smuggling case from J. J. that I jumped right into when I arrived. I realized how much I had missed investigating criminal activity and, as luck would have it, the case took a good turn for me not long after I started working it.

Being a member of a federal task force required that I now enforce federal law, which was somewhat different than state law. Making cases using state law involved charging suspects with what was found in their possession, no more and no less. We charged them with the actual amount of drugs we found on their person or under their control.

Federally, we could charge a person who had a history of bad acts, as long as we could prove that the target had distributed or received the illegal narcotics, either by eyewitness statements or statements from co-conspirators. Federally, I may make an arrest for two kilos of cocaine, but after the arrest, I am able to prove that he had been dealing two kilos of cocaine on a regular basis. Whatever I am able to prove is what he can be indicted on and subsequently charged with.

As I mentioned, my marijuana-smuggling case started to move when we stopped a van headed for a house in Charleston. It was loaded with multiple pounds of marijuana. We ended up at the house in question and were able to seize additional marijuana from chest freezers in the garage.

On the basis of the traffic stop and a search warrant of the house, we were able to identify the main supplier of the marijuana, which had been previously unknown.

One of the main players was "JL," whom I had known from working the streets. He was now a much bigger player in this marijuana-smuggling operation and was responsible for dealing many multiple pounds of marijuana per week.

His supplier was identified as "KG," who was living in a large house on a barrier island a block from the ocean at a nearby beach resort community. He also owned, as a front, a skateboard shop on one of the busiest streets in downtown Charleston as well as an indoor skate park in North Charleston. KG had started out in business in town as the owner of an escort service, which was how he met his wife. He graduated from the escort business, which was located in a second-story apartment on King Street, to the skateboard business just down the street.

We spent many hours of surveillance after the aforementioned traffic stop before we ever closed in on the actual smuggling operation. We determined that the marijuana was smuggled across the Mexican border into Texas, then was shipped to KG's skate park in North Charleston. There it was then broken down, weighed, bagged, and then "fronted out" to people like JL and others. It seemed as if daily we were identifying more and more players including some Mexican nationals living in our immediate area.

When it came time to arrest the players and conduct searches of the locations we had identified, we used all members of the task force. Simultaneously, we hit the homes of JL and KG as well as the skate park and the skateboard shop. JL was not at home, and it took more than a week to locate and arrest him. KG was not home when we arrived at the house, but his wife and children were.

The skate park was not open for business and was vacant when we arrived there. While searching the park, we found only a large wooden shipping box, large enough to contain a refrigerator, which had marijuana residue inside. KG had apparently had his shipments of marijuana delivered by truck to this location and used the out of the way and quiet location to weigh and package the marijuana for resale.

KG was present when we arrived at the store, and he was a smartass in front of his friends, putting on a show. He changed his tune later, however, when he found out how much we had on him—to the point he was near tears. I spent many long hours with my co-case agent Johnny and KG's attorney, debriefing—KG, along with Internal Revenue Service investigators, who were deep into KG's bank accounts. We seized cash and Rolex watches from the safe in the store, as well as bank account records.

Another benefit I never had access to prior to working federal cases was the opportunity to work closely with IRS investigators. Since the big players in the drug world had so much money, they had to put it somewhere safe, and the IRS guys helped us regularly by looking closely into banks accounts and commodities, including stocks, bonds, and various other investments. With them on our side, we were able to place money-laundering charges on most of our targets, even if we did not catch them red-handed with the drugs.

KG hired a very well-known attorney, a former South Carolina attorney general, to represent him. During one of our last debriefings with

KG and his attorney, KG was having a hard time understanding how his drug money, which he had mingled with his legally earned money made from his two businesses, was eligible for seizure. After one of the IRS investigators explained why all of his bank accounts, all his cash in safe deposit boxes, and any cash in the safe were subject to seizure, he became irate. It was at this meeting when he finally realized that we had him cold and that all of the money he thought his wife would have access to while he was in prison would now be gone forever, all as a result of our seizure proceedings and months of investigation. We also seized his beach house, which was worth between $500,000 and $700,000.

During the course of the investigation, we also determined that he had a second skate park in the Virginia Beach, Virginia, area and that KG had shipments of marijuana trucked to that location, which also originated in Mexico, through Texas, then to the east coast. One day Johnny and I drove to Virginia and picked up another large shipping box containing 650 lb. of marijuana. This shipment was intercepted after we had arrested "KG," so we added this to his growing historical list of smuggled marijuana that we would eventually charge him with.

"JL" was finally located and ended up cooperating with us and filled in many of the blank spaces regarding other players in the organization and quantities of marijuana that he moved weekly. He assisted us in identifying the Mexican nationals who were living locally and responsible for getting the marijuana from Mexico to Texas and packaged for shipment to "KG." We were able to confirm that prior to "KG" having marijuana shipped 500 to 700 lb. at a time, he often had tractor-trailer loads of marijuana unloaded in rural portions of Charleston County.

It was a shame to see how a local street-level drug dealer graduated to the big time. He was now facing serious prison time in a federal penitentiary. He readily admitted that greed motivated his actions. Because he helped us as much as he did, he received assistance in the form of a reduced sentence for his actions. I do not recall exactly how long he was sentenced to prison for, but it was more than ten years. "KG," of course, received considerably more time, because he was charged with multiple counts of Money Laundering in addition to his drug charges. In the end, Johnny and I were able to prove that "KG" was responsible for smuggling more than 40,000 lb. of marijuana, multiple pounds of cocaine, and numerous firearms violations in the Charleston, South Carolina, area.

The case also netted nine arrests with an additional seventeen indictments still pending when I left the unit. Seizures of assets exceeded three quarters of a million dollars as well as submitted drug evidence totaling over 1,000 lb.

Buddy was the case agent in an investigation of illegal manufacturing and trafficking of methamphetamines in the Charleston area. Over a long period, Buddy was able to identify the main source and his associates, and he targeted them. Even though much intelligence and circumstantial evidence had been obtained and documented, the organization was impossible to infiltrate.

We knew that the organization in Charleston was responsible for virtually all of the ecstasy and the date or club drug "Georgia Home Boy" (GHB). The chemical name for GHB was Gamma Hydroxybutyrate, which was a central nervous system depressant that was approved by the Food and Drug Administration (FDA) for use in the treatment of certain sleep disorders. GHB was odorless, colorless, and tasteless and was frequently combined with alcohol or in water bottles in local bars in the downtown Charleston area frequented by local college students. GHB had recently been linked to one kidnapping, three rapes, and two overdoses in our area. In most of the cases, males were placing the GHB in unsuspecting girls' drinks or water bottles, then taking advantage sexually when they passed out.

One day we received a call from the Naval Investigative Service (NIS) in Jacksonville, North Carolina, requesting assistance regarding a search warrant it had executed near Camp Lejeune. They netted just two capsules of methamphetamine known as ecstasy, but they were able to get the person that they arrested to reveal his source and to arrange for an undercover purchase from two individuals identified as suppliers with a Charleston connection. This case brought us almost two hundred miles to a well-known tourist stop on I-95 known as "South of the Border," which was located just south of the North Carolina state line in South Carolina.

Buddy was able to debrief one of the individuals, who revealed his source as coming from Charleston. We immediately returned to Charleston and were going so fast, we were stopped twice by the highway patrol on I-95 South.

We prepared the search warrant and woke up a local judge to sign it. We hit the apartment just before 4:00 a.m. We ended up netting methamphetamine powder, a pill press, and weapons. After debriefing this person, he agreed to make several undercover pickups of methamphetamine and delivered marked money while doing so. With these pickups complete, the next level of supply was now positively identified and arrested with methamphetamine, cocaine, marijuana, and pills along with a quantity of cash. We were not surprised to find sophisticated video surveillance cameras around the house with monitors on the second floor, so the suspect had enough time to dispose of drugs in the house or to arm himself.

Through many countless hours of surveillance and intelligence gathering by many members of the task force, the actual chemist manufacturing the Ecstasy and GHB in the Charleston area was positively identified. This turned out to be the exact person Buddy had originally targeted and identified six to eight months prior.

It was common to work these long and crazy hours, and my guys never complained one bit. They all thrived on the adrenalin that came with the constant pace, especially when they were successful in their endeavors. They would go home, get a few hours rest, and be at it again a short time later.

During the course of the investigation over many months, Buddy, Kevin, "Lunch," and Jim had compiled piles of information about the target and the three locations he frequented. They had identified the house in an upscale community he lived in with his family and a house that he rented in a middle-class neighborhood, where we believed he cooked his meth. The target had been identified but probable cause was needed to get into the locations. One day we were comparing notes as a team, brainstorming on how to get enough information for a search warrant. I suggested that a trash pull at his cookhouse could very well give us enough information.

It is legal for law enforcement personnel to go through a person's trash if it is left at the curb for pick-up. When citizens leave trash at the curb for garbage pickup, they give up any expectation of privacy. Therefore, any evidence of illegal activity found in the trash can be used to further an investigation. Conducting a trash pull is best described as Narcotics Training 101, and it was this simple task that broke the case.

Buddy had heard that there had been a fire in the cookhouse that may have occurred while the target was cooking a batch of methamphetamine. Buddy was able to get a copy of the report submitted by the fire department, which listed the kitchen fire as a flash fire on the stove that spread quickly, which is a common occurrence while cooking meth.

The guys conducted their trash pull and were able to gather enough evidence along with the information about the fire to prepare a search warrant. We hit the cookhouse at the same time we hit his residence and netted our target, who shall be referred to by his initials, "JT."

JT was arrested without incident while preparing to leave the house for work. In the cookhouse, so much evidence was on scene that we had to call a contracted hazardous material disposal company from Atlanta to respond. The entire garage was loaded with so much chemical precursor to the manufacture of methamphetamine and GHB that it filled a truck.

We then went to the business and located even larger quantities of chemicals in drums and large storage cans that had been shipped directly to the business for storage. JT hid them in the wooded area adjacent to his office and would then take what he needed to his cookhouse as he cooked each batch of meth or GHB. The hazardous material disposal team also disposed of this evidence.

The search warrants and the arrest of JT netted so many chemicals used to manufacture ecstasy and GHB that this case virtually shut down the availability of methamphetamine and GHB in the Charleston area for years to come. This case was the first identified clandestine drug lab in the Charleston area since the 1980s, during my first tour in METRO.

The one phone call from NIS in North Carolina that netted only two pills was responsible for breaking this case wide open. The better part of a year's worth of investigation and surveillance came to a head because of a simple phone call from another narc sharing information.

One member of JT's organization was a guy closely affiliated with active and former motorcycle gang members, and when the time came to arrest him, we wanted to do so in a low-key manner. The day of his arrest, he was under tight surveillance, and we had arranged for a uniformed deputy to be waiting nearby so he could be quickly transported away from the location of the arrest. I was the closest to the target and pulled up next to him. Before he knew what had happened, I had him handcuffed and placed in the backseat of the waiting marked police car. I left my car at the scene and rode with the deputy to the office, which I mentioned before was in a bank building. During the short, ten-minute ride, he assumed that he had been arrested by Charleston County for an outstanding arrest warrant, and I did not let on through our conversation otherwise. We went to the back door of the building and walked him up the back stairwell where he continued to exhibit his cocky attitude, that is until I walked him to the entrance of our office, which had a metal plaque stating Drug Enforcement Administration. It was not until he saw the sign that he knew he had been had and in a low tone said, "Oh shit, I'm fucked."

JT and others in his organization were eventually convicted to long prison terms and ordered to forfeit all of their property and bank holdings. This case was in the works for many months before my guys had enough information together to make their move. Just like a murder case in which months of additional investigation after the fact are spent, the same was true for these long and involved drug cases. This case involved significant real estate holdings, bank assets, and involvement from players out of state. By the time JT went to trial, there were no secrets to his life..

In April of 1999, the sheriff presented a long Letter of Commendation to me and my team and recognized us for our productivity within the task force. He noted that among the six teams subdivided within the office, Charleston County investigators captained three. He also noted that the Charleston County members of the task force were responsible for more than half of all arrests made since January 1, 1999. This award was presented at a monthly Command Staff Meeting with all of my guys present. This award was like a shot of adrenalin to them because it made them work even harder, if that was at all possible. Recognition for a job well done always has positive results.

At the same meeting that the sheriff presented my guys the Letter of Commendation as a group, he also recognized Buddy individually because I had nominated him as Deputy of the Month for his great work in the "JT" case.

***

Quite often, Kevin, "Lunch," and Jim would interdict with mules traveling up and down Interstate 95, who were found to be involved with active and ongoing investigations within the system. When a person was stopped, his or her name was run through an internal computer system that kept track of all persons involved in previous stops and those who had already been identified in active drug investigations. This network was often responsible for breakthroughs in cases close to culmination. It was and remains mysterious to me that the same players continued to make the trip to points north with large quantities of cocaine. Interstate 95 between Miami and New York is aptly referred to as the "I-95 Corridor." Cops between New York and Washington refer to Interstate 95 as "Cocaine Alley," while cops in Georgia and the Carolinas refer to Interstate 95 as "Cocaine Lane." These nicknames come because of the distinction of being the nation's busiest drug-smuggling corridor.

In the fall of 1999, Jim decided he was ready to retire. He had purchased four years of Marine Corps time and was maxing out his retirement with thirty-seven years of service. We decided to have a luncheon for him at a local seafood restaurant, which was attended by over a hundred of his friends and family. Well, his retirement luncheon turned from a quiet lunch to a celebration of Jim's career. I started by telling a few funny stories about Jim, and when I was done someone else grabbed the microphone, and we started telling more stories. His luncheon turned into one of the funniest roasts of a person that I ever witnessed. It was an appropriate way for Jim to leave because he was a funny guy to work for and with. He retired and went to the upstate of South Carolina to become the person in charge of civilian security in a federal courthouse there. I still talk to him from time to time and keep him up on what is going on in Charleston.

***

Part of my routine on a daily basis was to go to the METRO office once a day to get our mail. While there, I would check in with my captain, Keith, and sometimes shoot the breeze with the chief, Marvin. My two bosses were pleased with what his guys were doing at the task force and especially loved the large seizures of cash because they often supplemented the sheriff's helicopter budget, helping to defray the high cost of aviation fuel.

In November of 1999, Keith approached me with the idea of transferring to METRO to run the unit there. I was extremely happy in the DEA Task Force, but I was excited about taking charge of the unit that I loved to work in the most. I had last been in METRO in March of 1989, when I was promoted to sergeant. I had now been a lieutenant for more than seven years and jumped at the opportunity and took over just after the first of the year.

I had worked with a great crew of guys at the task force and felt I was leaving them in good hands because my old partner John and I were switching positions. Buddy was eventually promoted to sergeant and then to lieutenant and into my old position in Judicial Operations.

Kevin and Lunch stayed in the unit until after 9/11, and both left the Sheriff's Office and became US Air Marshals. I still keep in touch with them via e-mail and Facebook.

When it was known that I was leaving, Phil, the group supervisor and my direct DEA superior in the task force, sent a very nice Letter of Appreciation to my sheriff, thanking me for my work in the unit and mentioning specifically the large marijuana smuggling case that I was the case agent for. The letter stated in part the following:

Lieutenant Wright has done an excellent job bringing a major marijuana/cocaine smuggling investigation to completion. During this specific case, the investigation showed a conspiracy involving in excess of 40,000 pounds of marijuana, twenty kilograms of cocaine and numerous firearms violations. To date, nine arrests have been effected with an additional seventeen indictments expected within the next ninety days. Seizures and assets exceeding one half million dollars as well as drug evidence totaling over a half ton have been made.

Phil's letter was greatly appreciated and was presented to me with a cover letter from the sheriff at a Command Staff Meeting. I also received a leather-bound certificate signed by the Director of the Drug Enforcement Administration.

METRO AGAIN

25

I HAD BEEN MANAGING A DELI IN DOWNTOWN Charleston for the past five years, and the owner sold the business in mid-December. The owner of the deli and I decided to go in together on another endeavor, which was a hot dog restaurant not yet open, located on the campus of the College of Charleston. The college is known locally as "C of C" and is located in the middle of downtown Charleston and is surrounded by old and stately homes more than 150 years old.

My partner was again going to be a silent one and left the restaurant, which was completely ready to open, for me to run as I saw fit. I decided to highlight the hot dogs by deep-frying them and offered burgers and chicken sandwiches.

Since I had worked days primarily in the task force, my new position as the supervisor of METRO was to work nights again from 7:00 p.m. to 3:00 a.m. I reinstituted these hours, which had gone by the wayside in the past several years. Drug dealers deal at night and sleep in the daytime, so the obvious time to be on the streets was nighttime.

I would be at the restaurant from nine in the morning, work through lunch until two, then go home to shower and be at METRO at 3:00 p.m.

until at least 11:00 p.m. Do the math: getting off at 3:00 a.m. only left six hours of free time in my day.

My buddy Keith and my immediate boss had been promoted to the rank of major and transferred to the detention center to be the assistant administrator there. He retired several years ago as a chief deputy and the administrator of the detention center.

My new captain was now Andi, my old partner during my first assignment in METRO. She had been promoted to captain and was happy to return to her old stomping grounds as well. She later rose to the rank of chief deputy and served several years as the assistant sheriff before her recent retirement.

Our boss was Marvin, the Chief Deputy of Executive Concerns, which consisted of METRO, the Aviation Unit, the Marine Unit, and the Bomb Unit. I had first worked for Marvin when he was a lieutenant, and he had risen through the ranks to become chief deputy. He was a great guy to work for, and Andi and I were friends, so there was absolutely no stress in this new assignment.

METRO had moved several years prior from headquarters to a building that once housed an old trucking company. It was a good thing for a narcotics unit not to be near headquarters, but the facility was inadequate for the number of people assigned. There was a large warehouse on the property, which is where we housed our undercover vehicles and seized property. The lot was adequate to store the more than fifty seized vehicles on hand, but the office was just too small to accommodate personnel. The good news was that a new facility was being built in a secluded area, less than a half mile away.

The very first day that I worked, I met with the guys and told them what I expected of them, which had become common practice. They knew that I had a strong background in investigations and drug enforcement. I asked them if they had any gripes, and they all agreed that they would like to have more time to work cases and not be forced to close a case because too much time had passed. I told them that we would be working evenings exclusively, unless a deal or circumstances required that we work days. They all seemed pleased with that decision. I told them that I would not be an absentee boss. I would be on search warrants with them and drug deals with them. I told them that I expected hard work and loyalty, and if anyone ever got into a jam, I would be there for them, as long as they were honest with me. I told them that I would go all the way to the sheriff with them if they screwed up and were honest about their mistake, which is something I told every unit I ever supervised. I did not think that there was any question that they believed me because they all worked their asses off for me.

I now had three sergeants, one in Narcotics, one in Vice, and one in Technical Operations. I had thirteen investigators, with two assigned to the Highway Drug Interdiction Team, which I mentioned in the previous chapter. Two of my guys worked Interstate 95 five days a week and worked with other members from two other law enforcement agencies. They were available to me if I needed manpower for larger operations. I also had two uniformed deputies who were assigned to the federally funded "Weed & Seed" drug program. They too were available if needed.

Due to all of the money seized and turned over to the sheriff, my unit was provided with state-of-the-art equipment. We had all of the latest surveillance tools, two outfitted surveillance vans, and very nice late model, undercover vehicles for each deputy. Because of all of the sophisticated electronic equipment available, I had a sergeant who was trained in operating all of it. When we did any drug deal, we included that sergeant and his equipment in the Operations Plan.

The case agent was responsible for preparing an Operations Plan for his deal. The Ops Plan was written and presented to all personnel involved in the deal. This ensured that everyone knew his or her assignment and responsibilities for each specific deal.

Marvin, my chief, had not changed one bit from his days when he would purposely fire up his sergeant, sometimes chastising him for the lack of unit seizures. Knowing this, I knew he would expect positive results from me. I had promised higher productivity to him when I came over and knew that he would expect that as soon as possible.

Within a week or so of my arrival, we brokered a deal with a guy for a quantity of marijuana to be delivered to a hotel room. This was probably the first actual drug deal that I went on with the guys, and they did a great job with it. When we hit the room where the gym bag of dope was delivered, we made entry without any issues, but we had one loud-mouth guy who decided he was going to resist, which was a big mistake for him.

When one of my guys opened the gym bag, he looked in and said, "That looks like about fifty pounds." I looked in the bag and said, "No, that looks like about thirty-five pounds." When we counted the one-pound bags, there was 36 lb. The narc who said there was 50 lb. could not believe how accurate I was, but little did he know how much marijuana I had seen and worked with in the last two years working the DEA Task Force. The boss was pleased with the bust because it also resulted in some cash being seized.

We started to get into the groove and were doing search warrants on a regular basis, not quite like we did back in the 1980s, but a definite change was taking place. Just as with any other unit, positive results result in positive attitudes with the troops. Nightly seizures and arrests kept their attitudes positive, and life was good.

One night while sitting at my desk, I got a call from an informant who wanted to provide me with some valuable information. He had joined the Navy and was awaiting a date from his recruiter to tell him when he was leaving to attend boot camp. He provided a wealth of information, but most of it was for people who were dealing in an adjoining county, where we had no jurisdiction.

In speaking with him, I learned that he had an outstanding cocaine charge, where he was found to be in possession of a small quantity, which more than likely would result in probation, if convicted. I knew his attorney very well and told him that I would be able to help him with his arrest if he were to help us facilitate a deal for some illegal drugs. His only arrest on his record was the outstanding cocaine charge, and I knew that the Navy would not accept him unless that charge was expunged or dismissed.

Helping informants was common, and getting a minor charge dismissed in return for a bigger fish was the name of the game. I spoke for a long time with this informant and arranged to meet him. After meeting with him the next day, I hooked him up with one of my guys, and we were able to arrange for the informant to have someone he knew to deliver 50 lb. of marijuana to us in Charleston. The dope was ordered and would be in town in a day or two, which gave me time to make some phone calls regarding his pending cocaine charge.

I called my counterpart in the narcotics unit of an adjoining county, and after speaking with him at length, he agreed that they would drop their charge in return for the deal he was arranging for delivery to us. This is the way these things work, and I have been doing this for a long time and had made many such deals over the years. A cop's word is his bond, even if it is to an informant. During our conversation, I also agreed to provide him with several pages of notes I had taken while debriefing the informant, which was all information that would be beneficial to him in his county. After a thirty-minute conversation, I felt comfortable that my informant would now be able to enter the Navy after he finished the deal with us.

About twenty minutes later, I got a call from the lieutenant I had just dealt with, and he informed me that he had told his captain about our arrangement, and his captain told him that there would be no deal. He was very apologetic over the change in plans, and I was very vocal about his captain and his decision. I told him that I had been a cop for eighteen years and *never* had another cop go back on his word to me. His captain did not have a good reputation as a cop and was part of the reason we never worked with that county on joint operations.

About ten minutes after our second conversation, I received another call. This time it was the captain who had nixed the deal. He started the conversation by identifying himself and by saying, "I understand you are not happy with my decision." My response was "No, I'm not," and the conversation went downhill from there. I explained that we were all doing the same thing, getting drugs off the street, and it should not matter where it was being done, as long as it was getting done. He proceeded to tell me that the informant should have provided him with the information. I explained that 90 percent of the information that the informant provided to me was of no use to me because it all pertained to drug activity in this captain's jurisdiction. I offered to provide the written debriefing to him for his use, and he remained adamant that he would not consent to the dismissal of the informant's minor drug charge. I told him that I had never had a fellow law enforcement officer fail to cooperate with me over something as insignificant as this. The conversation ended when I told him that I thought this was all bullshit, and I hung up. Hanging up on someone is something that I feel is an ultimate insult and have never hung up on anyone before or since that day.

I have always been known to be a man of my word, even when making a promise to a former drug dealer. I had, in fact, promised to get his charge dismissed in return for providing a quantity of drugs to my unit. His attorney was a friend I had known since he was first out of law school and had served as an Assistant Solicitor in our Solicitor's Office, which was the office that prosecuted all of our General Sessions Court

Offenses. I called the Solicitor's Office that prosecuted the cases in the adjoining county in question and actually arranged to have his case dismissed because he was helping to facilitate a large quantity of marijuana. I also knew that he would never ever get into the Navy with that charge hanging over his head. I figured that if he had enlisted in the Navy, he was certainly trying to clean up his act and go on the straight and narrow.

I mentioned that the captain who nixed the deal did not have a great reputation in the local law enforcement community. It is because of him that no other police agency ever wanted to work with his agency. I have always used the adage "what goes around comes around." It sometimes takes a while for things to catch up with people who do wrong. It can sometimes take months or years, but what is right always prevails in the end. It took more than twelve years, but that captain, who had since risen to the rank of major, the second in command of his agency, has been under investigation for various unethical improprieties that took place while he was a sworn deputy, some dating back to the mid-1980s. As a result of the investigation, he recently retired.

After arranging for the informant's charge to be dismissed, the 50 lb. of marijuana was on the way to Charleston County. Strangely enough, the marijuana was coming from New York, which was a little out of the ordinary. The informant kept in cell phone contact, and we knew where he was on the road for two hours prior to his arrival. We set up on Interstate 26, the only interstate that came to Charleston, and that intersected I-95. I had arranged for "Odie," one of my highway drug interdiction guys to make the actual stop. He was also a drug dog handler and had made hundreds of felony traffic stops. Once he made the stop, we would converge to assist. The vehicle was spotted, and "Odie" pulled up behind the target vehicle, and the vehicle pulled off the interstate to an exit ramp and finally stopped on the overpass over the highway. When "Odie" ordered the driver out of the car and the driver failed to respond, he let his dog loose, and his dog grabbed the driver's left arm and removed him from the vehicle. Sure enough, he had our 50 lb. of marijuana in the trunk of the vehicle. The whole deal that I have described was put into motion by one telephone call from an informant to my office. I always preached to my guys to take the time to speak to people who want to provide information because it is most often good information. There is nothing like a bitter ex-wife, a scorned girlfriend, or a pissed-off friend to provide valuable and accurate information.

***

I was thoroughly enjoying being back in METRO again. Even though I was now in charge, I managed to be involved in enough of what the guys were doing to always know what was going on. I accompanied them on most search warrants and hung back to allow my guys to investigate and develop their individual cases. Case management was a key to keeping up with what the guys were doing, and I stayed on my sergeants to review their cases regularly.

The first week of May we finally moved into our new facility, which was spacious compared to what we had been used to. Every investigator had his or her own workstation in a large office with separate computer stations tied in to the network. This room also had a large white board approximately eight feet wide, which is where we presented our Operations Plan before going out on search warrants and drug deals. Two sergeants shared a large office, and I had an office across the hall, located between my captain and chief. Compared to the office I worked from in the '80s and the facility we just moved from, where we were sharing desks, this was the Taj Mahal. Adjacent to our building was a huge warehouse that stored our undercover vans and seized property.

Adjacent to that were acres of fenced-in lots to accommodate the dozens of vehicles we had seized that were awaiting auction.

We had barely moved into our new facility when a drug deal came along that seemed about as routine a deal as we ever conducted. We learned from the beginning of our career, however, that *nothing* in a cop's job is ever *routine*. We hammered this point into those in training. I had been teaching Officer Survival to recruits for years and was a huge proponent of never becoming complacent.

We regularly purchased drugs in an undercover capacity from various locations. We then returned with a search warrant to that location within ten days, which was dictated by law. Upon our return, we would search the premises and look at any cash in the location to see if the marked money we used to make the purchase was still there. It did not have to be there, but if it was, it just made our case better for prosecution.

In the deal that was being planned, my guys had an undercover informant who was working off some charges and had arranged to purchase a half ounce of cocaine for the price of $550, which was the going rate for that amount at the time.

The deal was arranged by Kevin, the case agent, to happen sometime after 9:00 p.m. in the front parking lot of a local convenience store on a very busy four-lane thoroughfare. This purchase was going to be what is referred to as a "Buy-Bust" and was used in the drug enforcement trade very often. Since the undercover informant was unable to make a purchase from a house, the next best option was to purchase it directly, hand to hand, from the target in the parking lot. We had done this common drug transaction countless times before. Because we did not know the exact identity of the target and only had a nickname, "KC," we elected to do the deal this way because we would never allow that much money to walk away without knowing whom we were dealing with.

Prior to leaving the office to make the transaction, Kevin presented the Operations Plan and went over step by step each and every individual's assignment and used the diagram of the convenience store and the parking spots on the white board.

We had the advantage at the time of having two highly equipped surveillance vans at our disposal. My technical support sergeant, Mike, was assigned to set up just across the street that bordered the left side of the store and to monitor the recorded conversation of the undercover informant and the target, as well as videotape the entire deal with the state-of-the-art video equipment in the van. The van was equipped with more than $100,000 worth of surveillance and sound equipment. We tried to use this asset as often as possible, and using it in this particular deal proved to be extremely beneficial.

I was not assigned to be any part of the deal, nor was the narcotics sergeant, Robby, who rode with me. We planned to just hang back and keep a visual on the deal just in case anything went wrong. We were not dressed out and were in jeans and short-sleeve shirts. I did, however, have a weapon on my person, as always, but not visible.

We had an undercover cop, another Mike, who was assigned to drive the informant to the convenience store and to pull right up to an empty parking spot nose-in to the store. Once the target arrived, the informant was to exit his undercover vehicle and get into the target's car when he arrived. As soon as the informant got the cocaine and exited KC's vehicle, we had a car loaded with four deputies dressed like the common SWAT Team cop would be, all in black with SHERIFF'S OFFICE in big letters and a badge on their chests and backs. The way they were dressed, there was no question they were, in fact, uniformed law enforcement. Their vehicle was assigned to pull their front bumper right up to the rear bumper of KC's vehicle, preventing him from leaving his parking space.

We also had a marked police cruiser manned by my two Weed & Seed deputies, who were assigned to arrive when the takedown vehicle did and to standby on the perimeter as a chase vehicle in the event that the target was able to get away.

The plan was in place, and everyone suited up with holsters and vests and started to head to each assigned location to wait for the deal to develop. I took a minute and called home to tell my wife that I would be home in about thirty to forty-five minutes after we did a small cocaine deal nearby. My wife was used to the phone calls after hours and acknowledged she would see me soon.

We were all suited up and waited for Mike in the van to set up in the best possible position so he could videotape the entire parking lot. The convenience store was on a corner and was the old style setup with about eight parking spots out front, where the cars pulled right up to the storefront windows, with a cement walkway between the parking spaces and the storefront. A street bordered the left side of the store, and the entire right side of the store was bordered by a brick, two-story building that went all the way out to the street.

When Mike said he was in place with the van, we all left the office, which was a three- to four-minute ride. Drug deals almost never go on time, and we never expect any deal to go when scheduled. Robby and I met Mike, the undercover with the informant, and we activated an undercover microphone on the informant behind a business a block or so away.

When Mike in the van let us know he was ready, a recorded phone call was made to KC, and he responded that he would be at the store in three to four minutes. The undercover Mike and the informant then left our location, and we kept a visual on them and saw them pull up into the extreme right-hand space against the brick wall of the adjacent building. Within three minutes, KC pulled up in a four-door Toyota Camry with heavy tinted glass all around, with a second guy in the car. He pulled into the parking space directly next to Mike and the informant. When KC pulled up, his passenger got out and went into the store. The informant did just as he was instructed to do: he got out of the undercover car and walked over and got into the right front passenger seat of KC's car and handed the marked money to KC and took the cocaine and exited the vehicle. He was in the car for no more than two minutes. When the informant exited KC's car, the signal was given for my carload of narcs to pull into the lot and block KC in. This happened so fast that Mike and the informant had not yet backed out of their parking space as the takedown vehicle arrived.

My guys pulled in bumper to bumper, exited their vehicle, and approached KC's car with two guys on each side. They loudly identified themselves by yelling "Sheriff's Office, get out of the car!" When KC saw my guys hollering commands to get out of the car, KC did not respond. Roger had managed to open the left, rear door of the car, but KC had then apparently locked his driver's door because Ray was trying to get that door open to get KC out of the car. Roger made eye contact with KC, who looked over his shoulder, as he was literally three feet from him in the open apex of the left, rear car door.

KC then made the decision to slam the car into reverse and ram our takedown vehicle in an attempt to flee the scene. As he did so, Roger was caught in the already opened left rear door, and as KC slammed the car into reverse, the car door caught Roger's left leg and threw him violently away from the car. At the same time, the force of the first contact between cars pushed our parked car back approximately ten to twelve feet, also striking Mike's undercover vehicle that was still backing out of his parking space. As Roger was thrown and the takedown vehicle and undercover vehicle were struck, the front tire of KC's car also ran over the foot of Scott, the fourth guy in the takedown vehicle. At the time that all of this was happening, Robby and I, who were not to participate in the deal, saw what was happening and pulled into the parking lot. Robby bailed out to the right and ended up having to jump out of the way of Mike in the undercover vehicle as it was rammed, almost catching him between that vehicle and the brick building that bordered that side of the lot.

To our trained eye, we immediately knew that the deal was not going as planned, which is why we elected to quickly exit my Dodge Durango. I found out only later how close Robby came to being seriously injured after the dust had cleared, and we compared notes. My instinct and training made me react directly toward KC's vehicle, so I was at the driver's door as he violently rammed the vehicles. Because of this, I was right there when Roger rolled out of the way and recovered in time to fire into the vehicle. At the same time, Scott was recovering from having his left foot run over, and he responded by firing one or two times into the windshield from the front of the vehicle. Simultaneously, I pulled my Glock Model 27 handgun from my waistband and fired twice into the driver's window.

Ray and Kevin, the case agent, who were part of the four-man takedown team, were also members of the SWAT Team. They had extensive training in "shoot/don't shoot" situations and were trained to have the discipline to fire only at the appropriate time, or not. Because of the risk of crossfire and possibly hitting another police officer, they rightfully made the tough decision not to fire their weapons.

After Scott, Roger, and I each fired twice, KC threw the car into drive and went forward several feet, preparing to ram the vehicles again to get away. At that point, I made the decision to reach into the left rear door that was sprung and locked in the open position and yelled at KC. When I saw his right hand on the transmission shift lever getting ready to repeat what he had already done, I fired two rounds into the top part of his left shoulder from a distance of less than three feet and recovered from my position. In hindsight, after having the luxury of reviewing the videotape, it is amazing to see how your years of training kick in when you are forced to act. The video shows my entry into the rear door in a perfect two-handed shooting stance that was the result of years of repetitive practice.

I then gave the command to get him out of the vehicle. The driver's door was jammed shut because of the sprung rear door, but Scott, who was a bodybuilder, pretty much ripped the door from its frame and pulled KC out so medical assistance could be rendered.

I then immediately ran to my vehicle, grabbed my walkie-talkie, and radioed in the following radio transmissions:

My radio call designation at the time was "25."

25 to Headquarters

I need EMS ASAP, Ranger and Dorchester, Lil Cricket, shots fired, we've got a Code 49 (someone shot) of a suspect, get me a supervisor out here.

25 to Headquarters

Notify Captain C and Chief K, negative 33, not at this time, we've got a suspect Code 49, we got an injured Metro officer, was hit by a vehicle, injured leg, advise EMS the suspect has multiple gunshots torso.

25 to Headquarters

Headquarters, how about telling the first supervisor to get here to put crime scene tape out so we can secure this parking lot.

25 to Headquarters

If you haven't already, notify the lab.

25 to Headquarters

If you haven't already, I haven't been listening, make sure you notify the Detective Office.

While making the radio transmissions I was standing fifteen feet from KC, who was being administered first aid by a passing off-duty rescue technician. As I stood there, I saw KC take his last gasp of breath.

To this day, we do not know what ever happened to the passenger that KC let out of his car before the drug deal went down. In the confusion, he was able to remove himself from the situation and got away.

I had just called Paula a short thirty minutes prior to this situation to tell her I would be home soon. I did not want her to see or hear about this incident on the ten o'clock news, so I called her again to tell her what had happened and that I was safe. She only wanted to know whether I was safe and if my guys were OK. Once I told her that, she said she was going to bed. Not much bothers that girl!

It did not take long for cops from all over to respond to the scene. Within minutes, there were fifty cops on scene, all wanting to help. While waiting for the brass to arrive, I remembered that my son Doug was working the nightshift that night and was probably listening to the police radio in his jurisdiction, just fifteen miles away. I called him, and he too responded within minutes. He, in turn, called my next oldest son, Pete, who was also a cop, who on the way also called my daughter so she would not be alarmed in the event that the incident was on the ten or eleven o'clock news.

After making these two quick phone calls, my phone started to blow up with incoming calls. Andi, my captain, called me first, and when I answered all she said was "Talk to me." I had worked with her for so long that I knew exactly what she wanted. I gave her the quick lowdown on what had happened since she had to call the chief, who was also responding from his house.

The first supervisor to arrive was an old buddy, Mike, who was the patrol commander that night for the district. He had once been one of my patrol sergeants and was now a lieutenant. He came right to me, and

I relinquished the weapon that I had fired to him for submission as evidence. I told him that Scott and Roger had also fired their weapons, and I assumed that he collected their weapons too.

Among those who responded was the sheriff, who could always be counted upon to respond to serious or major incidents, especially when they involve injured deputies. He was always listening to his radio.

There is also a very well-known local attorney named Andy, whom most cops called when in need of legal assistance. He is a true friend of cops and has represented dozens of us over the years. He was also listed as a Fraternal Order of Police (FOP) attorney and the go-to guy, in my eyes. Mike, the duty lieutenant who assumed custody of my weapon, came back over and asked me if I wanted him to call Andy for me. It was a no-brainer, and I answered, "Yes, please call him for me." When I arrived at my office no more than thirty minutes later, he was there waiting along with his investigator, my longtime friend Bobby, a retired county lieutenant.

We were able to leave the scene once control of the crime scene was assumed by the Criminal investigations Division Supervisor. We had to leave our vehicles in place, as they were part of the crime scene. Someone gave me a ride back, and to my surprise, there were fifty to seventy-five cops in the parking lot and inside the building. It was great to see the support from my fellow brothers and sisters in blue. Little did I know at the time, but this was just the beginning of a very long night.

When I walked into the building, I was immediately greeted by my sons Doug and Pete. We embraced, and I assured them I was fine. Somehow, they had already viewed the videotape and told me I had done the right thing. Andy and Bobby scooted me into my office, and I shut the door. Andy advised me to give only one written statement and that would serve as my version of the sequence of events for the record. He knew from experience that Internal Affairs investigators would want a statement for their internal investigation. Andy also knew that the shooting itself would be investigated by the State Law Enforcement Division (SLED), which is customary, and it too would be requesting a written statement.

I left the office and met with an inspector from Internal Affairs. Lewis happened to be a guy I had known for almost twenty years and at one time served on my squad in the Patrol Division. I told him I had been advised by counsel to write only one written statement, and he agreed that this was no problem. By now, SLED Investigators began to show up to handle the formal investigation, and to my surprise, my old buddy John, who was my fellow sergeant in Criminal Investigations in the early 1990s was its lead investigator. When I was promoted to lieutenant in 1992, he left the Sheriff's Office and became a special agent for SLED. Unfortunately, when John saw that I was one of the shooters, he told me he would have to recuse himself from the investigation because of our friendship. I was a little disappointed but understood completely.

I went into my office and began to type my statement from memory. I knew for a fact that Mike, my tech sergeant, had immediately returned to his office, which was a large room with a desk and shelves upon shelves of electronic sound and camera equipment. He made a master copy of the tape and put it aside, knowing that SLED and Internal Affairs would want the original copy for their investigation. Guys from all over were gathering in his office to view the video. I did not want to see the video before I typed my statement because I wanted it to be my own recollection, not one influenced by knowing exactly what the video showed.

Because of all of the commotion in the office, my statement took hours to write. At one point, Ricky from the crime lab showed up to take pictures of the undercover vehicle that Mike was in while trying to leave the parking lot. Because it had some body damage, I showed Ricky where the vehicle was, and he documented it with photos. I then thought about the white board in the squad room that had the entire Operations Plan written on it. I brought Ricky in there and asked him to photograph the board close enough to make sure it was readable in a photograph, knowing it may end up in court someday.

After he took the photos, the sheriff came in, came right up to me, and immediately showed his support for our actions. Roger and Scott were still at the hospital being treated for what turned out to be minor injuries. My attorney, Andy, walked in and was surprised to see the entire written Operations Plan on the board. He recognized it because he and Bobby had already gone back to the scene of the shooting to inspect for themselves. His comment when he saw it was "I'm impressed." I told him that we did that with every deal we did.

There was a large, open space at the bottom of the white board, and the sheriff walked up, grabbed a black marker, and wrote the following:

It's about choices he made

He chose to sell drugs

He chose to attempt to flee

He chose to drive in a way that put deputies in danger

He chose to ignore warnings to stop

He chose to continue to attempt to flee with the result that he and he alone is responsible

For deputies to have acted differently may well have cost a deputy his life. The actions you took very likely saved lives

When he was done writing, there was no question by anyone in the room that he would support us through the entire process that we were about to endure.

I finally completed my written statement in the wee hours of the morning and handed it to Andy to read. He said it was good, and we made copies because both Internal Affairs and SLED wanted them. I was never interviewed that night, and my written statement was my documented version of my actions that night. I was then presented with a letter placing me on Administrative Leave with Pay. This is normal procedure when incidents like this happen. I had already relinquished the weapon that I fired that night. I did have another county assigned weapon and was allowed to keep it, along with my identification and badge. Normally, when someone is placed on Administrative Leave, he or she must give up the privilege of having his or her assigned vehicle, but Scott, Roger, and I were all allowed to keep our vehicles. We were advised to stay away from the office, but that could not last long.

By now, it was 5:00 a.m., and Andy and Bobby finally left. Andi, my captain, had also been there for the duration, and she left when I did. The chief and other brass, including the sheriff, had stayed around until about two in the morning.

I made the short, twenty-minute ride home and crawled into bed by five thirty for maybe an hour before Paula had to get up to get to school. It made no sense trying to sleep anyway because my cell phone was blowing up with people calling me. They had no way of knowing that I had been out for twenty-two hours; they just wanted to call to check on me.

That afternoon we somehow all ended up in Wild Wings, a chicken wing restaurant that had all-you-can-eat wings every day for lunch. I have no idea how it came about, but every guy involved in the deal and some who were off the previous night showed up, and lunch ended up lasting hours, along with the consumption of many buckets of bottled beer. Billy, my Vice sergeant had been in Myrtle Beach with his wife the previous night and heard about the shooting on the late news there. He drove back the next morning to be with his buddies. Being out drinking alcohol with my guys was not something that I ever did. Times were different now, and it was something I had not done since my early days in narcotics, working deals in bars and restaurants. This gathering turned out to be something that needed to happen and served its purpose as a way for the guys to bond. I do not recall that we even spoke about the incident; we just needed to be together as group.

Of course, the morning headline of the local newspaper was POLICE SHOOT MAN IN DRUG STING, which was not surprising. While I was out all night, my brother and his wife were driving to Charleston from New Jersey to visit my mother, on their way to their vacation in Florida. My wife, son, and I were going to meet them for dinner in a local seafood restaurant. We were catching up because I had not seen him in a while, and he asked me about that morning's news headline. He knew what I did and to that point, I had not told a soul in the family about what had happened, except my children. I told him to keep it quiet for now since I planned to tell my mother later in the evening.

The newspaper account the morning after the incident was accurate, and I expected it to stay in the news for a few days until the story died down and another story took its place. This was not to be. The local black community organizers, that included several outspoken clergy, formed a protest march that began at the site of the shooting and went directly to the Sheriff's Department Headquarters about two miles away. One particular clergyman was on the news nightly touting how the police were killing innocent black people. Instead of a two- or three-day story, it went on for weeks. As stated earlier, the sheriff supported all of us 100 percent. None of us could ever ask for anything more from a boss.

One aspect of this incident that I really have not spoken enough about was the great job that my tech sergeant, Mike, did in the surveillance van. He was forced to sit one hundred feet away watching in horror as the incident unfolded before his eyes through the lens of the camera. He was helpless in the position he was assigned, but it was his great work that allowed the three of us to be cleared to return to duty as quickly as we were. Shootings like this sometimes take three to six months, if not more, before an officer involved in a shooting is cleared. Because of

Mike's expertise, he was able to sit through the incident and continue his videotape, which he too knew was important. I will be forever grateful to him for the job he did that night. He went on in later years to become a lieutenant himself and assumed the position I held as the lieutenant of METRO.

Another role that needs to be recognized was that of Mike, the undercover narc, who drove the informant to the drug deal. He too was helpless to intercede. Because of the discipline and restraint he showed after being rammed and seeing the shooting occur right before his eyes, not twenty feet away, his actions were instrumental in keeping the informant safe. He was able get away without a scratch.

The weekend passed, and I went to my restaurant to work since I was on Administrative Leave. I worked a few days through the lunch rush and went home, worked in the yard, or hung around the pool. I was still getting numerous daily phone calls from people I worked with over the years. The newspaper and TV news was hard to ignore, but I was confident it would end soon, but it did not. I even got a phone call from my old buddy Chuck from our SCAT Team days. He had read about the shooting online from his home in Indiana.

I was summoned to the local office of SLED regarding my actions in the shooting. By now, about two weeks had passed, and an investigator still had never interviewed me. I went to the SLED office and met with a special agent who had the videotape ready to play. Their only issue with my actions was to explain why, after the three of us initially fired our weapons, that I chose to make entry and take the action I did. It is obvious by watching the videotape that I briefly entered the car door, and you could hear my two shots, but what I said was inaudible. I explained that after our initial shots, I still perceived the threat that KC posed behind the wheel of his car. Roger had hopped away on his bad leg, and Scott had also hopped away after the tire ran over his foot. The vehicle was in the motion of going forward, and KC was in the process of shifting the car into reverse, to possibly ram our vehicle again. With all of that information registered in my mind, I then made the decision to eliminate the threat and take the action that I did. The only other thing they asked was what I yelled to KC when I entered the open door. When I entered the rear door of the vehicle, I immediately yelled, "Put your hands up!" When KC failed to comply, and continued fumbling with the console gearshift, I then fired twice.

About two weeks after the shooting, we had an Incident Debriefing of all participants in the shooting incident, which included the entire shift of communications personnel who monitored the radio that night. This debrief was monitored by a trained grief counselor and was very productive. It too was important that the dispatchers and telephone clerks were involved because we never thought how hearing the events unfold on radio or by incoming 911 calls would affect them. They were in tears as the meeting progressed, and we were all glad that we had the opportunity to share our feelings.

By late May, Paula, who was a teacher, was out of school for the summer as well as my youngest son, Joe. Since I was on paid leave, we decided to take a trip to New York and New Jersey. At the time, my sister and her husband had a house down on the Jersey shore, and we went there for a few days to get away. I, of course, drove my bosses crazy calling the office daily to check on any developments on the incident. There were none.

After a few weeks, my immediate bosses recognized our restlessness and allowed us to come to the office and do administrative work around the office, a job that narcs just are not good at. They were champing at the bit to be on the streets and drove my bosses crazy.

In the state of South Carolina, criminal cases are prosecuted by a system of solicitors, the same role as some states who have district attorneys, just a different title. The state is broken down into judicial districts with an elected solicitor running each of the districts. The Ninth Judicial Solicitor's Office was investigating our shooting, in conjunction with SLED, and after seventy-seven days, SLED and, more importantly, the Ninth Judicial District Solicitor finally exonerated us. On August 14, the three of us received a letter from Internal Affairs stating we were able to return to full duty status. This quick clearance was, in my mind, due to the fact that the entire incident was videotaped, a luxury that is usually not available.

During the investigation by SLED and the Solicitor's Office, several versions of the videotape were produced by SLED, full speed, slow motion, and a stop-and-explain version. On the day that we were exonerated, the solicitor held a press conference in which he showed the three versions of the videotape to the local news media, as well as a diagramed timeline of events and actions of each officer. Specific aspects of the autopsy results of KC were also made public, which indicated that one of the rounds that Roger fired was fatal as well as the two rounds that I fired into KC's shoulder. Our seventy-seven-day ordeal was over, and we all finally went back to work. It was a long, hot summer, and we were all pleased to be productive again.

One of the first deals we did after returning to full duty was a state money-laundering case that I instituted. I had learned how easily it was to make a money-laundering case federally while in the DEA Task Force so I decided to make a case in state court. A local used-car dealer was a thorn in the side of law enforcement. The owner had a few nightclubs in the area as well as this particular car lot that was managed by his daughter, but he was an active employee of the business.

I had the idea that if an undercover cop went into the business posing as a drug dealer and bought a car with perceived drug money, we would be able to make a case against the sales person for money laundering. We recruited a black deputy from patrol to be the undercover. We wired him up wearing the finest "Mr. T starter kit" you ever saw. We gave him a wad of cash in big bills as well as a plastic bag with small, dummy packages of cocaine. He went in, and while negotiating the deal with the owner and his daughter in the office, the undercover "accidently" dropped his ball of cash and fake dope in the floor. When he left, there was no question that they knew he was drug dealer. He bargained with them and purchased an old Cadillac sedan with marked money.

I remember going back to the office after the deal to tell the chief, Marvin, about the deal. I had worked for him for years, and I knew how to get a rise out of him. When he asked what was going on I said, "Boss, I've got some good news and some bad news." When he asked what the good news was I said, "We finally got 'JW' and his daughter and got a Cadillac out of the deal." When he asked what the bad news was, I responded, "We paid for the Cadillac!" After a long string of profanity-laced comments, he calmed down, and I explained what we had done exactly, and he ended up being extremely pleased with the outcome.

Another deal that happened in August or early September concerned a significant crack cocaine dealer. One of the guys had targeted this well-known drug dealer in Charleston very close to a large mall. Since I managed all cases, I was aware that the target was the younger brother of "Jimmy B," whom I had found hiding under his mother's bed after receiving a Crime Stoppers tip that he was there. "Jimmy B" knew me well and was very vocal at his bond hearing back in 1992 when we arrested him. You may recall that my buddies John and Mike were upset because they had just made an undercover purchase of drugs from him, and I had left "Jimmy B's" cash on the bed where he was hiding.

The target's house was the very same that I had been in eight years prior, and I was pleased that we would be able to make this a family affair and arrest his younger brother! The guys were able to make a controlled purchase of drugs from the house in question and a search warrant was prepared and signed, ready to be executed.

On the day we were to hit the house to execute the warrant, we got a crew all suited up, and we piled into a large panel truck that we referred to as "The White Elephant." Because I was very familiar with the exact house we were to search, I drove the truck. About six or seven of my guys were all suited up and ready to bail out of the back on my command. When it came time to execute the warrant, we drove slowly down the street, and as we approached the target house on the driver's side of the truck, luck was on our side because the target and one of his buddies were sitting right on the front porch steps. I yelled this information back to the guys in the back. As I rolled up, both parties on the front porch were immediately taken into custody on the front lawn. Even though the target was in custody, we still had to enter the house and clear it of any persons and prepare to conduct our search.

The only occupant of the house was the target's mother, who had been napping. Of course, she started to hyperventilate and eventually fainted, which was all an act, in my opinion. So now, our only occupant needed medical attention. We called EMS, and they quickly responded and transported Mama to a local hospital.

We were very lucky in that the target was in possession of ninety-six grams of crack cocaine and cash when we arrested him outside. The crack was still in cookie form, and some was already broken down into rocks for sale on the street.

When crack is cooked, it ends up in the shape of a large cookie about three to four inches in diameter. When it cools, it is either broken into small rocks or cut in strips that are called slabs. There are clientele who prefer to purchase crack in slabs, which is of course, more expensive. We were lucky to catch our target with cookies, which resulted in more weight for criminal-charging purposes. It did not take long for a crowd to gather in the neighborhood, as everybody around knew who lived in the house we were about to search. A large, city-controlled complex of low-rent apartments was just down the street, and thugs hanging on the corner began to straggle down toward our location.

When we have a search warrant for drugs, we are allowed to search anywhere in the house that any amount of drugs can be hidden. We had a system of searching and did this for a living, so we knew what we were doing. While searching a bedroom for example, we would first toss the mattresses and bed linens then systematically place items found in drawers or closets on the bed. I have personally found thousands of dollars hidden in pockets of jackets hanging in closets. By the time we were done with our search, the house was a mess. Well, here we are—Mama is in the hospital, the target and his buddy are under arrest, and we are within ten minutes of being ready to leave the premises.

All of a sudden, "Jimmy B" pulled up in his car out front and wanted to go inside. As soon as he saw me, he remembered me as the one who pulled him out from under his mother's bed back in 1992. He then angrily asked who was in charge, and I told him I was, which surely did not improve the situation. I managed to calm him down and reasoned with him and advised him of the circumstance that brought us to his house. He had already served six or seven years for the charge that I arrested him on and had since returned to the area. I had heard through the grapevine that he was running a recording studio in North Charleston, and our conversation confirmed that fact. I was aware that he too was now probably also involved in illegal drug activity, but on this day, we were here for his little brother.

"Jimmy B' was concerned about the condition of his house inside because he knew we were known for redecorating. When I told him the condition of the house, he went ballistic and started to cause a scene in the street and deliberately tried to incite people on the street to protest our presence. In the middle of this, one of my guys rode up in our target's customized Cadillac and parked in front of the house. When I saw the response from the crowd, I immediately told my guys to "Get that car the hell out of here!" I ordered my guys to expedite their paperwork so we could get the hell out of there too! The Cadillac had been seized in another search at a second location executed simultaneously.

We loaded the two prisoners into the back of the truck, and when we were sure we had everything, I quickly maneuvered the truck through the crowd. As I looked in my side-view mirrors, I could see them all shaking their fists at us and yelling more loudly. We got safely back to the office, processed our evidence, and had someone take our two prisoners to the jail. Between the two search warrants, we arrested three players and seized a half-kilo of cocaine in fifteen separate bags, as well as the ninety-six grams of crack cocaine, $7,800 in cash and two vehicles. The two we apprehended on the porch were each arrested on five separate charges. The most serious carried a minimum sentence of twenty-five years, if convicted. Both were convicted and are presently enjoying room and board provided for them by the South Carolina Department of Corrections.

***

About this time my wife and youngest son, who by now was eight years old, expressed the fact that they really enjoyed having me home each night for the seventy-seven days while I was on administrative leave because of the shooting at the convenience store. I had never thought about the impact my hours had on them and realized that I had not spent very many evenings with them since Joe was born.

Joe had progressed well in school, and his form of autism allowed him to be a high-functioning, productive student who was doing quite well in school, the result of extra assistance that my wife and I pursued in the school system. Joe had gone through much testing, and he was reading at the level of a second-year college student at the age of eight. We accepted the fact that he would never be a star in sports because of his motor-skill issues, but there was no other person who knew at his age what he knew about sports and geography. He read everything he could get his hands on and would rather go to Barnes and Noble than to the playground. At the age of three, he was able to identify every state by shape and memorized their capitals. What his autism took from him was replaced by many more other gifted and talented traits.

I began to seriously reflect on my time with the agency and, more importantly, my future. I had been on a fast track in making sergeant and lieutenant. I had now been a lieutenant for eight years, and I knew why. I knew the incident that resulted in my suspension without pay was the reason for the fact that my advancement was at a standstill, and the prospect of ever being promoted to a higher rank was probably remote. Subordinates who had worked for me were now advancing to a point where they were being promoted right past me. I had worked for eighteen years at the very best law enforcement agency in the state of South Carolina, but I was now considering new challenges.

I had no one to blame for this but myself, and I never once complained or cried over spilt milk. It was the result of my doing, and I understood that fact completely. I started to put my feelers out, and within two weeks, I heard through the grapevine that the assistant chief of police at a local beach-resort community had resigned to pursue a career in real estate. I knew the chief there casually but not professionally. I knew his wife, Carol, pretty well because she had been my secretary in the early 1990s while in CID and was now the secretary of METRO, where I worked at the time.

I made telephone contact with the chief, and we met for lunch one day in a local restaurant and had some very serious discussion about what I could offer to him and his department in the way of experience. I left that meeting with a positive feeling, and when the position was posted in the newspaper, I immediately filled out an application and submitted it with my resume.

Within a few weeks of submitting my application, I was called for an interview. I met with the chief, the mayor, the city administrator, and the chairman of the public safety committee and answered questions for almost an hour. After a week or so, I met one on one with the chief. He offered the position to me, and we agreed on my salary.

I had more than 520 hours of annual leave (vacation) accrued, as well as over 1,450 hours of sick leave because in 18 years I had taken sick leave only when I had two minor surgeries. I would lose all of the sick leave because there was no way of being compensated for that time. Regarding the 520 hours of annual leave, I elected to take a week off and receive payment for a lump sum of the remaining 480 hours, which was 90 days of pay. My decision surprised many people, but I know I made the right one and was looking forward to now being home every evening with my wife and young son. I had a great run for 17-plus years and had faithfully served in every bureau of this highly respected law enforcement agency.

My starting date for my new job was the first week of November, so I had three weeks of not working, which drove me absolutely up the wall. I almost never took time off and never called in sick ever in my entire career, so being home without a job was something I had not experienced since I left the Marine Corps in 1972, twenty-eight years earlier.

My guys from METRO had a party for me at a downtown watering hole and presented me with a beautiful plaque with an engraved badge, which read,

**Presented To
Lieutenant Raymond F. Wright**

**For Your Dedicated Leadership of the METRO Major Case Unit
January 2000 – October 2000**

*"Leaders Aren't Born, They Are Made and They Are Made Just
Like Anything Else,
Through Hard Work"*

I was very proud of my guys and have remained close to them over the years. The inscription indicates to me that they recognized that I was a hardworking lieutenant, who did everything they did and never asked them to do anything I would not do.

Except for Scott, who left law enforcement, all remain on active duty today. Ray and Mike now work as US Air Marshalls. Robby, who was my narcotics sergeant, was later promoted to lieutenant and recently went to work for another local police agency. Mike, my technical sergeant, later made lieutenant and returned to METRO in my old position. Kevin and Roger were both promoted to sergeant and lieutenant, where they both still serve. Kevin was just recently promoted to captain. Alan has been promoted twice and is presently a lieutenant. "Odie," one of my highway interdiction deputies, left the agency and served numerous tours as a civilian contractor in Iraq and Afghanistan. He is now in charge of the entire K-9 program in the Middle East for his company. Joe, my other highway interdiction deputy later left the agency but went to work for another agency and continued to serve in its highway interdiction unit, where he now serves as a lieutenant. These guys were all leaders and proved that to me then and now as I continue to follow their careers.

In almost eighteen years with Charleston County, I worked with some great people, but more importantly, I worked for some of the best bosses anyone could imagine. It is to those leaders in particular, that I am forever grateful. Thank you, Marvin, Eddie, Ernie, and Larry.

A few weeks or so prior to my departure, my daughter Christy told me she was ready to get out of the retail business. The hours were not conducive to a good family life, and with a small child and a cop husband who worked crazy hours, she needed to make a career change. She had always wanted to be a paralegal and went to school with that direction in mind. I told her I knew some people within the county and would speak to someone who might be able to help. I spoke to a friend who supervised all summary court personnel, and she agreed to interview Christy for a job. Christy was hired by Charleston County Government and went to work for a local magistrate, starting on the same day I did with my new agency. I was happy that she was now in a much better situation with great benefits and hours.

Note: In all chapters of my law enforcement career I have referred to my superiors by name, but always preceded their first name with their rank at the time. I did this to describe who they were and never called any one of them by their first name on the job. The first names that I used were all actual first names. The agency that I worked for was and remains a Para-military organization that would never allow a subordinate to refer to a superior by anything other than his or her rank. I most often referred to my superiors as "Boss," which was an accepted way of addressing superiors by most. Every suspect that I mentioned was referred to by their actual nickname or real initials.

ASSISTANT CHIEF OF POLICE
26

After three weeks off and climbing the walls because I was not actively working, I started to work in my new endeavor. I now answered to only one person, the chief, which was something new to me because I was used to large chains of command in the past.

Paula drove me to work that first day because I would be taking my assigned vehicle home with me that evening. Paula is a beach lover and grew up on the Jersey shore, spending all of her summers at the beach. As we drove over the connector highway onto the island toward the ocean and got to the highest point, we looked out through the windshield and saw the beautiful Atlantic Ocean across our immediate front, with a few shrimp boats scattered for effect and a large ship just getting out into the open ocean after leaving the Charleston Harbor. My comment to Paula was "A tough place to come to work, huh?" Before that day, she had never been to the Isle of Palms. She could not believe where I now worked and how beautiful it was.

The agency was small, consisting at the time of eighteen sworn officers, eight dispatchers, two Animal Control officers, one secretary, and four part-time Beach Services officers. Since the agency was small, everyone knew everyone's business. There were no secrets. Except for the chief, only two of the officers knew who I was because they both previously worked for Charleston County with me. I knew that some were apprehensive because I was invading their domain from another department. Tim was a detective sergeant, who I had worked with in my first tour in METRO in the mid-'80s. Lester too worked in METRO with me, when he worked for another agency. He would soon replace Tim as the sole investigator for the department.

The atmosphere at the department was great, and everyone made me feel at home. The police department was in a building that was built after Hurricane Hugo obliterated the old police department building in 1989. The building was shared by City Hall and was split down the middle, with the police department occupying both floors in one half and City Hall in the other half. The bottom half of city hall was City Council Chambers, which doubled as a courtroom twice per month. Even though the building was only nine years old, it was inadequate in size to properly accommodate the department.

My new area of responsibility was now a barrier island almost seven miles long, the majority of which was public beach. Located at the far northern end of the island was Wild Dunes, a gated community that had two golf courses and a large hotel and every other amenity you could think of. Wild Dunes consists of 1,500 acres and is a getaway destination for many high-profile people, such as actors , sports stars, college football and basketball coaches, and other well-known celebrities and politicians. Some own their own homes, and some just vacation there to get away.

The entire island had approximately 5,000 year-round residents, which grew to 12,000 during the warmer months. Of the homes on the island, more than 1,300 are rental units, long and short term.

Before Hurricane Hugo changed the face of the island, most of the homes were small and cozy, with many used as second vacation homes. There was a business district that fronted to the beach that catered to day-trippers. The beach was also a popular destination for the thousands of military personnel stationed in Charleston, so there were quite a few watering holes that they frequented.

Some of the original occupants of the island enjoyed a carefree, quiet way of life, and the island incorporated into the City of Isle of Palms in 1952. The island was, at the time, only accessible by a swing bridge and a short ride through the neighboring Sullivan's Island before you got to the Isle of Palms. I spent many of my Reserve Police Officer hours in 1982 directing traffic at the turn that led to and from the Ben Sawyer Bridge. Traffic would back up for miles after each bridge opening, which allowed tall boats access to and from the Intracoastal Waterway. The winds of Hurricane Hugo blew that steel bridge right off of its cement pedestal, leaving it dangling dangerously in midair. Tom, my new boss, was at the time a patrol officer and was driving the last vehicle that crossed the bridge before the 120-plus-mile-per-hour winds blew the bridge off the pedestal.

Several days prior to the hurricane's arrival, Charleston County officials gave a mandatory evacuation order, which was obeyed by most, but the loss of the use of the bridge stranded those who desperately wanted to return to their homes on the two islands. There were several altercations between residents who wanted to return by boat to see their property, or what was left of it, so that shots were fired by the then chief of police to warn those trying to return to turn back. There were some very heated words exchanged by residents to the press, which was reported nationally, but sanity prevailed, and eventually they were allowed to return.

The Isle of Palms was devastated by a storm surge that was estimated to be anywhere from fourteen feet to twenty feet as it crossed the island. Hundreds of homes were lost, never to be seen again. Some washed off their foundations and were located blocks away. The morning after the storm hit, members of the police and fire department and a few city government employees returned by boat and stayed on the island until the bridge was repaired and reopened in October, about a month after the hurricane did its damage. They used four-wheel-drive vehicles that they commandeered from damaged homes and worked hard to make the island safe for habitation.

Due to the Federal Emergency Management Agency (FEMA) regulations, if a home in a flood plain is more than 51 percent damaged, it must be rebuilt on pilings or a breakaway foundation at least twelve feet above ground. Those homes that were damaged under the 51 percent threshold of damage could be repaired, and residents could eventually return to those homes. The effect that the hurricane had on the Isle of Palms resulted in a positive one. Hundreds of new homes sprouted up, bigger and better than those that were lost or damaged beyond repair. As a result, the island changed its face and became an even more desirable place to live and to vacation. The land was extremely valuable and multimillion dollars homes were now being built right on the ocean, on previously vacant beachfront land. The result was that those old homes that survived the hurricane and that were worth no more than $100,000 anywhere else, were now worth $400,000 to $500,000. The high-end new homes built on pilings now ranged from $800,000 to $7 million each.

Many investors have built the high-end homes and used them as vacation homes for their families or as rentals for anywhere from $1,500 to $15,000 per week, depending on their size, during the season (May to September).

As a result of the hurricane and the issues that arose after the mandatory evacuation and the problems that occurred post-hurricane, construction began on an 11,700-foot bridge from Mount Pleasant across the wetlands and the Intracoastal Waterway to the middle of the island. The bridge was more than three miles long and, at its highest point, sixty-five feet high, which easily accommodated the many sailboats and tall craft that negotiated the waterway. Evacuation, in the event of future weather issues, was now made easier, and the existence of the bridge now made going to the beach a whole lot easier for visitors than in the past.

Charleston County then purchased primo front-beach property and built a park with secure parking and amenities such as restrooms, showers, snack bar, and a small boardwalk to enter the beach, as well as hiring lifeguards. Placing the park where it was made the Isle of Palms the most desirable beach destination in the entire county. It has become so popular, in fact, that on many days during the season, the entire three-mile length of the bridge is full of bumper-to-bumper traffic for those trying to get to the beach.

I made it a point to become familiar with the island and spent a few hours a day driving around and learning where everything was. As I drove around, I introduced myself to merchants and citizens.

At a large agency, each ranking person has set responsibilities with set limitations dictated by his or her specific rank. My new position of responsibility allowed me to be involved in every aspect of the police department, which is something I enjoyed becoming proficient at in the coming years. I had input on the annual budget of $2.8 million and purchased everything for the department except for computer equipment. Only those with the rank of a major or chief were allowed to be involved in such things at my old agency.

About two weeks after my arrival at the Isle of Palms, I received notification that I was cleared by the US Department of Justice for my involvement in the shooting of May 19. It took seventy-seven days for SLED and the Solicitor's Office to clear me and my two guys as far as the state was concerned, but this took just days shy of six months to be cleared and exonerated. The letter said in part,

Dear Officer Wright:

The Criminal Section of the Civil Rights Division enforces the federal criminal civil rights laws, such as the willful abuse of authority by public officials that deprives individuals of liberties and rights defined in the United States Constitution or federal law. We evaluate allegations of civil rights violations to determine whether the evidence and circumstances of the case warrant a federal criminal prosecution.

After carefully considering the information obtained by the FBI as a result of its investigation, we concluded that the evidence is not sufficient to establish a prosecutable violation of the federal criminal civil rights statutes. Accordingly, we have closed our investigation. Please be advised that our conclusion in this matter does not preclude other components of the U.S. Department of Justice from taking action, where appropriate, under their separate enforcement authority.

The Division is dedicated to the enforcement of federal criminal rights statutes. We appreciate your cooperation in our shared responsibility to ensure the impartial and effective enforcement of our laws.

*A short paragraph between the first and second paragraph was omitted, because it listed the name of the person who lost his life by our hand.

I could essentially breathe a sigh of relief now that the federal government cleared us. As one might be expected, the family of the victim did not agree with these findings.

I was eager to learn and asked many questions over my daily lunches with the chief. We did not usually talk business, but when we did, it was usually me asking him questions. He and I went to lunch together every day unless he was out of town, and our topic of conversation was usually sports because we were both deeply into baseball and football. Unfortunately, he was from Michigan originally and was a diehard Detroit fan, so I had to often feel sorry for him.

My responsibilities included Patrol Commander, Communications, Investigations, Records, and Professional Standards Officer, and Fleet Manager. I also served as the prosecutor in Municipal Court for all misdemeanor traffic and criminal cases made by all officers. If a person asked for a jury trial, I then turned the case over to a City Attorney, with whom I worked very closely. I was extremely pleased that our municipal judge was a fulltime county magistrate whom I had known for years. She was the same retired English teacher that I spoke about in the SCAT Team chapter, after arresting four of her former students for marijuana possession.

I made it a point to review all pending court cases and started to work with the City Attorney in adjudicating them. There were also hundreds of traffic tickets pending due to defendants asking for continuances on their case. I started to work closely with Amy, the Clerk of Court, whose office was right across the hall from the police department. This working relationship, along with my long working relationship with the judge, resulted in clearing the backlog of the outstanding cases.

The department was in the process of becoming nationally accredited and was due to be assessed by a team of assessors in December of 2001. It was well on its way to becoming compliant with The Commission on Accreditation for Law Enforcement Agencies, or CALEA, which was the credentialing authority. This accreditation was accomplished through the joint efforts of law enforcement's major executive associations: the International Association of Chiefs of Police (IACP), National Organization of Black Law Enforcement Executives (NOBLE), National Sheriffs Association (NSA), and Police Executive Research Forum (PERF). These agencies set almost five hundred national standards that accredited law enforcement agencies must comply with. It was not an easy accomplishment to become nationally accredited, and many hundreds of man-hours were expended in the process to prepare for the assessors' arrival. The assessors were police executives themselves, some retired, who worked for accredited agencies.

I was very familiar with the concept of accreditation and had been responsible for writing some policies while with Charleston County. That department too was in the process of becoming accredited and was scheduled to be reviewed by assessors in the summer of 2001.

Not long after my arrival, I was put to the test in my capacity as Professional Standards Officer. I was essentially a one-man Internal Affairs Office. In that capacity I investigated all complaints made from any source, internal or external. Within a month of my arrival, I was forced to conduct an internal investigation into one of my patrol supervisors who had committed several violations of policy that drew my attention. My in-depth investigation lasted several weeks and resulted in his departure. No one knew what a cancer he was to this small department until he was gone, but his departure immediately uplifted the morale of the department.

This problem didn't go away as easily as his resignation, however, because he ended up filing a federal lawsuit against the City, the City Administrator, the chief, myself, as well as another female supervisor. The lawsuit went on for more than two years, and we settled just hours before a jury was to be selected.

As you can well imagine, complaints at a beach resort community were abundant. Not only did I handle all complaints regarding my officers, all other complaints too were forwarded to me for immediate action. It amazed me that someone who comes to our city and pays thousands of dollars a week for lodging can make such a fuss over a $15 parking ticket. Because parking on the island is at a premium, it must be strictly enforced. I stayed on the telephone handling parking complaints. Citizens would often come to City Hall, which is where tickets are paid, and give the girls who worked there such a hard time that I often had to run across the hall due to the loud and irate recipient of a parking ticket causing a disturbance and berating the girls.

I quickly found out that people on vacation switch to a different mode when they arrive at our beautiful beaches. They ignored signs that clearly posted parking regulations and beach regulations in general. Unlike a nearby beach community several miles away, our city did not allow the possession of alcohol anywhere on our beaches. There was no way to enter any portion of the beach without passing a white sign with black letters that clearly stated that no alcohol was allowed. My officers regularly walked the beach in uniform and, on occasion, in plainclothes. It was common for my people to spend an hour on the beach and issue tickets to a dozen beachgoers who were in violation.

On the average, I received less than ten complaints a year against my employees, which I feel is extremely low for the volume of people they encountered on a daily basis. I mentioned earlier that the population of those staying on the island grew from 5,000 to approximately 12,000 during the season. This does not include the 20,000 to 25,000 additional people who visited the beach on a daily basis, who we referred to as day-trippers. On any given day during nice weather, almost all of them were on the beach. At the peak of the season, it was common for four or five children to become lost or separated from their parents or guardians. Because so many people were tending to their children or in the water, they also left themselves wide open to becoming the victim of a theft. It amazed me that unthinking people left all of their vacation cash and credit cards lying on a towel unattended. Beachgoers also left themselves wide open to having their vehicles stolen by leaving their keyless remotes out in the open. The thief would just walk to the nearest parking lot and find the car and either steal from the car or steal the car itself.

I had worked for a busy law-enforcement agency with over 280 sworn deputies where a shooting, stabbing, or homicide was commonplace.

According to the chief, to his knowledge, there had never been a homicide in our jurisdiction. I understood that crimes that occurred here were different. Although there had never been a homicide, aggravated assaults, rapes, domestic abuse, burglaries, and thefts were very prevalent. There was an obvious need for more than one investigator. I often assisted the investigator with cases, which I thoroughly enjoyed. The biggest thing for me to get used to was the fact that the first eighteen years of my law enforcement career were spent serving in a nine hundred-square-mile county. Almost everywhere I went I had law-enforcement jurisdiction. Charleston County was ninety miles long, which ran along the east coast. Now, my jurisdiction covered just seven of those ninety coastal miles, which took some getting used to.

One issue that I quickly became aware of was the fact that many of our victims did not live locally, which made the criminal cases harder to solve. The first thing I observed in my new position was the lack of accountability in cases assigned for investigation. They were not being properly cleared, and pertinent questions could not be answered when I asked questions. I saw the need to assign all cases for investigation myself, which immediately eliminated the problem. I instituted a large log, identical to the one I kept twenty years prior as a sergeant in Criminal Investigations. Some concepts of management are tried and true.

Sometime in the Spring of 2001, my old chief, Marvin, from the Sheriff's Office made contact with me to advise that a nationally known police training company, In the Line of Duty, wanted to produce a training video regarding my shooting of the previous year. I was very familiar with In the Line of Duty and had viewed many of their training videos over the years. The chief told me when they would be in town, and they would conduct their interviews in the conference room at the METRO office.

The production crew from In the Line of Duty had the benefit of having studied the videotape of the shooting and was familiar with all of the details of the incident. They were eager to meet all of the participants and would interview each individually, then edit the interviews into their finished product, using the video that we provided.

In the Line of Duty is owned by a former police officer, so the interviews could not have been more professional. As former cops, they asked all of the right questions and produced a great training tool for law enforcement use nationwide. The Charleston County Sheriff's Office still shows the video to all of its new employees.

I am proud that the video highlights the great job that my guys did that night. We planned and executed a tactically sound textbook Buy/Bust and did everything that we had planned and trained for and managed to overcome the twist in fate that forced us to use deadly force. Fortunately, our years of training and experience allowed everyone to go home safely to their families that night.

***

At the time, we had a dormant Reserve Police Officer Program, and the chief expressed an interest in trying to revive the program. When your manpower is limited to eighteen, having the assistance of reserve officers is necessary. We were able to bring on an already certified Reserve officer, who did such a good job that we hired him as a full-time police officer six to eight months later.

During this same period, my oldest son, Doug's, father-in-law became a Reserve Police Officer at his department, where he and his brother-in-law worked. Doug convinced his father-in-law, William, to come from another department because he had intended to become a full-time police officer too. Well, as luck would have it, my new hire, Derrick, ended up being William's roommate at the police academy. William was forty-eight, and Derrick was in his mid-twenties. It was common for me to receive a phone call from them late in the evening as they were studying for legal tests to ask me a question or to have me explain something they did not quite understand. My instructions to all recruits attending the police academy were to call me if they needed anything, and this fit that category.

Our police department was a very desirable place to work as a cop. We never had any problems filling positions, and we were one of the few in the area that hired without prior experience. We tended to attract two distinctly different types of applicants. They were either young kids, twenty-one or twenty-two, just out of college, or cops who were near the end of their career and wanted to take it slow until retirement. There were always those, though, who were certified cops coming from a larger agency and were dying to be hired. A quick phone call usually indicated they were on their way out of the door for violation of policy or procedure. I became inundated with cops I knew who thought I would hire them to save their careers. I had to explain that we had a hiring process that we could not deviate from and that usually was all the explanation I needed. I did not have the power to hire or fire, but I was part of all of the interview process of all employees sworn or civilian. I would make my recommendation after the chief and I gave each applicant his or her final interview.

The chief and I also understood that hiring a person with no experience usually resulted in the person becoming restless to work at an agency that had more crime or one that was busier. We knew that these young people with no experience would also be gone to another agency within three years. Understanding that, we still never hesitated to hire someone without prior experience.

I had participated on so many police interviews while spending seven years on the county hiring board that I became very adept in seeing through people and reading into an application. My practice of trusting no one still worked and was very helpful in some of my interviews. I will admit that I did make some mistakes over the years by selecting a person or two who did not measure up to expectations.

***

By now my youngest son, Joe, was ten, and his knack for memorizing odd facts had been noticed. A teacher who worked with Paula, who ran the high school Academic Team recognized his talent, and she encouraged us to bring Joe to a match in the Columbia, South Carolina, area the Saturday after 9/11. Joe participated in several matches in a tournament of Junior Varsity players, and all of his opponents were amused by his small stature and young appearance as compared to all of the other high school participants. This turned out to be the first day of seven years of his involvement with the school's Academic Team. None of the so-called geeks, who were usual participants, ever knew any of the answers to any sports questions, and Joe excelled in geography and mapping, which were his specialties in knowledge.

God rewarded and blessed Joe with this unusual trait to offset his little setback in life, autism. Paula and I ended up spending our weekends traveling around the southeast competing in academic tournaments. The team also traveled to national tournaments and competed in Chicago, Boston, and Washington, DC, to mention a few. Instead of taking long weekends off, I now used my vacation time to take a long weekend to travel to the various tournaments where Joe and his team participated.

***

Our inspection team arrived in early December of 2001 to make the determination of whether our police department was worthy enough to become nationally certified through CALEA. We welcomed the team on

Saturday, and they stayed until the following Wednesday morning. We passed with flying colors and received the team's written report a month or so after its departure. One of the most glaring notations made in their comprehensive report was that our facility was busting at the seams, and we needed more room. This report was the first written notice to the city administrator, mayor and city council that confirmed what the chief had been saying for quite some time.

We received our national accreditation award several months later. At the time, we were the smallest nationally accredited law enforcement agency in the state of South Carolina.

In January of 2002, Derrick and William graduated from the South Carolina Police Academy and returned to their departments to begin their field training. The chief and I attended all graduation classes that our officers attended. The chief liked to take his new graduate and his or her family to lunch, and Derrick had a large, extended family. I told Derrick over lunch that his nine weekends of being off were over and told him when and where to report to begin his field training with a seasoned training officer.

Our police family had now grown with the newest addition of William to the profession. We now had my oldest son, Doug, my middle son, Pete, my son in-law Timmy, now William, and me. We pissed off our wives at family gatherings because there was always a corner where the five of us went to talk shop. William was extremely proud of his new job and the fact that he fulfilled his lifelong dream of becoming a cop. At an age when most are looking ahead to a retirement date, William was putting his affairs in order. He remedied the fact that he never graduated from high school by going to classes and obtaining his GED, which was the minimal educational requirement to enter the police academy. He was determined and had achieved his lifelong goal.

***

In the Spring of 2002 we started to see a noticeable influx of out-of-state college students visiting the island. We had an ongoing problem of underage drinkers, which was the source of many of our problems. It appeared that these large groups of students were occupying the large rental homes that accommodated up to twenty-five people. When that many people contribute to the rent, it can make for a very affordable spring break, without having to travel all the way to Florida. Since it is warm enough in March in our area and the ocean water temperature is warm enough to allow swimming, our island had become a popular destination with college students from the northeast.

We had enough issues in just dealing with the local high school and college students coming to the beach to cause problems, without the added out-of-state influx of potential trouble.

One underage alcohol incident comes to mind when one of my guys rode up on the beach one night and encountered a group of ten to twelve college students sitting around a campfire, which was prohibited. When they saw the officer, most of them ran to a nearby beach house, so the officer followed. Because the officer saw enough evidence of underage drinking going on, he was able to enter the house and charge them. The officer smelled an aroma of burned marijuana, and all present denied that there was anybody smoking marijuana. The officer then saw an open plastic container on the kitchen table with individual bags of marijuana in it. Each of the bags had the name of every occupant in the house on it, so all were charged with possession of marijuana. Nobody ever said they were very smart.

***

I had now been at the Isle of Palms for two years, and we went through our major seasonal events that required all available personnel. Memorial

Day weekend was big and mandated that officers work extra shifts to cover the influx of visitors to the beach. Once we got over Memorial Day weekend, we began planning for July Fourth. Because we were busiest in the summer, we did not allow people to take vacation during the busy months. Being at a beach-resort community, we constantly received requests to have events on the beach. Since I was the coordinator for all special events, I had the task of screening each and every request.

For the entire time I worked on the Isle of Palms, I never took a vacation longer than a long weekend. Since I was normally off on Saturday and Sunday, I would from time to time take a Friday or a Monday so I could have three days off to attend Joe's competitions. Our vacation policy was unpopular with some, but we told them when they were hired what we expected from them. I took some time in the spring for the three of us to go to Florida and attend Yankees spring-training games. The absolute end to our season was a connector run, which is an annual run and walk for charity and an event that required that we close the connector bridge so the 1,200 to 1,500 participants could do their thing.

FAMILY TRAGEDY

27

November 19, 2002, was a date that was a dark and devastating day to my family. Doug, who was now a sergeant and still working with the Drug Interdiction Unit on Interstate 95, heard a radio transmission come across his police radio, stating that two officers were down on Boone Hall Road in the Summerville city limits. Doug knew that his father-in-law, William, was working the evening shift and would have just left roll call prior to hitting the street. Doug called his dispatcher from his cell phone and asked the dispatcher, "Is William Bell one of those officers down?" The dispatcher would not answer him and began to cry as he pressed her for an answer. The dispatcher finally relented, and through her own tears and emotions told Doug that William was one of the two down. Doug was more than thirty miles away and ran Code 3, which is police radio code for lights and siren, responding to an emergency. It did not take Doug long to make the trip, and while making that trip, he called me. He often called me while working, and I always have to tell him to turn the volume down on his radio so I can hear what he is telling me on the cell phone. When I answered, I knew immediately that something bad had happened because I recognized the tone of his voice, and I could tell from the background noise that he was driving well over a one hundred miles per hour. I had just finished eating dinner, and when I answered, Doug said, "Dad, I think William has been killed." He then told me what he thought had happened and wanted me to come to the scene in Summerville, which was thirty miles from where I lived. I told him to calm down and be careful and told him I was on my way. I immediately called my other son Pete, who was a cop now at another local police agency and told him about Doug's phone call. I told him that I was on my way to pick him up because he lives about a mile away from me.

I hauled ass over to Pete's, and we then traveled Code 3 in my police cruiser to the scene. By now, we had received additional information by talking to my daughter on the trip to Summerville. Her husband, Timmy, was a motorcycle traffic officer for the Summerville Police Department and had responded to the accident scene. The information we received was that William rode up on a disabled motorist with a flat tire on the side of the road, and he and a Berkeley County Sheriff's Deputy, who was off duty stopped to change the tire for the distressed female driver. While both were changing the left rear tire, a pickup truck driven by a male subject ran off the road and plowed right into William's cruiser then into the two officers changing the tire, killing them instantly. A tractor-trailer driver following behind stopped to assist and had to physically restrain the driver who ran off the road from trying to leave the scene of the accident on foot.

While Doug was making his trip to the scene from the opposite direction, he realized when he heard the exact location of the accident that his wife was at home, a half mile away from the accident scene with my two grandsons and would certainly hear all of the sirens in the area. He knew that his wife, Valarie, was aware that her dad William was working that night. Doug knew that he had to tell Valarie something, and he called to tell her that her dad had been in an accident, and he didn't know how badly he was hurt. He is not a very good liar, and she knew right away that he was not being completely truthful with her. Desperately, she then began to call her dad on his cell phone, and of course, there was no answer.

When Doug arrived at the scene of the accident, knowing that the worst had happened, he tried to remain calm as he saw the two covered bodies lying near the accident scene. He was escorted to where William and the deputy were, and he kneeled down and lifted the blanket to see the lifeless body of his father-in-law, William. Doug said that the first thing he noticed was that William was wearing his department issued wooly-pulley sweater because it was a chilly November evening. Doug viewed the extent of William's injuries and knew that he had probably died instantly, and he now knew he had to get to his wife right away.

After Doug saw William, the identity of the off-duty deputy was still unknown. The deputy was wedged partially under the truck that struck them. Officials at the scene asked Doug if he knew who the deputy was, and he looked at the parked Berkeley County deputy's cruiser and recognized some distinguishing features and realized that the other lifeless body was that of Deputy Marion Eugene Wright (no relation), who lived with his parents in a nearby neighborhood. He told the officials that they had better get to his parents' house before they found out the wrong way.

After Doug positively identified the two downed officers, Pete and I arrived and went immediately to Doug. I declined an offer to see William since I had seen enough death in my career, and doing so would have served no purpose. Pete and I both reminded Doug that he had to get to Valarie right away. I would not have wished that task to even my worst enemy. Valarie was very close to her dad and was still dealing with her dad's divorce from her mother a few years prior. William often came by the house on a meal break while working, and Valarie would fix him something to eat while William doted on his only two grandchildren. His namesake, William Cole, was going to be one on December 18.

His first and oldest grandson, Douglas Tanner, was going to be three on November 24. They were, at the time, his only two grandchildren, and he was extremely proud of them both. He would, unfortunately, be absent for Tanner's third family birthday celebration, which had been planned for the upcoming weekend.

The coroner arrived on scene and removed William and Eugene then released them to their respective funeral homes for preparation for their upcoming funerals. Doug knew that William had been disfigured because he had already seen him. He did not want any family member to see him in the condition that he had seen him, so he and Timmy went to the funeral home and asked the funeral director if they could have some private time with William. Doug and Timmy paid their quiet respects then meticulously cleaned him up to the best of their ability and covered him up. Knowing the relationship Doug had with William, I know that this was an extremely hard thing to do. It was a unique relationship because William was a forty-eight-year-old rookie, and Doug was his superior by rank and had been responsible for recruiting him to the Summerville Police Department.

In the meantime, all of William's family members were brought to a local Episcopal church that opened its doors, so a remote meeting place was present. Cops did what they do best when a fellow brother in blue is hurt or killed. They just began showing up from all over to express their condolences to the family members. That is just what cops do. When I arrived at the accident scene, there were easily one hundred cops on scene from at least six different agencies. If a cop is badly injured, they will generally go en masse to the hospital. Valarie, her sister Gail, and William's former wife arrived, and I went to the three of them as they all cried uncontrollably and put my arms around all of them at the same time and told them, "Your dad was a hero, and he gave his life helping someone in need." We hugged for a while, and I could see the hurt and pain in their eyes. Valarie was extremely close to her dad and had been enjoying seeing him interact with her boys. Cole was only eleven months old and never got to really know his grandfather.

By now, a few hours after the incident, the facts of the accident were materializing. The woman who had the flat tire on the side of the road had a suspended driver's license and should not have legally been out on the road. The driver of the pickup truck that struck William and Eugene also had a suspended driver's license and had a history of seizures and a long history of driving offenses while under suspension. Eugene had apparently stopped first and parked in front of the disabled vehicle, and when William drove up, he stopped and parked behind the disabled vehicle. Eugene had been on the cell phone with his girlfriend and told her he was stopping to change a flat tire. His girlfriend asked him not to stop, but he said he would not be long. All three vehicles were well off on the shoulder of the road. The pickup truck first struck William's police cruiser, then struck William and Eugene, then came to rest against Eugene's cruiser. Evidence and witnesses indicate that Eugene was kneeling down changing the tire and William was to his right holding a flashlight on the tire and handing lug nuts to Eugene when they were struck.

After a few hours at the church, we all went home for the night. Doug was left to deal with his inconsolable wife and to tell his oldest son, Tanner, that his "Pop Pop" was gone and would not be at his birthday party. We agreed to meet in the morning after he asked me to come to the police department. He wanted my assistance in making the family decisions at the funeral home after our meeting. Doug knew that William wanted a Marine Corps funeral, if possible, and the reason for meeting at the police department was to see if a copy of his military record was in his personnel file. Otherwise, a military funeral would not be an option.

The arrangements were made, and the funeral was set for Friday, November 22, 2002. As the funeral procession left the funeral home for the five-mile ride to the church, we turned onto the main road that led into the town of Summerville to Interstate 26, which is lined with businesses. As we came out and got into line to begin our procession, we were overcome by the response from the citizens of the town who had lined the street on both sides, standing in reverence as the procession passed them by. Men and women were holding their hands over their heart as we passed. An even more moving tribute was when we passed underneath two fire department ladder trucks that had their ladders extended and touching from either side of the six-lane street with a huge American flag hanging down over the roadway as we passed underneath.

When we arrived at the church, the parking lot was full of police cruisers from all over. There were at least 1,000 people in the sanctuary, with all of the police officers filling the left side of the church, and all civilians on the right and in the middle behind the family. In the tri-county area, there are approximately 1,200 law enforcement officers, and at least half of them attended. Doug then did something that I never would have been able to do: he delivered William's eulogy and did a wonderful and respectful job. After a moving service and a celebration of William's life, we walked out through the walkway lined with many hundreds of police officers. I had been on the Charleston County Sheriff's Department Honor Guard for over seven years and had worked many police funerals, but the role was now reversed. I was now a member of the grieving family, a very different feeling indeed.

After the procession to the cemetery, Marine Corps Honor Guards met the hearse and removed William with precision, led by a first sergeant. William was loaded onto a caisson provided by the Charleston Police Department and led to his grave site. The short service ended with a rifle salute and the flag folded and presented to the family by the first sergeant. Before everyone left the grave site, a Summerville police radio speaker blared William's radio call number three times, after the non-response to William's number, the radio code for out of service was called, and everyone in the crowd lost it. Over the years, I have been to many military and police funerals, but this was by far the most moving that I have ever attended. Most of the officers present then went off to another church and attended Eugene Wright's funeral service.

The town took great care of the family and fed them that entire week. That evening, the fire department cooked a great meal for anyone who wanted to attend, and we all sat and talked for hours in the fire department garage bays. I was very impressed by the closeness that the department exhibited, and I now knew for sure that Doug and my son in-law, Timmy, were working at a truly fine police department. This was the department's first line of duty deaths, and it did all of the right things to accommodate the family respectfully.

The scumbag who killed these two fine cops was tried and convicted on two counts of Reckless Homicide and sentenced to two consecutive twelve-year sentences. Consecutive means that the second term is served after first, so he would serve twenty-four years. If the sentences had been concurrent, then they would be served together. The judge made the sentences consecutive to ensure that the driver served more than twelve years. When he was sentenced, the family thought that we would be done with him until his release, but that thought was quickly quashed when we realized that after four years of his sentence, we would need to attend annual parole hearings and speak to the board that heard these cases. Every year for the past six years, the family has circulated petitions to be presented to the parole board. We have also attended the remote video sites set up to speak directly to the board to plead our case that the prisoner will not be released. Each time, the prisoner has waived his right to be present for the hearing, but he appears just minutes before each hearing, thus playing games with the family. He is due to max-out on his sentence in 2014, so his release in inevitable.

The following week an Incident Debriefing was held in the town's visitor center. In attendance were at least fifty people who were involved in the incident, directly or indirectly, and they were monitored by trained Police Grief Counselors. Valarie was still so consumed with grief that Doug thought it best that she not attend because he did not want to put her through that ordeal. The debriefing was a meaningful one. Many tears flowed in the room, and many emotions were shared. These debriefings should be required after all major incidents, as they are highly productive and insightful. These were the first line-of-duty deaths that the department ever had, and it handled the aftermath well. Again, just as the debriefing of my officer-involved shooting two years prior, this debriefing identified the extent that the communications personnel working at the time of the incident were affected. This debriefing turned out to be especially beneficial to them.

What this man did to our family is unfathomable. I have seen my daughter-in-law suffer and have seen her transformation from a happy-go-lucky, cheerful mother and wife to a defeated and clinically depressed mess of a person. She finally sought psychiatric help and was diagnosed with Post Traumatic Stress Disorder and had to be medicated to control her mood swings just to get through the day. I am happy to say that she has, for the most part, overcome the bad and has turned her life around. She had dropped out of college and eventually married Doug and used the educational benefits now available to her as a result of her dad's death to complete her Bachelor's degree and went on to obtain her Master's degree in Communications. She made the Dean's List and worked as an adjunct professor. She became active in the nationally known organization, Concerns of Police Survivors (COPS), which was organized in 1984 with 110 members. It has now grown to 50 chapters nationwide with more than 15,000 families, made up of spouses, children, siblings, significant others, and coworkers of fallen law-enforcement officers. Valarie even surprised us all and became an elected officer in her chapter.

It has been wonderful to see Valarie turn the death of her dad into something positive. This past fall she was awarded a full scholarship to obtain her doctorate degree in Communications at Ohio University. I mention this because she has devoted her doctoral research to investigating the deaths of law-enforcement officers in the United States, as well as Post Traumatic Stress Disorder in law enforcement. I have no doubt that she will be successful in her endeavor.

Even now, more than ten years after William's death, I continue to see evidence of the pain inflicted on my family. When Doug, Valarie, and their children visit, I can often see tears in Valarie's eyes as she watches me play with her children in the pool or interact with them. They are tears of sadness because she is watching what she wishes her dad could experience. The pain will never go away; it just gets a little easier to deal with.

Patrolman William Boland Bell
End of Watch–Tuesday, November 19, 2002
Deputy Marion Eugene Wright
End of Watch–Tuesday, November 19, 2002

BACK TO WORK
28

After almost a week of spending time with family members bereaving William's death, I tried to get back into the groove of working again. Upon my return, I had a desk full of paperwork to deal with, which took my mind off family issues.

My son Pete had started his work in law enforcement as a patrolman at the Summerville Police Department but felt like he was under the shadow of his older brother and brother in-law, so he had left and worked for two other police agencies. After William's death, there was, of course, and opening available, and Pete was asked to reapply to return to where he started his law-enforcement career. The chief thought it would be fitting and proper that Pete was the one to fill the vacancy made available by William's premature death. He was offered the position, and within two weeks, Pete was back at Summerville working with his brother and brother in-law again.

Cops are a weird breed of people because they will change their police job for a $500 raise in pay or to work for an agency that has nicer police cars. It is common for someone to end his or her career having worked for several police agencies along the way. Law enforcement in the south is very different from most anywhere else because we are not unionized.

Because we are not unionized, the starting salaries of local law enforcement agencies vary as much as $15,000.

***

We did not have many serious crimes occur in our jurisdiction, but because we were so proactive, we continued our higher-than-average clearance rate. Because of the atmosphere of the beach, most year round residents were very lax in their home security. They often failed to lock their homes as well as their vehicles.

One high-profile resident of the island was a well-known football announcer for ESPN. He had owned several homes on the island as investments and had recently built a beauty of a home facing the ocean for him to live in. He left his brand-new Acura SUV parked in the garage located under his house, with the key in the ignition. Since new homes must be constructed on pilings at least twelve feet off the ground, the ground floor was usually enclosed with latticework and used as a garage and storage area. One night a thief found the unlocked SUV and stole the vehicle. He then left our jurisdiction and was chased by an adjoining jurisdiction for a speeding violation but managed to get away.

In our area, it is extremely unusual not to recover a stolen vehicle within a few days of the theft. They are usually used for joyrides until they run out of gas and are usually abandoned. This particular Acura was missing for two weeks and was not recovered until it was used to facilitate a restaurant burglary and a bank robbery in nearby Mount Pleasant. I read the daily Crime Analysis Reports from all surrounding jurisdictions and read that Mount Pleasant indicated that video surveillance tape and a witness observed a white SUV after a restaurant burglary and a bank robbery. I then heard that a white SUV was chased by another jurisdiction the night of the vehicle theft and asked for a copy of the police video to see if there was a connection. My investigator, Dawn, and I worked together with Mount Pleasant Police investigators and determined that the stolen SUV from our jurisdiction was used in their burglary and bank robbery. The thief was identified and determined to be working at a construction site on our island. He had apparently taken cash from the bank robbery and purchased a used car, which was conveniently parked at the jobsite when we arrived. He was taken into custody without incident.

***

A beach atmosphere was also conducive to its share of sexual assaults. I am very proud that our agency cleared every sexual assault case that occurred during my tenure. These crimes were usually committed when alcohol was involved and generally occurred on the deserted beach late at night.

Because of the socioeconomic makeup of the majority of the residents on the island, we had to be extremely careful to ensure that we were not manipulated when summoned to affluent homes to report domestic disturbances. In my prior law enforcement experience, domestic disputes usually involved two parties in an estranged relationship. They were usually low- to middle-income people either renting a home or an apartment, owning one possibly two cars, and, for the most part, had no other sign of monetary worth. These disputes were easy to resolve, and it was easy for the cops who responded to get the entire picture during their response to the home.

Now, dealing with a domestic dispute may involve a situation in which the occupants were more highly educated, and the house they were living in was worth a million dollars or more, with two or more cars in the driveway, valued at $100,000 or more. The homeowners may have a large boat parked outside, or in some cases docked at the dock in their yard, not to mention their unknown mutual worth through investments. It became all too clear in some cases that husbands or wives often tried to set up their spouses by reporting insignificant arguments in preparation for separating. This action was to start the chain of documentation through police reports to provide their respective divorce lawyers in preparation for a beneficial separation and eventual divorce settlement. I warned my officers to be careful when dealing with such incidents and saw this happen quite often.

One thing that bothered the hell out of me was that some of the affluent often thought of the local police as a necessary evil and were quick to complain when things were not done to their satisfaction. Some of the complaints that I handled were laughable and totally without merit. Some of the old-timers remembered when the island was wide open and full of bars and drunken visitors, and the necessary cops were there to keep the peace. Over the years, some of the older residents never noticed that their police department had transformed into a nationally accredited law enforcement agency that adhered to the same standards of agencies in large, metropolitan cities. For the most part, our officers and the administration won over these people through hard work. We organized community meetings, attended civic group events, and made believers of those who were not aware of the changes that had been made over the years.

I was also surprised by the number of people who decided to come to our pristine beaches to end their lives. I guess the solitude of sitting on the beach watching the waves roll in was appealing to those misguided few who decided to make the ultimate decision to end their troubled lives by committing suicide on the beach. The affluence of our population made no distinction in the national rate of suicide either, as we had our share of local residents who chose the ultimate act to end their troubles by committing suicide.

One such suicide comes to mind in which a man rented a condominium unit and committed suicide while talking to his girlfriend on the phone. We responded, investigated the incident, and removed the body. All of his personal property was inventoried and left in the condominium unit because he had paid the rent in advance. Arrangements were made for a family member to come from out of state to retrieve the property. Unknown to us, a civilian security guard had access to the condominium after our departure and decided to steal property owned by the deceased individual. He stole credit cards, a camera, and a few other minor items. When the family member arrived to accept ownership of the property, he noticed that some credit cards were missing. We did a computer search of the account and discovered many local purchases made with the stolen cards after the death of the owner.

It did not take long to track the crime back to the civilian security officer who provided security to the gated community within our jurisdiction. I prepared a search warrant, and when we arrived at the apartment occupied by the employee and his girlfriend, he played dumb and was uncooperative with us. I separated the girlfriend and Dawn, my investigator, and I spoke to her. She was wearing a brand-new engagement ring recently purchased with one of the stolen credit cards. She was unaware that the ring was purchased with a stolen card and reluctantly took the ring off and gave it to me, at my request, where she then proceeded to tell us where other items were that were fraudulently purchased. That was not a hard case to solve, but it was unusual and interesting to say the least.

We were targeted each season with new groups of innovative thieves who put a severe strain on our resources. Since there were so many rental homes on the island, they were often the target of burglaries. The kink to our investigation was that affluent and absent owners often unknowingly hindered our investigations. The owner would build a rental home or buy a completed home with the intention of keeping it occupied as much as possible. They would outfit an entire home with four or five flat-screen TVs, with VCRs or DVD players, and often have a state-of-the art stereo system available for the pleasure of their renters. When a theft occurred, they were never able to provide serial numbers of the electronic equipment in their rental property, which made them extremely hard to track through local pawnshops or to identify as stolen when we conducted search warrants. We had several groups over the years who managed to double and triple our yearly number of burglaries, as well as adding to the monetary value of reported thefts in our jurisdiction.

One season we had burglars who were tied in with a group of house cleaners who cleaned the homes after each weekly rental. Since the house cleaners had access to the keys to each rental property, we immediately targeted several cleaning companies who provided house cleaner service. We even went so far as to meet with all of the rental company personnel, who were forced to change or adjust their policy and procedure regarding key access and quality control. The temptation to low-income and low-paid personnel was usually the motive. In the course of several investigations, we recovered electronic equipment as far as eighty miles away.

After providing countless reams of crime statistic reports to the City Council, it finally decided to add two police officers to the Patrol Division. The City Council funded the entire cost of the personnel, their equipment, and vehicles, which exceeded $200,000. At the same time the council also decided that there was a need to fund a third position dedicated to the enforcement of what they considered livability issues on the island. This allowed us to add three full-time law enforcement positions, bringing the size of the department to twenty.

We now had to advertise for the positions and go through a hiring process, but we were able to hire in time for our new budget, which commenced on July 1. There are times when twenty officers are not quite enough to get the job done, but twenty seemed like a perfect size for the task.

In 2006, I encountered more and more freshly discharged military applicants as I reviewed every application submitted. Over the years, after spending so many years as a member of the police hiring board at Charleston County and now being a part of every hire at this department, I always favored the hiring of veterans. I have found that an applicant who has a military background usually turns out to be a superior employee. There have been a few exceptions, however. I, of course favor Marine veterans, and have never been disappointed in any former Marine who was hired. They are disciplined, know the importance of chain of command, understand how to follow orders, and are always dependable.

One such applicant was deep into the hiring process and had just returned from his second tour in Iraq. I noticed from his military record (DD-214) that he had a Purple Heart and two Bronze Stars. During his final interview with the chief and me, I asked him to tell me about how he earned his Bronze Stars, and he became emotional as he thought about what I had asked him. I had to stop him because I could tell that it was too hard for him to discuss. We hired him, but within three weeks of being hired, he was recalled to active duty, and we never saw him again.

I bring this up because there is an ever-increasing number of former military entering the job force who want to become cops. After seeing how emotional that one applicant became, law enforcement agencies will need to be extremely careful in their psychiatric testing during the hiring process to ensure that they are not hiring people suffering from Post-Traumatic Stress Disorder (PTSD). The war has lasted so long that I fear there are many more veterans suffering from PTSD than is actually known. Military personnel tend not to report symptoms of PTSD because they do not want to be labeled or identified, which would hinder their military career.

Just recently, I heard of a freshly discharged soldier who was hired by a local sheriff's office. He had attended twelve weeks of the police academy and returned to complete his field training. About a month into his field training, he told his training officer that he did not think he could do this, and he quit his job that night. He told his training officer that he was a sergeant in the Army and was used to being given an order, completing the task, then returning to his superior for another assignment. He just could not handle driving around looking for something to do. He went back to his recruiter, rejoined the Army, and was given his stripes back.

Being a veteran of Vietnam, I always thought PTSD was a cop-out to a certain number of malingerers who were looking for benefits they did not necessarily deserve. I have done a complete turnaround over the years in my thinking after seeing how just one life-threatening or traumatic event can cause PTSD to take over a person's entire life. After almost thirty years as a cop, I have seen cops suffer from PTSD after just one life-and-death, fight-for-life experience. If a cop is alone and placed in a situation in which he or she has to fight for his or her life and keep an assailant from taking his or her weapon and turning it on him or her, that one incident can be enough to cause that cop to suffer from PTSD.

Cops are just like military personnel; they do not want to share or admit to a superior or a friend, for that matter, that they are suffering inside. They tend to become depressed and deal with their issues by turning to alcohol or prescription medication or by just ignoring the symptoms entirely and continuing to suffer. This suffering many times causes marital problems at home, then problems on the job. I have great respect for the military warriors who are coming home daily. When I go to the VA facility for my twice-annual physical, I listen to the young guys telling doctors and nurses the problems they are experiencing because of

PTSD. I thank my lucky stars that it never affected me and pray that those suffering will overcome.

Unfortunately, PTSD has resulted in a record number of military suicides. In 2012 alone, there were 325 military suicides, more than who died in combat in Afghanistan for the same calendar year. I fear that the end of the war will result in many more, especially with the economy the way it is, because it will be extremely hard for the influx of veterans again entering the job force. The option for them to stay in the military has also been decreased because of mandated budget cutbacks by the present administration that will affect the military.

***

One of my responsibilities was to serve as the Public Information Officer to the police department. There are several highly respected and professional news reporters in Charleston, and I have dealt with some for more than twenty-five years. I received daily calls from various media outlets asking for details or wanting an interview to support a story they were reporting on. I have learned over the years who I could trust with off-the-record information. For the most part, the TV reporters were young and just starting out in the business and working their way to larger TV markets in the country. I have also made the determination that some venues would rather create the news rather than report the news. As a result, some outlets often reported inaccurate information.

In the summer of 2007, we had the worst possible incident occur that could happen to a beach resort. One warm afternoon, a little after four in the afternoon, we had a nine-year-old boy bitten on the lower leg by a shark in knee-deep water while riding a boogie board. His dad saw that he was in distress and grabbed his son and carried him to the beach. The victim told his dad that he tried to release his leg, but the shark would not release its jaw from him. As soon as the word got out, that section of beach was immediately closed, which was not very popular among the many thousands of beachgoers forced to get out of the water. Just a few minutes later, and four miles north on the island, a second person was bitten by a shark twenty-five to thirty yards from shore. This thirty-year-old victim's injury was more serious, causing a severe ankle laceration and dislocation. Of course, we now had to close the entire seven miles of beach. The local media listening to their police radio scanners heard the word *shark*, descended to the Isle of Palms, took to the beach like the movie *Jaws*, and started asking ridiculous questions to those remaining on the beach. Within an hour, national media outlets began to call—CNN, NBC, CBS, and FOX—wanting information. I referred all of these requests to the city administrator, who gave several telephone interviews. The beach remained closed for the rest of the day, but we had the Coast Guard and Sheriff's Department helicopters fly over periodically in an attempt to ensure the safety of those who ignored our orders to stay out of the water.

The next morning I started receiving my daily press inquiries, and, of course, the topic was the two shark bites of the previous day. One female TV reporter, new to that particular station, called and asked me, "How is the investigation of the shark bites going?" My response was "There is nothing to investigate." She seemed incredulous that there was no investigation. Her next question was "Can you tell if the same shark was responsible for both bites?" I could not resist, so my answer was "I don't know yet. I'm waiting on dental records to come back now," and I began to laugh at her ridiculous question. She asked why I was laughing at her question, so I began to laugh harder and told her to think about what she had asked. I then told her that there was no possible way that we could ever tell, and it was unlikely that the same shark bit both people. We were very fortunate that both bites appeared to be from small species of sharks and did not seem to affect the volume of visitors to the beach in the days following the attacks.

***

The fire department's main station was heavily damaged after a large storm passed through. While workers inspected the roof and wall damage, they determined that cracks in the walls from the storm damage had caused mold to form, and firefighters were beginning to get physically sick while staying in their quarters. They were temporarily placed in a nearby hotel and finally were placed in trailers that were purchased to house their offices and sleeping quarters. The city determined that they would demolish the existing building and would rebuild on the same lot and would finally alleviate our lack of space by building a new facility to house the fire and police departments.

Ground was broken in the spring of 2008, and construction began on this more than $7.5 million project. The chief and I had much input into what we wanted and needed in the new facility, which would be known as the Isle of Palms Public Safety Building. The building was designed to withstand hurricane-force winds and was built in such a way that the first floor consisted only of public restrooms, sheltered parking for police vehicles, and fire department garage bays. One-half of the second story was police department and the other half office space for the fire department, as well as a state-of-the art training room that we shared. This room doubled as an Emergency Operations Center in the event of disaster. The third floor housed the fire department sleeping quarters and a fully equipped gym.

We moved in in August of 2009, had more than enough room, and brought only some filing cabinets. All of the furniture in the new facility was new and greatly appreciated by all of our employees. Many trips to various venues to shop for office equipment were required, and we now enjoyed the benefit of our choices. By virtue of the fact that I purchased all equipment for the department, I remained heavily involved in the extra maintenance now required to run a building of this size. I never once complained after spending more than eight years in the old and small facility. We had, fortunately, properly planned and built into our budget the funds needed to accommodate the higher costs involved in properly maintaining this much-larger facility. We split much of the operating costs with the fire department, but trivial unexpected things like providing bathroom supplies for the public restrooms and keeping them clean remained minor issues that were remedied.

***

In February of 2010, my youngest son, Joe, was now a senior in high school. He had overcome his autistic shortcomings, had managed to maintain good grades, and had even taken an advanced course in history that earned him college credits. We wanted him to attend college locally, preferably the College of Charleston, so he could live at home. Presently, there was just no possible way that he could live independently.

An admissions representative from The College of Charleston scheduled interviews for thirty-three prospective students at his school. These interviews would be for immediate approval or rejection to their institution, without having to wait. We assisted Joe in putting together a resume and a portfolio of all of his accomplishments and writings and highlighted what to emphasize during the interview. Paula works in the same high school that Joe attended and was on pins and needles out in the hallway as he entered the conference room for his one-on-one interview. Paula met Joe out in the hallway as he exited the interview, and Joe calmly announced that he had been accepted. He was one of only ten students selected that day out of thirty-three interviewed for admission to The College of Charleston. Paula called me to announce the great news and we cried tears of joy together over the phone.

After all of the problems Joe had in his life and dealing with the cards that life had dealt him, he was now accepted to college and ready to begin a new chapter in his life. On top of this great news, he would be able to attend college tuition-free because of a Purple Heart Scholarship program provided by the State of South Carolina to children of Purple Heart recipients.

Joe's high school graduation was a big deal, and the entire family attended the event. We had a family party at the house, attended by some former teachers and family friends.

***

The police department maintained its national accreditation status, and we were recertified in 2004 and again in 2007. We were due to be inspected again in December 2010 for the fourth time and spent our time in earnest preparation.

While preparing for the upcoming visit by the CALEA inspectors, I began doing some math regarding my retirement benefits. The state of South Carolina Police Retirement System allows each member the opportunity to purchase up to six years of military time. The purchase price of each year of service is computed by paying the retirement system a set percentage of your current salary, which is deducted from each paycheck at a reasonable interest rate until paid in full. My five years, ten months and twenty-eight days had been paid off for several years now. I was computing what my monthly retirement check would be if I retired and was pleased to see that my monthly benefit for my thirty-five years of service would be more than what I made by actually coming to work. The generous formula available to police retirees made it a no-brainer—why was I still working? I was now sixty-two and eligible to also receive Social Security. People have always said that you will know when you are ready to retire. Now I knew!

I went home and told my wife, Paula, and she agreed that retirement should be considered. The first thing she said after that was "You know you can't just sit around and do nothing. You have to be busy, or you will go crazy." I agreed and told her I had been thinking about contacting several of the local attorneys in town and would like to start a business as a process server. It was a business that really only required a car and a phone, and I was certain that my years of contact with local attorneys would pose no problem to establishing my business.

I planned an immediate trip to the Police Retirement Board in Columbia to meet with them to confirm my calculations and to get some advice from them regarding the best time to make my move. My wife Paula traveled with me because she, as a teacher, was also in the state retirement system and eligible to retire several years after me. While at this October 2010 meeting, I made the decision to retire on Friday, April 1, 2011. On the trip home, we discussed my imminent retirement, and I felt extremely comfortable in my decision. The time was right, and I was still a young sixty-two. I wanted the opportunity to enjoy my retirement and to do other things with my life. Too many times, I have seen guys on the job push themselves too far and never get to enjoy life post-retirement. I vowed that I would not be one of those.

My next day back at work my chief walked into my office and closed the door because he was eager to know all of the details of my trip to the retirement board. He too had more than enough time to retire, but he was about ten years younger than I was and needed to stay where he was for several more years. I filled him in on the details, and he was pleased to see that my retirement check was even more than we had calculated on paper.

I informed him that my plan was to retire on Friday, April 1, 2011, more than five months away. We agreed that I would keep my plans quiet because he needed time to decide what to do in the form of a replacement for my soon-to-be vacated position. I told him that I thought I should advise the city administrator of my plans, and he agreed that would be wise.

I now had to think about how to make the transition to retirement after April 1 because I had worked since I was a teenager. I had lunch one day with two attorneys from a very prominent law firm in Charleston and told them about my plan to start a process service business. I told them I planned to write letters to dozens of local attorneys, soliciting their business. They immediately shut me down and said that I could have all of the process service business for their law firm, which had seven working attorneys. That proved to be a very successful lunch.

I wanted to work only enough to keep from being bored and to keep involved with my friends in law enforcement and to continue the friendships I had established with local attorneys over the years.

Our December on-site inspection by CALEA for reaccreditation went well, and we were again awarded our third national reaccreditation.

***

In January of 2011, the chief of police of another local beach community suddenly resigned. This job opportunity was very desirable to me. This beach community was less than five miles from my home, and the salary of the chief there was very appealing. There is not a cop alive who would not want to end his or her career as a Chief of Police if he or she had the opportunity.

About ten years ago the South Carolina Police Retirement System (PORS) began to allow cops eligible for retirement to retire, thus freezing their benefits, then allow them to come back to work at their old position after taking fifteen days off. They were allowed to receive their previous salary, as well as their retirement benefits. The City of Isle of Palms did not allow its employees to participate in this program because the administration thought it would be bad for morale because it would not allow others to advance.

Even though I planned to retire on April 1, I applied for the position. I told my boss of my intentions, and he agreed that I would be well suited for the position, and if I was allowed to retire and return to work, the situation would be very beneficial to me financially. Over the previous eleven years, my chief and I had become close friends. We estimated that we had eaten more than 2,400 lunches together and had solved the problems of the world many times over. Along the way, he had entrusted me with much responsibility and had prepared me well, should I be successful in the process. The day-to-day problems and issues that I dealt with were the very same encountered at the agency that I was applying to.

After submitting my paperwork, I was contacted for an appointment for a telephone interview within the next week or two. I prepared my research and laid out dozens of talking points on the kitchen table for the interview. I was interviewed at length by two council members, which I thought went quite well. The next portion of the hiring process was a very long interview with a psychiatrist who asked me dozens of questions regarding my background, to include my family and my career, as well as my time in the Marine Corps. This report was submitted to the department's Human Resources, and about two weeks, I was informed that I was a finalist for the position, out of more than forty-five applicants. I was next scheduled for an interview with the mayor, several council members, and the director of Human Resources. I was questioned at length, and it was obvious that some of the interviewers' questions came from the report submitted by the psychiatrist. At that interview I was told that I was one of two finalists. Everyone in the room was then asked to leave the room, and it was then a thirty-minute one-on-one session with the mayor, which seemed to go well. I was then taken to lunch with the panel of those who interviewed me, and we had a great time talking for another hour in a nearby restaurant.

I now knew that the other applicant was from out of state, and I now had to wait for him to travel to Charleston to participate in the same interview process that I did. It was now a waiting game and mid-February. I was receiving daily phone calls from lawyers wanting to assist and updating me on what they had heard through the grapevine. All of the information I was hearing seemed positive, but I kept quiet and waited for some sort of notification. The following Friday I received a hand-delivered letter from the mayor advising me that he had hired the other applicant. I was somewhat disappointed, but since my retirement was now imminent, I went into the chief's office and told him that my April 1 retirement date was a go because I did not get hired for the other position.

After keeping my retirement plans quiet since October, I could now make my intentions public. Because the law-enforcement community is so tight, the word about my consideration for the other position had, unfortunately, gotten out. You cannot keep a secret like that in this town. Because I kept my impending retirement quiet, there would be some who would speculate that I was now retiring because I did not get the chief's job. I did not care what anyone thought. I had done my twenty-nine plus years and was mentally ready to pull the pin and retire. I never regretted not getting the position but just felt gratified that I was one of two finalists.

The last week of March was just like any other, and I worked as hard that week as any other I have ever worked. The department was in the process of hiring police officers and some beach services officers. I chaired an interview board most of Thursday, and we finished several other interviews on April 1, my last day on the job.

Several people in the department organized a luncheon held in the training room, and at noon, I was surprised to see that my wife, Paula, my three oldest children, and their spouses were present. Joe was attending a class and was unable to attend. A few friends from the Sheriff's Department also attended as well as pretty much everyone who was working in the city that day. I was presented with a beautiful plaque, a shadow box, and some other small mementos of my career.

Believe it or not, I still had some work to do at my desk. I had already, for the most part, taken all of my personal property out in boxes, but I truly needed to finish the March Monthly Report for submission since it was April 1. At about 3:00 p.m., I walked into the chief's office, put my building keys, badge, identification, and car keys on his desk, and I told him I was ready to go if he was OK with letting me go an hour early. He smiled and we shook hands, and I was done. I had already been issued a new ID card that said *RETIRED*. My twenty-nine plus years in law enforcement was over, and I was now officially retired. I walked downstairs and met Paula, and we drove home.

After almost six years in the Marine Corps, and twenty-nine plus years in law enforcement, my thirty-five years in uniform was at an end.. It was a great run, but it went way too damn fast!

RETIREMENT

29

I HAD AN UNEVENTFUL WEEKEND OFF, AND MY first project was to clean my garage. Monday morning, bright and early, I went out in the garage and emptied everything in it onto the driveway and started to fill several trashcans with junk. While cleaning the garage, I got a phone call from Jon, one of the attorneys in the law firm that stated they would give me their process service business. Jon wanted me to serve some papers, and I had to tell him I was in the middle of a big project and would really like to take a week or two off before I started my new endeavor. He understood, and we laughed a minute about him calling me so soon.

While in the garage cleaning, I ran across a Rubbermaid bin that contained all of my work from a book I had started back in 1989, twenty-three years prior. I had filled several legal pads with writings by hand and some of the research that I had obtained at the time. My original plan was to write only about my tour in Vietnam. I spent about an hour going through the contents of the container and thought for a minute about picking up where I left off, but I quickly scoffed at the idea and told myself that too much time had passed for me to renew the project.

I spent the first week working with a business attorney to get my business legally established and to get bank accounts started and business cards and letterhead printed.

The Saturday after my retirement weekend, I was invited to go to the VFW Hall on the Isle of Palms to receive an award for my service to the city. Dawn, my investigator, had called during the week to notify me of the event. Joe had gone to work at the grocery store where he worked, and Paula and I were getting dressed to go to the event. I was dressed and ready to go, waiting for Paula, as usual, when I received a phone call from my old buddy Jim. Jim, you recall, was my sergeant in METRO in the 1980s, and he later worked for me while in the DEA Task Force. He called to tell me that he was sorry he could not attend my retirement party that evening because he was in North Carolina dealing with one of his daughters. I assured him that it was all right and I got off of the phone and told Paula, "Something weird is going on here," and I told her about the call. She shrugged me off and hustled me out of the door and on to the VFW.

During the thirty-minute ride to the Isle of Palms, I, of course, wondered what was really going on at the VFW. When Paula and I walked in, I was not totally surprised there was a party, but floored by those in attendance. At least a dozen of my friends, who were attorneys, some of whom I had not worked with for over twenty years, my four children, Christy, Doug, Pete and their spouses, and Joe, who Paula had allegedly been taking to work two hours prior, were all there. The mayor, the city administrator, family friends, neighbors, Harve, a local TV reporter and longtime friend, a judge, cops I had worked with at Charleston county, and at least a dozen cops from the police department were all there to provide a very memorable night and one that I shall never forget.

My four children presented me with a beautifully engraved Seiko watch, which is a prized possession. The mayor presented me with a gold-plated key to the city, and we enjoyed the fellowship and the telling of war stories until the keg of beer was empty.

I later found out that Paula had sent an e-mail invitation to my friends, and Doug had copied all of the more than two hundred phone numbers I had saved in my cell phone to contact people to invite. They all kept a great secret until Jim's phone call. Paula has never met Jim, but assured me she would kill him if she ever did!

We had planned for weeks to gather the entire clan together the next day to take family photos. After the photo session, we had a party to celebrate Paula's and Christy's birthday, which was April 1. I had already purchased the food to feed all sixteen of us. As it turned out, we had the leftover food from my retirement party, and I did not even have to fire up the grill. I refer to this gathering as a pool party, but it was still too cold to swim, so we just gathered around the pool and had a great day with the entire family.

Our favorite thing to do is to cook for the family and to enjoy the grandchildren, and it is not often that all sixteen of us are able to attend. All had a great time, and we enjoyed a family party that included everyone. I felt a little guilty in that I planned my retirement on Paula's birthday, which took away from her day somewhat, but I think she understood.

***

It was time to start my new professional endeavor. I never advertised or promoted what I was doing. All of the business I received was strictly by word of mouth. In addition to my process service business, I was contacted for a few consulting jobs and ended up also conducting quite a few private investigations. I pledged to work no more than twenty hours per week and have kept that promise, except for handful of weeks when I was very busy. In almost two years of retirement, I have not had one day where I did not have anything to do. I have been blessed and have enjoyed every minute of retirement thus far.

For more than eleven years, while working at the Isle of Palms, I had not taken any vacation time, except for a Friday or a Monday to hook onto a weekend off. I certainly had not taken any time off in the summer, so being off and able to now vacation whenever I wanted was a bonus. We took a trip to Florida to see our Yankees, and in early August, Paula, Joe, and I went on a cruise to the Bahamas on a Carnival Cruise ship that is ported in Charleston. That was a very nice getaway and recharged my batteries.

Since Joe's spring break does not coincide with Paula's spring break from her job, Joe and I take that time to drive to Tampa, Florida, and watch our Yankees in spring training.

Several weeks after my retirement, a longtime friend and attorney called me and asked if I was still interested in being a chief of police. He told me that the chief of another small police department had just resigned, and he had some pull if I was interested. My response was "Not only no, but hell no!" I told him that I appreciated him thinking of me, but I was enjoying retirement and extremely happy with what I was doing.

Many times in the year after my retirement, I have reflected on my working career of forty-five years. Not counting my teenage jobs while still at home, I have been continuously employed since I entered the Marine Corps in 1966 at the age of seventeen. My six years in the Marine Corps, my ten years for the most part in the trucking business and sales, then twenty-nine plus years in law enforcement just went too fast! My only thought while reflecting was how quickly time had passed by and the many friends made over the years.

It was while reflecting that I made the decision to write this book. I decided to change direction from the first project that I had started in 1989. That project was to be just about my experiences in Vietnam. I had realized the impact that the Marine Corps had made in my life, transforming a young smartass kid from New Jersey to a man with core beliefs embedded in my being for life. I realized the immense influence the Marine Corps had in making me a successful marine, businessman, cop, leader, and most importantly, father. After thinking about my life, I decided that I would write about it.

My story is no different from many other former marines I have known, but I just happen to be one of the few who have chosen to write about it. If I never sell one copy of this book, I am still proud of what I have accomplished in my life, and I will die some day at least knowing that my children and grandchildren have this book to better understand why I am the way I am and why I do some of the things I do.

MY PROMISE TO MY CHILDREN

30

AS LONG AS I LIVE, I AM YOUR parent first and your friend second. I will follow you, lose my temper on you, lecture you, drive you crazy, hunt you down like a dog when necessary, and be your worst nightmare, all because I love you! When I am sure that you understand all of that, I will then know for sure that you are a responsible adult. You will never, ever find anyone who loves, prays, and worries about you more than I do. If you have not hated me at least once in your life, I have not done my job.

My children all know that I was a strict father who made them do things that at the time they may not have understood. Maybe now they will now understand why. As I watch my three oldest children raise my seven grandchildren, I feel confident that I did a pretty good job. They are great parents and great spouses to their husband and two wives.

I was honored to be the best man at Doug's and Pete's weddings, and we have a very special father/friend relationship. I talk to all three of my older children every day, and they all know they can come to me for anything. For the two years that Christy and Timmy lived in North Carolina, we spoke each day, without fail.

Christy, my oldest, is now an assistant to the Charleston County Attorney, and her husband is a motorcycle deputy with my old agency, the Charleston County Sheriff's Office. They have two great boys, Jeremy, my oldest grandson, who begins college in the fall of 2013 and hopes to pursue a career as a music minister, and Lucas, a freshman in high school who could probably pursue a career as a stand-up comedian.

Doug is still is a lieutenant with the Summerville Police Department and is a sought-after nationally known trainer in the drug interdiction field. He is also the executive director of a nonprofit criminal enforcement association with over 5,200 members nationwide. His wife, Valarie, is at Ohio University pursuing her doctorate in communications. Their children are Douglas Tanner, a fine young man who will go far, and wants to be a marine, and William Cole, a nature lover who would rather play with bugs and wildlife than anything. Their youngest, and our only granddaughter, Mason, is a beautiful little girl who will break many hearts as she gets older.

Pete left law enforcement after approximately six years and has pursued his college degree while being Mr. Mom. He will graduate from the College of Charleston in 2014 and plans to teach high school history. His wife, April, is a registered nurse and has blessed us with the last two grandsons of the clan. Jackson is as smart as a whip and enjoys anything military, wildlife, or anything in the water. Sawyer is my sweet, little, redheaded boy, who also loves wildlife and the beach.

I am equally proud of all of my children but have special pride of my youngest son, Joe, who continues to thrive and is presently a rising senior at the College of Charleston. He attends every basketball game, baseball game, and soccer game and would go to football games if the college had a team. He plans to pursue a career in communications and hopes to work in TV or radio. His autism has never once been a hindrance to any of his goals in life.

Paula, my wife of twenty-two plus years, is still teaching high school business and hopes to retire herself in June of 2015. She endured more than twenty years of my law enforcement career and never once ever complained about me being called out in the middle of the night, working late and ruining many dinners, working holidays, nights, weekends, days off, birthdays, anniversaries, etc. She has stood by me without question and has always supported my profession 110 percent. She allowed me to put in the extra time necessary to get the job done properly, and it is for this that I was as successful as I was in my career. Everyone should have a wife as good as mine, and I am truly a blessed and lucky man. I thank her for allowing me to commandeer the dining room table for the past thirteen months while writing this book.

Semper Fidelis!

GLOSSARY

Cruisin — Driving around with no particular place to go.

NHRA – National Hot Rod Association

Head – Bathroom

Rack – Bed

Scabbard – Hard cover for bayonet or knife.

Bends & Thrusts – An exercise involving bending at the waist over on your hands then thrusting your legs back and into the pushup position, then pulling legs back to bent position, usually done for punishment.

Confidence Course – An extreme obstacle course designed to instill recruits' confidence.

NCO – Non-Commissioned Officer which is pay grade E-4 and E-5.

Irish Pennants – Loose threads on any part of the uniform.

AIT – Advanced Infantry Training.

C rations — Canned Combat Rations.

MOS –	**M**ilitary **O**ccupational **S**pecialty, a four-digit designation assigned to signify each individual marine's job.
Quonset Hut –	A corrugated metal building shaped in a semi-cylindrical shape.
E-Club –	Enlisted Man's Club.
Hootch	Any type of covered place that a marine would live in.
Brig –	A military jail.
Fixed Wing –	An aircraft with permanent wings. Generally speaking, not a helicopter.
VC –	Viet Cong soldier who generally wore either black, pajama-type clothing or civilian clothing to better blend into the population.
Medevac	Medical Evacuation
1st Air Cav	First Air Cavalry, Army combat unit that traveled everywhere by helicopter.
Sundrie Pack –	A boxed ration with enough large cans of food to feed an entire platoon.

GLOSSARY

Chopper – A helicopter.

KIA – Killed in Action.

WIA – Wounded in Action.

S/A – Small arms.

A/W – Automatic Weapons.

NVA – North Vietnamese Army, uniformed soldier who wore a uniform and hard-shell helmet, usually very well equipped.

Fam Fire – Familiarization Fire, test-firing a weapon.

Grunts – An endearing slang term used to describe fighting marines.

R&R – Rest and Recuperation.

HE – High Explosive.

WP – Willy Peter, a type of artillery round or bomb with white powder explosive that burns upon impact and is designed to maim personnel.

Satchel Charge – A handmade explosive with a strap for carrying or to sling at personnel.

SITREPS –	An abbreviation for Situation Report, calling in via radio with exact your location.
Amtracs -	Amphibious Tractor, a tracked, box-like armored vehicle designed to transport troops and sometimes also referred to as tracs.
I & I Staff –	**I**nspector & **I**nstruction Staff were marines permanently assigned to local Marine Corps Reserve Units in various cities around the country.
AWOL –	Absent Without Leave.
LST –	The Navy designation for **L**anding **S**hip **T**ank, a flat-bottomed ship that carried several hundred troops, and opened at the bow to discharge tracked vehicles.
PX –	Post Exchange.
H&S –	Headquarters and Support.
PT –	Physical Training.
Pvt. –	Private (E-1).
PFC –	Private First Class (E-2).
L/Cpl. –	Lance Corporal (E-3).

GLOSSARY

Cpl. – Corporal (E-4).

Sgt. – Sergeant (E-5).

S.Sgt. – Staff Sergeant (E-6).

LSD – **L**ysergic **A**cid **D**iethyamide, also known as acid, a semisynthetic drug known for the psychological effects on the user.

PR-24 – A particular type of police nightstick that has a handle.

PD – Police Department.

Signal 46 – Radio code for "officer needs immediate assistance."

EMS – Emergency Medical Service.

CID – Criminal Investigations Division.

SLED – **S**tate **L**aw **E**nforcement **D**ivision, the state police of South Carolina.

COMP Time – Compensatory Time, time taken off in lieu of being paid overtime.

CPSIA information can be obtained
at www.ICGtesting.com
Printed in the USA
LVHW080841051020
667920LV00019B/200